CAPITALISM RELOADED

The Rise of the Authoritarian–Financial Complex

Peter Bloom

BRISTOL
UNIVERSITY
PRESS

First published in Great Britain in 2025 by

Bristol University Press
University of Bristol
1–9 Old Park Hill
Bristol
BS2 8BB
UK
t: +44 (0)117 374 6645
e: bup-info@bristol.ac.uk

Details of international sales and distribution partners are available at bristoluniversitypress.co.uk

This publication was supported by the University of Essex's open access fund.

British Library Cataloguing in Publication Data
A catalogue record for this book is available from the British Library

ISBN 978-1-5292-3385-8 paperback
ISBN 978-1-5292-3386-5 ePub
ISBN 978-1-5292-3387-2 OA PDF

Cover design: Liam Roberts
Front cover image: Unsplash/Arthur Mazi
Bristol University Press uses environmentally responsible print partners.
Printed and bound in Great Britain by CPI Group (UK) Ltd, Croydon, CR0 4YY

This book is dedicated to all of my
colleagues in the COVER Research Centre
and the Management and Marketing Group
at the Essex Business School who every
day help imagine a world beyond the need
for control

Contents

Preface

In his prescient 1961 farewell address, President Eisenhower warned of the burgeoning power of the military–industrial complex – the symbiotic relationship between the armed forces, defence contractors, and politicians that promoted vested interests over the public good. He declared:

> We have been compelled to create a permanent armaments industry of vast proportions. ... This conjunction of an immense military establishment and a large arms industry is new in the American experience. ... Yet we must not fail to comprehend its grave implications. ... In the councils of government, we must guard against the acquisition of unwarranted influence, whether sought or unsought, by the military-industrial complex. The potential for the disastrous rise of misplaced power exists and will persist. (Eisenhower, 1961)

However, in the ensuing decades, capitalism has undergone a profound transformation, extending beyond the quest for new markets and armaments to encompass increasingly sophisticated technologies and mechanisms of control, allowing them to extract value by bringing all aspects of human life – even dissent – under their domain.

Capitalism has long portrayed itself as the antidote to authoritarianism and totalitarianism, claiming that free markets, individual liberty, and the pursuit of profit are the best defences against the concentration of tyrannical power in the hands of a few. In the decades since the end of the Cold War, the triumph of capitalism over communism has been hailed as a victory for freedom and democracy, with the spread of market economies seen as a key driver of political liberalization and social progress. The reality of the past half-century tells a different story. Far from eliminating or lessening repression, capitalism has in many ways facilitated its growth and evolution. The same technologies and techniques that have enabled the expansion of global markets and the creation of vast wealth have also been harnessed by both explicitly authoritarian and increasingly repressive democratic regimes to monitor and control their populations with unprecedented efficiency and precision.

Indeed, authoritarianism has become a major growth industry in the era of globalized capitalism. The rise of surveillance capitalism, in which the tracking and monetization of personal data has become a key driver of economic growth, has created new opportunities for repressive governments and their corporate partners to expand their power and influence. Companies like Google, Facebook, and Amazon have built vast empires by collecting and analysing the personal data of billions of users, creating detailed profiles of individuals that can be used for targeted advertising, political manipulation, and social control. And, perhaps even more terrifying, all of this is being done in the name of creating a supposedly more safe and secure world.

Modern authoritarian regimes led by leaders like Putin in Russia and Xi in China have driven an obsessive focus on securitization, as these autocrats consolidate power through repression, economic control, and manipulation of public opinion. They cultivate national pride intertwined with security notions, viewing challenges to their authority as existential threats. To maintain control, these regimes and even democratic societies have turned to advanced surveillance technologies and data techniques. Examples include China's vast camera network, facial recognition software, and social credit system, as well as the United States' expanded domestic surveillance post-9/11.

The proliferation of smart devices has further accelerated data collection and analysis opportunities, reflecting a growing reliance on surveillance across various political systems in pursuit of security. The integration of tracking technologies with personal and national empowerment characterizes modern securitization. Governments and individuals rely on data-driven solutions for various challenges, from tracking infectious diseases to predictive policing. However, smart technologies also create vulnerabilities exploitable by authorities and employers. This digital monitoring enhances power structures while benefiting technology producers, allowing for precise tracking of individuals and groups.

We have entered a new historical era characterized by the rise of an 'authoritarian–financial complex' fundamentally different than past complexes focused on resource exploitation and industrialization. This complex centres on financially securitizing all aspects of society to maximize their monetary value and ensure populations remain profitable assets. The emphasis is on employing authoritarian tools for command and control not just to extract raw materials but to transform all human thoughts and interactions into opportunities for further profit. This complex interweaves repressive governance, invasive surveillance, personal empowerment, and ideologies of security to justify the financial predation of communities and lives.

The convergence of state, capital, and technological interests creates a system that subjects populations to invasive monitoring and over-policing, linking freedom with commodification and securitization. This 'repressive cycle of financialization' intensifies authoritarian control over destabilized communities as economic conditions worsen. The system exploits vulnerable populations through predatory practices while containing unrest, creating profitable feedback loops of criminalization and punishment. To maintain this system, complex partnerships form between authoritarian states and corporations, exchanging data and resources to enhance surveillance capabilities, secure favourable regulations, and profit from militarized policing and mass incarceration.

The ideology of financialized security fosters a self-surveillance mentality, with individuals viewing themselves as brands requiring constant risk management. This mindset becomes a discursive addiction fueled by big data's promise of total knowledge and personal optimization. Simultaneously, technological narratives of empowerment and convenience mesh with this financial imperative, luring users with visions of enhanced connectivity and artificial intelligence-amplified capabilities. However, these advancements demand comprehensive data extraction, habituating users to perceive surveillance as a necessary cost of progress rather than its opposite.

Financialization, thus, generates and depends upon a political economic pathology of insatiable control. The endless need to maximize monetary value sets in motion state–corporate forces of continual monitoring, prediction, and manipulation that become self-reinforcing. No domain can escape the colonizing logic of financial risk reduction and profit maximization. Family relations, political dissent, social bonds, workplaces, urban spaces, and human cognition become objects of ceaseless cataloging, segmentation, and securitization. Only renewed democratic accountability can disrupt this dystopian trajectory. The stakes in confronting the authoritarian–financial complex are no less than the future of human dignity, creativity, and liberation

This book sounds a warning call about the terrifying potential of boundless authoritarianism, while affirming the power of social movements to reclaim our future. Through tracing the origins and contemporary acceleration of an authoritarian–financial complex linking population control to the generation of massive and growing profitable industry, it highlights an incredibly dangerous consolidation of power over human autonomy, dignity, and democracy itself. There is thus an urgent need to unpack the hidden drivers, questionable assumptions, and baked-in biases behind authoritarian capitalism's standards, systems, and imperatives if concrete dangers of automated totalitarian creep are to be mitigated, much less resisted through organized demands for accountability, transparency, and the struggle for emancipating economic and political systems. This work aims to spark such crucial conversations before freedom fades fully into optimization and securitization.

1

Capitalism Reloaded

Introduction

The dawn of the 21st century has ushered in a new phase of capitalism, marked by the convergence of financial interests and increased security and population control, giving rise to the 'authoritarian–financial complex' (AFC; Mishura and Ageeva, 2022). This complex, characterized by financialization (Christophers et al, 2020), has led to a concentration of wealth and power among the elite, weakening democratic institutions and eroding socio-economic rights (Albertus and Menaldo, 2018). Transcending authoritarian regimes, it has become a pervasive organizing principle, utilizing financial instruments and technologies for social control (Mattioli, 2020) and fostering 'surveillance capitalism', where data is exploited to monitor and influence behaviour (Zuboff, 2019a).

The AFC marks a shift from 'militarization' to 'securitization' as the primary method of power, control, and profit, centring on securing populations and regulating behaviour to maximize financial value (Arrighi, 1994). This evolution is evident in the use of surveillance technologies (Feldstein, 2021) and debt as social control tools (Lazzarato, 2012), with financial instruments shaping conduct and extracting value through daily life securitization (Langley, 2008). The complex is driven by an elite alliance of financiers, tech companies, and governments (O'Neil, 2016; Srnicek, 2017), creating a repressive feedback loop that legitimizes the quest for control through the datafication of life and advanced surveillance. As capitalism shifts from industrial production to immaterial assets like data, intellectual property, and financial instruments (Moulier-Boutang, 2011), wealth and power concentrate among tech and financial giants, exacerbating inequalities (Piketty, 2014) and fostering precarious work regimes (Standing, 2011). Continuous surveillance and data-driven optimization are presented as empowering, reinforcing the desire for control in a 'society of control' (Deleuze, 1992; Lupton, 2016a; Han, 2017).

The society of control has evolved into a pervasive psycho-social complex that permeates all aspects of contemporary life, driven by an obsessive pursuit of control that continually adapts to new social, technological, and personal contexts. This fosters a state of perpetual anxiety and self-monitoring, where individuals constantly strive for self-improvement and control over their lives. The complex exhibits remarkable flexibility across professional, educational, and domestic spheres, where mandates to monitor, evaluate, and enhance performance are increasingly prevalent. This cyclical pursuit of control not only fuels but also emerges from the development of ever more repressive and profitable technologies. The AFC, thus, marks a fundamental reconfiguration of capitalism, uniting financial interests in the pursuit of security and control over populations. By tapping into individuals' deepest fears and desires, it establishes a form of social control that is both highly effective and deeply insidious, producing a state of perpetual self-regulation that is difficult to resist or escape. In this era of high-tech surveillance and quantification, the traditional 'Big Brother' is increasingly none other than ourselves.

Aims and scope of book

The purpose of *Capitalism Reloaded* is to explore the emergence of a new form of capitalism driven by the convergence of financial interests, technological advancements, and authoritarian tendencies, termed the AFC. It seeks to unravel how this complex operates as a distinct configuration of power, one that fundamentally reshapes social, economic, and political landscapes. The book contends that contemporary capitalism has evolved far beyond the industrial and military foundations that defined previous eras, now centering on financialization, data commodification, and pervasive control mechanisms. Through this lens, it critically examines how systems of governance, market dynamics, and cultural practices intertwine to produce a society that normalizes repression, commodifies control, and perpetuates insecurity.

The scope of the book extends across a range of interconnected domains: economic systems, political structures, technological developments, social conditions, and cultural ideologies. It analyses how the AFC consolidates power through the financialization of everyday life, transforming social relations, institutions, and even individual subjectivities into commodities to be controlled, predicted, and exploited for profit. The discussion moves beyond traditional critiques of capitalism that focus on class exploitation or industrial production, positioning control itself as a primary engine of capital accumulation in the 21st century. By framing control as both a means and an end, the book illuminates how capitalism is not only an economic system but also a mode of governance that extends into the intimate domains of life, influencing how people think, behave, and relate to one another.

A central focus is to reveal how this new capitalist configuration perpetuates itself through the strategic use of 'complexes'. The term refers to the interconnected networks of institutions, corporations, governments, and ideologies that collectively exert control over society. These complexes do not merely represent alliances of convenience between powerful entities; rather, they constitute an evolving system where financial, technological, and state interests reinforce one another to ensure stability and growth at the expense of democratic freedoms and social equity. The AFC marks a departure from the military–industrial complex that defined the 20th century, shifting the focus from armaments and defence to the commodification of data, securitization of social life, and financial speculation.

The historical analysis situates the rise of the AFC within broader developments in global capitalism, tracing shifts from industrial capitalism to financialized and digital capitalism. It shows how each phase has reshaped the dynamics of power, control, and exploitation. By exploring the roots and evolution of modern capitalism, the book provides a comprehensive understanding of how the present configuration came to be and where it might be headed. Drawing on diverse theoretical perspectives, from Marxism and political economy to psychoanalysis and cultural studies, it offers a nuanced critique of contemporary capitalism that addresses both its structural dynamics and its psychological impacts.

This shift is not just a change in economic drivers but represents a transformation in how power operates, becoming more diffuse, pervasive, and insidious. The book maps this new terrain of power, highlighting how the AFC uses advanced surveillance technologies, algorithmic governance, and financial instruments to penetrate all aspects of life. It explores how everyday activities – from social interactions to financial transactions – are monitored, categorized, and optimized in ways that serve the interests of capital. This pervasive surveillance goes beyond state control, with private corporations playing a significant role in shaping the norms, policies, and practices that determine the limits of individual freedom and collective action. By tracing the evolution of these control mechanisms, it provides a deeper understanding of how contemporary capitalism manages to appear both liberating and repressive, presenting itself as a necessary safeguard against chaos while continuously expanding the scope of what must be controlled.

Critical to this investigation is an analysis of the socio-economic and psychological dimensions of modern capitalism, examining how insecurity and instability are deliberately cultivated to maintain control. Conditions of precarity – whether in the form of job insecurity, financial instability, or social anxiety – are considered integral to the functioning of the AFC. The discussion shows how this manufactured precarity creates a market for security solutions, data analytics, and risk management services, all of which profit from managing the very insecurities they help to perpetuate.

This approach expands the understanding of capitalist exploitation beyond traditional labour relations, considering how contemporary capitalism extracts value from the governance of social relations, emotions, and even human consciousness.

A significant part of this work is, thus, devoted to theorizing a new form of power, referred to as 'complex power'. This concept challenges conventional understandings of domination as a top-down exercise of authority, instead framing power as something that operates through dispersed networks, ideologies, and practices. Complex power does not reside solely in the hands of the state or corporations but is diffused across systems that govern social life – markets, legal frameworks, technological infrastructures, and cultural norms. The analysis examines how these systems interconnect, forming a self-reinforcing apparatus that makes the control of populations appear natural and unavoidable. By analysing how complex power manifests through the normalization of surveillance, the commodification of risk, and the financialization of social relations, it uncovers the ways in which contemporary capitalism shapes not only institutions but also the very fabric of everyday life.

While it paints a critical picture of the AFC and its far-reaching implications, the book, nonetheless, emphasizes that these systems of control are not monolithic or invincible. Resistance can manifest at various levels – political, economic, social, and cultural – and the book calls for a rethinking of what it means to resist in an era where dissent is easily co-opted or neutralized. It challenges traditional notions of resistance that focus solely on policy reforms or revolutionary upheaval, advocating instead for a multifaceted approach that targets the very infrastructures and ideologies that sustain the complex. This includes technological redesigns that prioritize privacy, community-based economies that resist commodification, and democratic reforms that restore accountability and limit the concentration of power. By mapping out the interconnected mechanisms of modern power and offering pathways for resistance, it provides a critical framework for understanding and challenging the deep entanglements of contemporary capitalism before they solidify into a techno-authoritarian order.

Foundations of the authoritarian–financial complex: key terms and their interconnections

In *Capitalism Reloaded*, key terms like capitalism, power, complexes, precarity, and resistance form the backbone of the analysis, shaping an understanding of the AFC. The term 'capitalism' here refers not only to an economic system characterized by private ownership, profit motives, and market relations, but also to an evolving and adaptive system that maintains its dominance by reshaping the way power functions and is increasingly commodified. It goes beyond industrial production and labour exploitation to focus on financialized capitalism, where speculative investments, data commodification, and the control of social relations have become central to economic accumulation. This shift emphasizes the extraction of value not just from goods and services, but from the regulation, prediction, and manipulation of behaviours, with surveillance capitalism serving as a prime example. The AFC thrives on this transformation, finding profit in the constant need for securitization and the intensification of control over economic activities and human behaviour.

Power, as used in this analysis, extends beyond traditional notions of authority imposed from above. Rather, it is conceived as a diffuse and pervasive force, one that operates through multiple layers of society, influencing social relations, behaviours, and knowledge. Drawing on the critical theories of Michel Foucault and Giles Delueze, power is presented not merely as a coercive tool wielded by elites, but as something embedded in daily practices and ideologies, exerted through normalization and subtle mechanisms of control. Within the AFC, this manifests in technologies and infrastructures that condition individuals to behave in ways aligned with capitalist imperatives, from surveillance technologies to algorithmic governance and financial instruments. Power thus becomes insidious and difficult to resist because it is not only applied externally; it is internalized through systems that appear neutral – markets, data-driven tools, and financial systems – embedding compliance in everyday life.

The idea of 'complexes' builds on Dwight D. Eisenhower's notion of the military–industrial complex but extends far beyond, incorporating financial, technological, and surveillance networks into a new framework where control and economic accumulation converge. In the AFC, public and private interests blur together, creating a symbiotic relationship that perpetuates economic inequality and social repression while reinforcing each other across domains like technology, culture, and governance. Unlike traditional forms of hegemony that rest solely on state power or direct domination, these complexes diffuse their influence by embedding it in systems that seem impartial, expanding their reach while masking the extent of their control. This diffusion extends into social norms, desires, and fears, shaping policies and ideologies in ways that make the structures of domination appear necessary or even beneficial.

Socio-economic complexes are deeply intertwined, in this respect, with psychological complexes, shaping both external social structures and internal mental landscapes. The AFC exerts power not only through institutions and technologies but also through its influence on desires, fears, and individual subjectivities. Control mechanisms extend into everyday life – through surveillance, financialization, and data-driven behavioural interventions – shaping how people perceive their own identities, aspirations, and insecurities. The relentless demand for security and optimization fosters a psychological complex marked by a constant need for self-monitoring and control, where individuals internalize the imperatives of surveillance capitalism and financial risk management. This dynamic creates a feedback loop, as socio-economic systems govern behaviour externally while conditioning individuals to seek out the forms of control that perpetuate their own subjugation. Consequently, the psychological need for stability and empowerment transforms into a commodity, with people increasingly turning to the market for solutions to existential anxieties, thus reinforcing the reach of the AFC across both material and mental realms.

Precarity is a crucial aspect of this analysis, representing not just economic instability but a mode of governance that disciplines populations by making insecurity a constant condition. It encompasses the erosion of job security, income stability, and social safety nets, but goes beyond being a mere side effect of neoliberal policies. In the AFC, precarity becomes a deliberate strategy, serving as a tool to ensure compliance by keeping individuals in a state of anxiety and dependency. This state of precariousness not only facilitates the exploitation of labour but also supports the growth of industries dedicated to managing insecurity, such as private security firms, data analytics, and risk management services. Precarity thus feeds back into the complex itself, making populations easier to govern while creating new markets for the industries that perpetuate it.

Resistance is framed as more than just defiance against overtly authoritarian policies; it is a deeper struggle against the normalization of control and the commodification of everyday life. Resistance must confront the economic, technological, and ideological frameworks sustaining the AFC. Traditional protests or policy reforms may be insufficient, as the complex has developed methods to neutralize opposition, including co-opting resistance movements or using predictive analytics to anticipate and counter activist strategies. Effective resistance therefore requires a fundamental rethinking of economic and social systems, advocating for democratic accountability, community-based economies, and efforts to decommodify public life. It also involves reclaiming autonomy from the relentless demands of financialization, whether through new technologies aimed at privacy, local networks of mutual aid, or democratizing workplaces.

The terms defined here – capitalism, power, complexes, precarity, and resistance – are not separate concepts; they interact and reinforce one another, shaping the framework of *Capitalism Reloaded*. Capitalism is not simply an economic exchange system; it integrates power dynamics and social relations to sustain itself. In this framework, power operates through complexes that embed capitalist imperatives deeply into society, making economic and social conditions appear inevitable. These complexes manufacture and maintain states of precarity, creating conditions that ensure populations remain manageable and compliant. Resistance must challenge not only the visible manifestations of these structures but also the underlying networks of influence that connect them.

The AFC exemplifies how these terms interrelate to describe a contemporary capitalism where economic and social life are governed by principles of securitization, surveillance, and financialization. This complex transforms social control into a profitable venture, continually expanding the reach of data-driven mechanisms and financial speculation. Power is exercised not merely through direct state control or corporate influence, but through the normalization of insecurity and the commodification of everyday experiences. The resulting precarity is an intentional feature, designed to keep populations in a state of dependence while enriching the industries that profit from managing risk and uncertainty. In such a context, meaningful resistance involves more than merely contesting individual policies or leaders; it requires dismantling the entire apparatus of control, from the economic incentives that drive financialization to the technological systems that surveil and manipulate behaviour.

The interconnectedness of these concepts reflects a deeper insight into the evolution of capitalism in the 21st century, characterized by a shift from a focus on industrial production and national defence to one centred on financial speculation, data commodification, and social control. This transformation indicates a new mode of power, where control is not just a means of maintaining order but a fundamental component of capitalist growth. Understanding capitalism today necessitates an analysis of how power operates through interconnected networks, how precarious conditions are manufactured and commodified, and how effective resistance can be organized to challenge this multifaceted system.

Big Brother Inc.

Financialization, marked by the dominance of financial markets over the real economy (Epstein, 2005), is closely linked to the global rise of authoritarianism and illiberalism (Bruff, 2014; Boffo et al, 2019), rooted in neoliberalism's emphasis on free markets, deregulation, and privatization (Harvey, 2005; Jessop, 2019). Neoliberalism has evolved into a political project reshaping state–market–civil society relations (Bruff, 2014; Tansel, 2017), with an 'authoritarian turn' involving coercive measures to enforce market discipline, criminalize dissent, and weaken democratic institutions (Bruff and Tansel, 2020; Bloom, 2023). Financialization has accelerated this shift, blurring public–private boundaries, concentrating power, and undermining worker protections (Krippner, 2012; Sallai and Schnyder, 2021). This global trend manifests in forms such as Asia's 'authoritarian capitalism', China's state-controlled market reforms (Duckett, 2020), and Latin America's legacy of neoliberal repression (Huneeus and Undurraga, 2021). The erosion of democracy in the 21st century reflects the crisis of neoliberal globalization, with rising inequalities, weakened political representation, and the influence of financial elites over policy (Berberoglu, 2020; Biebricher, 2020). While populist movements challenge neoliberalism, they often exhibit authoritarian tendencies (Yalman, 2021), as financialization disconnects the interests of elites from the needs of ordinary citizens, intensifying social and political tensions (Harrison, 2020).

Digital technologies have reshaped authoritarianism, giving rise to 'digital authoritarianism', where state repression merges with hyper-financialized neoliberal capitalism (Turner, 2019; Jamil, 2021). This phenomenon uses advanced data analytics, algorithmic governance, and 'smart city' infrastructures to monitor and control populations (O'Hara and Hall, 2018; Zuboff, 2023). Central to this is 'surveillance capitalism', in which tech giants commodify personal data for profit, creating detailed profiles to manipulate behaviour for corporate gain (Foster and McChesney, 2014; Zuboff, 2019b; Darmody and Zwick, 2020). Authoritarian regimes collaborate with tech companies to access personal data and surveillance tools, enabling unprecedented monitoring, intelligence-gathering, and suppression of dissent (Feldstein, 2021). Technological advancements like smartphones, social media, and data analytics facilitate the manipulation of public opinion and enforcement of social control with minimal accountability (Gohdes, 2020; Topal, 2022). Techniques such as internet censorship, keyword filtering, and deep packet inspection allow regimes to monitor online activity, block dissenting content, and target perceived threats using data-driven analysis (Bak et al, 2018; Steinberg et al, 2021; Chan et al, 2022).

The internal contradictions of neoliberalism have necessitated expanded state powers to enforce compliance and control unrest (Klein, 2007a; Evans and Sewell, 2013; Monbiot, 2016). This dynamic is intensified by the growing influence of tech giants, who act as gatekeepers of the digital economy and enable digital authoritarianism (Doctorow and Giblin, 2022). Digitalization has created new tools for population management and profit generation, with social media allowing autocrats to stifle dissent (Jones, 2022). The result is the integration of coercive state power into capital accumulation – the financialization of authoritarianism (Davis and Walsh, 2016) – where unaccountable security agencies merge with arms manufacturers and data analytics firms, creating a sprawling ecosystem that propels the expansion of the monitoring state through threat inflation and intrusive technologies.

Several key mechanisms enable this financialized authoritarianism:

1. *Private prisons and security firms*: Incarceration and coercive security provision morphs into a for-profit industry. Maintaining imprisoned population levels becomes an economic end unto itself rather than

a necessary evil. Lobbying entrenches hyper-criminalization and immigration detention as profit drivers.

2. *Arms manufacturers*: The unceasing war on terror provides cover for huge public investments into high-tech military and surveillance capacities which find further lucrative applications in civilian population management, enriching contractors. Creating overseas threats sustains this domestic authoritarian complex.

3. *Big Tech and data analytics*: Digital platforms monetize user data through advertising. State contracts offer additional revenue streams by harnessing these surveillance capacities, often compromising privacy rights. Data becomes a plundered commodity aggregated into profiles of targetable behaviours and dispositions.

4. *Lobbying networks*: Revolving doors between government, industry, think tanks and media outlets create an ecosystem of officials, consultants, and commentators invested in justifying an expansive monitoring state. Threat inflation and technological solutionism morph into default policy.

5. *Automating governance*: Algorithmic administration, predictive policing, facial recognition and digital ID systems deskill public sector workers while embedding top-down command and control logics into bureaucratic routines. Technology brands domination as modernization.

Interlinked economic and political interests drive the relentless expansion of the surveillance state, fuelled by hyper-financialized capitalism's demand for pre-empting instability through pervasive discipline. Digital authoritarianism emerges from the disturbing fusion of state repression with the imperatives of hyper-financialized neoliberalism, leveraging advanced data analytics, algorithmic governance, and surveillance technologies to enhance authoritarian regimes' capacity for comprehensive population control. The global surveillance industry has grown into a profitable sector that not only protects capitalism but drives economic growth (Venkatesh, 2021), blurring the lines between state and private interests as companies collaborate with governments to share data and develop new technologies. This globalization of surveillance integrates practices across borders, with private actors playing a central role, leading to a 'data gold rush' where vast amounts of personal data, or 'data oceans', are exploited for valuable insights and competitive advantage (Ebeling, 2021).

The contemporary economy incentivizes the capture and exploitation of data for commercial gain, driving extensive public and private surveillance through collaborations between private companies and state agencies with little transparency or accountability. In the pharmaceutical industry, postmarketing surveillance gathers vast amounts of patient data to monitor drug safety (Haque et al, 2017), while internet companies fuel a 'surveillance advertising industry' that monetizes personal data through targeted ads

(Crain, 2021). The privatization of security services and the proliferation of smart security cameras have transformed security into a data-driven market, particularly in Europe, where private security has grown due to privatization and increased security demands (Van Steden and Sarre, 2007). The convergence of security and intelligence now sees private firms and intelligence agencies collecting personal data for sophisticated decision-making, with biometric technologies becoming essential for managing global population movements (Humphrey, 2022). The international market for advanced surveillance technologies reshapes global power dynamics, as countries like China expand influence by deploying surveillance equipment worldwide, particularly in Africa (Woodhams, 2020). Companies like Huawei and ZTE play key roles in China's geopolitical strategy, collaborating closely with the state to form a repressive 'surveillance–industrial complex' that exports surveillance tools for domestic and global use (Greitens, 2020; Jili, 2022). This marketization of surveillance not only enhances security but facilitates global data collection and the spread of authoritarian practices.

Complex security

The commercialization of population control has established a 'new surveillance normal', where collecting and exploiting personal data is essential for the global economy (Price, 2014). Surveillance technologies have advanced the idea of a Foucaultian 'panopticon' society, where constant monitoring serves as a tool for shaping public opinion, influencing politics, and maintaining social control. This shift has turned population monitoring into a lucrative industry, concentrating power among private companies and state agencies incentivized to monetize data capabilities. The expansion of the global surveillance industry marks a shift from state control to a booming market driven by high data demand and profitability, with emerging powers like China exporting surveillance technologies to expand geopolitical influence. The 21st century has seen the military–industrial complex evolve into the AFC, prioritizing the extraction of value from personal data and the commodification of security (Hayes, 2012; Hester and Williams, 2020). This trend reflects a broader economic shift towards financialization and securitization, where the monetization of security often undermines individual privacy and civil liberties (Rigakos, 2016). Consequently, new socio-economic complexes have emerged, transforming the traditional military–industrial complex into an engine for authoritarian control and capital accumulation (Der Derian, 2009; Höglund and Willander, 2017).

The surveillance–industrial complex includes government agencies, private corporations, and research institutions collaborating to develop, produce, and deploy surveillance technologies (Hayes, 2012). Driven by the demand for advanced monitoring and analysis under the pretext of public safety and national security, this complex uses rapid advancements in data collection, storage, and processing to amass vast personal information, from biometric data to social media activity, which can be monetized for targeted advertising, risk assessment, and predictive policing. Similarly, the cyber security industrial complex has arisen in response to increasing cyber threats and reliance on digital infrastructure. This sector features collaboration among government agencies, private security firms, and technology companies to develop cyber security solutions. The evolving nature of cyber threats, from state-sponsored hacking to organized cybercrime, creates a continuous demand for enhanced security measures, driving industry growth. The cyber security complex not only reacts to threats but also shapes discourse on cyber threats, emphasizing digital vulnerabilities to justify its expansion. This has led to the militarization of cyberspace, with nations engaging in covert operations, espionage, and sabotage, blurring the lines between war and peace.

The somatic-security industrial complex represents, conversely, a more social and, in many ways, intimate form of this complex evolution from militarization to securitization. It seeks to transform the human body into a new frontier for profitable control, by harnessing the power of biological data and advanced technologies such as genomics, biometrics, and neurotechnology. The goal is to develop new means of identifying, monitoring, and manipulating individuals based on their biological characteristics, ostensibly in the name of security and public health. It relies upon the increasing 'informationalization' of biology, which renders the human body as a source of valuable data that can be collected, analysed, and monetized through the decreasing cost of genome sequencing, the proliferation of wearable health devices, and the development of sophisticated algorithms for processing biological data. The complex also exploits the growing public interest in personalized medicine and wellness, capitalizing on the idea that biological data can be used to optimize health outcomes and prevent disease.

The role of international financial institutions, such as the International Monetary Fund (IMF), is crucial in enabling the expansion of these new security based accumulation regimes (Breen and Doak, 2023). By promoting policies that prioritize financial stability and economic growth over individual rights and freedoms, these institutions create conditions for the proliferation of surveillance capitalism and the consolidation of the military–industrial complex. The IMF's surveillance and monitoring practices have been criticized for reinforcing power imbalances and undermining democratic accountability. This convergence of state power, corporate interests, and technological capabilities creates a self-reinforcing system that prioritizes surveillance, security, and military for political control and financial gain. The integration of advanced technologies across domains blurs the lines between civilian and military applications, with innovations in artificial intelligence, biometrics, and cyber capabilities rapidly commercialized and weaponized, fuelling continuous technological competition. The global reach of these complexes allows for the export of surveillance, security, and military technologies worldwide, shaping international power dynamics. As capital seeks new frontiers, it turns to the commodification of security, evolving control from a political necessity to a globally expanding economic opportunity.

The financialization of security has created interconnected complexes that capitalize on the growing demand for surveillance and protection, turning security into a lucrative market. The surveillance–industrial complex provides the infrastructure for mass data collection and analysis, which feeds into the cyber security complex that safeguards digital networks, and the somatic-security complex that generates biological data for surveillance and cyber algorithms. These complexes support global financial markets by securing the infrastructure needed for capital accumulation and reinforcing power structures (Golash-Boza, 2009; Kuldova, 2022). The financialization–securitization link is evident in the use of financial instruments to profit from security risks (Breen and Doak, 2023), resulting in new forms of social control like 'techno-securitization' (Petit, 2020a) and 'pacification through surveillance' (Rigakos, 2016). This system spans various domains, from border security (Palacios, 2017) to health and wellness (Ford et al, 2021b), creating a pervasive network of surveillance and control driven by the imperatives of capital accumulation.

Controlling desires

The digitization era has ushered in high-tech securitization, where digital technologies manipulate social desires and drive individuals towards control through data tracking and quantification, a shift known as 'Lifeworld Inc' (Thrift, 2011). This political economy of security exploits vast amounts of personal data (Webster, 2010), encouraging people to seek new forms of control, especially in uncertain times when appeals to fear and security sway support for authoritarianism (Feldman et al, 2021). Digital technologies create 'imperfect imaginaries', offering a semblance of empowerment while reinforcing power structures and deepening inequalities (Willim, 2017). The Pentagon, Hollywood, and the gaming industry accelerate this trend by blurring the lines between reality and fiction, normalizing surveillance and militarization (Cousineau, 2011; Kaempf, 2019). Social media algorithms perpetuate cycles of consumption and commodification (Jago, 2022) and shape public opinion, as seen in the manipulation of political discourse and rise of digital authoritarianism, particularly in the Middle East, where technology suppresses dissent (Jones, 2022). This convergence of digital technology and security exploits drives a pervasive culture of surveillance and control, distorting perceptions and undermining democratic discourse (Marwick and Lewis, 2017; Harris, 2023).

The concept of 'algorithms of desire' highlights how digital platforms anticipate and shape users' desires, driving cycles of consumption and commodification (Lacković, 2021). This shift has fuelled 'digital authoritarianism', where individuals actively seek new forms of manipulation under the guise of empowerment, as seen in the quantified self movement's embrace of self-tracking (Hepp et al, 2021). Security has become an individualized consumer product, appealing to desires for control and predictability in a world marked by technological change, economic instability, and social fragmentation. As traditional institutions erode, people increasingly turn to the market for security, using digital tools to monitor and optimize various aspects of life – from smart home devices to wearable health trackers. However, these technologies, while promising empowerment, also enable new forms of surveillance and control by corporations and governments. The data they collect supports targeted advertising, behaviour modification, and social engineering, blurring the lines between personal choice and external influence. Despite the risks, the market for security products continues to grow, fuelled by marketing that taps into fears about crime, disease, and ageing, transforming security into an emotional commodity. Consuming security products has become a form of self-expression, signalling one's values and lifestyle, much like political ideologies once did, aligning individuals with specific communities and worldviews. The integration of security products into daily life creates new social stratification, as access to these technologies becomes a status marker, while also fostering social cohesion through shared values around risk management, as present-day capitalism commodifies security and transforms the desire for safety and autonomy into an insatiable demand for technologies that enable surveillance and control, turning external impositions of control into internalized necessities. In this way, present-day capitalism has not only enabled new modes of external control but has also co-opted the very human desire for security and autonomy, transforming it into an insatiable consumer demand.

The rise of the authoritarian–financial complex

This book introduces the emergence of a new AFC, revealing repression and control not as incidental elements but as fundamental imperatives within contemporary capitalism. With neoliberal policies exacerbating inequality and social fragmentation, financial interests have increasingly found profitable ventures in punishment, surveillance, and the apparatus of security states. Consequently, private capital is directly stimulating and investing in processes of criminalization, mass incarceration, militarized policing, personal security, and the expansion of monitoring systems as new avenues for accumulation and catalyst for production.

In contrast to previous eras, present-day capitalism exhibits a contradictory reliance on perpetuating insecurity and conflict. Crimes, protests, and terrorism are no longer anomalies to be resolved but occasions to develop new security infrastructure convertible into assets for global financial markets. This creates a repressive cycle of finance, where instability becomes the basis for fresh investment in control amidst widening inequalities, contrasting sharply with ideals of political–economic harmony. Or more precisely, such hegemony is now secured exactly through producing ever new instances of insecurity requiring control.

To theoretically unpack the symbiosis between financial power and social control, the book introduces the concept of 'complexifying power'. Unlike simplistic notions of a ruling class imposing its will, complexifying power links the purported 'truths' upheld by private and public elites to the dissemination of specific desires, anxieties, and ideological premises throughout society. Crucially, the neoliberal paradigm aligns state priorities with the profit motives of corporations and banks, as police, military, and intelligence agencies prioritize capitalist stability as national security while private sectors capitalize on public infrastructure. This hegemonic programme subtly reinforces free market ideals about personal responsibility and optimization while naturalizing inequality.

Yet, ideological conditioning alone isn't sufficient for the expansive rise of repressive-speculative complexes without the fostering of psychological yearnings for security amidst destabilizing social relations. Complexifying power thus signifies the reciprocal interaction between prevailing regimes of political–economic truth and the mass production of individual mentalities desiring control. As detailed in the book, the authoritarian–financial nexus capitalizes on consumers' yearning for safety and predictive certainty against perpetual crises by securitizing infrastructure and extracting data. These resonant anxieties are amplified by sensationalist media systems that turn public fears into justifications for commodified monitoring solutions.

The notion of the 'repressive cycle of finance', crucially, reveals the self-perpetuating dynamic whereby instability catalyzes investment in coercive measures. As will be shown throughout the book, financial agents precipitate fiscal austerity, eroding public infrastructure and compelling reliance on credit systems. However, the resultant increase in inequality, precarity, and social unrest simultaneously presents opportunities for corporations to market surveillance, incarceration, and sophisticated techniques for expansive population control as a means for providing ever greater security. The societal volatility and existential malaise engendered by finance consequently generate record profits, thereby incentivizing the allocation of additional resources to forcibly manage the residual fallout. This repressive cycle persists as long as the inherent contradictions of financialized capitalism remain unresolved. Conflict is perpetuated because the repression of its consequences remains a highly lucrative endeavour.

This dynamic between structural and subjective forces is vital for understanding the emergence of contemporary techno-policing within everyday life. A key aspect of the AFC, thus, is its ability to construct and exploit a pathological desire for employing authoritarian technologies and techniques to assert control over all facets of individual and collective existence. This complex fosters a pervasive sense of insecurity and anxiety, which is then leveraged to market surveillance, data aggregation, and repressive measures as essential tools for regaining a sense of control and predictability in an increasingly volatile world. By framing granular monitoring and behavioural tracking as empowering solutions, the complex encourages individuals to internalize and normalize the very mechanisms of their own oppression. This manufactured desire for control becomes a self-perpetuating feedback loop, as the more people seek to assert control through these technologies, the more they inadvertently contribute to the expansion and entrenchment of the authoritarian–financial apparatus. This pathological need for ever greater security serves, thus, to reinforce the power of the complex, as it compels individuals to actively participate in their own subjugation while obscuring the systemic sources of their insecurity and alienation.

Outline

This book provides an original analysis of the rise of an AFC in which state and private power elites reinforce exponentially expanding systems of control, surveillance, and extraction across society. The insatiable imperatives of authoritarian–financial regimes to continuously maximize intrusive data extraction, predictive analytics, life optimization, and population management for commercial gain signal profoundly disturbing potentials for technological totalitarianism. Through ten chapters, it traces the historical origins, contemporary dangers and future trajectories of this totalitarian threat to human rights, freedom and democracy.

Chapter 1 has introduced the AFC, in which political and corporate interests merge to manage populations for profit through invasive surveillance, predictive analytics, automated repression, and technological domination destroying privacy.

Chapter 2 examines the concept of 'complexifying power' in which public and private authorities leverage psychological and social complexes to legitimate the supposed necessity and inevitability of their unchecked domination across economic, governmental, and technological domains.

Chapter 3 highlights the contemporary origins of the AFC in the financial imperatives to 'secure markets and populations' that morphed into an unrestrained industry for monitoring and controlling individuals and society, anchored in asymmetries of identity privileging white male technologists as sole experts.

Chapter 4 historically situates the roots of today's authoritarian capitalism in 20th-century discourses of 'financial securitization' initially deployed to justify enhanced state power ensuring debt repayments before morphing into the violent imposition of market rule over society against public resistance through 'shock doctrines'.

Chapter 5 shows how financial securitization birthed contemporary authoritarian financial markets anchored in the endless expansion of 'security wars' on concepts like drugs and terror that continue to fuel a global private policing and incarceration industry as control is increasingly privatized to violent corporations.

Chapter 6 interrogates the rise of a precarious society marked by insecure workers under algorithmic management and disciplines of invasive digital surveillance, alongside vulnerable populations experiencing heightened tracking through immigration enforcement or global supply chains enabling a detention industry to flourish.

Chapter 7 explores how the normalization of total data surveillance and control cultures feeds an insatiable fantasy of perfect securitization through personal/collective quantification – enabling comprehensive monitoring, optimization, and policing of human life itself behind technological veil.

Chapter 8 discusses the oppressive extractive economies that financialized authoritarianism spawns as humanity and nature get recast as resources for exploitation, plunder, and surveillance to serve capital accumulation.

Chapter 9 highlights how capitalism's financial contradictions require perpetual crisis across society – divisions, disasters, and downturns furnishing authoritarian profits and power amidst collapses they simultaneously deepen and have an interest in sustaining.

Finally, Chapter 10 offers hopeful visions for challenging the AFC through workplace democracy, mutual aid networks, policy reforms and technological redesign that ruptures capitalist totalitarianization of economy and psyche.

The ultimate aim of this book is to provide a comprehensive understanding and critique of the rise of an AFC, a formidable combination of state and corporate power that seeks to profitably maximize control, surveillance, and extraction across all spheres of society. By tracing the historical roots and contemporary manifestations of this complex, the analysis will hope to expose the disturbing potentials for technological totalitarianism, where humanity itself is reduced to a resource for exploitation and optimization in the relentless pursuit of profit and shareholder value. Through its analysis of the intricate connections between authoritarianism, financialization, and the normalization of invasive surveillance practices, it paints a chilling picture of a world in which individual freedom, privacy, and democratic values are under constant assault. However, it also offers at the end a profound sense of hope, suggesting avenues for resistance and envisioning alternative models of governance, economic organization, and technological development that prioritize human rights, community empowerment, and a more equitable distribution of power and resources. One where the desire for security is found not in the global expansion of financialized control but in the struggle for a more free, fair, and democratic society.

2

Complexifying Power

Introduction

The current era is defined by intricate systems of power known as complexes, where elite interests converge and institutional control spans political, economic, military, and cultural domains. The concept of 'complexifying power' helps explain how these interconnected networks blur boundaries to perpetuate dominance, shape social reality, and form influential alliances with significant coercive capacities, resources, and ideological influence. While direct coercion persists, complexes increasingly rely on sophisticated methods to manufacture cultural fantasies and harness collective aspirations, offering symbolic compensation for the social tensions they create. This marks a shift in the political economy, where social control and regime stability take precedence over economic optimization, with industries like defence, mass persuasion, and internal policing driving economic activity. The fusion of political aims with economic incentives makes social and political control central sources of profit, as elite interests shape the symbolic realm and redirect unconscious investments to sustain their dominance. Through complexifying power, these arrangements become unconscious frameworks for human experience, legitimizing domination and ensuring the expansion of elite control.

This chapter highlights the intricate relationship between fantasy and power within contemporary complexes, where fantasy shapes subjectivity, desire, and identification, providing the affective support for individuals to invest in repressive power structures as sources of enjoyment and self-realization. These fantasies are adaptable, evolving with changing social and political landscapes, enabling complexes to absorb and recode resistance and critique, ensuring their perpetuation. Genuine emancipation must address the affective and fantasmatic infrastructures supporting hegemonic domination, alongside its material and institutional aspects. This theory of complexifying power formations reveals how control and authoritarianism constitute and spread capitalist relations across economic production, social provisioning, and cultural conditioning. As complexes gain influence in policy making, governance, and social relations, their logic infiltrates society, reshaping institutional arrangements that support economic activity and cultural reproduction. Complexes evolve from sectoral alliances of state–corporate networks into dominant paradigms that reorganize society around control, embedding their priorities across economic relations, knowledge transmission, identity construction, and technological design. These realms ultimately serve elite complexes, entrenching their power over public welfare, environmental limits, or democratization.

Critically untangling the military–industrial complex

The military–industrial complex highlights the interplay between diverse interests, institutions, and power dynamics in shaping socio-economic realities. Initially aimed at bolstering national security, it has evolved into a force that profoundly influences economies, geopolitics, and political decision-making globally (Dunne and Sköns, 2010). Understanding this multifaceted entity requires a multidimensional approach, examining its organizational underpinnings, ideological foundations, and societal implications, which reveal its evolution into the authoritarian–financial complex (AFC) and the nature of complex power. The military–industrial complex is sustained by an extensive web of relationships and institutional arrangements that blur the lines between public and private sectors. An organizational perspective shows how military bureaucracies, defence contractors, and political actors collaborate to perpetuate the financially lucrative military–industrial enterprise (Adams, 1968). Public and private complexes merge into distinct yet reinforcing institutions (Hartung, 2010; Dunlap Jr, 2011). The complex's dynamics highlight administrative and managerial structures that arise during war mobilization (Dunne, 1993; Barnes, 2008), facilitating the consolidation of power, resources, and decision-making authority, enabling significant influence over global economic and political spheres (Aspaturian, 1972; Pavelec, 2010). Furthermore, global conflicts have fostered institutional arrangements that solidify a complex status quo, making it increasingly entrenched and difficult to challenge or dismantle (Shkaratan and Fontanel, 1998; Glassman and Choi, 2014).

The military–industrial complex is not merely driven by individual or institutional desires; it has become a depersonalized entity with a life of its own, transcending the influence of any particular interest or firm (Moskos Jr, 1974; Brunton, 1988). This can be understood through the concept of 'cyborg' entities, which incorporate diverse elements into a larger composite, creating a dominant logic for arranging social and economic relations. This logic includes private contractors, defence lobbying, a culture of constant preparedness, and the acceptance of large-scale public investment in military endeavours (Conca, 1997). The military–industrial complex embodies not only war profiteering but also a worldview and governing ethos embedded in society (Pilisuk and Hayden, 1965; Jencks, 1980). The ideological foundations of the military–industrial complex are reinforced by the perception of military production as fundamental for national economic growth and personal financial well-being. The push for greater military spending often arises from material concerns related to employment, social mobility, and economic security rather than patriotic fervour for war (Adams and Adams, 1972; Abdolali and Ward, 1998). The link between national security and personal economic security reveals the interplay of political, economic, and social factors that sustain the military–industrial complex (Rundquist, 1978; Byrne, 2010).

The military–industrial complex reflects systemic corruption, incentivizing actors to undermine collective goals for narrow self-interests (Baack and Ray, 1985; Pavelec, 2010). This dissonance creates institutional hypocrisy, where the professed aims of security, prosperity, and national strength diverge from the complex's true priorities and operational imperatives (Bernstein and Wilson, 2011; Hiltzik, 2015). These contradictions are evident in the diversion of public resources into private corporate coffers under the guise of national defence and the perpetuation of conflicts to justify further military–industrial expansion. The complex has become a self-sustaining entity, pursuing growth under national interests while subverting the principles it claims to uphold. A significant consequence is the emergence of a control logic, where political domination facilitates economic accumulation, and economic power reinforces political control (Cuff, 1978; Davis, 2019). This dynamic is evident in the relationship between government officials and defence contractors, where unchecked defence budgets and contracts are exchanged for political financing (Wasson and Grieveson, 2018; Wicaksono and Perwita, 2020). Consequently, the state prioritizes maintaining the complex and its social order above all else (Ledbetter, 2011; Epstein, 2014).

The influence of the military–industrial complex extends beyond the economic and political spheres, infiltrating various aspects of society and culture. It shapes critical cultural institutions such as academia, with universities serving as crucial agents in its political and economic propagation (Hartung, 2001; Ottosen, 2009). Academic experts provide intellectual justifications for the expansion of the defence industry, playing up global dangers that necessitate continuous growth, while economic analyses support the importance of military investment for economic development (Feldman, 1989; Schlosberg, 2017). This formal intellectual complicity reinforces the narrative that links personal, political, and economic safety, further reinforcing the need for this military–industrial complex within changing geopolitical environments and eras (Baack and Ray, 1985; Pavelec, 2010).

Critically, untangling this complex reveals the existence of a self-perpetuating system that transcends traditional boundaries between the public and private sectors, the economic and political spheres, and even the material and ideological realms. Its organizational dynamics facilitate the consolidation of power and resources, enabling it to wield significant influence over global economies and political decision-making processes. At the same time, its ideological foundations are deeply rooted in the popular consciousness, where military production is perceived as indispensable for national prosperity and personal well-being. However, perhaps, the most insidious aspect of the military–industrial complex lies in its ability to normalize systemic corruption and institutionalized hypocrisy across the social order. By incentivizing actors to prioritize narrow self-interests over collective goals, it generates profound and strategically productive contradictions between its professed purposes and actual priorities. This dissonance between rhetoric and reality is further amplified by the emergence of a control logic, where political domination and economic accumulation become mutually reinforcing imperatives.

Producing complex political economies

The proliferation of multifaceted complexes in capitalist economies challenges the conventional view of the economic realm as an independent sphere governed by objective laws and market rationalities. The growth of neoliberal complexes highlights the recalibration of the capitalist economy to reflect these embedded structures, revealing the evolving complexity of capitalist systems with security apparatuses, technological hierarchies, and financial institutions transcending traditional state–corporation divisions (Peterson, 2002; Jessop, 2010). Rather than being autonomous, the economic sphere is embedded within and driven by political priorities, elite power relations, and governance dynamics (Guzzini and Neumann, 2012; Guizzo, 2021). Complexes epitomize this interconnectedness, as profit motives and market mechanisms are subordinated to ideological imperatives of social control, hierarchies of advantage, and political legitimacy (Flores, 2012).

Complexes reflect a political economy where power and domination organize politics, economics, and society. Functions historically necessary for ruling class stability – organized violence, mass surveillance, and pervasive persuasion techniques – now serve as dominant economic drivers. Internal security, weapons innovation, and information control reshape capital flows, investment patterns, growth cycles, and technological progress based on elite political calculations (Tellmann, 2009; De Lima, 2010; Springer, 2012). This fusion of political aims with economic incentives means the means to sustain a dominant economic system become key drivers and sources of accumulation.

Michel Foucault's theoretical insights provide a valuable lens for understanding the political-economic logic of contemporary complexes and their power dynamics. In *Discipline and punish*, Foucault expands on Marxian analyses of the capitalist state by describing 'disciplines' – enclosed microcosms blending human knowledge cultivation with increased political subordination (Foucault, 1977; Kelly, 2015). Institutions like schools, clinics, military camps, and prisons foster individual economic capacities while creating 'docile bodies' – compliant individuals subjected to orders, hierarchies, and subjugation rituals for optimal social control (Foucault, 1977: 138). Foucault's notion of productive power structures that restrict and depoliticize human capacities highlights the deeper political-economic logic of contemporary power complexes. These complexes fully realize their potential when multifaceted disciplines extend from specific institutions into generalized socio-economic drivers across corporate–governmental networks (Hardt, 1998; Lazzarato, 2006). Complexes represent a political economy focused on control, stabilization, and risk elimination rather than shared prosperity or collective welfare.

In 'The subject and power', Foucault expands his analysis beyond disciplinary institutions to propose a tripartite conceptualization of power operating across multiple dimensions. The first dimension involves networks of force relations that produce domination through strategic manoeuvres and tactics by various actors. Power is not merely top-down but involves complex actions modifying others' potential actions. The second dimension concerns how power shapes and restricts human capacities, cultivating abilities aligned with its objectives while suppressing potentials that may challenge hierarchies. This dynamic regulates what individuals can become. The third dimension revolves around the constitution of regimented communication systems and sanctioned knowledges, controlling discourse and rendering alternative worldviews illegible (Foucault, 1982).

Foucault argues that these three vectors – force relations, capacity modulation, and discursive circumscription – are interwoven and mutually reinforcing, creating a cohesive ensemble that reconstitutes hierarchical social architectures. Power perpetuates itself by internalizing individual and collective aspirations, values, and modes of thinking into its reproductive structures. This internalization makes subjects invested in sustaining regimes of truth and domination, believing prescribed beliefs and ambitions represent authentic self-actualization rather than instruments of subjection. Foucault thus describes power as an interconnected strategic situation, infiltrating diverse sites and domains, shaping subjects by binding them to frameworks that perpetuate hierarchies. Overcoming these entrenched power structures requires dismantling not just overt mechanisms but also the interlocking networks of knowledge, desire, and capacity-regulation that support their hegemony.

In his influential 1992 work 'Postscript on the societies of control', Gilles Deleuze builds upon and extends Michel Foucault's analysis of disciplinary power to theorize an emerging new mode of domination – the societies of control. Deleuze argues that the 18th- and 19th-century disciplinary societies analysed by Foucault, characterized by enclosed institutional spaces like prisons, hospitals, schools and factories, are giving way to more fluid, dispersed and pervasive forms of power and subjugation. While the disciplinary societies operated through confinement and the rigid partitioning of space and time, the emerging societies of control modulate flows and codes in an open, continuous environment (also see Martinez, 2011). Central to Deleuze's conception is the idea that power in control societies is not confined to specific enclosed sites, but becomes a decentred, ubiquitous force shaping how individuals understand themselves and relate to one another across all domains of life. Disciplinary institutions like the family, school, workplace, and so on are being reconfigured and integrated into an overarching 'corporation' that subsumes their functions.

Instead of the individual being moulded and confined, Deleuze describes processes of 'dividuation' whereby the mass distribution of sample data, codes, and monitoring mechanisms produces a constant modulation and reshaping of subjectivities. Discrete sites of enclosure give way to mobile, free-floating control – a self-deforming 'universal system of deformation' without fixed positions. This new power operates through the continual recombination of communications networks, digital flows of information, and computer tracking rather than older paradigms of static spatial segmentation. Deleuze emphasizes how emerging technologies like computing enable these generalized cybernetic control systems to permeate society in a supple, metastable manner.

Most critically for understanding complexes through this lens, disciplinary power for Deleuze was still linked to older institutional enclosures, however distended. But control inaugurates a new immanent mode of domination – it decodes flows to extract value and administer life itself. Power complexes can thus be seen migrating from localized sites to become unmoored operational matrices for modulating human behaviour and infrastructure on a planetary scale. By becoming more transferable, extending into every aspect of the social field instead of being concentrated, complexes embodying power in the control societies amplify their capacities for environmental design, productive mobilization and perpetual logistical reconfiguration. Their territorializing strategies bypass institutional restrictions through polymorphous circulation across bodies, spaces, codes and networks. In this sense, complexes come to embody a new abstract social subjection – continual modulation and disciplining of populations into data streams and valorized capital-flows under the administration of flexible, decentralized digitalized automation.

Complex political economies, thus, expand and take these societies of control to their logical conclusion, as their power no longer needs or relies upon rigid confinement, but instead advances a self-perpetuating cybernetic enclosure without external limits.

As this complex power becomes more diffuse, adaptive, and all-pervasive, it becomes increasingly difficult to identify, locate, and resist. The traditional boundaries between the state, the economy, and civil society become profoundly blurred, as power operates through a complex web of institutions, technologies, and discourses that span across these domains (Guizzo, 2021). The very notion of resistance, hence, becomes problematic, as power co-opts and incorporates potential challenges into its own operations, neutralizing and absorbing dissent into the reproduction of its hegemony. The expansion of human capacities, which Foucault identified as a key site of resistance, is increasingly subordinated to the imperatives of control and risk management (Foucault, 1982; Kelly, 2015). The resultant effect is the emergence of a closed but ever amorphous complex system that perpetually reinforces its own power structures and forecloses the possibility of genuine alternatives and emancipatory transformation.

In light of these dynamics, complexes can be theorized as embodying a distinct political economy centred on the expansion of control as both a means and an end. This conceptualization highlights the fundamental shift in the nature and purpose of economic activity within complex systems. In traditional political economic theory, the primary focus is on the production, distribution, and consumption of goods and services, with the aim of generating wealth and material prosperity. However, in the context of complexes, the central organizing principle becomes the expansion and intensification of control over human behaviour, thought, and social relations as the very means for generating profit and securing power.

Complex hegemony

Complexes, thus, illustrate the strategic combination of political aims with economic incentives, whereby the very means employed to sustain a dominant economic system become, over time, one of its main material drivers. In the present age, it reflects the emergence of ever-expanding disciplinary societies of control, where regulating populations becomes the catalyst, as opposed to simply the byproduct, of capitalism. However, the ascendance of complexes within the economic sphere cannot be understood as a purely structural phenomenon or a unilateral imposition of elite interests. Crucially, complexes rely upon the construction and perpetuation of hegemonic ideologies and discourses that legitimize their power and shape social relations in ways that align with their agendas (Holborow, 2007; Gilbert, 2013). This hegemonic dimension is integral to sustaining the dominance of complexes and ensuring the active consent of subordinate groups to this prevailing oligarchic order.

Antonio Gramsci's theorization of hegemony provides an analytical framework for understanding how multifaceted complexes establish and perpetuate dominance within the socio-economic order. Gramsci argued that ruling class power hinges not only on control over state and capital but also on generating active consent and legitimacy through cultural and ideological leadership (Singer, 1990; Daldal, 2014). This hegemonic class rule is achieved through the formation of 'historical blocs' – convergences of political, economic, intellectual, and cultural forces that align their interests (Turner, 2002). These blocs, evolving into modern complexes, do not impose ideological homogeneity through compulsion alone but exercise influence by selectively incorporating cultural demands and material interests of oppressed groups while preserving fundamental hierarchies and power relations (Bonefeld, 2017a).

Through building bases of consent among subordinate groups, complexes universalize their narrow interests as collective ones, rendering their dominance hegemonic – a ruling philosophy diffused throughout social relations (Gramsci, 1971). They achieve this by controlling key meaning-making institutions and cultural sites, such as the media, education, think tanks, and policy networks, which propagate ideologies that present complex imperatives as societal goods (Gramsci, 1971). However, Gramsci emphasized that manufacturing consent cannot completely eradicate the contradictions and fissures that destabilize ruling class power. Hegemony is an inherently unstable accomplishment, vulnerable to counter-hegemonic narratives and oppositional movements that contest dominant meanings, expose the particularistic class interests beneath the rhetoric of universality, and activate new collective subjectivities (Laclau and Mouffe, 1986; Thomassen, 2005).

For Gramsci, hegemony requires a constant cycle of strategic recomposition and discursive recalibration, continually updating ideological discourses to incorporate elements of emergent counter-narratives that threaten mass consent. This rearticulation is the 'price of historicity' that those in power must pay to maintain their hegemonic rule against the subversion of new collective wills (Gramsci, 1971). It involves an exhaustive ideological-cultural struggle across symbolic, subjective, and material planes to suppress radical alternatives and present the existing order as the highest form of rationality, morality, and collective interest. Gramsci's theory elucidates that hegemonic governance relies on multidimensional ideological production and consensus-building, rather than just economic determinants or state coercion. It represents a synthetic unity of political, intellectual, and moral leadership, akin to 'trenches and fortifications' distinct from the spatially limited enclosures of earlier disciplinary power (Gramsci, 1971). Complexes embody such dominant historical blocs, emerging from the convergence and alignment of elite interests across political, economic, military, and cultural spheres. They legitimize their power by constructing a 'common sense' narrative that aligns their narrow interests with the collective well-being, security, and prosperity of the entire nation or community (Flew, 2014). Through strategic appropriation of everyday understandings and embedding their priorities within popular consciousness, complexes portray their dominant position as natural, inevitable, and representative of the general will.

The discursive theory of hegemony by Ernesto Laclau and Chantal Mouffe illuminates the role of complexes in shaping social relations and delimiting political and social possibilities within the economic sphere. According to Laclau and Mouffe, hegemony is sustained through constructing discourses that partially fix meanings, constraining the range of legitimate subject positions, identities, and socio-economic imaginaries (Laclau and Mouffe, 1986; Thomassen, 2005). Complexes exercise discursive hegemony by presenting their sectional interests as representative of the community's shared welfare and prosperity (Howarth, 2010; Remling, 2018). They create equivalential chains between signifiers like freedom, security, progress, innovation, and justice, associating these values with policies favouring elite interests, such as corporate power, capital accumulation, and market-driven individualism (Laclau, 2003; Selg and Ventsel, 2008). Alternative social relations, economic organization, and well-being that challenge complexes' imperatives are marginalized as impractical or threatening to stability and growth (Mumby, 1989; Fairclough, 2013).

Jason Glynos and David Howarth's theorizations on social logics complement this perspective, showing how complexes perpetuate hegemony within the capitalist political economy. Social logics are tacit, normalized rules that organize social life and economic activities around 'common sense' notions (Glynos and Howarth, 2007; 2008). Capitalist hegemony embeds market-centric, commercial, and individualistic social logics, naturalizing existing hierarchies and inequalities as rational and aligned with collective interests (Purvis and Hunt, 1993; Therborn, 1999). Complexes function as expansive hegemonic social logics by institutionalizing norms, practices, and modes of subjectification that legitimize elite control over production and reproduction processes as beneficial and essential for freedom, prosperity, and progress (Glynos and Howarth, 2007; 2008). They link their control-oriented and profit-driven interests with societal logics of social mobility, security, and empowerment (Holborow, 2007; Gilbert, 2013).

The ascendance of neoliberal reason since the 1970s exemplifies the evolving role of complexes in universalizing capitalist social logics as the pre-eminent conduits of individual and collective freedom, democratic pluralism, and general societal welfare. Neoliberal ideology frames human subjects as self-interested, rationally calculating, utility-maximizing consumers and entrepreneurs perpetually competing within various markets (Flew, 2014). These subjectivities and behaviours are posited as inherently rational, desirable, and emancipatory, facilitating the unrestrained commodification of social life and the unfettered pursuit of capital accumulation in ways that ostensibly generate individual and shared prosperity. Different values frameworks and practices privileging mutual aid, cooperation, public goods, or substantive equality are systematically dismissed as unrealistic, statist, authoritarian, or economically inefficient deviations from this neoliberal common sense (Singer, 1990; Daldal, 2014).

Complexes, hence, bolster and propagate this capitalist hegemony through the continual expansion of their discursive and ideological power across myriad cultural, political, and civic institutions. They mobilize a vast array of meaning-making apparatuses, including corporate media conglomerates, business-influenced think tanks, advertising agencies, lobbying groups, and public relations firms, to shape societal norms, values, desires, and modes of identification in ways that strategically reflect and reinforce the core capitalist imperatives of commodification, competitive individualism, and intensified class inequality (Turner, 2002; Bonefeld, 2017a). The manufacturing of this hegemonic common sense relies upon the deft appropriation of public frustrations and the selective incorporation of rhetorical engagements with certain subordinate group demands, while simultaneously suppressing or marginalizing fundamental challenges to the underlying structures of elite power and economic dominance (Glynos and Howarth, 2007; 2008). Through such strategies of selective concession and discursive capture, complexes are able to continually renew and maintain their hegemony by presenting themselves as fundamentally responsive and attuned to popular concerns, even as they work to preserve the core hierarchies, social relations, and modes of capital accumulation that serve their narrow class interests.

Complexification

This chapter has, thus far, established the intricate relationship between complex political economies and hegemony, highlighting the role of ideological and discursive power in sustaining the interconnected dominance of elite interests and actors. This section delves into the concept of complexification, a process through which complex forms of hegemony spread, adapt, and entrench themselves across diverse social, cultural, and geographic contexts (Peters, 2001; Springer, 2010). Complexification is underpinned by a fundamental transformation in the nature of production, characterized by the emergence of modes centered on the manufacturing and selling of goods and services associated with control (Jessop, 1990). These control-based modes of production represent a significant departure from traditional forms, as the imperative of control becomes the primary driver of economic activity (Clifton, 1977; Burawoy, 1990).

To understand the significance of this shift, it is crucial to define the mode of production. In Marxian theory, a mode of production refers to the specific combination of the means of production (tools, machinery, raw materials, and labour power) and the social relations of production (the relationships between people involved in the production process, such as owners and workers) that characterize a particular economic system (Jessop, 1990). It determines how goods and services are produced, distributed, and exchanged within a society and is shaped by prevailing social, political, and cultural conditions (Mafeje, 1981; Wolpe, 2023). Complexes are increasingly linked to the growth of an extractive and increasingly datafied mode of production, centred on the collection and processing of data and resources to better track, predict, and shape individual and population behaviour (Banaji, 1977; Karatani, 2014). This shift is driven by the sophistication and pervasiveness of surveillance technologies, data analysis, and behavioural modification, enabling economic and political elites to gather vast amounts of information and use it to shape choices, preferences, and actions to align with their interests (Peters, 2001; Springer, 2010).

The extractive nature of control-based modes of production significantly impacts capitalism's dynamics by creating constant competitive pressure to develop new markets and populations for profitable control (Gunder, 2010; Peck et al, 2018). As the ability to shape and direct human behaviour becomes a key economic value, complexes continuously expand their reach and influence, seeking new domains of social life to control (Brenner and Theodore, 2002; Prechel and Harms, 2007). Control becomes a valuable commodity, with those possessing the necessary skills commanding a premium in the labour market, while those subject to control face increasing precarity. This expansion is facilitated by the financialization of the global economy, which generates opportunities for extracting value from risk management and manipulation across borders and sectors (Broomhill and Sharp, 2007; Bakker and Gill, 2019; Valle, 2021).

A striking feature of this complex mode of reproduction is its capacity for political and social adaptation, maintaining hegemony amidst shifting contexts and challenges (Peters, 2001; Springer, 2010). This adaptability stems from complexes' ability to selectively incorporate elements of local culture, identity, and political discourse while advancing their control and accumulation agendas (Gunder, 2010; Peck et al, 2018). This fluid, 'protean' nature of power (Katzenstein and Seybert, 2018) allows it to shape-shift and modulate in response to societal changes and contested landscapes. Theorists like Aihwa Ong conceptualize capitalism and state power as mobile technologies, mutating in response to dynamic contexts while retaining underlying logics of commodification and discipline (Ong, 2006a; 2006b).

The spread of neoliberalism exemplifies the adaptability of complexes (Brenner and Theodore, 2002; Prechel and Harms, 2007). Neoliberal policies, encountering resistance and contestation, have undergone continuous political mutation and social adaptation, incorporating local elements while retaining their market-driven core and commodification principles (Bakker and Gill, 2019). Contemporary neoliberalism should be seen as an adaptive process of continuous ideological and policy mutations – 'actually existing neoliberalization'. It involves market rule principles intertwining flexibly with diverse institutions and cultures, with elites reworking policies, discourses, and norms to entrench commodification amid crises and contestations (Brenner and Theodore, 2002). Rural and urban spaces experience varied, unequal neoliberal restrictions mediated by socio-political conditions, with contingency rather than determinism defining this uneven development (Parnell and Robinson, 2012).

Complexes epitomize how fluid power can be constantly mobilized, expanding into new geographic contexts and social spheres. Mobilization denotes the coordinated expansion of mutable power formations into interlocking systems driven by underlying imperatives, continually absorbing new spaces and social energies. This 'complexification' method extends dominant structures' reach, embedding their visions within society's fabric. Hegemonic systems like capitalism reconstitute social meanings, identities, and subjectivities through this flexible process to normalize imperatives like individualism, consumerism, and competition. Complexes continually recalibrate their discourses and governance modes to remain relevant amidst dynamic conditions while retaining their essential purpose of control.

The political and social adaptability of complexes is facilitated by their ability to deploy discursive and rhetorical strategies that resonate with local concerns and aspirations (Broomhill and Sharp, 2007; Valle, 2021). By presenting themselves as aligned with diverse communities' interests and values, complexes generate legitimacy and consent while advancing their own control and accumulation agendas. By selectively engaging with critical voices and movements, and offering limited concessions and reforms, they defuse challenges to their hegemony while maintaining underlying power structures and inequality (Bakker and Gill, 2019). Complexification involves reconfiguring governance structures and institutions, aligning local decision-making processes with the imperatives of complex hegemony (Jessop, 1990). This often erodes democratic accountability and concentrates power in technocratic elites, deemed best equipped to manage global economic demands (Clifton, 1977; Burawoy, 1990). The spread of complexes through complexification is facilitated by the interconnectedness and interdependence of the global economy, creating opportunities for control and influence across borders (Katzenstein and Seybert, 2018; Bloom et al, 2021). As capital, information, and people flow freely across national boundaries, complexes' ability to shape and direct these flows becomes a crucial source of power and influence (Bakker and Gill, 2019).

Understanding complexification entails examining it across three interwoven dimensions:

- *Economic complexification*: Complexes' geographic, sectoral, and demographic expansion of profit-driven commodity production through colonizing new markets and workforces by perpetually revolutionizing technologies and business models in dynamically creating and capturing value.
- *Political complexification*: Growth of complexes' influence over governance and state capacities across local, national, and global scales by intertwining government policies, legal regimes, and regulators with corporate agendas amidst ongoing tactical reconfigurations to manage periodic legitimation crises.
- *Cultural complexification*: Diffusion of complexes' ideological common sense diffusing logics of hierarchical individualism, possessive consumerism, and capitalist social relations through continually updating discourses, identities, and desires appealing to popular sentiments while marginalizing alternatives.

Complexification is, thus, characterized by complexes' capacity to mobilize and spread their influence across social, cultural, and political domains through strategic discourses, narratives, and institutional arrangements that resonate with local concerns while advancing control and accumulation agendas. This dynamic form of social and cultural colonization embeds complex logics and practices within diverse contexts, reshaping local institutions, norms, and subjectivities to align with complex hegemony.

Psycho-social complexes

Building on the concept of complexification, this section explores how complexification links to the creation of the desiring subject by delving into its affective dimensions. It reveals that the consolidation of complex hegemony is strengthened through the formation of fantasies that individuals emotionally invest in to secure their sense of self, turning elite discourses into pathological social desires. These fantasies promise an imaginary resolution to the constitutive lack of subjectivity, eliciting emotional investment in hegemonic complexes despite contradictions and failures. The strategic cultivation of fantasy channels and contains the destabilizing nature of jouissance, harnessing affective energy while mitigating potential disruptions. Research shows that economic threat and instability can heighten authoritarian themes in media and attitudes in individuals (Jorgenson, 1975; Doty et al, 1991). Personality traits like social conformity, fear, and aggression are associated with right-wing authoritarianism, while autonomy and guilt are negatively correlated (Butler, 2000). Individuals with narcissistic vulnerabilities may be drawn to authoritarian leaders for validation (Frankel, 2022). Concerns about internet surveillance and privacy violations post-Snowden further highlight the psycho-social implications of authoritarian tendencies, contributing to fear, mistrust, and self-censorship (Fuchs and Trottier, 2017).

Cultural and political discourses can become social pathologies when they contribute to social problems, deviant behaviour, and structural inequalities. The concept of social pathology, viewed sociologically, emphasizes the role of broader social contexts and power relations in shaping these issues (Lemert, 2014). Pathological discourses reproduce and legitimize oppressive ideologies, unequal power structures, and systemic injustices (Laitinen and Särkelä, 2019). Economic conditions also influence social pathology, highlighting how political discourses shape resource and opportunity distribution (Horwitz, 1984). When political narratives prioritize economic growth over social welfare, they exacerbate income disparities, poverty, and unemployment, leading to higher crime rates, mental health issues, and family instability. The hermeneutic conception of social pathology focuses on subjective experiences and interpretations, showing how dominant narratives of individualism and consumerism foster feelings of alienation and anxiety among those who fail to meet societal expectations, thereby perpetuating social dysfunction (Laitinen and Särkelä, 2019).

The concept of cultural complexes, extending Jung's theory of individual complexes to the collective level, provides a framework for understanding social pathologies. Cultural complexes are emotionally charged, largely unconscious belief systems shared by a group or society, shaping attitudes, behaviours, and relationships (Singer and Kimbles, 2004). These complexes can be transmitted across generations, perpetuating group traumas and social tensions (Kimbles, 2006). This theory emphasizes the collective unconscious and the role of shared symbols, myths, and archetypes in shaping social phenomena, suggesting that social pathologies are rooted in the interaction between individual psychology and the broader cultural context (Alho, 2006; Lu, 2013). Furthermore, cultural complexes highlight the political dimensions of social pathologies, indicating that dominant ideologies and power structures create and reinforce complexes that maintain the status quo and marginalize certain groups (Alschuler, 2009). This perspective aligns with the critical conception of social pathology, emphasizing oppressive ideologies, unequal power structures, and systemic injustices in perpetuating social problems (Laitinen and Särkelä, 2019). The theory also underscores the role of discourse in shaping social realities. Valsiner (1995) introduces the concept of discourse complexes, suggesting that social sciences construct meaning systems that influence how societies understand and respond to social issues, resonating with the hermeneutic conception of social pathology (Laitinen and Särkelä, 2019).

In turn, psychological complexes, which are rooted in individual experiences of trauma, conflict, and unmet needs, find resonance and amplification within the broader cultural context. When these personal complexes align with the dominant cultural narratives and power structures, they can become entrenched and normalized, contributing to the emergence and persistence of social pathologies. This mutually reinforcing relationship between socio-economic and psychological complexes creates a powerful feedback loop that can be difficult to break. As individuals are shaped by the cultural complexes that surround them, they may unwittingly perpetuate the very social conditions that give rise to personal and collective suffering. At the same time, the collective weight of individual psychological complexes can serve to reinforce and legitimize the oppressive ideologies and unjust power structures that underlie socio-economic complexes.

The interplay between dominant psychoanalytical fantasies and hegemonic complexes is crucial for understanding the perpetuation of power structures in contemporary society. Drawing on Lacanian psychoanalysis, scholars have explored how fantasies shape subjectivity, desire, and enjoyment, sustaining ideological attachments and social orders (Glynos, 2001; Stavrakakis, 2007). Fantasy provides a sense of completeness to the inherently fragmented nature of the subject (Fink, 1995). Ideological fantasies, like those of the free market or nationalism, promise to fill the subject's lack, offering a sense of wholeness and purpose (Bautista, 2018; Maher, 2023). These fantasies mask the symbolic order's incompleteness, creating a strong affective attachment to the hegemonic complex (Glynos and Stavrakakis, 2008). Fantasies also structure desire around the unattainable *objet petit a*, luring the subject into an endless quest for satisfaction (Kirshner, 2005). Hegemonic complexes manipulate this dimension by directing desire towards objects and practices that sustain existing power relations, such as consumerism or nationalism (Bloom and Cederstrom, 2009; Krüger, 2019). By promising enjoyment through these pursuits, complexes secure the subject's complicity in their subjugation, even amid contradictions or failures (Newman, 2004).

The process of complexification, where hegemonic complexes adapt and expand across social domains, heavily relies on mobilizing fantasies. As complexes face new challenges or resistances, they reinvent and reconfigure the fantasies underpinning their legitimacy and appeal (Ormrod and Ormrod, 2014). This involves incorporating popular desires and grievances into the fantasmatic narrative, creating a sense of inclusivity while preserving power asymmetries (Wardle, 2016). Policy makers and institutions operate within a fantasmatic framework that shapes their perception of social reality and possible interventions (Gunder, 2014). Fantasies of control, efficiency, or technological solutions drive policies reinforcing hegemonic complexes, such as expanding surveillance or commodifying public goods (Krüger, 2019).

Neoliberalism's resilience, for instance, stems from presenting itself as a fantasy of limitless possibility and self-realization, adapting to cultural and technological changes (Maher, 2023). By tapping into fantasies of individual autonomy, creativity, and entrepreneurship, neoliberalism maintains hegemony despite crises and inequalities, demonstrating fantasy's power in sustaining ideological complexes (Bloom and Cederstrom, 2009). Similarly, authoritarian and nationalist complexes rely on fantasies of unity, purity, and historical greatness (Bautista, 2018). These narratives promise to restore a lost sense of wholeness and identity, eliciting strong affective investments from subjects even amid oppression or exclusion (Glynos and Stavrakakis, 2008). Fantasies of national revival or ethnic superiority obscure social order antagonisms and contradictions, securing the subject's attachment to the hegemonic project (Stavrakakis, 2007).

To fully grasp then the affective dimensions of complexification, it is essential to examine the intricate interplay between socio-economic and psychological notions of complexes. Hegemonic fantasies, such as those of national redemption, democratic salvation, or the wholeness of the nation-state, can be understood as a specific manifestation of cultural complexes (Tismaneanu, 2009). These fantasies offer a sense of coherence, continuity, and belonging in the face of the inherent incompleteness and contradictions of social reality. They provide a narrative framework through which individuals can make sense of their experiences and invest their desires, while also legitimizing particular forms of political and social order. They are not simply imposed from above but are actively taken up and reproduced by individuals through processes of internalization and identification (Singer and Kimbles, 2004).

The insights gained from exploring the relationship between social pathologies and cultural complexes reveal a profound and mutually reinforcing connection between socio-economic complexes and psychological complexes. This connection highlights the interdependence of individual and collective experiences, as well as the powerful influence of social, cultural, and political forces on the formation and perpetuation of both personal and societal dysfunction. At the heart of this connection lies the recognition that socio-economic complexes, such as those related to power structures, ideologies, and institutions, are not merely external factors that shape individual lives but are also deeply internalized and embedded within the collective psyche. These complexes give rise to shared belief systems, emotional patterns, and behavioural tendencies that are passed down through generations and reinforced through everyday interactions and cultural practices.

Complex repression

The entrenchment of hegemonic power structures in contemporary societies is maintained not just through overt coercion and repression, but through the subtle inculcation of desires, fantasies, and identifications that bind subjects to dominant ideologies. This process operates at the deepest levels of subjectivity, shaping individuals' self-perception, place in the world, and relationship to the social order. Louis Althusser's theory of Ideological State Apparatuses (ISAs) and Repressive State Apparatuses (RSAs) provides a framework for understanding how power shapes subjectivity and forecloses resistance (Althusser, 2014). In complex 'societies of control', however, the distinction between ISAs and RSAs blurs as instruments of repression become internalized and integrated into everyday life (Deleuze, 1992; Massumi, 2015).

Traditionally, Althusserian theory posits that RSAs enforce compliance through coercion and violence, while ISAs shape subjectivity and desire through institutions like education, religion, and media (Hirst, 1976; Althusser, 2012). RSAs represent overt state power, while ISAs subtly inculcate dominant ideologies and beliefs to secure consent and identification with the social order. In the context of complexes, this distinction blurs as repressive mechanisms integrate into daily life and cultural fantasies, making coercion and ideological interpellation increasingly indistinguishable (Cousins and Hussain, 1984; Montag, 1995). Complexes reveal a new dimension of Althusser's theory, one in which the traditional RSAs are transformed into ISAs, and repression itself becomes ideological (Rancière, 2014). The instruments of coercion and control, such as surveillance, policing, and carceral systems, are no longer experienced as external impositions but are instead internalized and embraced as essential components of individual and collective identity (Chimisso, 2015). This process of internalization is facilitated by the complex fantasies that shape subjectivity and desire, providing a sense of meaning, purpose, and enjoyment that is inextricably linked to the maintenance of the prevailing social order (Hunt, 1985; Ryder, 2013).

These complex fantasies operate at both conscious and unconscious levels, deeply embedded in the symbolic order that structures social relations and power dynamics (Jameson, 1981; Eagleton, 1991). They weave together the fabric of subjectivity, securing individuals' affective investment in perpetuating hegemonic power structures. Interpellation is not merely identifying with authority but involves a constantly renewed affective investment reinforced through daily practices and interactions (Althusser, 2000; Zake, 2002). These fantasies are ingrained in the social infrastructure and processes of social reproduction, shaping how individuals perceive themselves and their place in the world (Youdell, 2006; Bargu, 2019; Hall, 2020).

The concept of jouissance, from Lacanian psychoanalysis, is useful for understanding the affective dimension of interpellation in complex societies (Stavrakakis, 2007; Glynos and Stavrakakis, 2008). Jouissance refers to a form of enjoyment that is both pleasurable and painful, derived from submission to the dominant order (Fink, 1995; Kirshner, 2005). In complexes, interpellation becomes a form of jouissance, as subjects derive enjoyment from their subjugation and the perpetuation of repressive ideologies (Ormrod and Ormrod, 2014; Wardle, 2016). This jouissance is fundamental to the complex fantasies sustaining hegemonic power (Glynos, 2001; Maher, 2023). By offering transgressive enjoyment tied to subjugation, these fantasies create a powerful affective bond. Resistance or critique becomes a source of jouissance, reaffirming the subject's attachment to the dominant order even as it challenges it (Bloom and Cederstrom, 2009; Bautista, 2018; Krüger, 2019).

Moreover, these complex fantasies are not static but constantly evolve and adapt to changing social and political conditions (Laclau, 1990; Butler, 1997). They respond to the shifting desires and anxieties of subjects, offering new sources of jouissance and affective investment as older forms become exhausted or challenged (Puar, 2007; Berlant, 2011). This adaptability contributes to the resilience of hegemonic power structures, enabling them to weather crises and upheavals (Gramsci, 1971; Hall, 1986). The deep entrenchment of these fantasies in the symbolic order makes them difficult to dislodge, as they are intertwined with the material and social conditions that sustain them (Althusser, 1969; Williams, 1977). Challenging these fantasies requires a broader social transformation that addresses the structural and institutional bases of hegemonic power (Negri and Hardt, 2000; Harvey, 2005).

The complexity of this task is heightened by the way these fantasies are embedded in the language and practices of resistance and critique. As Slavoj Žižek and others have noted, even radical opposition often reproduces the very fantasies and power dynamics it seeks to overturn (Žižek, 1989; Butler et al, 2000). These fantasies are constitutive of subjectivity itself (Lacan, 1977; Foucault, 1978). The complex fantasies underpinning hegemonic power serve to perpetuate repressive interpellation, experienced as enjoyment and self-realization. By transforming RSAs into ISAs and integrating repression into cultural fantasies, complexes create a subjectivity deeply invested in maintaining the dominant order and resistant to change (Deleuze and Guattari, 1987; Spivak, 1988).

A growing complex configuration of power emerges where the fantasies and desires underpinning hegemonic ideologies become the very foundation of subjectivity. This internalization and affective investment make domination insidious, experienced not as an external imposition but as a source of enjoyment and self-realization. Resistance paradoxically perpetuates the dominant order, as critique or opposition reinforces the subject's attachment to the fantasies and power relations it seeks to challenge. This highlights the challenge for any emancipatory project, which must contend with both overt coercion and the deep psychic and libidinal investments securing mass complicity in structures of domination. Hegemonic complexes achieve durability by colonizing the psychic territory of desire, diffusing complex fantasies seamlessly into everyday life. Control and hierarchy become eroticized and libidinalized, with individuals developing unconscious investments in their own repression and the repression of emancipative alternatives to this system.

Perpetual complex

Socio-economic complexes, embodying the fusion of political agendas and capitalist profit motives, generate immense systemic contradictions and crisis tendencies through their relentless pursuit of elite enrichment at the expense of broader social welfare. However, in a striking departure from traditional theories positing that such endemic crises inherently disrupt and destabilize dominant power formations, the reality under complexes is that destabilization itself becomes a productive force for expanded entrenchment. Complexes do not merely navigate or withstand the volatilities wrought by their own accumulative drives; they actively politicize and strategically capitalize upon the very crises their policies manufacture and amplify. Rather than implementing substantive reforms to resolve fundamental contradictions, complexes leverage crisis as a pretext to institute fresh regimes of mass behavioural control, ideological regimentation, and intensified capital accumulation – all meticulously aligned with overarching corporate interests. In this paradoxical dynamic, complexes alchemically convert the fires of social unravelling they stoke into potent fuel for their own relentless self-perpetuation and territorial expansion.

Karl Marx's original critique of political economy provides a framework for understanding the politicization of economic life under capitalism (Marx, 1867). Marx rejected the notion of an autonomous economic realm governed by self-regulating market laws, identifying capital as a politically constructed social relation rooted in organized class power, maintained through legal and institutional means to ensure bourgeois dominance. He exposed liberal tenets like private property, market competition, and the profit motive as ideological mystifications concealing class exploitation and labour subjugation. Mainstream capitalist economics thus naturalizes political-economic relations that reinforce bourgeois rule over direct producers (Resnick and Wolff, 1989). Marxian analysis also identified the 'military–industrial complex' as a pathology where state–corporate capitalism transformed mass violence technologies into engines of capital accumulation, diverting resources from social needs into profitable warfare and insecurity industries (Melman, 1974). This politicization of economic reproduction around security priorities reached new extremes post-war, as theorists like Paul Baran traced the formation of a 'military economy' driven by militarized Keynesian policies merging state and corporate power.

The theory of complex power builds upon and transforms Marxian ideas of the base/superstructure by highlighting the fluidity and interconnectedness of political and economic realms. Complexes show that the economic base and ideological superstructure dynamically interact to perpetuate elite power. By integrating repression and ideological manipulation into everyday life, complexes blur traditional distinctions, demonstrating how power operates through economic mechanisms and cultural narratives, reinforcing political decisions in shaping economic realities. This analysis provides crucial insights into contemporary complexes, such as the prison–industrial, surveillance–security, and military–technological complexes, which supplant civic functions with resource pillage, mass coercive control, and rationalized dispossession (Morozov, 2022). These complexes exemplify Marx's critique of capital as a politicized relation that displaces civic development with governance technologies designed to force human potential into profitable power structures.

Mid-20th-century neo-Marxian theorists like Nicos Poulantzas and Ralph Miliband deepened the analysis of the state's role in concentrating capitalist power under advanced capitalism (Miliband, 1965; Poulantzas, 1978). Poulantzas rejected mechanistic 'base/superstructure' dualisms, highlighting how economic centralization and systemic turbulence dissolve the illusion of the capitalist state's 'relative autonomy.' He argued that the state must deeply penetrate and regulate capitalist economy mechanisms to uphold governance and accumulation imperatives (Poulantzas, 1978). As crises intensify, the state increasingly supports oligopolies through fiscal interventions, debt-financing, mass securitization, and technocratic-surveillance infrastructures, erasing the separation between economic and political realms. Miliband located this fusion of 'state' and 'economy' in the social networks linking corporate capital and state managers into an interwoven power bloc. He highlighted the institutional partnerships, shared class outlooks, and socialization patterns that create synergies between executives and bureaucrats, effectively making state capacities serve business dominance. Economic volatilities and legitimation deficits drive state–capital complexes towards further immiseration and authoritarian disciplines, as accumulation priorities override other social considerations in systemically reconciling crises.

This neo-Marxist analysis of state-capitalism's class recomposition into concentrated complexes of political and economic power finds stark contemporary validation. The cycles of financial implosion, capital strikes, and austerity militarism are radicalized expressions of monopolistic state-capital complexes rationalizing governance to uphold capitalist social relations against democratic forces. The interpenetration of corporate–securitarian control logics reorganizing civil society for mass population management and rentier predation is not an aberration but the aggressive universalization of complex capital's class rule as governance telos. For complexes, crises are not disruptions but opportunities for disciplinary restructuring, cementing dominant hierarchies and exploiting post-crisis conditions for more invasive state–capital enclosures. Under complexes, the political anatomy of crisis differs starkly from conventional portrayals. Crises are no longer deviations to be managed and corrected but spaces where state/capital complexes intensify assaults on social life. These dislocations become staging grounds where collective desperation is leveraged for accelerated privatization, austerity, and militarization of public policy. The state metamorphoses into a permanent crisis manager, organizing economies of insecurity for complex oligopolies, systematizing and commodifying contingencies of fear.

Complexes deliberately amplify dislocation to restructure environments, integrating social infrastructure into mass control trajectories and redefining capitalist 'progress' as the application of complex logics to perpetual crises. Precarity and structural failure become markets for control, with manufactured existential threats rationalizing complex governance under systemic resilience (Morozov, 2022). Healthcare collapses expand biometric databases and pharma supply chains; housing and food insecurity drive intrusive surveillance urbanization; and climate collapse accelerates infrastructure privatization and immiseration. Complexes strategically catalyse crises across geographies and social scales, extracting value from disruptions and transforming social experiences into control constellations while masking tensions with techno-utopian promises. Their proactive, globally synchronized crisis amplification rationalizes dislocation to reproduce control regimes, packaging dislocations as opportunities to rebuild environments around automated regulation, monitoring, and commodity flows, perpetuating capitalist relations and foreclosing social emancipation

Navigating global capitalisms: complexifying power in a fragmented world system

The term 'capitalism' in this analysis refers not to a singular, monolithic system but to a mode of economic and social organization characterized by the prioritization of capital accumulation, market relations, and private ownership as the primary means of organizing production and distribution. This understanding aligns with orthodox political economy but emphasizes that capitalism is not uniform; it takes different forms depending on historical, cultural, and institutional contexts. The concept of 'complexifying power' extends this analysis by viewing capitalism as a dynamic process that evolves through the interaction of economic practices with social and political structures. This evolution leads to the emergence of complexes – like the AFC – that combine elements of finance, state governance, and technological control to manage social order and generate profit.

By framing capitalism as a flexible and adaptive system, the analysis allows for the inclusion of different capitalist models, such as the liberal capitalism of the United States, the state-directed capitalism of China, and the oligarchic capitalism of Russia, within the broader processes associated with the AFC. The critical point here is not that all these systems are identical, but that they each contribute to and participate in the ongoing expansion of the AFC, albeit in different ways and with varying degrees of integration. The concept of complexifying power helps explain how seemingly divergent forms of capitalism can be interlinked through global financial networks, shared technologies of control, and overlapping strategies for maintaining social and political stability. The 'variegated capitalism' approach (see Peck and Theodore, 2007; Zhang and Peck, 2016) recognizes the diversity of capitalist systems across different geographical and institutional settings. According to this perspective, capitalism is not a uniform phenomenon but consists of multiple 'varieties' that manifest through different combinations of market mechanisms, state interventions, and cultural norms. For example, social-democratic capitalism in Northern Europe differs significantly from the more laissez-faire approaches found in the United States or the state-driven model in China. These differences shape how capital is accumulated, how labour is managed, and how the state intervenes in the economy.

The notion of complexifying power accommodates this diversity by viewing these different capitalist models not as entirely separate systems but as interconnected nodes within a broader global network of capital accumulation and governance. While the specific forms of capitalism may vary – shaped by national histories, political structures, and cultural factors – there remains a convergence around certain mechanisms of control and financialization that support the operations of the AFC. For instance, while China's state-directed capitalism emphasizes centralized state control over economic planning and technology, it still utilizes global financial markets, surveillance technologies, and data-driven governance techniques that align with practices found in the United States or Europe. The AFC's power does not lie in homogenizing these diverse forms of capitalism but in leveraging the capacities of each to reinforce a global system of control-oriented practices. Through complexifying power, different capitalist models can coexist within the AFC because they share a common reliance on financialization, securitization, and technological governance to manage social risks and ensure economic stability. The mechanisms of control may be implemented differently across regions – reflecting variegated capitalism – but the underlying imperatives of risk management, social control, and profit extraction are present across these diverse systems.

Specifically relevant to financial capitalism, it becomes possible to develop a more nuanced understanding of how complexifying power operates within the AFC. Building, for instance, on the work of Dixon (2011) and the variegated geographies of finance, what is uncovered are the dynamic ways in which the AFC integrates, adapts to, and shapes these diverse capitalist forms. Rather than imposing a single model of control, complexifying power exploits the variations within capitalism, turning institutional and geographical differences into strategic opportunities for deepening control and expanding influence. By utilizing local contexts and varied regulatory environments, the AFC can selectively deploy financialization and surveillance mechanisms that resonate with specific cultural, economic, and political conditions, effectively embedding its operations across different systems.

Critically, this approach to power does not rely on homogenizing global capitalism but instead involves orchestrating its diverse elements to create a complex, adaptable system of control. Different forms of financialization, shaped by local traditions and state–capital relations, act as entry points for the AFC's mechanisms of social and economic management. For instance, in state-directed economies, surveillance and financialization may be more overtly tied to state interests, while in liberal economies, these mechanisms operate through market-driven processes that appear to emerge naturally from private sector dynamics. By strategically navigating these variations, the AFC ensures that financial control and social regulation are continuously refined and recalibrated in response to local resistance, institutional constraints, or opportunities for deeper integration. This process reflects a form of complexifying power where the AFC not only accommodates the variegation of capitalism but actively reproduces it, using the differences as a way to distribute risk, shift regulatory burdens, and optimize profit opportunities. By sustaining the diversity of capitalist practices rather than erasing them, the AFC maintains the flexibility needed to expand its influence across different economic landscapes. The variegated nature of capitalism thus becomes a resource for the AFC, allowing it to perpetuate its control through an ever-changing configuration of financial, technological, and regulatory practices. In this sense, the AFC's power is not limited by the contradictions within global capitalism but thrives on them, continually turning these contradictions into opportunities for deeper entrenchment and global coordination.

World-systems theory, as articulated by scholars like Immanuel Wallerstein, provides another lens through which to understand the integration of various forms of capitalism within the global economy. It posits a hierarchy of core, semi-peripheral, and peripheral states, each playing different roles in the global division of labour. The core states (such as the United States and parts of Western Europe) dominate the production of high-value goods and control global financial flows, while peripheral states are often sites of labour-intensive or resource-extractive industries. Semi-peripheral states (such as China and Russia) occupy an intermediary position, combining elements of both core and peripheral functions. The AFC can be seen as a development within the world-system where traditional distinctions between core and periphery become more fluid, with the mechanisms of financial and social control spreading across different regions. As financial networks, digital surveillance, and control-oriented policies extend beyond the core states, they contribute to the formation of a transnational capitalist class that operates across national boundaries. This class consists of elites who, despite differences in their respective capitalist systems, share an interest in perpetuating the conditions that sustain the AFC. Their collaboration often involves coordinating on financial regulations, data governance, and the securitization of social life, even if tensions and rifts remain between states.

The existence of a transnational capitalist class does not imply a uniformity of interests across all elites; rather, it indicates a shared framework for engaging with global capitalism and managing its contradictions. There are indeed tensions, as seen in trade disputes between the United States and China or geopolitical conflicts involving Russia, but these conflicts do not negate the broader convergence around certain control-oriented practices. In fact, these tensions can themselves be commodified and integrated into the operations of the AFC, as they create new demands for risk management, surveillance, and technological solutions that benefit transnational elites. Thus, while divisions remain among capitalist powers, these divisions are incorporated into a complex global system where control itself becomes a transnational concern.

While important distinctions exist among capitalist elites in the United States, China, and Russia, these rifts reveal how the complex navigates and integrates divergent interests. Each capitalist model brings unique resources, capabilities, and constraints to the global system, which the AFC leverages in different ways. For example, the United States provides advanced financial markets and data-driven technologies that are central to the operation of global financial surveillance. China, on the other hand, offers a model of state-directed capitalism that demonstrates how centralized control can coexist with market mechanisms, influencing approaches to digital governance and infrastructural development worldwide. Russia, with its emphasis on energy resources and strategic military interests, adds another layer to the global system by influencing geopolitical dynamics that affect financial stability and security practices.

The AFC establishes, in this respect, a framework in which the commodification of control and the social desire for regulation can flexibly adapt to different forms of capitalism. By embedding mechanisms of control within both market-driven and state-directed contexts, the AFC enables the commodification of surveillance, risk management, and financialization to take on various forms that resonate with local socio-economic conditions. In liberal economies, this can manifest through market-oriented solutions that emphasize personal empowerment and consumer choice, such as financial products for risk mitigation or digital surveillance tools marketed as lifestyle enhancers. In more state-centric models, control may be commodified through state-sponsored programmes that integrate surveillance and financial monitoring as part of public policy, presenting them as measures for social stability and national development. This adaptability allows the AFC to align its operations with existing cultural and institutional norms, ensuring that the commodification of control does not appear as an external imposition but rather as a logical extension of local economic practices. As a result, the AFC can sustain and even deepen the social desire for control across different forms of capitalism, framing surveillance and financial regulation as essential elements for managing modern life, regardless of the specific economic model in place.

Conclusion

This chapter introduced the concept of 'complexifying power' as a new theoretical framework for examining consolidated institutional power networks exhibiting unique features. Rather than a phenomenon fixed to the current era, complexes represent durable formations where elite interests across military, economic, political and cultural spheres coalesce into influential blocs with considerable coercive capacities, resources, and ideological influence.

Crucially, such complexes retain and expand power across changing contexts not merely through direct state-backed coercion, but through sophisticated manufacturing of cultural fantasies and collectivized dreams that strategically promise symbolic compensation for profound societal tensions that reckless policies by complexes continually worsen over time. Skilful manipulation of psychic insecurity and desires thereby elicits periodic renewal of mass loyalty despite unrestrained complexes exacerbating inequality, precarity, and demoralization.

The notion of complexifying power theorizes complexes as manifestations of a distinct political economy where imperatives of social control and security maintenance override conventional economic optimization. What originated to secure regime viability comes to directly structure economic activity as complexes reroute investments and revolutionize accumulation priorities according to political dictates of capital enrichment, asymmetric benefit capture, and legitimacy restoration amid crises through weapons innovation, mass persuasion technologies, and internal policing apparatuses becoming growth industries in themselves.

A crucial advancement put forward in this chapter's original theory of complexifying power is demonstrating critical linkages between multifaceted institutional ecosystems of consolidated power and the psychological notion of unconscious 'complexes' in order to reveal deeper dimensions of sophisticated power arrangements dominating society. It importantly bridged this structural investigation of institutional power networks with psychoanalytic understandings of 'complexes' as charged clusters of unconscious thoughts, emotions, and associations that become semi-autonomous fixations that fundamentally structure desire and identity.

The analysis undertaken here highlights the intricate and multifaceted relationship between fantasy and the operation of power in contemporary complexes. What becomes clear is that fantasy is not merely an epiphenomenon or supplementary aspect of hegemonic domination, but is rather its very condition of possibility. The complex fantasies that circulate within the symbolic orders of these societies play a foundational role in shaping subjectivity, desire, and modes of identification. They provide the affective scaffolding that allows subjects to invest libidinally in repressive power structures, experiencing them not as external constraints but as sources of enjoyment and self-realization.

Simultaneously, these fantasies exhibit a remarkable degree of plasticity and adaptability, evolving and mutating in response to changing social and political landscapes. This capacity for metamorphosis enables complexes to absorb and recode forms of resistance and critique, ensuring their own perpetuation even in the face of concerted opposition. As such, any project of genuine emancipation must reckon with the affective and fantasmatic infrastructures that underwrite hegemonic domination, in addition to challenging its material and institutional manifestations.

The original theory of complexifying power formations and dynamics elaborated across this chapter critically examines a further dimension regarding complexes progressively dominating processes of economic production, social provisioning, and cultural conditioning underlying societal development. Namely, as complexes gain heightened influence across policy making, governance, and cultural ecosystems, their logics infiltrate sinews of society to materially reshape core institutional arrangements supporting economic activity and reproduction of culture/subjectivities. A central thesis is that complexes evolve from being sectoral alliances of self-interested state–corporate networks into dominant existential paradigms reorganizing society itself wholly around axes of capital accumulation, mass behaviour control, and ideological management.

This manifests in the complexification of economic modes of production – structural realignments embedding the control priorities and protectionist imperatives of complexes across interconnected domains of economic relations, knowledge transmission, identity construction, and technological design so that these realms fundamentally come to serve elite complexes entrenching their power over any alternative considerations of public welfare, environmental limits, or democratization. Under complexified reproduction, the sinews underlying human development such as workplace relations, community support, scientific research, and democratic process undergo thorough infiltration and reorientation around outcomes desired by capitalist oligarchies and their allies rather than standards of civic dignity, climate stewardship, or collective needs fulfillment. What originated as politically necessary for social control becomes the productive logic driving organizational design, labour dynamics, and resource flows.

The introduced conceptual framework spotlights a pivotal paradox – how institutional power formations become counterintuitively strengthened by the crises they generate. Complexes directly drive societal tensions and afflictions by prioritizing narrow interests over collective welfare. However, the ensuing turmoil and demoralization become distorted into opportunities for further expansion rather than accountability or restraint. Complexes exacerbate underlying issues through reckless policies that prioritize narrow interests over collective welfare. However, the resulting tensions and afflictions then allow those same complexes to entrench control by offering their unique managerial capabilities, resources, and visionary futures as supposed remedies for the manufactured volatility.

The foregoing examination underscores how complexes are fundamentally psycho-social phenomena, operating across both psychic and social registers. The manner in which hegemonic power structures are internalized and affectively invested in by subjects points to their status as symbolic-imaginary constructs that hold sway at the level of the unconscious. The complex fantasies that secure this investment are psychical formations, emerging from the interplay of unconscious drives and the constraints of the symbolic order.

Yet these subjective dimensions are inextricable from the social conditions and relations of power in which they are embedded. The fantasies in question are fundamentally social fantasies, providing the narratives, images, and scenarios through which societal complexes cohere and reproduce themselves. They serve to stitch subjects into the fabric of hegemonic ideology, aligning individual desires and modes of enjoyment with the perpetuation of dominant structures. As such, complexes reveal themselves to be phenomena that straddle and articulate the psychic and the social, the unconscious and the institutional. The circuits of affective investment and libidinal cathexis that sustain them simultaneously shape and are shaped by broader matrices of political-economic and cultural forces. Repressive interpellation operates not only at the level of overt discipline and subjugation, but also through the production of unconscious attachments and identifications.

Having introduced this theoretical framework, the next chapter will explore its concrete application through profiling the rise of a specific contemporary AFC defined by fusion between militarized policing capacities designed for internal security and ballooning financial sectors politically harnessing economic volatility for further security expansion and discipline.

3

The Rise of the Authoritarian–Financial Complex

Introduction

The movement from the military–industrial complex to the authoritarian–financial complex (AFC) reflects a significant reconfiguration of power dynamics, driven by financial markets, technological advancements, and population control. This complex brings together authoritarian regimes, financial institutions, and tech companies to develop surveillance and control mechanisms for profit. Financialization has prioritized short-term financial gains, making population control technologies attractive for their potential returns through commodified surveillance and behaviour modification (Epstein, 2005). Technology companies have capitalized on this, extracting vast amounts of personal data and advancing invasive tracking technologies (Hawley, 2021; Birch and Bronson, 2022). Operating within a 'moligopoly' of dominant firms (Petit, 2020a), the complex exploits crises like economic instability or public health emergencies to justify these technologies, eroding rights and deepening inequalities (Sawyer, 2013; Van der Zwan, 2014). By tapping into the human desire for control, the AFC develops systems to predict and influence behaviour for financial gain.

The AFC exemplifies the 'repressive cycle of finance', where increasing financialization fuels economic and social insecurity, driving demand for control technologies as people seek stability in a turbulent world. Surveillance tech providers and data analytics firms capitalize on this demand by offering products that promise security but simultaneously erode privacy, autonomy, and social cohesion, exacerbating the insecurity they aim to address. This commodification of repression ties the profitability of control industries to the perpetuation of insecurity, creating a vicious cycle where the more uncertain the world becomes, the greater the demand for these products (Epstein, 2005). The convergence of financial, technological, and political power creates a profitable paradigm of population monitoring and control, driven by securitization, where various aspects of life are transformed into tradable assets. Ideological narratives of empowerment and accumulation perpetuate this cycle, trapping individuals in a system where fantasies of individuation and actualization depend on submission to control technologies and policies.

This chapter examines the rise of the AFC and its implications for contemporary power dynamics. It begins by introducing the concept of the AFC and contrasting it with the previous military–industrial paradigm. The next section delves into the process of financialization, unpacking its role in the ascendance of this new complex and its relationship to capital accumulation. This is followed by an analysis of how financial and technological power have become increasingly intertwined, shaping the governing logic of the AFC. The chapter then explores the mechanism of securitization as a driving force behind the assetization of various domains, the commodification of security, and the creation of new markets premised on population control. The 'repressive cycle of finance' is introduced as a key conceptual framework for understanding how instabilities catalyse an incessant expansion of profitable securitizing interventions.

Financialized securitization

Securitization, as a process, has become central to understanding contemporary forms of governance and control under late capitalism. It represents not just a shift in how threats are managed but a fundamental restructuring of power, where economic, political, and technological imperatives converge to shape the landscape of social control. At its core, securitization involves the transformation of various risks – whether political, economic, or existential – into tradable, financialized assets. These risks are commodified, allowing for the generation of profit while reinforcing the power of those who control the means of securitization. This process extends beyond traditional forms of security, such as military power, to encompass social, economic, and personal domains, making it a cornerstone of the AFC.

Securitization operates through the commodification of uncertainty. The ability to anticipate, control, and mitigate risk becomes a valuable commodity in financialized capitalism, where the global economy is increasingly driven by speculation and instability. Financial markets are not simply reactive to crises but are deeply embedded in creating and amplifying conditions of uncertainty that necessitate securitization. This is evident in the proliferation of financial instruments, such as derivatives and credit default swaps, that transform future risks into present-day financial opportunities. These instruments allow financial institutions and corporations to profit from the very instability they help produce, turning insecurity into a profitable venture.

This economic dimension of securitization is intertwined with technological advancements that enable more precise and pervasive forms of surveillance and control. Digital platforms and data analytics technologies play a crucial role in facilitating securitization by providing the means to collect, process, and interpret vast amounts of personal data. The datafication of everyday life – where every action, transaction, and interaction becomes a data point – creates new avenues for monitoring, predicting, and managing behaviour. In this context, securitization is not merely about responding to perceived threats but about actively shaping social and economic environments to ensure compliance with the imperatives of financialized accumulation.

The intersection of financialization and securitization thus results in the development of control mechanisms that are both pervasive and adaptive. Financial institutions and corporations increasingly employ predictive analytics and algorithmic governance to manage risks and optimize control strategies. These technologies, far from being neutral tools, are deeply implicated in reproducing and reinforcing existing power structures. By framing security as a commodity, they mask the underlying dynamics of power that drive their development and deployment. The promise of security becomes a justification for the expansion of surveillance technologies and the erosion of personal autonomy, as individuals are increasingly subjected to algorithmic decision-making processes that prioritize financial and political stability over individual rights and freedoms.

Moreover, securitization extends beyond the individual level to encompass broader societal dynamics. The financialization of public goods and services – such as healthcare, education, and housing – has introduced new forms of risk management that prioritize profitability over accessibility and equity. In sectors like healthcare, for example, the rise of private insurance markets and the commodification of patient data have transformed health into a securitized asset, where the risks associated with illness and mortality are monetized and traded. Similarly, in housing markets, securitized mortgage-backed securities have not only contributed to global financial crises but have also reshaped access to housing, creating new forms of exclusion and inequality.

The role of the state in this process is also crucial. While securitization is often driven by private interests, it is facilitated by state policies and regulatory frameworks that prioritize financial stability over social welfare. In many cases, governments have actively encouraged the securitization of public goods through privatization and deregulation, creating new opportunities for financial markets to exert control over critical aspects of social life. This has led to the erosion of public accountability, as private corporations and financial institutions take on increasing responsibility for managing risks that were once the domain of the state. However, the state's involvement in securitization is not limited to enabling financial markets. In many cases, governments themselves become key actors in the securitization process, using the language and tools of risk management to justify authoritarian policies. This is particularly evident in the deployment of surveillance technologies during times of crisis, such as public health emergencies or national security threats. The state's role in securitization is thus twofold: it facilitates the expansion of financial markets into new domains while simultaneously using securitization to legitimize its own exercise of power.

The commodification of security, therefore, is both a product and a driver of broader processes of financialization. As security becomes a tradable asset, it is subject to the same logics of capital accumulation that govern other commodities. This has profound implications for how governance is structured and how power is exercised in contemporary society. Securitization not only transforms risks into opportunities for profit but also restructures the relationship between the individual and the state, as well as between private and public actors. The boundaries between public and private, and between economic and political power, become increasingly blurred as securitization infiltrates all aspects of life. In this regard, securitization must be understood as a deeply political process that goes beyond its economic and technological dimensions. It is a mechanism through which elites – whether financial, political, or technological – consolidate their power by shaping societal responses to risk and insecurity. By framing these responses in terms of security and control, they obscure the underlying drivers of instability, reinforcing a cycle in which crises are both manufactured and managed for the benefit of those in power.

This brings us to the broader implications of securitization for democratic governance. As securitization becomes more entrenched, it erodes the capacity for collective action and democratic decision-making. The commodification of security shifts the focus away from public accountability and towards private profit, weakening the social bonds that are necessary for democratic governance. At the same time, the increasing reliance on surveillance technologies and algorithmic governance further undermines democratic processes by concentrating decision-making power in the hands of unaccountable corporate and state actors. The result is a form of governance that is more concerned with managing risk than with promoting social justice or protecting individual freedoms. The intersection of securitization and financialization thus represents a fundamental transformation in the nature of power in contemporary society. It reflects a shift from governance based on public accountability and democratic participation to a form of control that is mediated through markets, algorithms, and surveillance technologies. This transformation has profound implications for how we understand the role of the state, the market, and the individual in the production and reproduction of social order. It also raises important questions about the future of democracy in a world where security is commodified and control is exercised through increasingly opaque and unaccountable mechanisms.

Securitization is not just a process of managing risk; it is a central mechanism through which financialized capitalism exercises control over individuals and societies. It commodifies insecurity, transforming risks into tradable assets, and uses surveillance technologies to enforce compliance with the imperatives of capital accumulation. By blurring the lines between public and private, and between economic and political power, securitization reshapes governance and deepens inequalities. It is a key tool in the consolidation of elite power, allowing financial, political, and technological actors to profit from and perpetuate the very crises they claim to manage.

The repressive cycle of finance

The AFC marks a significant transformation from the military–industrial complex, driven by the privatization and globalization of military operations, financial market influence, and advancements in surveillance, data analysis, and artificial intelligence (Lynn III, 2014; Smith, 2015). Private military and security companies operate outside traditional oversight, prioritizing efficiency and profitability over public interest, filling gaps left by military budget cuts post–Cold War (Dunigan and Petersohn, 2015; Singer, 2017). Financial markets now play a crucial role in shaping defence priorities, creating a symbiotic relationship between the military, defence industry, and finance sectors, all reliant on conflict and insecurity to fuel demand for new technologies (Pike and Pollard, 2010; Roland, 2021). Globally, this complex is reinforced by neoliberal policies and authoritarian governance, as seen in Turkey and the Global South, where privatization exacerbates inequality and violence (Wicaksono and Perwita, 2020; Nunes, 2023). In collaboration with state security agencies, private tech firms develop advanced surveillance and artificial intelligence systems to monitor and control populations, extending the complex's influence beyond military operations to public sectors like policing, raising concerns about transparency and accountability (Montgomery and Griffiths, 2015; White, 2015; Saglam, 2022a).

The privatization of security and financialization of economies, combined with the rise of sophisticated control technologies, exacerbates global power imbalances and creates a cycle where insecurity generates profit, which in turn perpetuates further instability (Tabb, 2021). This is especially evident in developing economies like Mexico, where privatized policing has intensified inequality and state violence (Müller, 2016). Unlike the state-centred military–industrial complex, the AFC includes private military firms, Big Tech, and financial markets, all profiting from commodified security and influencing defence and security policies with limited oversight

(Lavoie, 2012; De Goede, 2017). This shift commodifies human security and embeds financial logics into everyday life, maintaining dominance over labour, resources, and economic policies to sustain profit (Lai, 2016). Big Tech firms further leverage this system, using data-driven algorithms to expand their influence, while financial markets prioritize shareholder value and concentrate power among financial elites (Foster and Holleman, 2010a; Greene, 2019). Amidst this consolidation, resistance emerges from workers, consumers, and citizens demanding greater transparency and democratic control over the digital infrastructure shaping their lives (Prato and Sonkin, 2018; Wagner, 2021). Ultimately, the AFC reinforces inequality and societal discord, wielding formidable influence over global governance (Witko, 2016).

The shift from militarization to securitization has redefined how threats are perceived and governance is enacted globally (Wicaksono and Perwita, 2020). While the military–industrial complex once focused on state-centric violence and national sovereignty (Montgomery and Griffiths, 2015), the contemporary AFC uses securitization logic to privatize legitimate violence and manage risks through economic means (Saglam, 2022b). This approach commodifies entities into tradable assets, subordinating productive activities to financial interests and intensifying capitalist discipline worldwide (Lavoie, 2012; De Goede, 2017). Assetization processes have enabled new forms of rentiership, with corporations and academic institutions deriving profits from securitized technoscientific products (Birch, 2017). Financialized technologies now permeate welfare systems, surveilling marginalized populations and deepening authoritarian control (Bielefeld et al, 2021). Examples like Ukraine's 'forced credit' system and Turkey's vulnerability to volatile capital flows demonstrate how financialization fosters authoritarian dependency (Mattioli, 2018; Apaydin and Çoban, 2023). China's 'authoritarian capitalism' and Latin America's financial crises further highlight how financialization can entrench authoritarianism globally (Felix, 2019; Petry, 2020).

The pervasive logic of securitization has evolved into a potent force legitimizing the creation of ever-expanding markets predicated on controlling and governing diverse populations. This dynamic illustrates the insidious and insatiable capacity of financial rationalities to colonize realms previously insulated from the imperative of capital accumulation. Spheres hitherto exempt from the valorizing impulses of capital have been subsumed under the disciplinary gaze of finance. The historic rationale for securitization emerged from the necessity to stabilize the financial system. By transforming illiquid assets into tradable securities, securitization provided a mechanism to distribute risk and enhance liquidity within capital markets. This process aimed to fortify the integrity of financial institutions by converting their holdings into marketable instruments. However, the contemporary landscape bears witness to a striking reversal, wherein securitization has evolved into an end in itself. Rather than serving as a bulwark against instability, it has become a driving force propelling the relentless expansion of financialization. The logic has shifted from securitizing finance to financing securitization, whereby securitization has mutated into an insatiable imperative to commodify and monetize all aspects of existence, perpetuating the relentless expansion of authoritarian capitalist formations.

The 'repressive cycle of finance' highlights the intricate relationship between economic dynamics, technological innovation, and authoritarian control in contemporary societies. Financial speculation and crises create instability, which authoritarian governance and control technologies exploit under the guise of restoring order and security. This dynamic perpetuates cycles of instability while deepening societal dependence on surveillance and repression. The convergence of financial imperatives and technological advancements fosters a self-perpetuating system where each crisis fuels innovations that further entrench control and profit from repression. Narratives of securitization, combined with the commodification of previously insulated domains, legitimize the extraction of value through assetization and financial derivatives, promising future prosperity (Lysandrou, 2016; Walker, 2018). This mythos, championed by Silicon Valley and global capital, promotes a utopian vision of digital innovation and financialized society while obscuring the unequal distribution of risk and precarity, especially for marginalized groups (Haiven, 2023). Despite these inequalities, tech-finance elites present a seamless and prosperous future, glossing over the dystopian impacts of their economic and social policies (Gruin, 2019; Golka, 2023).

The authoritarian–financial fantasies propagated by securitization regimes reveal how the yearning for security has, thus, coalesced into an intricate psycho-social complex. These fantasies resonate at a personal level by appealing to innate human desires for stability and coherence that underpin our sense of self. The assetization of domains previously considered outside market logic seduces with the tantalizing prospect of transforming the fluctuations of everyday life into measurable, tradable commodities – a fantasmatic vision that seemingly offers refuge from the tumult of our ever-shifting modern existence. Simultaneously, this seductive appeal catalyses investments, both financial and psychological, in institutions that propagate techniques of surveillance, risk management, and algorithmic governance of populations. An entire economic system thrives by fuelling and catering to these investment desires rooted in the aspiration for psychic insulation against uncertainty (Leopold, 2009; Meissner and Meissner, 2017a; Whitener, 2019; Shih, 2020; Wray, 2021).

The narratives surrounding securitization perpetuate a damaging cycle where financialization spawns social, political, and economic instability, prompting the proliferation of control techniques and technologies that paradoxically reproduce precarity. Introduced as the 'repressive cycle of finance', this phenomenon reveals how the financial system sustains itself by profiting from control mechanisms. At its core is a self-perpetuating loop: financial speculation disrupts economic and social structures, leading to instability. Subsequent interventions, promising stability through enhanced governance and surveillance, capitalize on this precarity. Crucially, this feedback loop perpetuates itself, each wave of instability followed by authoritarian stabilization fostering technological innovations that expand control frameworks. This perpetual deferral of resolution compels subjects to invest in the illusion of security, reinforcing regimes that monitor and govern populations under the guise of stability. Political futures markets exemplify this trend, quantifying insecurity to manage it, yet deepening dependencies on systems that originally caused instability. The imperatives of capital accumulation drive increasingly sophisticated financialized securitization techniques and population control mechanisms, entrenching structural dependencies on cycles of instability they purportedly resolve (Aitken, 2011; Jessop, 2013).

Financial control mechanisms and the suppression of dissent are often justified as necessary for maintaining systemic coherence, yet this overlooks how the repressive apparatus thrives by perpetuating hardship to sustain its power. Crises are opportunistically exploited to justify authoritarian measures that expand financial influence into broader aspects of social life under the guise of restoring stability (Whitener, 2019; Shih, 2020). The deployment of digital surveillance during public health crises exemplifies this cycle, where crises enable authoritarian expansions masked as crisis management (Wray, 2021). Financialization triggers economic disruptions that drive technological advancements, which are then co-opted to enhance securitization efforts, trapping individuals in a paradox: seeking stability binds them to regimes perpetuating instability. Each wave of instability spurs new technologies that amplify control, yet these interventions only set the stage for future upheavals. In this cycle, external digital repression intersects with internal psychic repression, as individuals suppress aspirations for alternative societal models free from financial control. The allure of stability promised by financialized governance systems deepens dependence and compliance, stifling dissent and suppressing visions of more equitable social organization.

The repressive cycle of finance reflects, thus, a self-perpetuating dynamic where financialization spawns instability, prompting the deployment of control mechanisms that paradoxically perpetuate precarity. This cycle begins with financial speculation disrupting economic and social structures, leading to crises that justify enhanced governance and surveillance. These interventions, purportedly aimed at restoring stability, instead deepen dependencies on systems that profit from instability. Technological innovations arising from these crises are co-opted to expand securitization efforts, further entrenching structural inequalities. Individuals, driven by desires for security and stability, invest in regimes that promise protection but ultimately reinforce their subjugation. This perpetual deferral of resolution perpetuates a cycle where each wave of instability breeds innovations that enhance capitalist control, maintaining a status quo that undermines efforts for systemic change and perpetuates a reliance on authoritarian mechanisms of governance.

Empowering financial authoritarianism

The repressive cycle of finance has extended its influence into intimate aspects of life, transforming previously insulated domains into avenues for capital accumulation and governance strategies that securitize all facets of existence (Lucarelli, 2010). This biopolitical rationality commodifies life itself, infiltrating everyday experiences through financial mechanisms (Langley, 2020). Microfinance, for example, integrates impoverished populations into financial circuits under the guise of empowerment, masking their subordination to financial accumulation (Mader and Mader, 2015). Similarly, the financialization of critical sectors like the global food system consolidates corporate control, framing domination as efficiency and progress (Keenan et al, 2023). The digital realm has become a key frontier for these logics, where financial transactions are transformed into data streams ripe for extraction and algorithmic governance (Westermeier, 2020). Big Tech firms like Google and Amazon disrupt sectors like healthcare and education under the banner of innovation, establishing extractive systems that turn human well-being into profit centres (Ozalp et al, 2022). While these digital platforms facilitate global capital flows, they also impose new forms of surveillance and control, curating user experiences and shaping acceptable behaviour to serve financial interests, ultimately undermining collective autonomy (Bowers, 2016; Partycki, 2018).

Digital financial technologies, like payment platforms, overlay digital matrices onto physical economic infrastructures, shaping access to services, resources, and jobs around financial identities built from data extraction and commodification (Haiven, 2013). Non-compliance with these systems risks exclusion, deepening social and economic marginalization. Corporations like Walmart exploit the convergence of financialization and securitization to align employee behaviours with capital's logic, where workers internalize speculative investments as part of their labour (Jain and Gabor, 2020). Wage stagnation and benefit cuts push workers into volatile capital flows, further entrenching their dependency on corporate financial services, despite worsening debt and insecurity. Globally, fintech platforms like Paytm in

India, under the guise of financial inclusion, amplify vulnerabilities by regulating credit access through discriminatory risk profiles and punitive fees, trapping individuals in debt cycles (Jain and Gabor, 2020). Digital platforms such as Amazon and Flipkart foster consumer identities tied to aspirational consumption, framing perpetual indebtedness as a status marker (Haiven, 2013). These platforms, driven by data infrastructures and algorithmic governance, track transactions to regulate economic behaviours, reinforcing subordination to algorithmic scoring while eroding collective solidarities through individuation (Partycki, 2018).

The repressive cycle of finance employs adaptive authoritarian strategies tailored to individual profiles and predicted behaviours, enabled by the pervasive datafication of human life (Ozalp et al, 2022). This vast data collection allows for detailed user portraits that inform predictive analytics, managing deviations from financial norms by manipulating behaviours through incentives, nudges, and environmental adjustments (Westermeier, 2020). Digital platforms thus create a coercive feedback loop where surveillance and behavioural modulation serve financialized accumulation. This shift in authority moves away from overt state coercion, co-opting individuals' desires for empowerment and framing control mechanisms as sources of agency. Instead of traditional repression demanding obedience, control is presented as a personalized, attractive vision of individuality, creating an Orwellian dynamic where submission is seen as empowerment. The hierarchical relationship between oppressor and oppressed is redefined as a simulated dialogue, portraying control as responsive to personal preferences and desires.

Leveraging economic governance

The AFC thrives on the interconnectedness of global supply chains, government regulations, tariffs, and tax policies, all of which serve as mechanisms to extend financial control and social governance. These components help perpetuate the interests of the complex by weaving systems of economic surveillance and coercion into everyday life, where securitization and control not only shape market dynamics but become embedded as social imperatives. This framework creates conditions in which economic policies intersect with authoritarian practices, reinforcing the complex's grip on power while commodifying control and entrenching it as a central feature of contemporary life.

Global supply chains are at the heart of this process, serving not just as conduits for the movement of goods and resources but also as mechanisms for monitoring and regulating labour, trade, and even political activities. The highly integrated nature of global production relies on vast networks of logistics, data analytics, and surveillance to optimize operations and ensure compliance (see Levy, 2008). This degree of oversight enables corporations to extend control over workers, transforming them into monitored inputs whose productivity is constantly measured and adjusted to meet shifting demands. Workers in supply chains are often subjected to algorithmic management that uses real-time data to dictate schedules, evaluate performance, and enforce compliance (Graham and Anwar, 2019). This extends to gig workers, who experience precarious conditions where algorithmic surveillance governs not only their work output but also their access to economic opportunities (Woodcock, 2020).

The use of surveillance technology within supply chains serves as both a tool of efficiency and a means of enforcing social order. Companies justify the implementation of these technologies as necessary for ensuring ethical sourcing or environmental responsibility, but the data collected in the name of transparency often serves broader interests (Egels-Zandén and Hansson, 2016). It allows for the identification of patterns that can be used to suppress labour organization, predictively police protests, or even influence local politics to maintain favourable conditions for business. The normalization of these practices under the guise of 'ethical supply chain management' obscures the underlying motives of exerting control and maintaining stability in regions where social tensions may threaten production. Additionally, supply chain management serves as a geopolitical tool, with states and corporations using control over critical nodes to apply pressure or gain leverage in international relations. The strategic manipulation of resources, labour markets, and logistics networks can destabilize economies or coerce governments into policy changes that favour corporate or state interests. This form of economic diplomacy transforms supply chains into instruments of coercive power, where economic dependencies are exploited to shape political and social outcomes (Cowen, 2014). The result is a global system in which economic activities are not only subject to market forces but are deeply entwined with mechanisms of social control.

Government regulations further embed the AFC into social and economic life. While regulations are typically presented as safeguards for the public, they often operate as tools for legitimizing expansive surveillance and control. For example, data protection laws ostensibly designed to protect privacy frequently include provisions that mandate data sharing with law enforcement or intelligence agencies. These frameworks establish legal norms for surveillance that are difficult to contest, embedding the practice of monitoring into the very structure of governance. Regulations around financial activities, such as anti-money laundering and anti-terrorism measures, expand this infrastructure by providing governments with legal avenues to monitor citizens' financial behaviours. Such measures go beyond traditional financial oversight, creating a network that surveils not just economic transactions but social movements, political affiliations, and personal networks. This regulatory environment consolidates power within the AFC by integrating surveillance into the architecture of financial governance. By making certain aspects of life contingent on regulatory compliance, it becomes possible to normalize the surveillance of ordinary activities under the pretext of security and legal necessity (Amicelle and Favarel-Garrigues, 2012). For example, businesses are required to comply with know-your-customer regulations that necessitate detailed data collection, not just to prevent illicit activities but to feed into a broader ecosystem of financial monitoring. This creates pathways for corporations and governments to collect vast amounts of data on citizens, turning compliance with financial regulations into a means of social control.

The selective application of regulations further reinforces this dynamic, where compliance standards are used to penalize dissent or to suppress sectors that challenge established interests. Labour regulations can be enforced in ways that stifle union activities or silence worker advocacy, while environmental regulations may be applied to displace communities in favour of commercial development. In this context, regulation becomes a means of shaping the economic landscape to favour entities aligned with the complex, effectively leveraging legal frameworks to expand control and suppress opposition.

Tariffs and tax policies contribute to the consolidation of the AFC by influencing economic behaviour and creating incentives that align with the interests of financial elites and authoritarian governance. Tariffs, for instance, can be strategically applied to manipulate market conditions in ways that secure compliance or create economic dependencies. By imposing tariffs on essential imports or exports, states can disrupt supply chains to coerce governments or populations into conforming to specific political or economic demands. Domestically, tariffs may be used to protect industries that are closely tied to surveillance technologies, military contractors, or sectors considered strategically important for maintaining control over populations. Tax policies similarly shape the distribution of wealth and power by favouring certain industries while penalizing others. Tax incentives often promote investment in sectors like technology, finance, and private security, which are crucial to the operations of the AFC. These policies concentrate economic control in industries deeply integrated with surveillance, data analytics, and security, effectively creating a feedback loop where economic power reinforces social control. The preferential treatment given to these industries accelerates the commodification of data and control, embedding the economic logic of surveillance into the financial fabric of society.

Together, the manipulation of supply chains, government regulations, tariffs, and taxes reflects the rise of the AFC, where economic governance is not simply about managing resources or facilitating growth but about consolidating control over social life. The entanglement of these mechanisms within the financial and political domains extends the reach of surveillance, making it a normalized aspect of governance and economic activity. As financial incentives increasingly favour the securitization of life itself – through data commodification, predictive policing, and the regulation of behaviour – the pursuit of control becomes not only an economic strategy but a social imperative.

The rise of the authoritarian–financial complex

Financial authoritarianism has undergone a profound transformation, evolving from a political tool into an economic necessity within global capitalism. Initially a response to political instability and economic crises, authoritarianism was often used by elites to manage turmoil and maintain social order. Over time, however, its function has expanded, aligning with the imperatives of financialization. In the contemporary global economy, financial institutions and corporations hold significant influence over political systems, and their control has made financial authoritarianism a critical mechanism for preserving the conditions that allow financial markets to flourish. This shift reflects a growing dependence of modern economies on financial markets for stability and capital accumulation.

Financialization has, importantly, led to the subordination of productive activities – such as manufacturing and agriculture – to speculative investments and financial instruments. As speculative capital becomes more dominant, ensuring the stability and profitability of financial markets becomes paramount. Authoritarian measures, including austerity policies, deregulation, and the prioritization of financial stability over democratic accountability, emerge as essential tools to protect financial interests. Authoritarianism, once primarily a political tool, is now integral to sustaining the global financial order, ensuring that capital accumulation remains uninterrupted. Securitization plays a critical role in reinforcing financial authoritarianism. By transforming risks – whether economic, political, or social – into tradable assets, securitization enables financial markets to extract value from areas that were once outside their reach. This process has allowed financial institutions and governments to commodify various aspects of life, turning insecurity into a source of profit. In this sense, securitization extends the reach of financial markets into domains like health, education, housing, and personal data, creating new avenues for control and governance.

The connection between financial authoritarianism and securitization becomes especially apparent during times of crisis. When faced with economic, health, or security threats, financial institutions and governments often respond by expanding securitization efforts. Crises present opportunities to introduce new financial instruments designed to manage uncertainty, while governments implement authoritarian policies to maintain order. The convergence of these forces strengthens the financial-authoritarian complex, deepening its influence over both the economy and society. The financial crisis of 2008 is a clear example, as securitization – particularly of mortgage-backed securities – was a key factor in the collapse of global markets. In the aftermath, rather than addressing the underlying causes, financial institutions repackaged and resold these risky assets, while governments imposed austerity measures to stabilize their economies. This response reinforced the mechanisms of financial authoritarianism, prioritizing the continued profitability of financial markets over social welfare.

The COVID-19 pandemic further illustrates how financial authoritarianism operates through securitization. Governments around the world introduced widespread surveillance measures, justified by the need to monitor public health and control the virus's spread. At the same time, financial institutions created new financial products tied to pandemic-related risks, extending the commodification of uncertainty into the realm of public health. This alignment between financial markets and authoritarian governance shows how crises are leveraged to reinforce existing power structures. Rather than providing relief or promoting social welfare, financial authoritarianism intensifies during crises, ensuring that control is maintained through both economic and political channels. The entrenchment of financial authoritarianism is not limited to economic or political mechanisms but is also reinforced by a social pathology rooted in control and compliance. The processes of financialization and securitization have fostered a cultural mindset in which security and control are prioritized over autonomy and democratic participation. This mindset is evident in the proliferation of surveillance technologies, which have become central to financial authoritarianism's function. Surveillance is not just a tool of state control but a profitable industry, with digital platforms and data analytics technologies transforming personal data into financial assets.

Individuals are conditioned to accept and even embrace these forms of surveillance, often viewing them as necessary for personal security. This acceptance is fuelled by the commodification of security, as surveillance technologies are marketed as tools of empowerment and protection. Smart home devices, wearable health trackers, and other forms of self-monitoring technology offer the promise of control over one's environment, but they also facilitate the collection and commodification of personal data. By monitoring their own behaviours and health, individuals contribute to the broader project of financial authoritarianism, as their data becomes a valuable resource for financial markets. This self-monitoring creates a continuous dynamic of control, in which individuals internalize the need for compliance while financial elites benefit from the extraction of data and the expansion of control technologies.

This dynamic is exacerbated by ideological frameworks that legitimize financial authoritarianism. Neoliberal narratives of individual responsibility, self-reliance, and market-based solutions serve to reinforce the social pathology of control. In this context, individuals are encouraged to see themselves as responsible for managing their own risks – whether financial, health-related, or security-based. This ideology shifts the burden of insecurity onto individuals, who are expected to navigate complex systems of surveillance and financialization to protect themselves from harm. As a result, financial authoritarianism is not experienced as an external imposition but as a personal responsibility. Individuals willingly participate in systems of surveillance and securitization, contributing to the very structures that undermine their autonomy.

The social pathology of control extends beyond the individual level and into broader societal dynamics. The financialization of public goods and services, such as healthcare and education, has introduced new forms of securitization that prioritize profitability over accessibility and equity. In healthcare, for example, the rise of private insurance markets and the commodification of patient data have turned health into a securitized asset. The risks associated with illness and mortality are monetized and traded, transforming the basic need for healthcare into a financial opportunity. Similarly, securitized mortgage-backed securities in housing markets have reshaped access to housing, contributing to global financial crises and exacerbating inequality. Financial authoritarianism relies on this convergence of state and market power to maintain control over society. It blurs the lines between public and private sectors, allowing financial institutions to exert control over governance while simultaneously profiting from crises. In this model, the boundaries between economic and political power become increasingly fluid, with each reinforcing the other to consolidate elite control. This convergence represents a profound shift in how governance is structured and how power is exercised in contemporary capitalism.

The transformation of financial authoritarianism into a complex system of power is a reflection of the adaptability and resilience of contemporary capitalism. It demonstrates how financial markets, political institutions, and social pathologies are intertwined in a way that perpetuates control, accumulation, and compliance. This complex power structure allows financial elites to profit from crises while maintaining a firm grip on the mechanisms of governance. By integrating economic, political, and social forces, financial authoritarianism redefines the relationship between the state, the market, and the individual, creating a system in which insecurity is both manufactured and monetized. This form of power challenges traditional notions of authoritarianism, as it is no longer confined to overt political repression or state coercion. Instead, it operates through more subtle forms of control, using financial markets and securitization to govern populations and manage risks. By transforming security into a tradable commodity and surveillance into a profitable industry, financial authoritarianism reshapes the very foundations of contemporary society.

Conclusion

The AFC marks a departure from the traditional military–industrial paradigm, fusing financial, technological, and authoritarian forces to exploit and colonize new aspects of life. Through securitization, entities – from natural resources to human behaviour – are transformed into tradable assets, subsuming previously shielded realms under financial control. This process creates new markets based on the governance and control of populations, while masking its repressive nature with promises of technological advancement, individual empowerment, and societal improvement. These fantasies, however, serve the logic of capitalist accumulation and authoritarian population management, captivating individuals with illusions of prosperity. The 'repressive cycle of finance' highlights this paradox: financialization generates instability, making populations vulnerable to securitizing interventions that promise stability but instead tighten control. Each crisis invites more invasive measures, as individuals are lured into supporting the very systems that constrain them. In the pursuit of security, they become complicit in their own subjugation, trapped in a cycle where the mechanisms designed to provide safety perpetuate insecurity, fostering continuous dependence and ontological anxiety.

This simulated mastery is further entrenched through the increasing sophistication of governance technologies oriented towards granular subjective customization. The incessant datafication of human activity enables the construction of high-resolution portraits mapping the idiosyncratic contours of individual experience. These data matrices are subjected to predictive analytics that modulate control regimes in accordance with each subject's distinctive fault lines and prospective resonances. Subjugation is thus refracted into individuated and customizable spectra, each control paradigm tailored to enchant through the distinctive fantasies of empowerment it purportedly facilitates. In this affective system of repression, the traditional power hierarchies between the dominant and dominated blur into a superficial dialogue. Dominance perpetually reshapes its narratives to align with the consumptive desires of the subject it is seeking to profitably control. The next chapter will trace out the historical roots of this AFC beginning in the latter half of the 20th century.

4

Securitizing History

Introduction

This chapter explores the historical emergence of the authoritarian–financial complex (AFC), based on the needs by financial and political elites to introduce and entrench neoliberalism against mounting social dissent. As the free market paradigm encountered resistance from those marginalized by its policies, an alliance emerged between concentrated capital, authoritarian governance structures, and industries predicated on control and subjugation. This axis capitalized on manufactured fears and crises to legitimize its expansionist agenda under the guise of enhanced security. Concurrently, a pervasive cultural obsession with control and order took root, normalizing the erosion of civil liberties and the militarization of public spaces. The historical arc traced herein elucidates how the AFC metastasized from a desperate bid to safeguard elite interests into an all-encompassing force that has supplanted democratic norms with a regime of profit-driven oppression.

The roots of the AFC trace back to the post-Second World War era, when newly independent nations in Asia, Africa, and Latin America pursued rapid industrialization through developmental state models. Theorists like Albert Hirschman advocated for centralized governments directing investments into strategic industries, but this often required political repression to ensure repayment of foreign loans from institutions like the World Bank and International Monetary Fund (IMF) (Hirschman, 1965; Baran, 1968). In countries like South Korea under Park Chung-hee and Indonesia under Suharto, dissent and labour unions were suppressed to attract foreign capital, with Suharto's 1965 anti-communist purge leading to 500,000 deaths, and Park justifying human rights abuses in the name of economic growth (Cribb, 1990; Eckert, 2000; Pirie, 2007). These regimes exemplified how authoritarian governance merged with financial interests, laying the groundwork for the AFC. In the 1970s, this symbiosis took on a neoliberal character as Keynesian economics lost credibility, and laissez-faire capitalism gained traction (Harvey, 2005). The 1973 US-backed coup in Chile, which installed Augusto Pinochet's dictatorship, solidified this complex. Pinochet implemented neoliberal 'shock therapy' policies advocated by Milton Friedman, including privatization, deregulation, and austerity, dismantling Allende's welfare state and enforcing these changes through widespread repression (Lear and Collins, 1995; Solimano, 2012). Pinochet's regime was hailed as an 'economic miracle', legitimizing brutality as necessary for economic prosperity (Valdés, 1995). This period marked a significant evolution in the AFC, establishing repression as a key tool for enforcing pro-corporate policies in service of capital.

As neoliberal ideology spread and was institutionalized through the IMF, World Bank, and other global bodies, the AFC expanded through financialization, which extended finance sector dominance and infused financial logic into various aspects of social life (Duménil and Lévy, 2004; Soederberg, 2004; van der Zwan, 2014). State coercion became crucial for enforcing 'financial discipline' and suppressing opposition to wealth-concentrating policies (Gill, 1995), as seen in Margaret Thatcher's brutal suppression of the 1984–1985 UK miners' strike, where state violence was deployed to enforce economic reforms (Adeney and Lloyd, 1986; Milne, 2014). The US prison–industrial complex further exemplified how private industries profited from population control, turning incarceration into a profitable business model that disproportionately affected marginalized communities. This dynamic was fueled by 'tough on crime' legislation and militarized policing, aided by surplus military equipment from wars in Iraq and Afghanistan, creating a cycle of repression that advanced private interests at the expense of social justice. Beyond incarceration, the corporatization of control extended into private security, surveillance, and military contracting firms profiting from the societal fixation on 'security' (Singer, 2008). From technologies that monitored welfare recipients (Eubanks, 2018) to pervasive surveillance, biometrics, and predictive policing (Monahan, 2006; Ferguson, 2017), a vast industry emerged, eroding civil liberties and benefiting corporations (Neocleous, 2007). This security complex, driven by fear and crisis narratives, became a self-perpetuating system of manufactured insecurity and control, enhancing the economic and political power of the AFC. Initially a strategic alliance between political authoritarianism and financial interests to impose neoliberal policies, this complex evolved into a pervasive system of social control and capital accumulation (Bruff, 2014), normalized through mass surveillance, preemptive detention, and militarized policing under the guise of security (Neocleous, 2007), further expanding its reach while encroaching on civil liberties.

The chapter begins by analysing how militarization discourses evolved into narratives focused on securitization, laying the groundwork for the AFC. It traces this evolution back to the developmental state paradigm of the 1960s, where securing foreign investments required political control mechanisms for repayment. This paradigm shifted in the 1970s to legitimize authoritarian regimes like Pinochet's Chile, facilitating neoliberal policy imposition. The chapter critiques how financialization expanded state repression capabilities, exemplified by Thatcher's UK suppressing resistance to neoliberal reforms. It explores how this fostered new complexes like the prison–industrial complex, profiting from population control. State-sanctioned privatization intensified, serving a growing societal demand for security, normalizing civil liberty curtailments and public sphere militarization. Emerging technologies, like welfare monitoring, furthered this trend. The chapter charts the AFC's rise as a hegemonic force, using crises and cultural indoctrination to justify control commodification.

Complex transitions

The concept of 'complex historical transitions' involves the evolution of power structures where mechanisms of control initially arise in response to political necessities but gradually transform into profitable economic practices, ultimately becoming perceived social necessities. This process characterizes the transition from the military–industrial complex to the AFC, revealing how methods originally developed for state security and governance adapt to and reinforce new economic models, embedding themselves deeply in social life. A critical analysis of these transitions shows how these mechanisms evolve in stages, becoming increasingly difficult to disentangle from everyday norms and values, thereby consolidating power in a way that appears natural and even indispensable.

The first stage in this historical transition often begins with mechanisms of control implemented to address immediate political threats or crises. During the Cold War, for example, the rise of the military-industrial complex followed a perceived need for national defence against external threats, leading to significant investments in military infrastructure and technologies. This framework found political justification through rhetoric that emphasized protecting freedom, democracy, and economic stability, positioning military strength as an essential component of national security. At this point, the mechanisms of control – surveillance, military spending, and strategic industry partnerships – were presented as necessary, temporary measures to address urgent political challenges.

After these mechanisms integrate into governance practices, they start to create new economic opportunities, evolving beyond their initial political purpose. The industries benefiting from government defence contracts in the military-industrial complex grew into powerful economic actors with vested interests in maintaining high levels of military spending. What began with the aim of ensuring national security transformed into a profitable enterprise, where defence contractors, arms manufacturers, and related industries relied on continuous funding for growth and sustainability. The economic benefits derived from defence spending – job creation, technological innovation, and regional economic development – helped normalize these expenditures, making them an integral part of the economy. The profitability of these strategies and techniques of control leads to their entrenchment as economic necessities, with their role in economic growth and stability becoming self-reinforcing. Military expenditures, having created profitable industries, allowed the associated technologies, such as surveillance and communications, to find new applications outside the defence sector. This stage marks a critical shift where mechanisms of control transition from state-centric tools to market-driven practices, generating revenue streams independent of their original political context. The normalization of surveillance technologies extended into civilian life, with private companies developing products for commercial use and marketing them as solutions for personal safety, corporate security, and digital convenience.

The final stage in complex historical transitions occurs when these economic practices transform into perceived social necessities. As mechanisms of control move from political and economic realms into social life, they become embedded in cultural norms and everyday behaviours. At this point, their rationale extends beyond political or economic arguments, shaping social expectations and moral imperatives. Surveillance, initially a tool for military intelligence, now appears essential for preventing crime, protecting children, or enhancing workplace productivity. The pervasive integration of these technologies into daily routines makes them seem natural and indispensable, obscuring their origins as tools of state control and reinforcing their legitimacy as social norms.

This historical transition from political necessity to economic profitability and eventually to social necessity becomes evident in the shift from the military-industrial complex to the AFC. Geopolitical threats had diminished in the post-Cold War era, and economic and financial risks gained prominence as new sources of insecurity emerged. Governments and corporations began investing heavily in financial surveillance, data analytics, and risk management technologies, framing these measures as essential for economic stability in an increasingly interconnected world. The mechanisms initially designed for financial oversight and counter-terrorism evolved into sophisticated systems for monitoring financial transactions, social behaviours, and political activities, thereby expanding the scope of control beyond the original political rationale.

For the AFC, the political strategies and techniques of 'securitization' linked closely to the need to manage and repress resistance to neoliberalism, while addressing the social costs it generated, including increased inequality and unemployment. Neoliberal reforms dismantled welfare states, deregulated markets, and prioritized financial interests, leading to widespread social dislocation – job insecurity, reduced social protections, and wealth concentration. These outcomes fuelled social unrest, protest movements, and challenges to the legitimacy of the neoliberal project. In response, securitization emerged as a key political strategy for containing dissent and maintaining social order. Techniques such as financial surveillance, policing protests, and criminalizing social movements aimed to control marginalized populations and pre-emptively address disruptions that could threaten economic stability. Framing social issues as security threats enabled the complex to justify authoritarian measures under the guise of economic necessity, reinforcing neoliberal policies while mitigating their destabilizing effects on society.

The profitability of these mechanisms emerge once data collection and financial surveillance technologies created new markets and revenue streams. Companies specializing in data analytics, cybersecurity, and financial technologies emerged as key players in the economy, deriving profits from services that extended the logic of control into economic life. These regulations, initially justified as measures to combat terrorism or criminal activities, generated demand for technologies and services that monetized compliance and risk management, turning surveillance into a profitable enterprise. Once these practices became profitable, they also started shaping social expectations and behaviours, reinforcing their status as perceived social necessities. Financial monitoring became an accepted part of modern economic life, with consumers and businesses adapting to a world where compliance with financial regulations was not just a legal requirement but a marker of trust and legitimacy. The normalization of credit checks, identity verification processes, and data sharing between financial institutions and governments made financial surveillance an embedded aspect of daily life, shaping perceptions of privacy, security, and economic participation.

The move from political necessity to perceived social necessity results in these mechanisms of control evolving into pathological social complexes, where values associated with security, surveillance, and control become deeply ingrained in the collective psyche. As these mechanisms integrate themselves in daily life, they shape not only institutional practices but also cultural norms and individual behaviours. The normalization of surveillance and risk management leads to a pervasive sense of anxiety and hyper-vigilance, where individuals come to internalize the need for constant monitoring and control. This internalization turns social values of security and compliance into compulsive behaviours, fostering a society that prioritizes safety and predictability over freedom and spontaneity. The resulting pathological social complex manifests in a cultural climate where dissent is stigmatized, privacy is devalued, and the pursuit of control becomes an end in itself. The complex not only shapes policy and governance but also influences personal identity and social interactions, transforming the mechanisms of control from external impositions into internalized imperatives. This dynamic makes it even more challenging to recognize and resist the pervasive reach of the AFC, as the values it promotes become fundamental to how individuals perceive their world and relate to others.

This transition illustrates a broader pattern in complex historical changes, where mechanisms of control adapt to new conditions by evolving from state-driven practices into market-driven solutions, ultimately embedding themselves in social norms. The shift from military spending to financial surveillance reflects how different complexes reshape historical trajectories by repurposing tools of control for new economic and social contexts. It demonstrates the resilience of these complexes in adapting to changing circumstances while retaining their fundamental logic of control and domination, albeit in transformed guises. Moreover, the perception of these mechanisms as social necessities often conceals the underlying power dynamics and interests driving their implementation. Framing surveillance and financial oversight as essential for economic security obscures the potential for abuse and overreach. The discourse around security and stability serves to depoliticize these practices, presenting them as technical solutions to problems rather than as political choices with significant social consequences.

The evolution from the military–industrial complex to the AFC highlights how power becomes more diffuse and deeply embedded within society. As mechanisms of control transition from state prerogatives to economic practices and social norms, they become harder to challenge. The financialization of surveillance and control creates feedback loops that reinforce the necessity of these mechanisms; for example, the widespread adoption of data-driven risk management practices increases the perceived need for more data, justifying further investment in surveillance technologies. This cyclical reinforcement makes it difficult to disentangle the original political motivations from the subsequent economic incentives and social expectations, solidifying the role of the complex in structuring power relations.

The shift from the military–industrial complex to the AFC, thus, represents a broader pattern in complex historical transitions. The mechanisms of control that emerge in response to political necessities become profitable economic practices, which in turn evolve into perceived social necessities and pathological obsessions. This process illustrates how power structures adapt over time, repurposing tools of control to fit new historical contexts while embedding themselves deeply within society, making their presence appear natural, inevitable, and even indispensable.

Securitizing society

Neoliberalism represents a transition from militarization to heightened securitization, as powerful actors sought to solidify economic and political dominance in the context of global capital flows and social unrest. Post-Second World War militarization focused on projecting hard power and suppressing dissent, especially in developing countries where authoritarian regimes were supported to counter communism, as seen in US-backed regimes in Latin America (Kofas, 1995; Sáez and Gallagher, 2008; Yeung, 2017). In East Asia, the 'developmental state' model fused authoritarian governance with economic growth, exemplified by Park Chung-hee's South Korea, where state–business alliances drove industrialization while repressing dissent (Im, 1987; Yeung, 2017). As Cold War ideologies waned and neoliberalism gained prominence, the focus turned from militarization to securitization, reframing repression as a necessary means of ensuring economic and social stability amidst unfettered capital flows (Remmer, 1986; Oneal, 1994). Debt crises and structural adjustment programmes further emphasized the need to maintain order, protect property rights, and attract foreign investment, making securitization a technocratic necessity (Kisangani, 1987; Glassman, 2020). This narrative legitimized repressive measures in the name of law enforcement and stability, particularly through austerity and market reforms imposed by institutions like the IMF to secure financial aid (Frieden, 1991a; Kofas, 1995).

The interventions of international financial institutions and powerful nations, ostensibly aimed at economic stabilization and development, often concealed the consolidation of authoritarian governance and the erosion of democratic norms (Gibbon et al, 1992). Neoliberal restructuring programmes, with their emphasis on fiscal austerity, privatization, and market reforms, legitimized regimes that suppressed dissent in the name of maintaining law, order, and an investor-friendly climate (Oneal, 1994; Sáez and Gallagher, 2008). Democratic freedoms such as speech, assembly, and press were curtailed to prioritize deficit reduction, deregulation, and foreign investment, framing opposition as a threat to economic recovery. This technocratic approach sidelined democratic leaders and justified repressive measures against labour unions, social movements, and political dissent, portraying them as obstacles to economic liberalization and stability. The neoliberal project, seen in both developing nations and Western democracies, used securitization discourse to justify the curtailing of civil liberties and the consolidation of state power in favour of market reforms (Serra, 1979). Thatcher's aggressive economic restructuring in the UK exemplified how security narratives legitimized state intervention and repression of dissent (Huggins, 2017). From the 'war on drugs' to heightened border security, securitization framed erosions of civil liberties as necessary for safety, normalizing militarization and surveillance (Vieira, 2014). These changes were reinforced by cultural shifts towards individualism and consumerism, reshaping citizens into economic actors who prioritized personal security and wealth accumulation over collective rights and democratic values.

Underpinning these phenomena is an ideology reshaping societies to align with neoliberal principles. Economists like James Buchanan, influential in public choice theory, laid groundwork for a libertarian vision perceiving democratic institutions as hindrances to economic freedoms and corporate interests (Thrasher, 2019). This philosophy, fostering corporate power through institutional strategies over decades (MacLean, 2017), intersects with disaster capitalism and colonial legacies, forming 'disaster colonialism' (López, 2020; Rivera, 2022). Disasters perpetuate structural violence and colonial oppression, enabling capitalist exploitation that disproportionately affects marginalized groups and reinforces inequalities. The AFC, as elaborated in the preceding chapter, embodies this convergence – authoritarian governance, economic power concentration, and crisis manipulation to consolidate control and benefit elites at democracy's expense. Throughout history, upheavals have been exploited to reshape societies, often under guise of restoring order or enacting reforms. Today, neoliberal ideology and corporate capture exacerbate repression, concentrating wealth, eroding civil liberties, and perpetuating exploitation and oppression (Storey, 2008; Loewenstein, 2015).

The pervasive discourse around crime, terrorism, and social instability fostered a culture of perpetual insecurity, framing these risks as existential threats requiring extensive control and surveillance, often at the expense of civil liberties like privacy and due process (Sassen, 2006; Wacquant, 2009). This narrative normalized the sacrifice of individual freedoms in exchange for an illusion of security and order, perpetuated by media and political rhetoric that portrayed such measures as necessary for national safety (Neocleous, 2007). Concurrently, the erosion of community and solidarity under neoliberalism made individuals more susceptible to fear-based politics, amplifying acceptance of authoritarian controls. The shift from militarization to securitization reveals a deeper truth: authoritarian governance and repression are intrinsic to neoliberalism's structure, essential for maintaining economic hegemony and disciplining dissent (Gill, 1995; Dean, 2002). This symbiotic relationship between capitalism and authoritarianism is foundational rather than incidental, with securitization serving as a legitimizing discourse that binds economic doctrine and political control into a cohesive system of power.

The historical roots of financial securitization

The historical origins of the AFC trace back to the developmental state paradigm of the 1960s, which saw the intertwining of foreign financial investments, development loans, and the imperative of political control. This convergence of economic and authoritarian interests laid the groundwork for a system characterized by the alliance of state power, concentrated capital, and repressive governance. The developmental state model, notably prominent in East Asia's newly industrializing economies, relied on strategic state intervention in markets and long-term economic planning to drive rapid industrialization (Leftwich, 1995; Wong, 2020). However, this ambitious agenda required substantial external financing, prompting authoritarian regimes to forge alliances with international financial institutions and foreign investors to secure capital inflows (Öniş, 1991). Amid the Cold War, Western powers viewed these authoritarian states as crucial allies in containing communism, exemplified by Park Chung-hee's South Korea, where partnerships with chaebols and suppression of labour rights enabled export-driven growth financed by foreign investments (Park, 2011; Cumings, 2016).

International financial institutions such as the World Bank and IMF, alongside multinational corporations, wielded significant influence in ensuring the repayment of their extensive investments and loans to developing nations. This dynamic created immense pressure on recipient countries to maintain political stability and economic predictability to reassure investors (Pepinsky, 2008). Any form of social unrest, labour activism, or democratic movements was viewed as a potential threat, capable of disrupting production, deterring future investments, and jeopardizing debt repayments. Embracing this narrative, authoritarian developmental states portrayed stringent governance as indispensable for fostering investor confidence. For instance, regimes like Park Chung-hee's in South Korea suppressed trade unions, criminalized strikes, and implemented surveillance and repression justified as essential measures to attract foreign capital for industrialization (Lim, 1998; Hee-Yeon, 2000).

The pursuit of rapid economic development was seen as requiring insulation of economic decision-making from societal pressures. Civil society organizations, opposition parties, and grassroots movements advocating for democratic reforms were depicted as impediments that could hinder the singular pursuit of economic growth (Kim, 2007a). Any move towards political liberalization risked destabilizing perceptions among foreign investors. Thus, developmental states positioned themselves as enforcers of economic discipline and political stability. By exerting control over labour, public discourse, and policy making, authoritarian regimes ensured unwavering commitment to export-oriented industrialization and debt repayment schedules (Remmer, 1986). This alignment of interests between global finance capital and domestic elites solidified authoritarianism as essential for attracting sustained foreign investment inflows.

Foreign capital tended to concentrate heavily in export-oriented sectors and economic enclaves, exacerbating societal inequalities. Attempts at redistribution or shifts in development priorities were swiftly suppressed as threats to the established economic model (Lim, 1998). Dissent was framed as endangering the entire national development agenda funded by external loans and investments. Consequently, developmental states became locked into a path where political liberalization was seen as undermining the economic foundations and external financing crucial to their industrialization strategies (Hellmann, 2018). Authoritarian governance evolved from a tactical approach to an existential necessity, tightly linked to assuring global capital of protection for their interests and loan repayments, regardless of domestic repercussions.

The influx of foreign investments and loans thus imposed implicit conditions requiring the reinforcement of political control mechanisms. International financiers and multinational corporations sought stability, predictability, and property rights protection, aligning seamlessly with the authoritarian tendencies of developmental states (Pepinsky, 2008). This convergence fostered a symbiotic relationship where authoritarian governance was justified as vital for creating an appealing investment climate and ensuring loan repayment (Remmer, 1986). Moreover, the developmental state's focus on rapid industrialization mandated the suppression of societal interests potentially obstructing this agenda (Hee-Yeon, 2000). Movements advocating for labour rights, civil society, and democratic freedoms were perceived as threats to the state's ability to pursue its developmental vision and meet financial obligations (Lim, 1998). Thus, consolidating authoritarian control became crucial, enabling the state to mobilize resources, manage dissent, and maintain the steadfast commitment to economic transformation demanded by external financiers (Kim, 2007a).

Shifts towards authoritarian governance structures were not confined to East Asia but extended globally, particularly in the developing world where industrialization imperatives and external debt servicing requirements necessitated strong-handed regimes (Gibbon et al, 1992). In Latin America, for instance, military dictatorships and repressive governments were emboldened by their ability to enforce stringent austerity measures and structural adjustments dictated by international financial institutions (Kaufman, 1985; Frieden, 1991b). Throughout the 1970s and 1980s, as countries in the region grappled with mounting external debt, the IMF and World Bank wielded considerable influence. Their imposition of structural adjustment programmes and conditional lending practices coerced nations into adopting neoliberal economic reforms, triggering widespread public discontent marked by protests, strikes, and political turmoil (Kaufman, 1985). Authoritarian regimes, viewed as more capable of quelling dissent and enforcing economic discipline through censorship and suppression of labour movements, garnered favour with global financiers desperate for stability and debt repayment (Remmer, 1986; Sáez and Gallagher, 2008). Despite international criticism of authoritarian tactics, the imperative to honour debt obligations often overshadowed concerns for democratization and human rights, reinforcing the legitimacy of regimes that prioritized austerity and privatization to secure continued access to international lending (Richards, 1985).

The debt crises in Latin America fostered a disconcerting incentive structure where authoritarian regimes, willing to impose severe economic hardships to satisfy foreign creditors, gained increased financial backing and external endorsement (Kaufman, 1985). Democratic governments, hesitant to fully commit to neoliberal reforms, risked isolation and withdrawal of support (Kaufman, 1985). This dynamic entrenched the 'Baker Plan' paradigm across the region, where conditional foreign loans facilitated a rightward economic shift under authoritarian regimes unimpeded by democratic checks (Serra, 1979). The interplay between external finance, austerity measures, and authoritarianism thus perpetuated a self-reinforcing cycle of economic discipline enforced through political repression.

The ideological foundations of this paradigm trace back to public choice theory, championed by economists like James Buchanan, which viewed democratic institutions as impediments to economic liberties and corporate interests (MacLean, 2017; Thrasher, 2019). This framework provided the ideological framework for a radical libertarian vision that justified curtailing democratic norms to implement market-oriented reforms (Serra, 1979). As the developmental state model adapted to global shifts, the symbiotic relationship between authoritarian governance and financial imperatives strengthened. In Singapore, for example, the ruling party utilized the developmental state paradigm to consolidate authority over economic planning, social policies, and civil society (Rahim and Barr, 2019). Similarly, in post-democratization South Korea, remnants of the developmental state persisted in the government's efforts to maintain control over development initiatives and promote national ownership (Kim et al, 2013).

The globalization era and increased capital mobility have deepened the symbiotic relationship between authoritarian governance and financial interests. Regimes adept at managing economic shocks and maintaining financial control domestically garnered greater stability and investment (Wong, 2020). These dynamics incentivized the perpetuation of authoritarian structures, justified as essential for economic stability and investor confidence (Pepinsky, 2008). Concurrently, the discourse on authoritarianism shifted from militarization towards securitization, framing repressive measures as pragmatic responses to threats to economic and social stability (Kisangani, 1987; Glassman, 2020). The developmental state legacy, coupled with neoliberal economic restructuring and capital mobility imperatives, has forged the AFC – a potent alliance blending state power, concentrated capital, and repressive governance. This complex evolved from Cold War geopolitics into a self-perpetuating system legitimized by securitization and economic pragmatism. Within this paradigm, authoritarian governance is integral to neoliberal capitalism, not incidental but essential for safeguarding capital accumulation and financial interests through dissent suppression, civil liberties curtailment, and democratic norms erosion (Kisangani, 1987; Glassman, 2020).

Protecting neoliberalism

The AFC in the 1970s was redefined by the convergence of several critical factors: the collapse of the developmental state model, the rise of neoliberal economic ideology, and heightened Cold War tensions. As economic stagnation and fiscal crises exposed the flaws of the authoritarian developmental state, once seen as vital for industrialization, repressive governance structures reoriented their justifications away from modernization imperatives (O'Donnell, 1978; Cammack, 1982; Richards, 1985). Meanwhile, neoliberalism, led by figures like Milton Friedman and the Chicago School, promoted market deregulation and reduced state intervention, challenging the statist economic strategies that had previously dominated (Collier and Cardoso, 1979; Sáez and Gallagher, 2008). This ideological reorientation reframed the legitimacy of authoritarian regimes, aligning them with economic doctrines that prioritized market freedoms over state-led development. In Latin America, bureaucratic-authoritarian regimes, such as Augusto Pinochet's dictatorship in Chile, exemplified this realignment. Following the 1973 coup against Salvador Allende's socialist government, Pinochet enacted radical neoliberal reforms promoted by the 'Chicago Boys', Chilean economists trained in free-market principles (Silva, 1993). No longer justified by developmentalist goals, Pinochet's regime was now portrayed as a defence against communism and economic instability (Huneeus and Undurraga, 2021), illustrating how authoritarianism became deeply entwined with the rise of neoliberal economic policies during this era.

The Pinochet regime in Chile reframed its actions as necessary measures to protect the nation from socialist threats and economic collapse, moving away from developmentalist narratives (Oppenheim, 2018). State repression and violations of civil liberties were depicted as regrettable but essential to defend Chile from Marxist subversion. This rhetorical strategy justified the regime's brutality, presenting it as a defence against existential dangers, thereby shielding it from international criticism. The systematic suppression of dissent, political imprisonments, and media censorship were cast as necessary sacrifices to protect Chilean society from ideological and economic ruin, giving the regime a veneer of moral authority in its pursuit of neoliberal reforms under the guise of restoring stability. The Cold War context further bolstered this narrative, with US support portraying Pinochet's rule as a bulwark against communist expansion (Calderón and Cedillo, 2012). Across Latin America, similar regimes, such as Uruguay's military junta and Argentina's bureaucratic-authoritarian regime, adopted this framework, justifying repressive measures as vital for protecting private property and market reforms (Bogliaccini et al, 2021; O'Donnell, 2023). These 'neoconservative' regimes maintained authoritarian control while aligning with neoliberal economic policies and Cold War ideologies, consolidating a new framework for legitimizing authoritarian governance (Schamis, 1991).

Furthermore, the entrenchment of this new legitimizing paradigm had profound implications for the trajectories of political and economic transformation across the region. In nations like Chile and Brazil, the legacies of bureaucratic-authoritarian rule and neoliberal restructuring cast long shadows over the subsequent processes of democratization and development, shaping the contours of state–market relations and the distribution of economic power (González, 2008; Schneider, 2015). In Chile, the brutal legacy of Pinochet's 17-year dictatorship profoundly shaped the nation's transition to democracy in the late 1980s and beyond. Despite the return of electoral politics, the military junta had entrenched a new economic model based on privatization, deregulation, and subservience to international financial institutions (Silva, 1993). This neoliberal policy regime became deeply institutionalized, constraining the scope of action for successive democratic governments.

The Pinochet regime had systematically disempowered labour unions, privatized pension systems and public utilities, and cemented the dominance of powerful economic conglomerates aligned with the dictatorship's free market agenda (Oppenheim, 2018). Even after democratization, these vested interests retained immense structural power, tempering any radical departures from the core tenets of the neoliberal model. The Chilean military's self-granted amnesty for human rights abuses during the dictatorship cast a long shadow, hindering efforts at accountability and transitional justice (Huneeus and Undurraga, 2021). Likewise, in Brazil, a similar dynamic unfolded, albeit with distinct national particularities. The bureaucratic-authoritarian regime that took hold after the 1964 coup had aggressively pursued a state-led industrialization drive.

However, by the late 1970s, this developmentalist model faced a profound crisis amid mounting debt and pressures to liberalize the economy (Weyland, 1998). The subsequent embrace of neoliberal restructuring in the 1980s–1990s became inextricably linked to the dismantling of the authoritarian state apparatus and the transition to democracy (Schneider, 2015). Yet this process unfolded in a deeply asymmetric manner, with the bureaucratic-authoritarian regime's ties to domestic economic elites leaving an indelible imprint. The very modernization processes that precipitated bureaucratic-authoritarianism had strengthened certain capitalist class fractions aligned with the military's economic agenda (Geller, 1982). During Brazil's democratization, these entrenched interests retained considerable structural power, shaping the contours of market reforms and privatization drives.

The 1970s, therefore, marked a pivotal juncture in the evolution of the AFC. The embrace of neoliberal economic doctrine by repressive regimes, coupled with the resurgence of Cold War ideological struggles, facilitated the emergence of a novel legitimizing narrative – one that posited authoritarianism not merely as a pragmatic expedient but as an indispensable bulwark against the twin spectres of communist subversion and economic instability. This discursive shift not only recalibrated the rationales for perpetuating authoritarian rule but also paved the way for the forging of strategic alliances between military dictatorships and the global financial establishment, creating the basis for the AFC's subsequent ascendance.

Repressive capitalism

Neoliberal ideology and financialization reshaped the state's role, turning it from a protector of public welfare into an enforcer of social discipline, particularly in the 1980s when opposition to neoliberal 'reforms' was forcefully suppressed. Thatcherism in the UK epitomized this, as the restructuring of state–economy relations dismantled the post-war consensus and Keynesian welfare state (Peck and Tickell, 2007). Thatcher's project was not merely economic; it reshaped British society culturally and politically (Vinen, 2013). Central to her agenda was establishing ideological hegemony, framing unfettered capitalism as both an economic necessity and a moral virtue – a process described as accumulation by legitimation (Da Costa Vieira, 2023). This entailed marginalizing dissent, delegitimizing alternative viewpoints, and fostering insecurity (Tyler, 2013). Opposition to neoliberalism was cast as economically irresponsible, justifying repressive measures to maintain order. The Thatcher era illustrates how neoliberalism, while promoting economic freedoms, also reinforced authoritarian tendencies within democratic states. By framing dissent as a threat to economic progress, the state curtailed civil liberties and enforced repressive policies in the name of economic stability, reshaping both policy and democratic norms.

Thatcherism's authoritarian tendencies extended beyond rhetoric, manifesting in the state's use of coercive power to suppress resistance and enforce neoliberal policies. The brutal suppression of the miners' strike of 1984–1985 exemplified this approach. The state deployed a vast police force specifically to crush dissent and facilitate the dismantling of the coal industry (McIlroy, 1993). This episode highlighted the regime's willingness to use force to achieve its accumulation agenda, sacrificing democratic principles and civil liberties for market fundamentalism. During this period, the Thatcher government was resolute in its efforts to quell any opposition that threatened its neoliberal restructuring. The miners' strike posed a significant challenge to the regime's attack on organized labour and its plans to dismantle a crucial part of the nation's industrial base. The state's response involved a massive police mobilization, a calculated strategy to overwhelm and suppress the mining communities' resistance. This deployment of coercive resources underscored the state's readiness to sacrifice democratic rights and civil liberties to ensure the success of its accumulation imperative. The suppression of the miners' strike revealed the regime's commitment to dismantling established economic structures and imposing market orthodoxy, regardless of the human cost or the erosion of democratic norms.

Reagan's confrontation with the 1981 air traffic controllers' strike marked a similarly pivotal moment in the rise of a repressive neoliberal agenda, encapsulating the convergence of state power and market fundamentalism where accumulation imperatives trumped democratic norms and workers' rights. Nearly 13,000 federal air traffic controllers defied a presidential order to return to work, prompting Reagan to respond with force by firing the workers and decertifying their union, signalling a major shift in the state's stance towards organized labour (McCartin, 2011). This crackdown was a calculated strategy to dismantle a significant barrier to neoliberal restructuring (Morgan, 1984). Reagan's use of executive authority and public safety concerns provided a narrative that legitimized this repressive act (Meltzer and Sunstein, 1983), with broader implications that weakened labour relations and emboldened private sector employers to intensify union-busting efforts, thus eroding workers' bargaining power (Farber and Western, 2002). This approach echoed Thatcher's tactics during the miners' strike, highlighting the link between neoliberalism and the suppression of opposition (McIlroy, 1993). The strike's aftermath also paved the way for further privatization within the industry, mirroring the broader trend of dismantling public sector institutions and the welfare state under Thatcherism, pursued with authoritarian zeal despite fierce resistance (Goodwin and Duncan, 1989).

The repressive neoliberalism of Reagan and Thatcher marked a sharp departure from the post-war consensus, targeting the social compact that had previously tempered the extremes of capitalism. Both leaders used the state's coercive apparatus to enforce market fundamentalism, prioritizing accumulation and private profit over workers' rights, democratic norms, and the public interest. Suppression of dissent, from striking miners in the United Kingdom to air traffic controllers in the United States, was framed as necessary for economic stability and investor confidence, echoing the strategies of the developmental state in the 1960s and neoliberal dictatorships in the 1970s. This authoritarian approach extended beyond Britain and the United States, aligning with the geopolitical imperatives of the Reagan Doctrine during the Cold War (Donziger and Fine, 1989). Thatcher's support for repressive police and military forces in Central America highlighted the interconnectedness of neoliberal restructuring, financialization, and authoritarian governance (Huggins, 1987; Cottam and Marenin, 1989). Her foreign policy was closely tied to Reagan's efforts to counter communist and leftist movements globally, particularly in Central America, where revolutionary forces threatened Western hegemony. The collaboration between Thatcher and Reagan exemplified how neoliberal economic policies and authoritarian governance were mutually reinforcing, advancing a global strategy to maintain capitalist dominance.

The Thatcher government's alignment with the Reagan Doctrine was evident in its material support – training, equipment, and financial aid – provided to repressive police and military forces across Central America, aimed at countering perceived communist or leftist threats. This collaboration not only reflected ideological alignment but also facilitated the neoliberal restructuring and financialization central to Thatcher's domestic policies. By supporting authoritarian regimes open to neoliberal economic reforms and international financial institutions, the Thatcher administration sought to advance British economic interests and secure the global neoliberal order. Neoliberalism's authoritarian logic viewed democratic institutions and popular mobilizations as threats to capitalist hegemony, laying the groundwork for the prison–industrial complex (Harris, 2018). The repression of radical movements in the 1960s and 1970s expanded into a broader project of social control, criminalizing dissent through draconian laws and enforcement measures. This facilitated the growth of carceral institutions as tools for disciplining populations, suppressing oppositional ideologies, and reinforcing market-driven imperatives. The repression and criminalization of these perceived threats represented a deliberate effort to eliminate alternative visions and stifle challenges to the neoliberal paradigm.

This trajectory was not a localized phenomenon but a reflection of broader global trends. Across the Global South, the imposition of neoliberal hegemony and structural adjustment programmes sparked popular resistance movements, which were met with brutal repression by regimes aligned with international finance capital (Kohl and Farthing, 2006). The state's role as an instrument of social repression became inseparable from the imperatives of financialization and the consolidation of the neoliberal world order. Protecting property rights, enforcing austerity, and silencing dissent were framed as necessary measures to maintain investor confidence and sustain capital accumulation (Campesi, 2009). The authoritarian suppression of opposition to neoliberal reforms thus signalled a global pattern, where both democratic and non-democratic regimes increasingly deployed state power to promote and expand financialization. This dynamic reshaped governance and political economies while normalizing the erosion of civil liberties and the militarization of public spaces under the guise of security and economic necessity. As a result, the state was re-empowered as an instrument of discipline and control, shifting from a protector of public welfare to a force for social repression, deeply intertwined with the demands of financialization and neoliberal hegemony.

Popular disciplining

The development of authoritarian neoliberalism reoriented the state's role into an instrument for financial subjugation across diverse populations (Colaguori, 2005). This process extended beyond traditional law enforcement and penal systems, becoming a comprehensive strategy to make all aspects of social life subservient to capital accumulation (Soto, 2021). The integration of market orthodoxy with state coercion facilitated the spread of disciplinary mechanisms throughout society, targeting populations deemed unprofitable or resistant to neoliberal agendas with punitive measures that extended beyond prisons (Kilty and DeVellis, 2010; MacKinnon, 2012; Rankin, 2021). This strategy materialized in the criminalization of homelessness, invasive surveillance over welfare recipients, and the proliferation of spaces blurring institutional and community boundaries (Rains and Teram, 1992; McNeill, 2020). The logic of financial discipline permeated areas such as mental health, gender, and youth policies, reframing individuals as subjects requiring coercive control (Arrigo, 2001; Maidment, 2006). These developments trace back to the authoritarian tendencies within neoliberal restructuring, as advanced by leaders like Reagan and Thatcher (Samuel, 1992; Quart, 2006). As these regimes dismantled the post-war social compact and entrenched market dominance, they deployed a mix of coercive force and ideological dominance to suppress opposition and eliminate obstacles (Tyler, 2013).

These strategies suppressed labour movements and political activism while promoting a cultural narrative that equated market fundamentalism with moral virtue and national identity (Evans, 1997). As a result, the subjugation of marginalized and 'expendable' populations to the demands of capital accumulation gained ideological legitimacy (Grasso et al, 2019). This was evident in the expansion of mass incarceration and the rise of the 'prison–industrial complex', where prisons became sites of capital accumulation through the commodification of captive populations and the outsourcing of correctional services (Colaguori, 2005; Soto, 2021). Simultaneously, the emphasis on financial discipline weakened public support for the social welfare system, leading to punitive conditions for aid recipients, who faced intensified monitoring, sanctions, and the constant threat of benefit termination (Rains and Teram, 1992; McNeill, 2020). These dynamics, passed down across generations, entrenched neoliberal values and normalized coercive control mechanisms (Grasso et al, 2019), making the subjugation of marginalized populations to market discipline appear natural and rendering alternative visions difficult to realize (McNeill, 2018). As the boundaries between institutions and communities, and between punishment and welfare, blurred, it became clear that social control was tightly interwoven with the imperatives of capital accumulation (Soto, 2021). This system managed growing economic and social precarity, particularly in urban areas, while neutralizing so-called 'expendable' populations (Wacquant, 2008). The legacy of deinstitutionalization further compounded this reality, with the closure of mental health facilities pushing individuals into the expanding prison–industrial complex (Parsons, 2018).

Throughout Asia, the once-heralded developmental state model faced a profound legitimacy crisis as globalization and neoliberal restructuring challenged state autonomy and interventionist capacities (Carroll and Jarvis, 2017). Nations like Taiwan recalibrated their developmental strategies, pivoting towards sectors like biotechnology to align with global capital accumulation demands (Wong, 2005). This shift did not abandon the authoritarian impulses of the developmental state model but rather reconceptualized the state's role to ensure financial discipline and entrench market hegemony (Wong, 2005; Carroll and Jarvis, 2017). The last decades of the 20th century saw a reconfiguration of the state and government, transforming it into an apparatus primarily concerned with the financial disciplining of diverse populations. Empowered under neoliberalism, the state became a key actor in enforcing market discipline and subjugating individuals to capital accumulation imperatives. This shift manifested in proliferating disciplinary mechanisms across social domains, from the criminal justice system to welfare provision and urban governance, creating 'societies of control' where financial rationality and punitive consequences for non-compliance shape individual lives.

Securocratic societies

The reconfiguration of the state to promote and ensure financial discipline has created 'securocratic' governance, realigning state functions to focus on public and private security. This shift towards economic technocracy has led to a 'de-democratization' of politics, where market fundamentalism dictates state policy, subordinating public deliberation to capital accumulation imperatives (Kiely, 2017). Even in established democracies, 'authoritarian liberalism' has undermined the democratic ideals underpinning neoliberal governance (Bonefeld, 2017a; Kiely, 2017). This results in the normalization of exceptional measures and the embedding of securitization logics within governance regimes. In the Global North, the consolidation of a 'securocracy' is exemplified by entities like the US Department of Homeland Security (Garrett, 2023). Their growing prominence represents the embedding of securitization rationalities within core governing apparatuses, explicitly oriented towards producing insecurity and intensifying population control. This is reinforced through 'globalized policing' and 'securocratic wars of public safety', where militarized civil enforcement and surveillance are accepted for social control (Feldman, 2004). In 'Fortress Europe', the militarization and policing of interior borders have ideologically conflated immigration, terrorism, and existential threats to the nation-state's integrity (Linke, 2010), allowing authoritarian control forms to become naturalized within democratic policy making and discourse.

Similarly, in countries across Africa, security narratives have legitimized the actions of explicitly authoritarian regimes and repressive democratic governments as necessary parts of the broader 'securitization of development' (Fisher and Anderson, 2015). This has enabled governments like Paul Kagame's in Rwanda to legitimize systematic human rights abuses and entrench a highly securitized state under the guise of 'development' after the genocide (McDoom, 2022). The regime's 'securocratic state-building' project has centralized control over security institutions, enacted draconian media laws, and implemented pervasive surveillance, all framed as necessary for economic progress and stability. Similarly, in Ethiopia under the Ethiopian People's Revolutionary Democratic Front, development narratives justified intensifying securitization, from brutal suppression of protests to the internment of dissidents (Fisher and Anderson, 2015). Megaprojects like the Grand Ethiopian Renaissance Dam were positioned as vital for development, enabling the militarization of surrounding areas and forced relocation of indigenous groups.

In nominal democracies like Kenya, imperatives of securitization have subverted development priorities (Berman and Tettey, 2001). The war on terror and counterinsurgency operations have been used to justify land dispossession, extrajudicial killings, and curtailment of civil liberties, legitimized through rhetoric about eliminating threats to economic growth and stability in frontier regions. Similar processes unfolded in apartheid-era South Africa, where the provision of arms and aid to the Rhodesian government exemplified the regime's commitment to perpetuating white minority rule through repression of liberation movements (Baines, 2019). In the post-independence era, the consolidation of a 'securocratic state' in Zimbabwe has been predicated on the accumulation of excessive power by security sectors, enabling the entrenchment of authoritarianism under the guise of transition management (Ruhanya and Gumbo, 2023).

Donor institutions and multilateral bodies have increasingly promoted securitization as essential for 'good governance' and unlocking development finance in Africa (Fisher and Anderson, 2015). This has led to public sector computing projects aimed at surveillance and security sector assistance focused on population control, with development policies serving as vehicles for securocratic expansion. The adoption of securitization techniques and technologies is framed as crucial for stability and progress, indicating a deep infiltration of securitization rationalities into the mechanisms that define the relationship between governing institutions and the governed. This 'new securocracy' has internalized a 'police concept' within public sector identities (Oswick et al, 2008), emphasizing disciplinary subjugation and omnipresent population control as the main imperatives for public service delivery. Consequently, civil servants administering social welfare programmes have shifted from service provision based on citizen rights and social upliftment to treating aid recipients as potential threats needing constant monitoring and punitive measures. In public education, this 'police concept' has normalized draconian security regimes and the criminalization of marginalized student populations, transforming schools into environments resembling correctional facilities with embedded surveillance and containment logics.

The new reign of securocratic governance paradigms reflects a novel 'society of control' premised upon the relentless injunctions of financial securitization. Within this emergent socio-political order, the continual production of insecurity becomes a self-perpetuating *raison d'être*, inextricably intertwined with the unbridled dictates of capital accumulation. All sectors of the economy – from governments to corporations to communities and even individuals – are expected to carefully monitor society and populations to secure their financial viability. Autonomy and self-determination, hence, are supplanted by the injunction to render all spheres of existence legible to the securocratic gaze and amenable to the dictates of financial control.

Conclusion

This chapter has traced the historical evolution and multifaceted manifestations of the AFC, elucidating its transformation from an elite strategy to entrench neoliberalism into an all-encompassing apparatus of control and subjugation. The analysis began by examining the discursive shift within the neoliberal project, transitioning rhetoric from militarization to an overarching preoccupation with securitization. Precipitated by neoliberalism's prioritization of unrestrained capital flows and market integration, this change recast authoritarian governance as a pragmatic necessity for fostering stable conditions conducive to capital accumulation. Repressive measures were reframed as essential for upholding law, order, property rights, and mitigating perceived economic threats, normalizing erosions of democratic norms as sacrifices for investor confidence.

This securitization paradigm created fertile ground for the ascendance of the AFC by intertwining authoritarian governance with financial imperatives. The analysis highlighted the origins of this change in the 1960s developmental state model, where foreign capital influxes necessitated relationships between authoritarian regimes and global financial institutions, a dynamic amplified by Cold War geopolitics positioning such states as bulwarks against communist expansion. This evolved during the 1970s–1980s debt crises, further cementing linkages between authoritarianism and financial subjugation. International creditors empowered military juntas to enforce market reforms and austerity, establishing a narrative portraying authoritarianism as a bulwark against economic instability and ideological 'subversion'. This paradigm shift extended to the Global North, where the decline of the post-war welfare state and the rise of neoliberalism reframed state power as an instrument of capitalist hegemony and social repression. This shift birthed 'societies of control' characterized by expanding mass incarceration, eroding welfare, and imposing punitive conditionalities, all underpinned by an 'authoritarian liberalism' that prioritized financial discipline over democratic inclusion.

The proliferation of securocratic societies exemplified a new governance model premised on perpetually producing precarity as an extractive instrument under neoliberal policy regimes. Conflating market orthodoxy with state coercion enabled disseminating disciplinary mechanisms throughout the social fabric, rendering autonomy a fraught endeavour haunted by securocratic intervention and economic immiseration. All aspects of society were turned into people and things to control, with an increasingly privatized state reconstituted to primarily ensure financial security. The next chapter will explore how this emerging AFC transformed the subjugation and disciplining of populations into a lucrative commercial enterprise. Initially pragmatic enforcement of financial conformity in the latter half of the 20th century developed into expansive profit-generating realms predicated on cultivating insecurity. Privatizing economic coercion opened new capital accumulation frontiers across public sector domains like criminal justice, education, and welfare – transforming them into sites for monetizing fear and deriving surplus through marginalized groups' subjugation domestically and globally.

5

Growing Global Authoritarian Markets

Introduction

The authoritarian–financial complex (AFC) represents a unification of political and economic power, transforming techniques and technologies of control into a profitable industry (Saglam, 2022). Previously, financialization's reliance on securitization practices since the 1960s was explored, revealing how the AFC has commodified social control, creating a global market for oppression as marketable products and services. This complex adapts to diverse socio-economic and political contexts, infiltrating both authoritarian and democratic environments. In Mexico, power concentration among elites, lack of transparency, and institutional co-optation have led to resource misallocation, competition suppression, and perpetuated inequality, hindering inclusive growth (Gonzalez Reyes, 2016). Patronage networks and clientelism sustain the complex, limiting political opposition and civil society space. In South Africa, the complex intersects with the political economy of surveillance, where state and private sectors collaborate to monitor and control the population, disproportionately targeting marginalized communities and reinforcing racial discrimination (Kuehn, 2019). These examples illustrate common themes: concentration of power and wealth, co-optation of state institutions, and use of surveillance technologies to maintain social order and suppress dissent.

The global trend towards authoritarianism has provided fertile ground for the AFC to flourish, as governments exploit democratic weaknesses such as ineffective digital regulation, eroding public trust, and political polarization for oligarchic gain. These vulnerabilities enable authoritarian actors to expand their influence and undermine democratic processes (Rak, 2022). Securitization advances as regimes deploy surveillance technologies, manipulate social media to spread disinformation, and use cyberattacks to target rivals' digital infrastructure. China has become a prominent player in this geo-digital competition, exporting its model of digital authoritarianism to enhance surveillance, censor information, and shape public opinion (Liu and Liu, 2020). Similarly, Russia projects power globally through digital disinformation, sowing discord in democracies and executing cyberattacks against critical infrastructure and political institutions (Rak, 2022). These authoritarian practices have led to the formation of networks of mutual support among regimes, undermining democratic norms (Cooley, 2015). For instance, the Shanghai Cooperation Organization facilitates collaboration on security, economic development, and counter-terrorism, while exchanging technology and expertise on surveillance, censorship, and propaganda. Additionally, growing cooperation between China and Russia in media and information control helps develop technologies for monitoring and manipulating public opinion. These networks foster an environment conducive to the AFC, further entrenching authoritarian power and the capitalist interests that sustain it.

A financialized global political economy of control emerged in the late 20th century and continues into the new millennium, exemplified by the prison–industrial complex, the war on drugs, and the war on terror. This system prioritizes profit and control over human rights and social welfare. The prison–industrial complex, fueled by privatization and the criminalization of marginalized communities, has become a profitable industry where private prison companies lobby for harsher sentencing laws and benefit from cheap inmate labour, disproportionately affecting communities of colour. The war on drugs, rather than addressing addiction, has become a tool for social control, criminalizing poverty. Similarly, the war on terror has expanded state surveillance, eroded civil liberties, and militarized policing, with private security firms and defence contractors profiting from perpetual war, while Muslim communities face profiling and state-sanctioned violence. These policies are justified by exploiting a pathological social desire for heightened security, which those in power manipulate to maintain control and generate profit. A narrative of constant threat – whether from criminals, drugs, or terrorists – creates public support for increased surveillance and stringent measures, all underpinned by a financialized logic that prioritizes profit over the well-being of individuals and communities. The AFC operates globally, shaping state power and social control under the guise of security and profit.

This chapter will explore, thus, how the financialization of the global political economy has given rise to a lucrative market for innovative and high-tech forms of control. This economy of control is exemplified domestically by the prison–industrial complex and the welfare–industrial complex, which rely on the commodification of social control and the extraction of profit from the most vulnerable populations. On a global scale, this economy of control is manifested in the perpetual security wars waged against the nebulous threats of drugs and terrorism. These wars have fostered a massive authoritarian market, where private corporations increasingly undertake the implementation of repressive domestic policies and global security initiatives. The pursuit of these aims relies heavily upon the continuous production and procurement of cutting-edge, privately produced goods and services designed for surveillance, control, and repression. Thus, the AFC operates at the intersection of financialization, privatization, and militarization, shaping the contours of state power and social control in the name of security and profit.

Drivers of change: how complexes reshape economy and society

Complexes serve as drivers of change by continuously reshaping economic structures, governance practices, and social norms, a dynamic that also underpins their crucial role in historical transitions. As analysed in the previous chapter, complexes adapt control measures to address shifting political, economic, and social contexts, enabling them to transform initial responses to political crises into profitable economic practices and, ultimately, into normalized social values. This adaptive capacity allows complexes to influence the trajectory of history by embedding mechanisms of control within legal, cultural, and economic frameworks, ensuring that practices initially justified by political necessity become institutionalized as economic imperatives and internalized as social norms. In this way, complexes not only respond to historical changes but actively shape the conditions and directions of these transitions, turning temporary solutions into enduring features of society that guide future developments. The dynamics within a complex enable it to adapt to changing conditions, repurpose existing forms of control, and foster new organizational approaches that facilitate the pursuit of power and profit. Through these adaptive processes, complexes act as catalysts for significant shifts in both economic structures and social relations, creating conditions that redefine what becomes considered normal, necessary, and desirable.

At the core of how complexes operate lies their capacity to leverage crises, opportunities, and emerging needs to extend their influence. They thrive on the ability to respond to perceived threats or disruptions, utilizing controls that emerge during crises to establish new standards and practices. For example, the military–industrial complex grew significantly in response to wartime needs and the perceived threat of foreign aggression. Military spending, surveillance technologies, and defence-related industries expanded dramatically, with states prioritizing national security. These approaches became institutionalized, transitioning from temporary wartime measures to permanent features of the economy, thereby shaping long-term economic priorities and social values. The complex did not only respond to existing needs but also created new economic dependencies, establishing military spending as a key driver of growth and technological innovation.

As complexes evolve, they expand the scope and application of their controls. What starts as a solution to a specific problem – such as military defence, financial oversight, or social welfare – can grow into a more generalized approach to governance and economic management. The transition from the military–industrial complex to the AFC illustrates this adaptive capacity. Approaches initially developed for military purposes, including surveillance technologies and logistical coordination, found new applications in financial governance and social control. In today's context, financial surveillance, predictive analytics, and data-driven decision-making have become central to state and corporate strategies, moving beyond their original functions to reshape how societies get managed. This expansion reflects the complex's ability to repurpose tools originally designed for state security into profitable economic practices that integrate deeply into social life.

The control strategies of complexes also drive economic restructuring. Through the evolution of these systems evolve, they reconfigure the relationships between different sectors, redistributing resources and shifting the focus of economic activities. Within the AFC, financialization and surveillance have become not just tools for governing but also lucrative industries. The creation of markets for data analytics, cybersecurity, risk management, and compliance services shows how the complex facilitates the emergence of new economic sectors. These industries, often supported by government policies, regulatory requirements, and public–private partnerships, capitalize on the commodification of control and security. The financial incentives generated by these markets encourage further investment in tools of control, perpetuating a cycle where the economy increasingly revolves around managing risk, enforcing compliance, and maintaining social order.

The transformation of social issues into economic opportunities represents, thus, a critical way in which complexes drive change. Approaches such as securitization, surveillance, and regulation convert social problems into marketable commodities, thereby aligning economic incentives with the imperatives of control. For instance, the securitization of social problems such as drug use, immigration, or terrorism has led to the growth of industries focused on policing, incarceration, and border security. This process involves framing certain behaviours or populations as threats, justifying the deployment of extensive control measures. The resulting industries generate profits from monitoring, managing, and punishing marginalized groups, embedding control measures within the economy itself. These dynamics do not merely expand existing markets; they actively shape social policies and public perceptions, promoting control as the primary solution to social challenges.

The adaptability and increased possibilities provided by complexes further facilitates change by integrating emerging technologies and innovations into their existing structures. This ability to incorporate technological advances enables complexes to remain relevant and effective in new contexts, driving further changes in the economy and society. The rise of digital technologies, for instance, has transformed the approaches of the AFC, allowing for more sophisticated forms of surveillance, data collection, and risk management. The integration of artificial intelligence, machine learning, and big data analytics into financial services, law enforcement, and social governance expands the reach of control measures. These technologies enhance existing capabilities while creating new opportunities for profit through the monetization of data and the automation of decision-making processes. The embrace of technological innovations by the complex reflects its capacity to adapt and evolve, using new tools to reinforce established patterns of control while fostering economic growth in related industries.

The evolution of complexes in driving change is revealed in the way they respond to resistance and adapt to opposition. When social movements, activists, or policy makers challenge control measures, the complex can co-opt, neutralize, or absorb these challenges by adjusting its strategies. For instance, increased scrutiny of surveillance practices has led some companies and governments to adopt more transparent data policies or invest in technologies that claim to enhance user privacy while still collecting data. Similarly, when traditional forms of policing face criticism, the complex may shift focus towards predictive policing, community policing, or other strategies that appear more socially acceptable while maintaining the underlying logic of control. This ability to adapt to resistance enables the complex to evolve in response to changing social attitudes, maintaining its relevance while minimizing disruptions to its power and influence. As these cycles continue, the practices of the complex shape not only current policies and methods but also the trajectory of future developments. The result is a society where economic and technological change gets continuously directed towards expanding the reach and capabilities of the complex, embedding control deeper into the structures of governance and everyday life.

Profitable domination

The financialization of the global economy has facilitated a new political economy of profitable control, marked by the privatization and commodification of policing, punishment, and security. This shift is driven by neoliberal ideology, global capital flows, and innovative surveillance and repression technologies (Amott and Krieger, 1982; Wright, 1991; Gordon, 2005). The private security industry has grown exponentially, often outnumbering public police officers in many countries (South, 1988;

Forst, 2000), fuelled by perceived inadequacies of public police, demand for specialized services, and government cost-cutting efforts (South, 1994). Privatization includes outsourcing specific functions and replacing public forces with private companies (Rawlings, 1991; Rosky, 2003). Concurrently, policing has become militarized, especially in the United States, with military tactics, equipment, and culture increasingly adopted by police forces under the influence of the 'war on drugs' and 'war on terror' (Kraska and Cubellis, 1997). The security and risk management discourse emphasizes the need to protect property and maintain order in a perilous world (Beckett, 1999; Gest, 2001). Media sensationalism of crime and fear of marginalized communities (McCann, 2017) has led to public demands for more security and punishment, expanding the private security industry and the criminal justice system (Beckett, 1999; Hunt, 2019).

The privatization of punishment is central to the new political economy of profitable control. In the United States, the prison system has expanded due to the privatization of prisons, with private companies increasingly providing essential correctional services such as food, healthcare, communication, and transportation, contributing to the rise of the 'prison–industrial complex' (Carl, nd; Beckett, 1999; Hunt, 2019). These companies exploit incarcerated individuals as cheap labour to produce market goods and services (Hunt, 2019). Privatization also intersects with education through the 'school-to-prison pipeline', where punitive school policies and security measures criminalize student behaviour, funnelling them into the criminal justice system (Simmons, 2014). The growth of the school security industry, driven by fears of violence, promotes surveillance technologies, metal detectors, and armed security personnel (Simmons, 2014). Similarly, the increasing reliance on private military companies for logistical support, training, and combat services in conflict zones highlights the expanding role of private actors in military operations since the post-Cold War era (Rosky, 2003). Governments have turned to private military firms to provide specialized skills and reduce the political costs of military interventions, while a global security industry has emerged offering services like risk assessment and intelligence gathering (Cook, 2010). The privatization and commodification of both punishment and security underscore the broader trend of integrating market principles into public and military services, reshaping the landscape of control and discipline.

The privatization of security functions has allowed these companies to capitalize on the fears and insecurities stemming from deeply entrenched social divisions and disparities. The outsourcing of policing and security functions to private companies in both authoritarian and post-authoritarian contexts reflects the emergence of a new political economy centred around profitable control. This system not only generates substantial economic gains for private security providers but also reinforces existing power structures and inequalities by enabling the wealthy and powerful to acquire exclusive access to advanced security services. Consequently, the evolving nature of policing in these contexts has become intertwined with the pursuit of profit and the consolidation of socio-economic hierarchies, further entrenching the marginalization of disadvantaged communities.

This system perpetuates a cycle of marginalization and control over those perceived as potential threats to the capitalist order, while simultaneously ensuring the continuation of economic dominance and wealth concentration in the hands of the capitalist class. Equally important, and perhaps more insidiously, this very system of repression has been transformed into a lucrative market in its own right. The production of goods and services designed to facilitate and maintain this control, such as surveillance technologies, weapons, and private security services, has become a thriving industry. Corporations have eagerly seized upon the opportunities presented by the privatization of policing, punishment, and security, recognizing the immense potential for profit. Thus, the political economy of control not only protects capitalist interests but also creates a profitable market for those who seek to capitalize on the business of control itself.

The complexification of punishment

The financialized political economy of control is epitomized by the prison–industrial complex, a system that commodifies punishment and exploits incarcerated individuals for economic gain. It intertwines state power, private interests, and the management of surplus populations, thriving on the criminalization and marginalization of certain communities (Schlosser, 1998; Papageorgiou and Papanicolaou, 2013). This complex represents a symbiotic relationship between state desires for social control and private corporations' profit pursuits, commodifying human bodies and perpetuating oppression cycles. The state enacts laws that disproportionately target marginalized communities, ensuring a steady supply of inmates to fuel the demand for prison beds and cheap labour. Private corporations build and operate prisons, exploiting incarcerated individuals' labour for financial gain. The profit motive, rather than public safety, primarily drives the prison–industrial complex, with private entities and state agencies extracting financial benefits from incarcerating and exploiting racial and ethnic minorities (Brewer and Heitzeg, 2008). Facilitated by the neoliberal economic order, this system encourages privatizing public services and expanding market logics into criminal justice (Hartnett, 2008; Rawal, 2014), generating immense profits for private prison operators while perpetuating poverty, trauma, and marginalization in affected communities (Eitches, 2010).

The racialization of crime and punishment is a key feature of the prison–industrial complex, disproportionately targeting and incarcerating people of colour, especially African American men (Smith and Hattery, 2010; Brown, 2014). This disparity stems from a history of systemic racism, economic inequality, and discriminatory policing and sentencing, driven by political and economic interests expanding the carceral state (Brewer and Heitzeg, 2008; Raza, 2011). The complex perpetuates racial oppression and white supremacy by systematically removing individuals and communities of colour from mainstream society (Davis, 2022). Utilizing prison labour generates profits for private corporations and undermines workers' bargaining power by creating a pool of cheap, exploitable labour that undercuts wages and working conditions (Schlosser, 1998; Rawal, 2014). Additionally, public policies and political rhetoric prioritize punishment over rehabilitation, criminalizing marginalized communities (Hartnett, 2008). Policies like mandatory minimum sentences, three-strikes laws, and the war on drugs have exponentially grown the prison population without addressing crime and social inequality's root causes. Political discourse often relies on racialized stereotypes and fearmongering, promoting a retributive culture that justifies expanding the carceral state.

The intersection of the prison–industrial complex with other systems of oppression, such as immigration and foster care, highlights the pervasive nature of the financialized political economy of control (Díaz, 2011). The criminalization and detention of undocumented immigrants have created an 'immigration industrial complex', generating profits for private detention operators and undermining immigrant rights and dignity (Díaz, 2011). Similarly, the foster care system often acts as a pipeline to the criminal justice system, with youth experiencing trauma and instability being more likely to be criminalized and incarcerated. This intersectionality extends to the education system, where punitive disciplinary policies and the criminalization of youth behaviour contribute to the school-to-prison pipeline (Heitzeg, 2016). Students of colour and those with disabilities are disproportionately affected, facing harsh disciplinary measures that increase their likelihood of future incarceration. The financialized logic of the prison–industrial complex infiltrates education, criminalizing youth to feed the demand for incarcerated bodies and cheap labour (Schlosser, 1998). Zero-tolerance policies and increased law enforcement presence in schools exacerbate this issue, as minor disciplinary incidents lead to arrests and entry into the juvenile justice system. This pipeline ensures a continuous supply of young individuals for the criminal justice system, perpetuating cycles of marginalization and incarceration, and generating profits for private corporations.

The geographic and economic dimensions of the prison–industrial complex illustrate its deep roots within the financialized political economy of control. Building prisons in economically depressed regions, especially rural areas, has become a strategy for generating employment and revenue, making communities dependent on the carceral economy for survival

(Streeter, 2004; Schept, 2022). This dependence creates perverse incentives for prison expansion, prioritizing the economic benefits of incarceration over social and moral costs (Streeter, 2004; Rawal, 2014). While prisons are touted as economic development tools promising job creation and increased tax revenue, the reality is that the jobs are often low-paying, and tax incentives for private prison corporations drain resources from essential public services. The presence of a prison perpetuates stigma and reinforces negative stereotypes, hindering residents' employment opportunities and access to opportunities outside the carceral economy. This reliance on the prison industry creates a vicious cycle, where communities become increasingly dependent on incarcerating individuals, primarily from marginalized populations, to sustain economic viability, perpetuating systemic injustices within the prison–industrial complex.

The globalization of the prison–industrial complex extends the financialized political economy of control beyond the United States, embedding the AFC on an international scale. As neoliberal economic policies spread, so do the logics of the carceral state, with multinational corporations and international financial institutions profiting from the privatization of prisons and exploitation of prison labour (Rawal, 2014). In many Global South countries, structural adjustment programmes and neoliberal reforms prioritize foreign investors and creditors over the needs of local populations, leading to the privatization of public services, deregulation of labour markets, and erosion of social safety nets. This fosters inequality, poverty, and social instability, fueling the criminalization and incarceration of marginalized communities (Gordon, 1999; Papageorgiou and Papanicolaou, 2013). The privatization of prisons in the Global South mirrors the US model, with corporations like G4S and CoreCivic profiting from constructing and operating prisons under contracts that promise cost-efficiency while exploiting prison labour and cutting essential services. Incarcerated individuals in these regions often work under inhumane conditions for little or no compensation, producing goods for both domestic and international markets. This exploitation is enabled by weak labour protections, the limited bargaining power of incarcerated workers, and the complicity of host governments and corporations that prioritize profit over human rights.

The criminalization and incarceration of marginalized communities in the Global South are intertwined with broader processes of economic and social dispossession, where the carceral state removes and contains populations viewed as obstacles to neoliberal development. This is evident in the expropriation of indigenous lands and the violent policing and mass incarceration of the urban poor as tools of social control (Rawal, 2014). The global expansion of the carceral state intersects with militarization and securitization, with private security companies, militarized policing, and surveillance technologies prioritizing control over individual rights (Papageorgiou and Papanicolaou, 2013). At the same time, the prison–industrial complex embeds itself in targeted communities, creating social and economic insecurity that fuels further opportunities for profit and control. Mass incarceration fractures families, disrupts social networks, and erodes economic stability, making entire communities vulnerable to secondary exploitation. Children of incarcerated parents become enmeshed in the foster care system, itself a site of privatization and profit-seeking, while the healthcare needs of incarcerated individuals and their families create markets for private providers who prioritize cost-cutting over quality care. This economic instability leaves communities dependent on predatory lending, exploitative labour practices, and other forms of financial extraction. The commodification of incarceration thus generates a cascade of profitable opportunities, perpetuating a cycle of social and economic marginalization and contributing to a broader AFC that feeds off the vulnerabilities it creates.

The complexification of welfare

The financialized political economy of control has found a profitable avenue in the privatization of welfare services, turning social support for economically marginalized populations into a lucrative industry. This trend involves private corporations increasingly administering and delivering welfare programmes, utilizing digital technologies to monitor and discipline recipients, and commodifying social needs into marketable products (Dunleavy, 2006; Henman and Fenger, 2006). In countries like the United States and the United Kingdom, welfare reform has prominently featured outsourcing services to private contractors, driven by neoliberal ideology and a desire to reduce government spending on social programmes (Blomqvist, 2004). Companies like Lockheed Martin and Maximus have capitalized on these opportunities, using their IT and management expertise to secure profitable government contracts (Hartung and Washburn, 1998). The deployment of digital technologies in social programmes, such as electronic benefit transfer systems and automated eligibility determination, has streamlined administrative processes but also created sophisticated surveillance systems to track and discipline welfare recipients (Dunleavy, 2006; Henman and Fenger, 2006).

The deployment of digital technologies in welfare administration has produced 'indigital peripheries' (Palmer, 2006), subjecting marginalized populations, particularly indigenous communities, to invasive data collection and surveillance under the guise of efficiency and accountability. For instance, the Bureau of Indian Affairs' adoption of Geographic Information Systems to manage indigenous reservations has enabled the creation of detailed community profiles, often without full consent, which are used to inform policies prioritizing external interests. Similarly, the use of biometric identification systems, such as fingerprinting and facial recognition, in administering welfare benefits has disproportionately targeted communities of colour, subjecting them to heightened surveillance and control (Magnet, 2019). These examples illustrate how the digital divide in welfare administration reflects the broader colonizing power imbalances of the financialized political economy of control, as the poor and disadvantaged are disproportionately targeted by systems of monitoring and discipline (Dunleavy, 2006; Henman and Fenger, 2006). These mechanisms of control are internalized by individuals as pathological social desires, such as the desire for efficiency and convenience, while simultaneously generating new opportunities for profit, as the data collected can be monetized and sold to third-party actors (Eubanks, 2018).

The privatization of welfare services has given rise to the 'corporate social worker', where social service professionals operate within private companies that manage welfare programmes (Frumkin and Andre-Clark, 1999). These workers navigate the tension between profitability and social responsibility, reflecting the contradictions of the financialized political economy of control, in which capital accumulation clashes with the social obligations of the welfare state (Henman and Fenger, 2006). Basic necessities like food, housing, and healthcare have been commodified into profitable markets, with private companies offering products and services such as electronic benefit transfer cards and privatized job training programmes, exemplifying the financialization of everyday life (Lacity and Willcocks, 1997; Hartung and Washburn, 1998; Winston et al, 2002). This outsourcing of welfare provision worsens the stigmatization of the economically disadvantaged and moralizes the financialized political economy, framing social assistance as a consequence of moral failure and personal irresponsibility rather than structural inequalities (Murray, 1999). Welfare-to-work programmes, often run by private entities, rest on the assumption that unemployment results from personal shortcomings rather than systemic barriers, mandating job readiness classes that emphasize 'soft skills' and perpetuating the idea that poverty is a result of individual failings (Soss et al, 2011).

The financialized political economy of control, evident in welfare privatization, operates as a colonizing force that profits from and sustains unequal power relations. This system classifies people into financially responsible and irresponsible groups, mirroring colonial distinctions between 'civilized' and 'uncivilized' populations, thereby legitimizing the marginalization of economically disadvantaged communities. It fosters a belief system that legitimizes exploitation and control, internalized by both the marginalized and society at large, maintaining these power imbalances. Privatized welfare, with its focus on individual responsibility and the moralization of poverty, expands this colonizing force, profiting from society's most vulnerable members. The prevalence of sanctions and punitive measures in privatized welfare administration, such as financial penalties or benefit termination for those not complying with programme requirements, reinforces the narrative that poverty stems from personal irresponsibility (Soss et al, 2011). This punitive approach obscures the structural roots of inequality, framing social issues as personal failings rather than consequences of broader economic forces (Blomqvist, 2004). As welfare services become commodified, the relationship between the state and its citizens is fundamentally altered, transforming basic human needs into profit-driven enterprises for the AFC. The commodification of human welfare enriches corporate interests while eroding social solidarity and mutual responsibility. As necessities like food and healthcare are monetized, the ethical foundations of the welfare state are undermined, replacing collective responsibility with a culture of individualism and self-interest.

Profitable prohibition

The commodification of incarceration and welfare provision exemplifies the evolution of Deleuzian 'societies of control' into a capitalist complex, where control techniques and technologies have become amorphous, universal, and profitable. Privatization in these areas has created perverse economic incentives, turning the subjugation and marginalization of vulnerable populations into lucrative business ventures. This environment encourages the innovation and proliferation of control mechanisms for financial gain, evident in invasive surveillance technologies and profit-driven 'welfare-to-work' programmes, transforming social services and criminal justice into vast markets. The legitimization of these control mechanisms depends on their economic viability and their infiltration into public consciousness, embedding within society as a cultural narrative that moralizes poverty, stigmatizes the marginalized, and valorizes individual responsibility. This narrative normalizes and justifies the system, shaping individual and community subjectivities to accept and desire the subjugation and exploitation of the vulnerable. The war on drugs illustrates the global expansion of the AFC, merging state power and corporate interests into a militarized, transnational endeavour, perpetuating violence, inequality, and oppression in affected communities (Corva, 2008; Watt and Zepeda, 2012).

Framing the drug war as a national security issue has had profound international consequences, particularly in Latin America, where it has justified increased military spending and interventions, eroding democratic principles and the rule of law (Bagley, 1988; Morales, 1989; Sanchez, 1991; Abbott, 1996). Programmes like Plan Colombia and the Merida Initiative illustrate this trend, with the United States funnelling billions in military aid to Colombia and Mexico, turning counter-narcotics efforts into large-scale military campaigns (Watt and Zepeda, 2012; Bourgois, 2018; Jenss, 2023). These efforts have devastated marginalized communities, leading to forced displacement, extrajudicial killings, and widespread human rights abuses carried out by security forces and paramilitary groups (Bourgois, 2018; Jenss, 2023; Masullo and Morisi, 2024). The AFC behind the drug war underscores the financial sector's growing involvement in drug enforcement, militarizing financial surveillance and eroding privacy rights (Amicelle, 2017). Asset forfeiture laws allow law enforcement to seize assets allegedly linked to drug trafficking without requiring a conviction, creating incentives that disproportionately harm marginalized communities and erode due process (Schack, 2011). Financial surveillance tools, like suspicious activity reports, turn the financial sector into an extension of law enforcement, monitoring transactions and flagging suspicious activities (Amicelle, 2017). This entanglement creates profit opportunities for private prison companies and military contractors, who provide equipment and support to law enforcement and military agencies engaged in drug enforcement (Schack, 2011; Lindsay-Poland, 2016).

The war on drugs has been a tool to advance neoliberal policies and illiberal governance practices, using national security rhetoric to justify policies that erode civil liberties, increase surveillance, and suppress dissent (Gordon, 2006; Lafer, 2020). Neoliberal globalization of the drug war has transnationalized these practices, legitimizing exclusionary policies and maintaining social control over marginalized populations under the guise of combating drug-related violence (Coleman, 2007; Osuna, 2020). This militarized approach has resulted in increased violence, displacement, and human rights abuses in affected communities, prioritizing state security over human security and neglecting root causes like poverty and inequality (Gautreau, 2012). The selective application of security protects those in power while criminalizing marginalized groups (Jenss, 2023). Media and private interests have shaped public perception and policy decisions by constructing narratives that perpetuate the conflict and obscure its underlying power dynamics (Van Zwieten, 2011; Robinson, 2017). First-person shooter video games depicting military conflicts, including the war on drugs, glorify military violence and reinforce American exceptionalism, while obscuring the complex factors and US foreign policy's role in perpetuating the drug war and advancing American interests (Van Zwieten, 2011; Robinson, 2017).

The war on drugs, therefore, despite its international scope, has come to embody a disconcerting trend in which state violence and militarization are turning inward, focusing on the mobilization of popular support for the eradication of social elements perceived as inimical to the production of financially responsible subjects. This sinister shift in the character of the drug war mirrors the all-encompassing influence of the AFC, as the imperatives of capital accumulation and social control unite to shape the priorities and practices of the state. The inward turn of state violence and militarization linked to the drug war represents a pernicious manifestation of the AFC, as the state becomes an instrument for the enforcement of market discipline and the production of compliant, financially responsible subjects. Even more so, it promotes an expansive economy of profitable prohibition.

Profiting off of terror

The war on terror exhibits striking parallels with the war on drugs, both fundamentally rooted in the discursive construction of existential threats to national security that justify extraordinary measures and the erosion of civil liberties. This securitization of societal issues, whether framed as the scourge of narcotics or the specter of terrorism, legitimizes the militarization of domestic law enforcement, the normalization of surveillance, and the concentration of authority within unaccountable bureaucracies. Both campaigns have also commodified security functions, fostering lucrative industries that thrive on perpetual conflict and insecurity, blurring the lines between public and private spheres and creating vested interests in the continuation of these efforts. As a result, the wars on drugs and terror have restructured the global political economy, reinforcing power dynamics, existing inequalities, and the exploitation of vulnerable populations. Security imperatives have facilitated the imposition of neoliberal economic policies, the consolidation of elite power, and the subjugation of popular sovereignty to the security apparatus.

The September 11 attacks marked a critical moment in the securitization of economic and political discourses, leading to a dramatic escalation in the rhetoric and policies associated with the war on terror. The attacks were framed as an existential threat, reshaping global security, governance, and economic power. In response, the United States launched military interventions, beginning with the 2001 invasion of Afghanistan to target al-Qaeda and remove the Taliban, followed by the 2003 invasion of Iraq, justified by dubious claims of weapons of mass destruction and terrorism links. This period saw security elevated as a central imperative, legitimizing extraordinary measures and blurring the lines between conventional and unconventional national security practices (Neal, 2009; Masco, 2015). The war on terror provided a pretext for privatizing security functions and outsourcing military operations to corporate entities (Ingram and Dodds, 2016), creating a lucrative industry driven by conflict and insecurity. Military interventions expanded the security–industrial complex, entrenching its interests within power structures, as the conflicts in Afghanistan and Iraq fuelled immense demand for military hardware, private security services, and defence-related products, driving profits for defence contractors and arms manufacturers. This convergence of securitization and commodification created a self-perpetuating cycle where escalating conflicts and sustained insecurity became tightly linked to the financial interests of the security–industrial complex.

The securitization of economic and political discourses has significantly expanded global governance structures and consolidated elite power (Heng and McDonagh, 2009). This dynamic is visible in international economic governance, where security imperatives justify the imposition of neoliberal policies and maintain Western hegemony. In the Asia-Pacific, for example, American strategic interests have advanced under the guise of the war on terror (McDonald, 2018), allowing interventionist policies and economic restructuring that reinforce power asymmetries and exploit vulnerable populations (Sharp, 2011). International financial institutions and donor nations impose conditionalities, tying economic aid to neoliberal reforms and security agendas, pushing developing nations to adopt deregulation, privatization, and trade liberalization measures that often worsen inequalities and erode social protections. Simultaneously, the war on terror has intensified intelligence cooperation, leading to unprecedented data-sharing and coordination of clandestine operations among allied nations (Svendsen, 2009). This cooperation fosters integrated surveillance networks, transcending national boundaries and entrenching a climate of secrecy. Counter-terrorism strategies emphasize hard power, prioritizing militarized approaches over human security and counterinsurgency (Gilmore, 2011), benefiting the security–industrial complex – comprising private military contractors, arms manufacturers, and security firms – which profits from sustained conflict and perceived threats. Media and entertainment industries further normalize these extraordinary counter-terrorism measures, shaping public perceptions and reinforcing the security–industrial complex's grip on power (Martin and Petro, 2006).

The commodification of popular control through information and popular culture during the war on terror mirrors the strategies used in the war on drugs, leveraging mass media and entertainment to shape perceptions, cultivate fear, and gain consent for extraordinary measures. Both campaigns use popular culture to propagate official narratives and reinforce securitization discourses, normalizing extraordinary measures and eroding civil liberties through the desensitization of the public with depictions of militarized responses and intrusive surveillance. The war on terror has provided governments a pretext to operate with unprecedented autonomy and transnational cooperation, facilitating profit-driven, militarized responses to perceived extremist threats under the guise of safeguarding global order. This dynamic has led to the consolidation of state power and the subjugation of populations resistant to corporate globalization. Governments have used the rhetoric of existential danger to justify deploying extraordinary measures, violating civil liberties, and circumventing democratic norms. The invocation of security imperatives has expanded state surveillance, militarized law enforcement, and normalized extrajudicial practices in combating terrorism. This transnational security apparatus has become intertwined with the AFC, comprising entities vested in perpetuating conflict and insecurity to sustain demand for security services, technological solutions, and ancillary offerings. The commodification of insecurity allows these actors to profit immensely from the perpetual cycle of conflict.

Growing authoritarian markets

The exercise of authoritarian control has undergone an important evolution, transcending the mere privatization of coercive functions and giving rise to a lucrative economic market centred around the commodification of authoritarianism itself. What this reflects is a paradigm shift challenging the traditional state monopoly over the instruments of coercion and ushering in a new era where the exercise of force and the suppression of dissent have become commodities to be traded in a marketplace driven primarily by profit motives, rather than principles of justice or the collective good. The emergence of this authoritarian market has been facilitated by the strategic construction of security threat narratives, which have cultivated a pervasive climate of fear and uncertainty that private military and security companies (PMSCs) have deftly exploited. Through the amplification of risk perceptions and the purported necessity of extraordinary measures, these private entities have positioned themselves as indispensable partners in the pursuit of security, offering a comprehensive suite of services that span the entire spectrum of authoritarian control.

This discursive framing has not only legitimized the presence of PMSCs within the security apparatus but has also fuelled an ever-increasing demand for their services, engendering a self-perpetuating cycle of insecurity and profit accumulation. By fostering a culture of fear and portraying their offerings as essential for public safety, PMSCs have effectively transformed the very notion of security into a commodifiable product that can be acquired by those with the requisite means. Furthermore, the ascendancy of PMSCs has been facilitated by the ideological tenets of neoliberalism, which valorize privatization and market-based solutions, even in domains traditionally reserved for state prerogatives. The rhetoric of efficiency, cost-effectiveness, and operational flexibility has been strategically deployed to justify the outsourcing of authoritarian control to private entities, obfuscating the profound ethical and democratic implications of such a paradigm shift.

The meteoric rise of PMSCs can be attributed to factors facilitating the outsourcing of authoritarian control to private entities. Proponents argue that the profit-driven nature of PMSCs promotes operational efficiency and cost savings for governments and international organizations. However,

PMSCs operate in a regulatory vacuum, largely insulated from oversight, allowing them to deploy personnel and tactics deemed unacceptable for state actors, providing clients with attractive, flexible solutions. The lure of profiteering from conflict and insecurity has fuelled this corporatization of security operations, with PMSCs commodifying authoritarian control into a profitable enterprise (Chesterman and Lehnardt, 2007). The marketization of authoritarianism has had acute consequences in regions like the Americas afflicted by the war on drugs. Neoliberal policies have facilitated the transnationalization of illiberal governance practices, leading to the militarization of law enforcement and erosion of civil liberties. PMSCs, operating without sufficient oversight, often disregard legal and ethical norms, creating environments conducive to human rights abuses and excessive force (Perret, 2023). Their presence destabilizes fragile regions, undermines governmental authority, and perpetuates cycles of violence, normalizing violence and eroding social fabrics, particularly in marginalized communities (Hobson, 2014).

PMSCs have leveraged their expertise, resources, and access to decision-makers to exert significant influence on security strategy formulation and implementation, often prioritizing commercial imperatives over societal considerations (Walker and Whyte, 2005). They have achieved this by capitalizing on their specialized knowledge and operational experience, positioning themselves as indispensable partners in security, and gaining entry to high-level decision-making. Their substantial financial resources are strategically deployed in lobbying efforts to sway policy makers in favour of their business interests, using well-funded advocacy campaigns and lobbyists with extensive networks and insider access. The revolving door phenomenon, where former military and intelligence personnel move into lucrative PMSC roles, blurs the lines between public and private sectors and creates potential conflicts of interest.

The outsourcing of authoritarian control to PMSCs has further entrenched the commodification of coercive power and eroded democratic norms and accountability mechanisms, particularly in international operations and post-conflict environments. Contracted by international organizations and non-governmental organizations, PMSCs often operate in regions with weak governance and limited oversight (Kawachi, 2018). This raises concerns about their potential to subvert local authority and legitimacy, exacerbate conflicts, and destabilize fragile regions. The presence of PMSCs in post-conflict environments, driven by profit motives under international mandates, can create power vacuums that challenge local sovereignty and self-determination.

The release of documents by WikiLeaks has shed light on the extent of the authoritarian market, exposing the willingness of private corporations to commodify the tools of repression and offer their services to authoritarian regimes across the globe. Perhaps one of the most striking examples is the proposed contract between the French company 2e Technologies and the Libyan government under Muammar Gaddafi, which sought to update and enhance the regime's repressive capabilities mere months before its eventual downfall. The technical proposal, titled 'Homeland Security Program – Technical Specification', outlined a comprehensive suite of solutions aimed at fortifying the Gaddafi regime's ability to monitor, intercept, and suppress dissent within its borders. This included the implementation of a 'legal GSM interception' system capable of simultaneously monitoring 128 calls across various interfaces, enabling the Libyan authorities to intercept communications based on calling numbers, called numbers, and other identifiers. Furthermore, the proposal detailed a powerful 'network monitoring' solution that would empower the regime to capture and reconstruct internet traffic in real-time, filtering online communications based on keywords, IP addresses, and geographic locations. This effectively undermined the remaining spaces for free expression and dissent within the digital realm, consolidating the regime's control over the flow of information.

Additionally, the company explicitly highlighted their expertise in providing 'convoy protection' through a mobile jamming system capable of blocking remote detonation signals for explosives within a 100-metre radius. This technology would enable the Libyan authorities to suppress potential threats to their movements, further entrenching their control over the physical space. The proposal also targeted the infrastructure responsible for managing citizen identities and mobility, offering to secure the Libyan passport database through encrypted data transmission and hard disk encryption. This comprehensive approach underscored the company's commitment to positioning itself as a crucial partner in the regime's efforts to monitor and control its populace.

The timing of this proposed contract is particularly noteworthy, as it was made mere months before the eventual downfall of the Gaddafi regime in 2011. This revelation highlights the extent to which private companies viewed even the most precarious of situations as potential opportunities for the commodification of authoritarian control. Undeterred by the mounting instability and the growing resistance to the regime, 2e Technologies sought to capitalize on the Libyan government's desperation to fortify its grip on power, offering a suite of repressive technologies under the guise of 'homeland security'. This willingness to engage with and enable authoritarian regimes, even as they teetered on the brink of collapse, underscores the profit-driven nature of the authoritarian market.

Furthermore, the leaked documents expose the symbiotic relationship between private security firms and state actors, wherein the former have become integral partners in the implementation of security policies and the projection of state power. For instance, an email from Hacking Team highlights the company's experience in working with the French authorities, including the French Army, the Ministry of Defence, and major corporations. This strategic positioning underscores the growing synergy between private security firms and state agencies, blurring the lines between public and private spheres and enabling the entrenchment of corporate interests within these global security efforts.

These examples reveal the extent to which private companies have developed sophisticated technologies and capabilities that were once the exclusive domain of state security agencies. For these private entities, the pursuit of commercial interests are the priority, and security simply a growing global market for it to exploit. Any situation, no matter how volatile or morally questionable, was viewed as a potential opportunity for the commodification of authoritarian control, perpetuating the erosion of democratic norms and the entrenchment of authoritarian practices. By positioning themselves as indispensable partners in the execution of security and counterterrorism initiatives, these private entities effectively legitimized and reinforced the discourses of fear and insecurity that justified both the expansion of authoritarian globally and their own profitable ability to supply it.

Conclusion

The AFC embodies the convergence of political and economic interests, transforming mechanisms of oppression into profitable products and services. The commodification of social control has created a global industry that thrives on the militarization of law enforcement, the normalization of surveillance, and the outsourcing of security functions to private entities. Campaigns like the wars on drugs and terror have not only perpetuated violence and inequality but have also fuelled a vast market for goods and services linked to social control. The privatization of policing, punishment, and security exemplifies this, with the prison–industrial complex turning incarceration into a profit-driven enterprise, incentivizing the mass imprisonment of marginalized communities. Similarly, the welfare–financial complex subjugates economically vulnerable populations as social services are outsourced to private entities governed by market discipline. This system of profitable control turns subjugation into a source of financial gain, with PMSCs capitalizing on demand for coercive services in conflict zones. The rise of the AFC has made repression and authoritarianism economically viable, transforming tools of social control into profitable commodities. Private companies and investors now benefit from industries built around surveillance technologies, security services, and carceral infrastructure, partnering with governments to provide the necessary tools for population control. This thriving market for control commodities incentivizes the expansion of repressive practices, embedding them deeply into the political and economic structures of societies, making them difficult to dismantle despite moral or ethical concerns.

The next chapter interrogates how the AFC not only profits from but also actively cultivates and perpetuates a state of insecurity and precarity among populations. By fostering vulnerability and instability, this system creates a captive market for its products and services, ensuring a steady demand for sophisticated control mechanisms. The chapter explores how the complex strategically manufactures and manipulates crises, conflicts, and threats to justify expanding its power. Through propaganda, disinformation, and fearmongering, it keeps populations anxious and susceptible to authoritarian solutions and false security promises. Moreover, it examines how the complex contributes to producing precarious subjects – vulnerable individuals and communities – by perpetuating inequality, eroding social safety nets, and criminalizing dissent. These marginalized populations become primary targets for control technologies and sources of profit. The chapter argues that as the AFC expands, it entrenches a vicious cycle of insecurity and control, where the proliferation of threats and precarious subjects is essential for its survival and growth.

6

Producing Precarity

Introduction

The global security industry and commodification of profit have intentionally propagated precarity as an economically produced phenomenon, permeating various social spheres (Neilson and Rossiter, 2008; Han, 2018). This pervasive precarity, marked by insecurity, vulnerability, and uncertainty, has become a defining feature of contemporary capitalism, reshaping work, life, and social reproduction. The deliberate production of precarity generates immense profits for the complex while normalizing it as an inescapable part of life, making it difficult to imagine alternative forms of stability. The proliferation of precarious labour, characterized by unstable employment, temporary work, and reduced social protections, exemplifies this trend (Durham, 2013; Wilson and Ebert, 2013). Corporations, in pursuit of profit, have facilitated the precarization of work by minimizing labour costs, maximizing flexibility, and transferring risks to workers (Chan, 2013; Vallas, 2015). This strategic cultivation of precarity has intensified post-financial crisis, driven by accumulation and financialization imperatives (McNally, 2009).

The deliberate production of precarity extends beyond the workplace, infiltrating essential aspects of everyday life, including housing, healthcare, and education, which are increasingly commodified and subject to market fluctuations (Mader and Mader, 2015; Parfitt and Barnes, 2020). Financial products targeting marginalized populations further entrench their precariousness (Mader and Mader, 2015). The global security industry capitalizes on this insecurity, turning it into profitable opportunities, as seen in the expansion of the carceral state and privatized prisons (Schram, 2015). This spread of precarity undermines traditional notions of economic security, which rely on stable employment and social protections, and instead forces individuals to navigate a world of pervasive insecurity (Parfitt and Barnes, 2020). Neoliberalism's emphasis on individual responsibility further erodes collective security, compelling people to face precarity alone (Schram, 2015;

Millar, 2017). Precarity is not merely a consequence of financialization but an intentional, politically contested process. The global security industry has facilitated the precarization of work and life, turning insecurity into a profitable venture (Worth, 2016; Jordan, 2017). This commodification has deepened social and economic inequality, as access to security depends on navigating market risks (Schram, 2015). The gendered nature of precarity exacerbates existing inequalities, with women – particularly from marginalized communities – bearing the brunt of precarious work and social reproduction (McCluskey, 2017; Adkins and Dever, 2018). Women face immense pressure from unpaid care work and emotional labour, balancing paid employment with domestic responsibilities, while intersectional forces of gender, race, and class further compound their vulnerability to precarity's effects, increasing economic insecurity and perpetuating cycles of disadvantage.

The remainder of this chapter will explore the ways in which the privatization of authoritarianism, as outlined in Chapter 5, has evolved into a global industry that preys on precarity. It will demonstrate how precarity has become a major growth industry, a condition that must be continually exacerbated and expanded to ensure ongoing profits. The chapter will then delve into how this has created precarious societal relations, where elites profit from precarity at the expense of the poor, who are rendered increasingly precarious. This analysis will highlight the role of the repressive cycle of finance in perpetuating class divisions in an increasingly financialized economy, where traditional notions of the capitalist working class are evolving and becoming less defined. The chapter will proceed to examine how the economic precarity caused by corporate globalization has been exploited to fuel a profitable global detention industry, capitalizing on mass human migrations linked to economic and political insecurity. It will then draw parallels to how economic insecurity has been transformed into a lucrative gig economy, characterized by invasive and controlling forms of algorithmic management. Similarly, in the social sphere, the chapter will explore how profitable forms of algorithmic control have emerged to take economic advantage of people's everyday precarity, ranging from housing to health. Through tracing the evolution of precarity from a byproduct of financialization to a deliberately cultivated and exploited condition, the chapter will shed light on the complex interplay between the global security industry, the authoritarian–financial complex (AFC), and the reproduction of social and economic inequality in contemporary capitalism.

Complex social production: creating conditions for expansion and control

To understand how complexes reproduce and expand, it is necessary to examine processes of complex social production, where social conditions are not simply reacted to or managed but are actively produced to sustain and enhance the complex's growth. The dynamics at play go beyond merely responding to crises or threats; they involve an ongoing process of generating, shaping, and institutionalizing social environments that perpetuate the complex's mechanisms of control. These processes reveal a deeper pattern where complexes not only adapt to existing conditions but actively manufacture the social, economic, and cultural landscapes that necessitate their continued expansion. In this theoretical framework, mechanisms of control move from being temporary crisis-management tools to structural components that continually reproduce the conditions for their existence.

Complex social production involves the deliberate shaping of environments in which certain risks, insecurities, and demands are continuously manufactured and intensified, creating a cycle where the need for control measures appears endless. This process entails normalizing and routinizing mechanisms of control by embedding them in everyday practices, legal frameworks, and economic structures. Over time, what was once an extraordinary response to a specific crisis becomes an entrenched feature of social organization, deeply intertwined with daily life and institutional operations. In this way, social production operates on both material and symbolic levels, as the processes of producing insecurity and risk are accompanied by narratives and cultural norms that naturalize these conditions.

The AFC exemplifies this dynamic by transforming the original political need to securitize neoliberalism into an expansive economy of control, where the social production of precarity serves as a key mechanism for reproducing the complex. The AFC did not merely respond to the social dislocations caused by neoliberal policies such as deregulation, austerity, and privatization. Rather, it took these conditions of economic instability and turned them into productive forces for its own expansion by generating markets for risk management, surveillance, and financial compliance. In this framework, precarity is not an unintended side effect of neoliberalism but a deliberately cultivated condition that fuels demand for the very mechanisms that the AFC supplies. This continuous production of social insecurity ensures that the need for control remains ever-present, embedding the complex's logic within the broader economic and social landscape.

One aspect of complex social production is the ability to make certain forms of instability appear natural and unavoidable. The AFC accomplishes this through the financialization of everyday life, where access to basic needs such as housing, healthcare, and education becomes increasingly mediated by financial markets. By turning these fundamental aspects of social life into commodities subject to market forces, the complex produces conditions where economic insecurity and indebtedness are common experiences. This financialization process does not merely affect individuals' economic conditions; it also transforms social relations, reshaping how people understand risk, security, and social responsibility. As financial instability becomes normalized, it creates a social environment in which the mechanisms of financial oversight, credit monitoring, and debt management appear necessary for functioning in society. The AFC thus continuously produces conditions that reinforce its own expansion by ensuring that financial surveillance and risk management become essential features of economic life.

The theoretical insight here is that processes of complex social production involve not just the generation of material conditions but also the shaping of cultural and ideological frameworks that sustain these conditions. Through discourses around personal responsibility, economic rationality, and risk management, the AFC promotes a worldview in which social problems are framed as individual issues that require surveillance and control rather than structural reform. This narrative shift reinforces the idea that social insecurity is a natural part of life, which can only be managed – not eliminated – through techniques of control. Consequently, the mechanisms of the complex become embedded in the cultural imagination, where surveillance, compliance, and financial risk management are seen as the logical responses to a precarious world.

The example of precarity within the AFC demonstrates how complex social production works to transform conditions of instability into engines of economic growth. The expansion of precarious labour, driven by algorithmic management, gig work, and the erosion of traditional employment protections, produces an environment where workers experience economic insecurity as a permanent condition. This insecurity drives demand for various products and services that claim to offer stability or mitigate risks, such as payday loans, insurance policies, and financial planning services. The economic value derived from managing precarious conditions reinforces the very dynamics that generate them, ensuring that the mechanisms of control remain necessary for navigating a world characterized by instability. The AFC thus reproduces itself by continuously producing the conditions for its own expansion, turning social vulnerabilities into opportunities for profit.

Moreover, the processes of complex social production involve the integration of mechanisms across different social spheres, ensuring that the logics of the complex permeate multiple dimensions of life. For example, the privatization and commodification of security functions – ranging from policing and incarceration to border control and private military contracting – blur the lines between state responsibilities and market interests. This integration not only creates new markets for control measures but also ensures that the practices associated with the AFC become deeply embedded in the structure of governance. By outsourcing traditionally public functions to private entities, the complex extends its reach and integrates its mechanisms into the core functions of the state, thereby normalizing the commodification of security and reinforcing the social production of control.

In this theoretical framework, the shift from driving change to producing the conditions for reproduction involves moving beyond reactive responses to crises to the proactive creation of environments that sustain and expand these complex relations. It is not enough for the complex to adapt to existing conditions; it must actively shape the conditions themselves to ensure that its mechanisms remain indispensable. This is achieved by embedding the mechanisms of control within legal, economic, and cultural structures, producing social environments that continually justify and necessitate their use. In the AFC, the perpetual production of precarity transforms economic and social instability from being challenges to be managed into permanent features of the economy that sustain growth in sectors dedicated to control and risk management.

Socially producing precarity

The transformation of precarity into a growing economic industry relies on its continuous amplification and spread to maintain profits. Precarious employment, marked by uncertainty and the erosion of social protections, has become a defining feature of contemporary capitalism, driven by neoliberal globalization and financialization (Lucarelli, 2012). This deliberate fostering of precarity has been facilitated by labour market restructuring, the weakening of welfare states, and the rise of new work modalities like the gig economy (Greer, 2016; Schor et al, 2020). The industry's growth is rooted in political and economic shifts over recent decades, characterized by the rise of neoliberal ideology and a global capitalist framework focused on profit maximization and labour cost reduction (Felix, 2020). The neoliberal agenda has dismantled social and institutional safeguards that historically provided worker security, such as labour unions, welfare provisions, and regulatory frameworks (Shin, 2013; Greer, 2016). In their place, a new paradigm of flexibility, individualization, and risk has emerged, forcing workers to bear the uncertainties of economic existence (Neilson, 2015; Paret, 2016).

The cultivation of precarity has been particularly pronounced in cultural and creative work, where the emphasis on innovation, entrepreneurship, and self-expression has normalized insecurity and exploitation (Gill and Pratt, 2008; De Peuter, 2011). The glamorization of immaterial labour in media, technology, and the arts obscures the precarious conditions many workers face, such as low wages, long hours, and constant unemployment threats (Bulut, 2015). This risk individualization is expedited by the erosion of collective bargaining and the rise of project-based and freelance work, undermining worker solidarity and resistance (Gill and Pratt, 2008; Lazar and Sanchez, 2019). Financialization prioritizes short-term profits over worker stability, leading to firm restructuring and labour outsourcing, thus proliferating precarious work without traditional employment benefits (Lucarelli, 2012; Greer, 2016). The platform economy exacerbates this trend, creating jobs marked by insecurity and the erosion of worker protections, where livelihoods depend on algorithms and digital platforms without traditional benefits (Heidkamp and Kergel, 2017; Schor et al, 2020). This environment intensifies surveillance and control, as workers face constant monitoring and evaluation by algorithms and customer ratings (Heidkamp and Kergel, 2017).

The cultivation of precarity as a profitable industry has also been expedited by the restructuring of welfare states and the rise of punitive and disciplinary forms of social policy (Greer, 2016; Massey, 2019). The erosion of social protections and the rise of workfare policies have contributed to the re-commodification of labour, as workers are increasingly compelled to accept low-wage and insecure jobs in order to survive (Greer, 2016). This has been accompanied by the criminalization of poverty and the rise of the carceral state, as the management of surplus populations has become a profitable industry in its own right (Paret, 2016; Massey, 2019). Moreover, the intersection of precarity with other forms of inequality and oppression has undermined the capacity for collective resistance and solidarity among workers (Ellis, 2015; Misra, 2021). The experiences of precarity are shaped by multiple and connected forms of disadvantage, including race, gender, class, and immigration status, which have contributed to the fragmentation and stratification of the workforce (Misra, 2021).

In the neoliberal financialized economy, precarity is not just a structural byproduct but a deliberately cultivated condition, serving to expand securitization industries that profit from controlling individuals and communities. These industries thrive on generating and exploiting insecurity, treating individuals and communities as raw materials for profitable securitization. Precarity is commodified, repackaged, and marketed by private entities like security firms, insurance companies, data brokers, and platform corporations. The subjective experiences of precarity, such as job loss apprehension and financial insecurity, are viewed as valuable commodities by economic elites rather than societal challenges to resolve. This creates a self-perpetuating cycle where precarity and securitization continuously amplify and perpetuate insecurity and vulnerability for profit.

Insecurity Inc.

Precarity has emerged not only as a structural inevitability of financialization but a burgeoning industry characterized by predatory practices aimed at exploiting widespread social and economic insecurity. This industry capitalizes on the enduring state of insecurity and vulnerability prevalent in contemporary society, leveraging the anxiety and uncertainty stemming from economic volatility, social upheaval, and the gradual erosion of conventional support structures. Central to the operation of this industry is a complex network comprising private enterprises, governmental bodies, and international entities, all capitalizing on the opportunities afforded by the securitization of precarity. These stakeholders have cultivated an extensive range of products and services tailored to surveil, regulate, and monetize the experiences of individuals and communities grappling with precarity. From sophisticated surveillance technologies and data management solutions to predictive policing algorithms and privatized security provisions, this industry has effectively transformed the phenomenon of precarity into a lucrative market, commodifying the very conditions of insecurity and vulnerability it ostensibly seeks to alleviate.

This thriving industry is uncovered in a range of released WikiLeaks documents. These leaked materials offer an unprecedented view into the burgeoning market for surveillance technologies, data retention solutions, and intelligence support systems that have proliferated in response to heightened security concerns and the normalization of precarity in the modern world. Revealed is an intricate web of private enterprises, governmental bodies, and international organizations that have seized upon the opportunities afforded by the securitization of precarity. They produce and sell an extensive spectrum of products and services engineered to surveil, scrutinize, and regulate the dissemination of information and the mobility of individuals worldwide, ostensibly aimed at upholding order and stability amidst the escalating uncertainty and instability characterizing contemporary global dynamics.

Aqsacom, a French company specializing in lawful interception solutions for telecommunications networks, exemplifies this trend. In a 2006 white paper, Aqsacom examines the implications of the USA Patriot Act for lawful interception, emphasizing how the legislation has expanded the scope and reach of electronic surveillance in the aftermath of 9/11. The document outlines key provisions of the Patriot Act, such as the expansion of wiretap authority, the introduction of 'roving wiretaps', and the extension of surveillance periods for non-US persons. Aqsacom emphasizes the profound implications of these provisions for lawful interception processes, necessitating the systematic organization of surveillance data and the coordination of criminal and intelligence investigations across multiple jurisdictions. The company positions itself as a solution provider, offering products that enable the secure collection, analysis, and sharing of intercepted communications data to assist law enforcement and intelligence agencies in navigating this complex landscape.

AGT International, a Swiss company, emerges as another significant player in the industry, offering customized security and safety solutions for clients in various sectors, including law enforcement, defence, and domestic security. AGT International's 2011 brochure reveals a significant shift in the security industry, as the company expands its focus from providing military solutions to offering a wide range of products and services aimed at civilian securitization. Touting its capabilities in providing 'sophisticated aerial, naval, and ground security platforms' for governments as well as solutions for 'managing and securing airports, ports, borders, large-scale events, etc.', the firm demonstrates the growing demand for comprehensive security solutions that extend beyond the realm of traditional military operations. This expansion into the civilian domain reflects a broader trend in the industry, as private companies increasingly recognize the lucrative opportunities presented by the securitization of everyday life. Moreover, AGT International's emphasis on implementing 'crime monitoring centers, first responders platforms, and intelligence solutions for police forces' highlights the blurring of lines between military and civilian security. The integration of these technologies and systems into urban environments and local law enforcement agencies suggests a growing convergence of military-grade surveillance and policing practices with the management of civilian populations. This convergence raises significant concerns about the normalization of militarized security practices in everyday life and the potential erosion of civil liberties and privacy rights as these technologies become more pervasive and entrenched in society.

The documents shed light on the role of major technology companies like HP in perpetuating a climate of insecurity and precarity in the post-9/11 era. In its own 2011 brochure on 'Investigative Solutions', HP explicitly capitalizes on the heightened security concerns and increased demands placed on law enforcement and service providers in the wake of the 'war on terror'. By framing its products and services as essential tools for addressing the challenges of 'today's converged communications services', it promotes itself as a key player in the growing market for surveillance and intelligence gathering technologies. Their emphasis on 'lawful intercept, data retention, and warrant management' solutions underscores the company's efforts to normalize and legitimize the widespread monitoring and collection of personal data in the name of national security. The brochure highlights the 'increasing data volumes, new technologies, and regulations around retaining records' as pressing issues that require 'standards-based, proven solutions' to mitigate risks and costs. This framing suggests that the erosion of privacy rights and the expansion of surveillance capabilities are necessary and inevitable consequences of the post-9/11 security landscape.

HP's assertion that 'law enforcement is asking more of service providers, in the form of both greater cooperation and expanded capabilities' provides further evidence of the increasingly intertwined relationship between technology companies and government agencies in perpetuating a culture of securitization. By presenting its 'comprehensive portfolio of intelligence support systems (ISS)' as a solution to these demands, the firm actively encourages the proliferation of surveillance technologies and the integration of military-grade capabilities into civilian law enforcement practices. The brochure's emphasis on HP DRAGON, the company's 'core platform that provides scalability, capacity, and functionality', further illustrates the industry's drive to normalize and expand the use of advanced surveillance technologies in the post-9/11 world. The platform's 'multidimensional scalability of performance, capacity, and functionality' is touted as essential for fulfilling 'requests for communications data', suggesting that the demand for ever-more invasive and comprehensive monitoring capabilities is a natural and necessary response to the challenges of the 'war on terror'. HP's marketing of its 'Investigative Solutions' can, thus, be seen as a calculated effort to capitalize on the climate of fear and insecurity generated by the 'war on terror', transforming it into a permanent state of precarity that requires constant surveillance and policing.

The expanding market for surveillance technologies is illustrated by the documents related to Security & Policing, the UK's premier security and law enforcement exhibition. This annual event serves as a platform for government agencies, police forces, and private companies to showcase the latest products and services in areas such as counter-terrorism, border security, and cybersecurity. The documents underscore the 'unique nature' of the event, which allows for the 'confidential display of sensitive equipment' and the 'formal overseas delegation management' by UK Trade and Investment. Exhibitors at this event encompassed a wide spectrum of companies offering state-of-the-art surveillance and intelligence gathering tools. AiSolve, for instance, provides advanced video analytics software for identifying and tracking individuals and objects in real-time, while Cobham offers integrated surveillance infrastructure for smart cities that leverages 'unique IP Mesh technology' to create 'a fluid, self-forming, self-healing network that adjusts even in rapidly changing, mobile situations'. These products are marketed as essential tools for maintaining public safety and security in an increasingly complex and uncertain world, promising to provide authorities with 'fast, reliable access to real-time visual, audio and location-based information'.

The case of PETER-SERVICE highlights, moreover, the disturbing trend of private companies repackaging and commercializing government-developed mass surveillance technologies as products and services to be sold back to states for domestic and international intelligence gathering and population monitoring purposes. A Russian company specializing in software and services for telecom operators, the firm has actively pursued partnerships with Russian intelligence agencies, offering them access to subscriber data and metadata through its various products and capabilities. One of the most troubling aspects of PETER-SERVICE's offerings is its Data

Retention System, which stores metadata on communications for access by authorities. This system, along with the company's interface for government surveillance under System for Operative Investigative Activities regulations, enables the Russian government to engage in widespread monitoring and tracking of its citizens' communications and online activities. By providing these tools to the state, PETER-SERVICE facilitates the expansion and normalization of mass surveillance practices, undermining the privacy rights and civil liberties of individuals. PETER-SERVICE's Traffic Data Mart and deep packet inspection products, designed for monitoring and analysing internet traffic, further demonstrate the company's role in enabling government surveillance on a massive scale. These technologies allow for the collection and analysis of vast amounts of data, providing intelligence agencies with unprecedented insights into the online behaviour and activities of entire populations.

What is also uncovered is how PETER-SERVICE has drawn inspiration from the National Security Agency's controversial PRISM programme, which gained notoriety following the revelations by whistleblower Edward Snowden. In a leaked presentation, PETER-SERVICE proposes an alliance for large-scale data collection and analysis, citing PRISM as a model for its own surveillance initiatives. This not only underscores the company's willingness to emulate the most invasive and controversial government surveillance programmes but also highlights the global nature of the surveillance industry, as companies and governments around the world share tactics and technologies to advance their monitoring capabilities. PETER-SERVICE's offer to coordinate its experience in surveillance technologies and 'big data' analysis into a national control system for digital networks underscores the company's aspiration to become a central player in the Russian government's surveillance apparatus. By consolidating and centralizing these capabilities, PETER-SERVICE aims to create an all-encompassing system for monitoring and controlling the country's digital infrastructure, providing the state with an unprecedented level of power and control over its citizens.

The case of PETER-SERVICE exemplifies the close interaction between private companies and government agencies in the global surveillance industry. By repackaging and commercializing government-developed mass surveillance technologies, companies like PETER-SERVICE not only profit from the erosion of privacy and civil liberties but also actively contribute to the expansion and normalization of these practices worldwide. The example of Cambridge Consultants reveals, even more so, how the surveillance industry is proactively anticipating and adapting to the evolving technological landscape, driven by the increasing demand for customizable and adaptable solutions that can keep pace with the rapidly changing nature of wireless communications. Through developing innovative technologies like the 'tiny base station' using commercial components, Cambridge Consultants demonstrates its ability to quickly respond to the needs of its clients and capitalize on the growing market for covert, flexible, and easily deployable surveillance tools.

This proactive approach to innovation highlights a key shift in the surveillance industry, as private companies take the lead in shaping the future of surveillance technologies. Rather than simply responding to the demands of governments and law enforcement agencies, companies like Cambridge Consultants are actively driving the development of new tools and capabilities that can be marketed to a wide range of customers. This shift reflects the increasing privatization of surveillance services and the commodification of precarity, as the industry seeks to monetize the growing demand for advanced monitoring and control technologies. As the documents show, Cambridge Consultants was developing technologies that address specific 'user needs', including 'smaller size units', 'fast deployment', 'scalable usage', and 'covert operation'. This emphasis on customization and adaptability illuminated how the industry was moving away from one-size-fits-all solutions and towards a more tailored approach that can meet the specific requirements of individual customers. This trend towards customization reflected, in turn, the growing recognition that effective population control requires a nuanced understanding of the specific social, political, and economic contexts in which surveillance technologies are deployed. In offering a range of customizable solutions, companies like Cambridge Consultants enable their clients to adapt their surveillance strategies to the unique challenges and opportunities presented by different environments, from densely populated urban centres to remote border regions.

The commodification of precarity has, thus, created a powerful incentive for the surveillance industry to continually innovate and expand its offerings. As governments and law enforcement agencies around the world seek to monitor and control increasingly precarious populations, the demand for advanced surveillance technologies continues to grow. This demand creates a lucrative market for companies like Cambridge Consultants, which could charge premium prices for their cutting-edge solutions and expertise. The increasing demand for interception and data retention solutions is further highlighted by presentations from companies like Utimaco, a German firm specializing in lawful interception and monitoring solutions, and Qosmos, a French company focused on deep packet inspection technology. These firms emphasize the challenges posed by the constantly evolving protocols and applications used by 'targets', as well as the necessity for specialized expertise and high-performance solutions to keep pace with the flood of data generated by modern communications networks.

Hence, by the second decade of the 21st century, a growing number of security and technology firms were not only responding to the demands of governments and law enforcement agencies but also actively shaping the discourse and policies surrounding security and surveillance. By framing the proliferation of surveillance technologies as a necessary response to the threats posed by terrorism, crime, and social unrest, these companies and agencies have contributed to the creation of a self-perpetuating cycle of fear and control, where the very solutions offered to address insecurity become a source of insecurity themselves. Through their participation in events like Security & Policing and their partnerships with intelligence agencies and research institutions, these companies played a significant role in defining the 'best practices' and 'industry standards' for surveillance and data analysis while simultaneously lobbying for legal and regulatory frameworks that align with their interests. The emergence of this growing high-tech industry of surveillance and control was indicative of the intensification of the AFC through the profitable production and spread of precarity.

Precarious classes

The convergence of finance-driven accumulation and authoritarian neoliberal governance has led to the rise of a transnational elite class that shapes contemporary politics, economics, and society. This elite, intertwined with the AFC, promotes pervasive cultures of precarity to maintain economic hegemony and political influence. At the core is the primacy of interest-bearing capital within finance-dominated regimes, which pursues supernormal returns through speculative ventures and leveraged debt (Lapavitsas, 2013). This relentless profit pursuit creates crisis tendencies, causing dislocations within the capitalist order and challenging its legitimacy (Seymour, 2024). In response, authoritarian neoliberal statism normalizes exceptional measures, routine coercion, and the erosion of democratic liberties (Boukalas, 2014). This transnational elite, encompassing corporate executives, political operatives, technocrats, and oligarchs (Durkin, 2022; Rushkoff, 2022), wields significant influence across various domains. A defining trait of this elite is its exploitation of cultures of precarity, creating insecurity, instability, and vulnerability in modern life. Through control over economic and political levers, the AFC shapes policies and narratives that normalize precarity as a disciplinary mechanism (Boaz, 2015; Ball, 2017).

In the realm of employment, the relentless pursuit of financial profits has fostered job insecurity, the rise of precarious labour arrangements, and the suppression of collective bargaining power (Evans and Sewell, 2013). This precarious workforce becomes a tool for disciplining labour, ensuring workers remain compliant and resistant to organizing. Likewise, the financialization of housing has intensified precarity, making homes increasingly unaffordable and insecure, benefiting financial institutions while weakening community power and heightening vulnerability (Bria, 2009; Hudson, 2020). Austerity measures have further eroded social safety nets, leaving individuals more exposed to economic shocks (Seymour, 2024). Simultaneously, the AFC has concentrated power, undermining legal safeguards and civil liberties, worsening conditions for marginalized and dissenting groups (MacKinnon, 2011; Maréchal, 2017). For economic and political elites, these cultures of precarity provide both profit opportunities and a means of consolidating power. The vulnerability of communities facilitates predatory practices like exploitative lending and asset stripping (Lapavitsas, 2013), which entrench precarity while generating immense profits. As elites accumulate assets and resources at discounted rates, their dominance deepens (Rushkoff, 2022). Moreover, precarity acts as a powerful disciplinary tool, with the constant threat of economic instability and social dislocation discouraging dissent and resistance, ensuring a steady supply of compliant labour and consumer markets (Ball, 2017).

Precarity permeates all levels of society, affecting even the elite who fear economic, social, and ecological insecurity (Rushkoff, 2022). This fear drives them to create secluded compounds and self-sustaining communities to ensure personal security, further embedding the cultures of precarity they propagate. The concentration of resources and securitization of elite enclaves exacerbates deprivation and vulnerability for the broader populace, increasing instability and insecurity (Durkin, 2022). This creates a repressive cycle: elite efforts to secure themselves intensify precarity, necessitating further securitization and fortification, reinforcing their economic and political dominance while subjecting populations to heightened surveillance, control, and repression (MacKinnon, 2011; Maréchal, 2017). Consequently, the AFC has fostered a transnational elite class that promotes and expands cultures of precarity to consolidate power and profits.

Precarity transcends traditional class boundaries, forming a new global class: the precariat, which includes migrant workers, contingent labourers, informal sector workers, and even segments of the middle class affected by financialization (Standing, 2011; Jørgensen and Schierup, 2016; Vij, 2019). Defined by shared experiences of insecurity and instability rather than traditional class markers, the precariat is particularly vulnerable, lacking the collective power and stable identities of the traditional working class (Standing, 2011). The production of precarity is a deliberate strategy by elites to enhance capital accumulation, creating a transient, insecure workforce devoid of occupational stability, adequate remuneration, or social protections. Policies promoting temporary contractual arrangements, the gig economy model, offshoring, outsourcing, and the weakening of organized labour have produced a surplus army of precarians, rendering them an exploitable resource for dominant economic actors. This manufactured vulnerability generates immense profitability for elites, as the precariat's lack of negotiating power makes it a leverageable workforce.

Detaining the world

The global detention industry exemplifies the AFC, exploiting the economic and political precarity created by neoliberal financialization. This cycle of relentless profit pursuit and human commodification has generated a vast pool of vulnerable populations, especially in the Global South, who are forced to migrate for survival and security (Waite, 2009; Lee and Kofman, 2012). The industry capitalizes on this precarity by mass incarcerating migrants and privatizing border control (Schierup and Jørgensen, 2016). Neoliberal economic restructuring, driven by financialization and corporate globalization, has eroded social protections and labour rights, leaving millions in chronic insecurity (Beer et al, 2016; Hürtgen, 2021). Climate change, political instability, and conflict have displaced millions more, intensifying this precarity (Vij, 2019; Akesson and Badawi, 2020). The detention industry markets itself as a solution to the migration 'crisis', offering privatized detention facilities and militarized border technologies to manage and control the flow of people (Dowling, 2017; Mattioli, 2019).

The financing of the detention industry has become sophisticated and globalized, with private equity firms, hedge funds, and other financial actors heavily investing in the sector (Appleyard et al, 2016; Fields and Raymond, 2021). This involvement ranges from direct investment in private prison companies to providing loans and financial services to government agencies responsible for immigration enforcement (Appleyard et al, 2016). In the United States, private equity firms like Blackstone and KKR have significant stakes in companies like CoreCivic and GEO Group, which operate many of the country's immigration detention centres (Fields and Raymond, 2021). These investments are driven by the expectation of steady returns due to restrictive immigration policies and the ongoing criminalization of migration (Ascher et al, 2022). Additionally, new financial instruments and investment vehicles, such as social impact bonds and public–private partnerships, have facilitated the transfer of risk from the public sector to private investors (Appleyard et al, 2016). Promoted as cost-reducing and efficiency-improving measures, these instruments have entrenched the power of financial actors and subordinated migrants' welfare to profit maximization (Lapavitsas, 2009; Ascher et al, 2022). Consequently, mass incarceration and human rights abuses are deeply embedded in the global economy, prioritizing the interests of private companies and financial institutions over migrants' rights and dignity (Ferreri and Vasudevan, 2019; Lesutis, 2021).

The expansion of the detention industry has been driven by neoliberal globalization, creating an environment conducive to the privatization and commodification of migration control (Gertel, 2019; Strauss, 2020). The financialization of this industry has intertwined the interests of financial actors with the state and private prison industry, forming a powerful lobby that profits from the criminalization and incarceration of migrants (Lapavitsas, 2009; Appleyard et al, 2016; Fields and Raymond, 2021; Ascher et al, 2022). Marginalized communities, particularly women and children, have borne the brunt of this system's violence and trauma (Fields, 2017; Ashiagbor, 2021). The racialization of migration, fuelled by xenophobic and racist discourses, justifies the detention of migrants from the Global South, creating a system where the free movement of capital is encouraged, but people are restricted and punished (McDowell et al, 2009; Palomera, 2014; Neimark et al, 2020; Silvey and Parreñas, 2020). This industry disrupts social and economic networks, perpetuating poverty and marginalization in migrants' home countries by separating families and interrupting remittance flows vital to local economies (Ettlinger, 2007; Hall, 2012; Lucarelli, 2012; Sproll and Wehr, 2014).

The weaponization of migrant precarity by right-wing political movements and populist governments has surged recently, exemplified by the anti-immigrant rhetoric and policies of US President Donald Trump and other far-right leaders worldwide (Robinson et al, 2019). Trump's 2016 campaign was rife with inflammatory statements about immigrants, especially those from Latin America and Muslim-majority countries, depicting them as criminals and economic burdens (Sanchez, 2018). His administration's draconian measures, such as the 'Muslim ban' and the 'zero tolerance' policy that separated thousands of migrant children from their families, were justified as necessary for national security, despite widespread condemnation from human rights organizations (Banki, 2016). In Europe, similar trends are evident, with far-right parties exploiting immigration fears to gain political ground. In Hungary, Prime Minister Viktor Orbán's anti-immigrant agenda includes a border fence and detention camps for asylum seekers, justified by portraying migrants as cultural threats (Sanchez, 2018). In Italy, the far-right Lega party, led by Matteo Salvini, has closed ports to migrant rescue ships and called for deportations, using rhetoric that paints migrants as criminals to stoke public fear and resentment (Banki, 2016; Jørgensen and Schierup, 2016).

The political weaponization of migrant precarity has produced devastating consequences for individuals and communities directly affected by these policies and has negatively impacted the broader social and political fabric. Migrants and refugees face human rights abuses such as arbitrary detention, family separation, and denial of asylum, while being demonized by political leaders and the media (Sanchez, 2018). This anti-immigrant rhetoric fosters xenophobia, racism, and intolerance, eroding social cohesion and undermining democratic values like pluralism and human rights (Jørgensen and Schierup, 2016). Moreover, scapegoating migrants distracts from addressing structural factors driving migration, such as economic inequality and climate change (Banki, 2016). The global detention industry exemplifies the AFC, where state repression aligns with private capital's profit motives. The commodification of human suffering and financialization of migration control subordinates migrants' lives to market dictates, with severe consequences (Matos, 2019; Graham and Papadopoulos, 2023). This precarity is not accidental but a deliberate strategy for creating a pliant workforce, integral to neoliberal capitalism's regulation of the global labour market (Lazar and Sanchez, 2019; Zembylas, 2019; Neimark et al, 2020; Lesutis, 2021).

Monitoring work

The financialization of the global economy has led to precarious forms of work, epitomized by the gig economy, which leverages digital technologies and algorithmic management to control workers profitably. Characterized by short-term contracts, freelance work, and platform-mediated labour, the gig economy exemplifies the precarity resulting from financialization (MacDonald and Giazitzoglu, 2019). As corporations prioritize shareholder value and short-term profitability over workers' well-being, they increasingly rely on flexible labour arrangements with minimal benefits and stability (Alberti et al, 2018; Westcott et al, 2019). Digital platforms and algorithmic management systems facilitate the efficient matching of labour supply and demand, granular monitoring of performance, and externalization of risk onto workers (Gandini, 2019; Duggan et al, 2020). Financial markets pressure corporations to maximize returns, making the gig economy a profitable frontier for extracting labour value (Muntaner, 2018; Liang et al, 2023). By classifying workers as independent contractors, gig platforms evade traditional obligations like minimum wages and social insurance (De Stefano, 2016; Todolí-Signes, 2017). Algorithmic management and data-driven surveillance allow platforms to exert significant control over workers, blurring the lines between employment and self-employment (Wood et al, 2019; Newlands, 2021).

The gig economy's repressive industry uses sophisticated technologies to monitor, evaluate, and discipline workers (Aloisi and Gramano, 2020; Jarrahi et al, 2021). Gig platforms employ surveillance technologies to track workers' physical movements, online behaviours, and communications (Ball, 2021). Ride-hailing apps including Uber and Lyft use GPS and accelerometer data to monitor driving patterns and collect data on acceptance rates and customer ratings (Rosenblat and Stark, 2016; Shapiro, 2018). Similarly, delivery platforms such as Deliveroo and Glovo draw on algorithms to assign tasks and evaluate performance based on metrics like delivery times and customer feedback (Tassinari and Maccarrone, 2020; Gregory, 2021). Additionally, gig platforms use facial recognition and biometric tracking to verify identities, monitor attention and emotions, and detect fatigue (Stark and Levy, 2018). This includes ride-hailing apps requiring driver selfies to match profile pictures and detect drowsiness (Ravenelle, 2020). Freelance platforms also monitor productivity through keystrokes and mouse movements (Wood et al, 2019). Platforms analyse digital interactions and online reputation scores to evaluate and discipline workers (Jarrahi et al, 2021; Sannon et al, 2022). Data on workers' online activities, such as search histories and social media posts, are used to assess their reliability, affecting their access to work, pay rates, and platform status (Lee et al, 2015; Rosenblat, 2018; Ticona and Mateescu, 2018a; Möhlmann et al, 2023).

This algorithmic management regime fosters an environment of constant scrutiny and evaluation, where workers face opaque decision-making processes that can abruptly end their livelihoods (Möhlmann et al, 2023). Gig workers often lack visibility into the algorithms that govern their work, struggling to understand penalties or deactivations (Rosenblat, 2018; Griesbach et al, 2019). Automated decision-making can also produce biased outcomes, amplifying existing inequalities. The psychological toll is significant, as workers internalize the logic of the algorithm and engage in self-disciplining behaviours to maintain their ratings and reputations, leading to perpetual anxiety and insecurity (Bucher et al, 2021; Sannon et al, 2022). Additionally, gamification and nudging techniques by gig platforms create a false sense of autonomy and empowerment, masking the exploitative power dynamics between workers and employers (Lehdonvirta, 2018; Woodcock and Johnson, 2018).

The gig economy and its associated technologies of control are not merely a reflection of the changing nature of work in the 21st century, but are deeply rooted in the broader processes of financialization and the AFC (Cushen, 2013; Bernards, 2020). The precarity and insecurity experienced by gig workers is not an accident or a byproduct of technological change, but is actively produced and exploited by a system that prioritizes the interests of financial capital over the well-being and dignity of workers (Anwar and Graham, 2021; Wood and Lehdonvirta, 2021). This system is sustained by the development and deployment of increasingly sophisticated technologies of surveillance and control, which enable the granular monitoring and discipline of workers' behaviours and performances (Aloisi and Gramano, 2020; Jarrahi et al, 2021).

Tracking society

Financialization has deeply permeated contemporary society, embedding precarious social dynamics across multiple spheres, including housing, education, and everyday life. The spread of digital technologies and algorithmic management systems has enabled the profitable surveillance and regulation of labour, reinforcing a coercive nexus between finance and authoritarianism. Everyday life is now intertwined with debt markets, necessitating financial discipline through data extraction and control, particularly over impoverished populations. In housing, financialization has exacerbated precarity and dispossession, particularly for marginalized communities. 'Dependent financialization' in semi-peripheral regions (Vilenica et al, 2023) has led to exploitative lending practices by foreign institutions, resulting in housing insecurity. The concept of 'mortgaged lives' (García-Lamarca and Kaika, 2016) highlights how mortgage debt governs households, commodifying housing and weakening social protections. In capitalist peripheries, mortgage securitization, foreign real estate investment, and public housing privatization have caused widespread dispossession (Aalbers et al, 2020). Rental housing platforms, through 'digital informalization' (Ferreri and Sanyal, 2022), bypass regulations and shift risks onto tenants, creating rental precarity. Landlords increasingly use algorithms for tenant screening, perpetuating racial and economic discrimination under the guise of 'risk management' (Rosen et al, 2021). The rise of 'platform landlords' (Nethercote, 2023), utilizing algorithms and data extraction, has imposed new controls over tenants' domestic spaces, further entrenching financialized control in the housing sector.

The widespread acceptance of algorithmic systems in workforce management and control extends to landlord technologies like rent estimation algorithms and tenant screening software, which facilitate 'automated gentrification' and displace low-income renters, prompting housing justice activism (McElroy and Vergerio, 2022). Integration of these systems into advertising, insurance, and credit decisions raises concerns about 'algorithmic redlining', perpetuating housing discrimination against minorities (Allen, 2019). Fintech's use of psychometric data scoring and alternative credit infrastructures, aimed at financial inclusion for the economically disadvantaged, also contributes to manufacturing precarity. Psychometric scoring assesses creditworthiness through personal data from social media, browsing habits, and smartphone use, raising privacy, data exploitation, and bias concerns. Alternative credit infrastructures use non-traditional data to provide credit access to those without traditional histories but can lead to the financialization of basic necessities. These systems institutionalize new forms of precarity and control by commodifying personal data from impoverished populations, subjecting them to financial institutions and algorithmic decision-making (Bernards, 2019).

The strategic production of precarity has given rise to an increasingly complex system of surveillance and control, as the imperative to maintain power and profitability in an era of widespread insecurity has necessitated the development of more sophisticated means for monitoring and managing populations. As the gig economy, financialization, and the erosion of traditional employment relations have rendered ever-larger segments of the population vulnerable to economic instability and social dislocation, those in positions of authority have sought to leverage new technologies and data-driven techniques to track, analyse, and influence the behaviour of precarious subjects. This growing surveillance apparatus encompasses a wide array of tools and practices, from the algorithmic management systems used to monitor and discipline gig workers to the predictive policing algorithms deployed to identify and preempt potential threats to the social order. By collecting and analysing vast troves of data on individuals' movements, communications, and interactions, these systems enable the granular tracking and targeting of specific populations, allowing those in power to anticipate and respond to potential challenges to their authority.

However, the very technologies and techniques used to monitor and control precarious populations also serve to create new forms of precarity, as the constant surveillance and evaluation of individuals' behaviours and performances creates a state of perpetual anxiety and insecurity. In this sense, the strategic production of precarity and the development of sophisticated systems of tracking and control are mutually reinforcing, creating a feedback loop in which the imperative to manage and exploit vulnerable populations drives the development of ever-more intrusive and oppressive forms of surveillance and discipline. The AFC, therefore, produces precarity so that it increasingly extends across all facets of contemporary life, subjugating individuals and communities to the imperatives of finance, authoritarianism, and technological control.

Conclusion

The deliberate production and perpetuation of precarity is a hallmark of contemporary capitalism, deeply embedded in the AFC. This self-perpetuating cycle, driven by profit and power consolidation, turns insecurity and vulnerability into marketable commodities. A transnational capitalist elite – comprising corporate executives, political operatives, technocrats, and oligarchs – propagates precarity to reinforce its dominance. Through control over finance, governance, and technology, this elite erodes economic security, making access to essentials like housing, healthcare, and education contingent on navigating financialized markets. Precarious labour arrangements, such as those in the gig economy, exploit vulnerable workers under constant algorithmic surveillance, commodifying basic needs and financializing poverty, further entrenching precarity while undermining privacy and autonomy. The global detention industry exemplifies this, turning the criminalization of migration and militarized borders into profitable enterprises, exacerbating displacement and exploitation. This system feeds a cycle of fear and xenophobia, creating a 'precariat' class defined by instability and lack of stable employment. Even elites are vulnerable to economic instability, social unrest, and climate crises, prompting securitization measures like gated communities and privatized security, which deepen cultures of insecurity and control. Advanced technologies and data-driven surveillance further monitor and manage precarious populations, reinforcing biases and eroding civil liberties, as the strategic production of precarity fuels a cycle of control and exclusion.

The AFC is now a self-sustaining entity, systematically undermining the foundations of collective security while profiting from the insecurity and instability it engenders. By consolidating their influence over global finance, governance structures, and technological systems, the transnational capitalist elite have positioned themselves as the prime beneficiaries of an increasingly precarious world order. The production and normalization of precarity are thus intentional strategies adopted by those in positions of power to reinforce existing hierarchies and concentrate wealth and influence. The repressive machinations of the AFC serve to buttress the hegemony of an elite minority by rendering the masses perpetually insecure, dependent, and vulnerable to the dictates of finance capitalism. In the upcoming chapter, the book will delve into how the proliferation of quantification and mobile tracking has spurred a novel fantasy: the quest for ever-greater personal control through data and surveillance. This phenomenon serves as an affective legitimization for the commodification of control, highlighting how the marketization of securitization is sustained through a universalizing psycho-social complex.

7

Insatiable Control

Introduction

The previous chapter explored the strategic manufacturing and spread of precarity as a catalyst for the repressive cycle of finance, characterized by the relentless pursuit of profit and the expanding commodification of control. This cycle has engendered a pervasive sense of insecurity and vulnerability, necessitating a deeper examination of the psycho-social dimensions of this phenomenon. This chapter uncovers the internalization of the desire for control by individuals, creating a paradoxical subjectivation that is simultaneously empowering and oppressive. The financialized commodification of control lies at the core of this process, transforming security and well-being into marketable products. As individuals become entangled in the web of surveillance technologies and data-driven behavioural modification techniques, they perceive these tools as indispensable for navigating modern life's complexities. The desire for control becomes a driving force, shaping their choices, relationships, and sense of self. However, the pursuit of control through these technologies subjects individuals to ever-greater levels of manipulation by the very systems they rely upon. This paradoxical subjectivation is predicated on the political economy responsible for expanding population control, creating a self-reinforcing feedback loop that entrenches the power of the controlling complexes.

The omnipresence of digital surveillance has profound psycho-social implications, shaping desires and behaviours through a complex interplay of discipline and desire (Morrison, 2016), amplified by persuasive technologies designed to influence human cognition (Fogg, 2002). Emotional contagion via social networks (Kramer et al, 2014) plays a key role in spreading misinformation, manipulating public opinion, and reinforcing power structures and inequalities. Organizations, driven by the need for data to optimize processes and gain competitive advantage, reinforce this reliance on personal data exploitation (Lanier, 2018). Tech companies manipulate behaviour on a massive scale, creating a dynamic where individuals and societies, fixated on security and control, fuel a self-perpetuating system of surveillance driven by fear and vulnerability. The surveillance industry, benefiting from this demand, lobbies to maintain and amplify the perceived need for enhanced security technologies. The complex relationship between surveillance and security reflects capitalist imperatives that commodify security, turning it into a lucrative product in a market fuelled by cultivated anxieties. This economy exploits personal data and behaviour manipulation for profit, exacerbating inequalities and vulnerabilities. The fantasy of empowerment through surveillance technologies paradoxically subjects individuals to the very systems of control they seek to harness (Hancock and Guillory, 2015; Lanier, 2018), reinforcing systemic control dynamics. As individuals increasingly rely on surveillance tools to navigate modern life's complexities, their desire for control deepens, shaping their choices and sense of self. Yet, even as they seek to assert control, they are further entangled in systems that manipulate and control them, becoming active participants in their own subjugation (Fogg, 2002; Morrison, 2016).

This chapter uncovers the interplay between the authoritarian–financial complex (AFC) and the psycho-social forces legitimizing this new control apparatus. It examines how digital self-tracking technologies create a paradoxical subjectivation that is both empowering and oppressive. The quantified self movement taps into desires for control and mastery while enforcing societal norms and enabling commodification. This dynamic reflects a shift from social securitization to personal empowerment through data, driving the expansion of the AFC. The chapter analyses how shaping human behaviour has become a lucrative frontier for capitalist exploitation through digital nudging and predictive analytics. It also interrogates the paradox of 'self-domination', where self-monitoring technologies reinforce subjugation to larger control structures, and explores the psychology and realities behind society's unquenchable desire for optimization technologies.

Desiring control

The production of complex social conditions does not merely transform the external structures of society but also penetrates deeply into the psyche, where it cultivates values and behaviours that reinforce the very mechanisms and technologies of control that perpetuate those conditions. This process goes beyond the material and institutional aspects of social production; it extends into the realm of individual and collective psychology, where the underlying values of security, risk aversion, and self-optimization become internalized. These values evolve into a psychological complex that shapes how people perceive themselves and the world, making the demand for mechanisms of control appear as a natural and desirable response to social and personal challenges. This psychological complex emerges through a feedback loop in which social conditions generate feelings of anxiety and insecurity, while the solutions offered for these feelings are the very technologies and control measures that reinforce the original conditions, thus creating a self-sustaining cycle.

Crucial to this dynamic lies the transformation of insecurity and risk into marketable emotions and experiences that drive demand for control technologies. The AFC, through its integration of surveillance, data analytics, and financial oversight, not only capitalizes on economic instability and social precarity but also leverages psychological dynamics to deepen its reach. By framing control technologies as tools for empowerment, self-management, and safety, the AFC taps into deep-seated anxieties and desires for security that arise from living in precarious conditions. As social, economic, and even personal life becomes more unpredictable, individuals increasingly turn to surveillance and data-driven solutions to manage these insecurities, leading to a cultural shift where control itself becomes a fundamental value. This transformation is not merely about addressing insecurity but about internalizing a mindset that equates safety, productivity, and even self-worth with the use of technologies that monitor, regulate, and optimize behaviour.

The normalization of self-surveillance and the quantification of everyday life play central roles in embedding this psychological complex. Practices such as tracking physical activity, monitoring financial transactions, and using data analytics to optimize performance have become routine, driven by the promise of self-improvement and protection. These practices encourage individuals to view themselves as subjects to be managed, measured, and optimized, reinforcing a culture where control mechanisms are seen as essential for achieving success, stability, or well-being. This internalization leads to a form of self-regulation where people actively participate in their own surveillance, not because they are coerced but because they perceive it as beneficial. The more individuals engage in these self-monitoring practices, the more they reinforce the social values that underpin the AFC's control measures, further embedding these technologies within the structures of daily life.

This psychological complex also involves the commodification of anxiety, where fear and uncertainty are not merely outcomes of precarious conditions but are actively cultivated to drive demand for control solutions. The more people feel anxious about economic instability, crime, health risks, or social status, the more they seek out technologies and services that promise to mitigate these risks. The AFC, through its pervasive integration of data analytics, risk management, and digital surveillance, positions itself as the provider of solutions to these anxieties, offering tools that appear to empower individuals by giving them a sense of control over their circumstances. However, these tools do not resolve the underlying sources of anxiety;

instead, they perpetuate the conditions that generate it by continuously expanding the scope of what is considered risky or insecure. This dynamic ensures that the demand for control remains insatiable, as the more one seeks to mitigate risks, the more one becomes aware of new or previously overlooked threats, creating a cycle where anxiety and the technologies designed to address it continually reinforce each other.

The relationship between the production of social conditions and the psychological complex is further intensified through cultural narratives that equate control with personal responsibility and moral virtue. In a society governed by neoliberal values, individuals are often told that they must take responsibility for managing their own risks, whether related to health, finances, or personal safety. This emphasis on individual responsibility shifts the focus away from structural causes of insecurity, such as economic inequality or inadequate social protections, and places the burden on individuals to monitor and manage their own lives through control measures. The widespread adoption of fitness trackers, budgeting apps, and social credit systems reflects how these narratives shape behaviour, encouraging people to embrace surveillance and data-driven management as the rational and morally correct approach to addressing personal and social problems.

By internalizing these values, individuals not only accept but also actively demand mechanisms of control, seeing them as essential for navigating an increasingly complex and insecure world. The psychological complex that emerges involves a form of obsession with safety, productivity, and optimization, where any perceived gap in security or potential for inefficiency becomes a source of discomfort that must be addressed through technological solutions. This obsessive demand for control does not merely seek to alleviate anxieties but actually amplifies them by continually raising the standards for what constitutes a safe or optimized state. The more technologies promise to protect or enhance one's life, the more aware individuals become of the risks and inefficiencies that could undermine these promises, leading to a perpetual cycle of seeking new forms of control.

This insatiable demand for control is also reinforced through social comparison and the fear of falling behind in a world where success and security are increasingly defined by one's ability to manage risk and optimize performance. The use of tracking technologies, performance metrics, and predictive analytics creates new benchmarks for what is considered 'normal' or 'acceptable' behaviour, making individuals feel pressured to conform to these standards to avoid being seen as irresponsible or unproductive. This social pressure intensifies the psychological complex, as people become not only concerned with their own security or efficiency but also with how they are perceived by others. The integration of social monitoring features in various apps and platforms further amplifies this dynamic, encouraging users to compare their data with that of their peers, thereby normalizing the expectation that everyone should be constantly striving for greater control over their lives.

The transformation of the underlying values of control into a psychological complex is thus a key process by which the AFC ensures its continued reproduction and expansion. The complex social conditions of precarity and instability generate a demand for control that goes beyond practical necessity, becoming a deeply ingrained cultural and psychological imperative. As the values associated with control are internalized, individuals come to see surveillance, risk management, and self-monitoring not as external impositions but as expressions of autonomy and self-empowerment. This internalization blurs the line between voluntary and coerced compliance, as people willingly adopt the technologies of control that the AFC promotes, believing that these tools are essential for achieving their own goals.

This process ultimately serves to depoliticize mechanisms of control, presenting them as neutral or technical solutions to problems that are framed as personal rather than structural. When individuals perceive surveillance technologies or risk management tools as necessary for their own safety, health, or success, they are less likely to question the broader social and economic structures that create the need for these tools in the first place. The psychological complex thus acts as a buffer that protects the AFC from critique, making its mechanisms of control appear as logical and inevitable responses to the conditions of modern life. This perpetuates a social order where the values of control, optimization, and risk management are paramount to individual and collective well-being, and where the technologies designed to support these values become integral to the functioning of society. Through these psychological complexes, the ends of control are, thus, reframed as the very means of personal and social empowerment, as they are no longer viewed as restrictive forces but instead embraced as essential tools for achieving greater security in an increasingly precarious world.

Insatiable control

The emergence of digital surveillance technologies has been legitimized through new social fantasies promising individuals enhanced personal agency and empowerment. These fantasies, embedded within the neoliberal paradigm, have normalized the authoritarian nature of such technologies, transforming them into coveted consumer goods. This shift exemplifies how authoritarianism has become a Lacanian capitalist fantasy, where digital control is the universal law, and the fantasies of psychic wholeness are highly personalized. This transition marks a shift from social to affective financial securitization, as explored through the logics of hegemony (Glynos and Howarth, 2007) introduced in Chapter 2.

The AFC cultivates a deep yearning for security, appealing to human needs for agency and self-determination. The neoliberal fantasy of the free market justifies digital control technologies, structuring desire and subjectivity while obscuring underlying power structures (Maher, 2023). Neoliberalism perpetuates a system of exploitation despite its contradictions (Swales, 2022). Datafication and digital reliance have introduced new forms of socially legitimized surveillance, with big data serving as both a scientific paradigm and a control fantasy (Van Dijck, 2014). This fantasy offers insights into personal lives while subjecting individuals to pervasive monitoring, relying on the misconception that data is a neutral and objective reality, masking its social and political construction (Dourish and Gómez Cruz, 2018).

Revealed is the profound linkage between political-economic and psycho-social dimension in sustaining the AFC. The libidinal economy of neoliberalism plays a critical role in transforming these digital technologies of control into desirable and profitable consumer goods and services. Psychoanalytic perspectives on datafication explore the perverse desires and fantasies that drive the obsession with data in the contemporary era (Piotrowski, 2018; Johanssen, 2021). Neoliberalism shapes desire through metaphors and discourses that promote the fantasy of endless growth and consumption (Ludwig, 2016; Bennett, 2017). Digital technologies are marketed as tools for personal empowerment and self-improvement, appealing to individuals' desires for control and mastery over their lives. However, neoliberalism structures feelings and emotions in particular ways, fostering a culture of anxiety and insecurity that fuels the demand for digital technologies of control (Freeman, 2020). The normalization of digital technologies of control and exploitation is reinforced by the reinvigoration of the supposed progressive spirit of capitalism, which promotes the fantasy of endless innovation and improvement.

Central to the AFC is the affective production of hegemonic fantasies of personal control. In the Lacanian framework, the law mandates the acceptance of digital control technologies as essential for participation in the neoliberal economy, while fantasies of psychic wholeness and empowerment remain highly individualized (Johanssen, 2021). Datafication creates perverse desires rooted in the individual psyche yet shaped by broader forces. This transformation of control technologies into profitable goods reflects how authoritarianism has become a Lacanian capitalist fantasy, supported by the neoliberal fantasy of the free market, which promotes the illusion of choice and autonomy while imposing pervasive control. The desire for control sustains neoliberalism by promising empowerment and mastery, integral to the 'greedocracy' that celebrates endless growth and consumption (Sim, 2017). This fantasy shapes desire through discourses of autonomy and self-determination but ultimately relies on pervasive surveillance and manipulation (Gilbert, 2017). Thus, the fantasy of control, while promising freedom, subjects individuals to new forms of domination and exploitation.

Individuals continuously desire new forms of control, creating an insatiable, ever-growing market. The rise of digital control technologies has normalized new forms of surveillance and manipulation, driving a demand for control commodified by the neoliberal fantasy of the free market, promising mastery over lives and behaviours. This commodification of control perpetuates a cycle of demand and supply, as individuals seek increasingly advanced technologies to keep pace with the digital landscape. The neoliberal paradigm promotes endless growth and consumption, drawing individuals into a futile pursuit of control over their lives and environments. The commodification of control profits from the anxieties and insecurities it creates, bombarding individuals with messages about the need for greater control while offering products and services to alleviate these concerns. This vicious cycle ensures the growth of the control industry, which in turn develops more advanced control technologies, perpetuating the cycle (Gilbert, 2017; Sim, 2017).

These control oriented desires are further reinforced by the affective dimensions of the neoliberal paradigm, which foster a culture of anxiety, insecurity, and precarity. As individuals are encouraged to bear the burden of responsibility for their own lives and well-being, they are simultaneously confronted with an ever-present sense of risk and uncertainty. This creates a powerful incentive to seek out technologies of control as a means of mitigating these risks and uncertainties, even as these technologies themselves contribute to the very conditions that give rise to these anxieties in the first place. In essence, the rise of digital technologies of control and exploitation reflects the way in which capitalist control has become an insatiable industry and desire. By commodifying control and transforming it into an affective and ethical imperative, neoliberalism has created a self-perpetuating cycle of demand and supply that feeds off the very anxieties and insecurities it helps to create. This cycle is sustained by the fantasmatic logics of the neoliberal paradigm, which promise individuals a sense of wholeness and completeness while simultaneously subjecting them to new forms of domination and control.

Shaping behaviour

In the first decade of the new millennium, the AFC evolved significantly, shifting from producing financially responsible subjects to profiting from the production of subjects themselves. This transformation extended the complex's influence beyond economic behaviour, aiming to shape human behaviour across all spheres of existence using advanced technologies and data-driven techniques to monitor, analyse, and manipulate choices, desires, and actions. This shift reflects the recognition of the immense value in shaping human behaviour, viewing the production of various identities and preferences as lucrative. The emergence of nudge theory by Thaler and Sunstein (2008) revolutionized the application of behavioural science in policy making by suggesting that subtle changes in the decision-making environment could influence behaviour without compromising autonomy. The rise of digital technologies has expanded the potential for implementing nudge theory on a large scale, using data from online activities to shape behaviour (Gandy Jr and Nemorin, 2019). This convergence of nudge theory and digital technologies, known as 'digital nudging', leverages personal data for behavioural modification, embodying a fantasy of control where data and technology are used to manipulate human behaviour.

This fantasy is based on the belief that personal data collection and analysis can create highly targeted interventions to guide behaviour, promising benevolent control through subtle influence rather than coercion (Leal and Oliveira, 2021). This fantasy has merged with political goals for digitalized population management, appealing to governmental and corporate desires to monitor, predict, and shape behaviour on a large scale (Leggett, 2014). Digital nudging offers a way to exert influence under the guise of 'choice' and 'empowerment', attracting liberal politicians aiming to advance progressive goals and align citizen behaviour with their ideology (Sunstein, 2014). The Obama administration's embrace of nudge theory and digital nudging, especially under Cass Sunstein, highlighted this shift, using behavioural science and digital tech to shape citizen behaviour (Sunstein, 2014). Initiatives like the Social and Behavioral Sciences Team (SBST) applied behavioural insights to policies ranging from retirement savings to college access (Halpern and Sanders, 2016). This marked a broader shift in population control strategies, expanding from national security and public order to health, education, and personal well-being, enabled by the availability of personal data and sophisticated digital technologies (Gandy Jr and Nemorin, 2019). Health apps and wearables like Fitbit encourage healthy lifestyles, while educational platforms like Knewton use adaptive learning to personalize instruction and improve outcomes (Abdukadirov, 2016; Halpern and Sanders, 2016).

Extending behavioural interventions into novel social spheres through digital technologies has created a new form of governmentality, blurring personal and political boundaries. This normalization of digital nudging as a population control tool has been bolstered by technology companies whose business models rely on monetizing personal data (Swagel, 2015). These companies promote the idea that digital technologies can effectively and desirably shape human behaviour, capitalizing on societal fascination with technology while advancing their commercial interests. For example, Google uses user data to develop targeted advertising systems, and Facebook's News

Feed algorithm shapes users' information consumption and social interactions through digital nudging techniques (Gandy Jr and Nemorin, 2019; Leal and Oliveira, 2021). As digital technologies advance and personal data collection becomes more pervasive, the desire to use these tools for behaviour control grows. This fantasy promises limitless ability to monitor, predict, and manipulate actions and choices under the guise of benevolent guidance and empowerment. Initially focusing on public health and education, these interventions now extend to all facets of human existence, from personal well-being and social interaction to economic and political life.

The fantasy of control is driven by an insatiable desire for more data, sophisticated algorithms, and precise behavioural targeting. Each technological advance is seen as an opportunity to refine behavioural modification techniques, resulting in a vast landscape of digital nudging where choices and actions are subtly manipulated for optimization. The political economy of control has shifted from creating financially responsible subjects to selling techniques and technologies for shaping behaviour. Previously focused on moulding productive economic actors, the emphasis now lies in commodifying behavioural modification tools and methods. This industry, by suggesting that subtle changes in choice architecture can influence decisions, has created a market for behaviour-shaping tools and strategies. Companies compete to develop and sell increasingly sophisticated means of monitoring, analysing, and manipulating human behaviour in various domains, including health, education, social media, and e-commerce.

The era of self-control

The ability to shape individuals' choices and actions has become a highly valuable commodity, driving the expansion of behaviour-shaping technologies into more intimate aspects of daily life. These technologies are often marketed as tools for personal empowerment and self-improvement, offering profound self-knowledge and value enhancement across economic, social, and personal realms (Lupton, 2016b). This industry profits from using data techniques and digital technologies to shape behaviour, creating a paradoxical discourse of personal empowerment that supports the AFC. The concept of the 'quantified self' exemplifies this, with self-tracking technologies allowing individuals to monitor personal metrics like steps, calories, sleep patterns, and mood (Neff and Nafus, 2016). Framed as empowerment tools, these technologies enable data-driven decisions to improve well-being (Sharon, 2017). The notion of 'data selves' (Lupton, 2019) illustrates how personal identities are shaped by digital data traces, constructed through algorithms and data infrastructures that reflect the biases of those in control (Selke, 2016). The 'computable body' is thus embedded within networks of power and control (Berson, 2015).

The discourse of empowerment has been crucial in legitimizing self-tracking technologies, positioning them as tools for personal growth and self-optimization. The 'datafication' of health and other aspects of life translates complex experiences into simplified, quantifiable data points for easy monitoring and manipulation (Ruckenstein and Schüll, 2017). Driven by technology companies, healthcare providers, and insurance firms, this process seeks profit and control (Ajana, 2018). However, the empowerment discourse obscures these underlying power dynamics, framing these technologies as individual choices. In workplaces, self-tracking technologies monitor and optimize employee performance, creating a 'quantified workplace' that emphasizes individual responsibility and self-discipline (Moore and Robinson, 2016). This neoliberal ideology encourages workers to measure and improve productivity, internalizing self-optimization logic (Fotopoulou and O'Riordan, 2017). Marginalized groups, however, may be disproportionately targeted for surveillance (Lupton, 2017). The constant need to monitor and optimize oneself can also lead to anxiety and pressure, though these consequences are often ignored in promoting self-tracking technologies as tools for personal development (Pantzar and Ruckenstein, 2015).

The increasing reliance on algorithms and data-driven decision-making in self-tracking technologies reflects a broader trend towards the automation of behavioural control (Dormehl, 2014). These technologies can exacerbate existing social inequalities and create new forms of discrimination based on personal data profiles (Wexler, 2017). They often reflect narrow, medicalized conceptions of health and well-being that prioritize individual responsibility over collective solutions to social problems (Dow Schüll, 2016). The 'more-than-human sensorium' (Lupton and Maslen, 2018) highlights how self-tracking shapes sensory experiences and perceptions, mediating relationships with bodies and environments in complex ways. Emotional and social motivations, such as the desire for self-improvement or control, drive self-tracking practices (Pantzar and Ruckenstein, 2015). This shift towards 'self-control' internalizes and individualizes self-surveillance and self-regulation, transforming the body and mind into entities to be personally monitored, quantified, and managed, extending Foucault's concept of disciplinary power.

The growing production and consumption of ever more innovative self-tracking technologies facilitates this process, enabling individuals to meticulously measure and analyse every aspect of their existence, from physical activity to emotional states, in the pursuit of socially promoted ideals of productivity, health, and well-being. What is particularly insidious about this shift is the way it co-opts the narrative of personal empowerment and self-optimization. Individuals are seduced by the promise of taking control over their lives through data-driven self-knowledge, oblivious to the subtle ways in which they are being coerced into conformity with dominant discursive regimes. The act of self-tracking becomes a form of self-imposed subjugation justified as a process regaining some sort of control over their lives and selves, leading individuals to internalize the imperative to continually monitor and adjust their behaviours to meet externally defined standards.

Personal colonization

The society of control, proposed by Deleuze, has thus evolved into a political economy of self-control, where individuals actively participate in their own surveillance and regulation, fuelled by the belief that doing so will lead to greater freedom, success, and happiness. The commodification of personal data generated through self-tracking practices further entrenches this system of self-domination. Corporations and institutions capitalize on this intimate data, using it to shape behaviour, influence consumer choices, and reinforce existing power structures, all under the guise of personalization and customization. In this era of self-domination, the body and mind are effectively reduced to objects of constant surveillance and control, with individuals willingly subjecting themselves to this process in the pursuit of an elusive ideal of self-optimization. The evolution from disciplinary power to internalized regimes of self-control marks a subtle yet profound shift in the techniques of social control, one that operates not through overt coercion but through the seductive promise of personal empowerment and self-actualization.

The quantified self movement has effectively outsourced surveillance and control to individuals, making them their own authoritarian overseers. They adjust behaviours and lifestyles to conform to idealized norms dictated by collected data, driven by a desire for personal empowerment that ultimately reinforces existing power structures and societal expectations. The data generated through self-tracking is commodified and exploited by corporations, entrenching the capitalist fantasy of personal empowerment. Self-tracking technologies encourage individuals to internalize societal norms, subjecting themselves to constant scrutiny and regulation. By embracing these practices, individuals submit their bodies, behaviours, and emotions to quantification and datafication, reducing their lives to measurable metrics and obsessively striving to optimize them. This process commodifies their existence and instils a sense of personal responsibility for meeting standards of productivity, health, and well-being, perpetuating the cycle of surveillance and control.

The AFC increasingly conflates personal identity and self-worth with the ability to digitally track, monitor, and regulate behaviour (Schüll, 2016). This commodification of control has spawned a thriving industry, with companies competing to offer advanced tools for self-monitoring and management. The market for personal data has grown rapidly, as individuals trade privacy for personalized services and recommendations. Wearable fitness trackers like Fitbit and Apple Watch exemplify how self-betterment is linked to digital technologies promising physical health optimization (Nafus and Sherman, 2014). Productivity apps like Todoist and RescueTime show how professional efficiency is mediated through digital tools that monitor work habits (Kristensen and Ruckenstein, 2018). These technologies promote capitalist fantasies of empowerment through self-discipline and self-management. The broader system of power relations embeds self-management, tying personal optimization to corporate and governmental interests (Galič et al, 2017). Corporate wellness programmes using digital tracking for health monitoring illustrate workforce optimization and cost reduction (Maturo and Moretti, 2018). Algorithmic decision-making in hiring, lending, and criminal justice shows the increasing delegation of power to opaque digital processes (Ajana, 2018).

The personalization of surveillance and self-management, enabled by the proliferation of digital technologies, has led to a profound shift in the nature of social control. Personalized news feeds, targeted advertising, and recommendation algorithms on platforms like Facebook, YouTube, and Netflix demonstrate how the power to shape individual preferences and behaviours is increasingly being wielded through the manipulation of digital traces and the exploitation of personal data (Ruckenstein and Schüll, 2017). This personalization of repressive techniques reflects the increasing influence of the AFC, which seeks to shape individual behaviour and preferences in ways that serve its own interests. As the boundaries between public and private, personal and political, become increasingly blurred, the very notion of the self is transformed, becoming a site of constant negotiation and contestation. The introduction of ever-more sophisticated 'quantified self' technologies and practices, such as mood tracking and sleep monitoring, illustrates how the project of self-understanding and self-determination is increasingly being mediated through digital technologies that reduce the complexity of human experience to a set of measurable and optimizable parameters for personal optimization (Nafus and Sherman, 2014). As a result, individuals are increasingly pressured to conform to narrow and normative standards of health, productivity, and well-being, and held responsible for meeting these expectations.

The AFC represents, therefore, a new form of internal colonization, where the insatiable search for new markets to conquer and exploit has turned inward, targeting the internal preferences and desires of individuals. This phenomenon builds upon earlier ideas of cultural colonization and psychic colonization but evolves them in a distinctly hyper-capitalist way, reflective of the contemporary neoliberal era. In the past, colonization was primarily concerned with the external domination and exploitation of physical territories and resources. Cultural colonization sought to legitimize this process by imposing the values, beliefs, and practices of the colonizers onto the colonized populations, while psychic colonization aimed to internalize these oppressive structures within the minds of the subjugated. However, in the era of the AFC, internal colonization takes on a new, more pernicious form. Rather than just legitimizing external military rule and economic exploitation, it seeks to transform one's beliefs, data, and actions into new markets to be controlled and exploited for profit. This process is driven by the relentless logic of neoliberal capitalism, which sees every aspect of human life as a potential source of value to be extracted and commodified.

In this context, the technologies of surveillance and self-management that have become so pervasive in our daily lives can be seen as tools of internal colonization. By constantly monitoring and quantifying our behaviours, preferences, and emotions, these technologies generate vast amounts of personal data that can be harvested and monetized by corporations and governments alike. This data is then used to create highly targeted marketing campaigns, personalized recommendations, and behavioural interventions designed to shape our desires and actions in ways that serve the interests of the AFC. Through encouraging individuals to internalize the demands for self-optimization and self-control, these technologies create a new form of psychic colonization, where the very notion of personal identity and self-worth becomes tied to one's ability to conform to the narrow and normative standards of productivity, efficiency, and well-being dictated by the market. This leads to a state of constant self-surveillance and self-discipline, as individuals strive to optimize every aspect of their lives in order to remain competitive and valuable in the eyes of the AFC. The result is a form of pervasive control that goes beyond physical boundaries, infiltrating the human psyche by colonizing our desires, beliefs, and behaviours on a deeply personal level.

Enjoyably controlling ourselves

The culture of internalized personal control endures through the construction of identities and social practices tied to digital monitoring and self-management. The financialized system persists not only through institutional surveillance but also by outsourcing policing functions to individuals in their daily interactions. Digital technologies and platforms facilitate tracking, quantification, and evaluation of personal and social life, fostering new forms of sociality and identity formation. People curate digital profiles, share experiences, and engage in self-branding, actively shaping identities and social relations. Monitoring others through digital platforms, such as rating drivers or reviewing products, has become crucial in everyday interactions, framed as consumer empowerment or social responsibility, reinforcing the system's norms. This decentralized, self-sustaining control system relies on individuals' active participation in monitoring themselves and others, driven by the desire for social recognition and resources. Thus, the financialized system persists through both formal mechanisms of control and individuals' willing participation in their own subjugation within a complex web of social and economic relations.

Rating systems, enabled by digital technologies, have become pervasive across social and economic spheres (Rosenblat and Stark, 2016; Zervas et al, 2017), contributing to a 'black box society' where opaque algorithms control various life aspects (Pasquale, 2015). These systems influence online marketplaces (Resnick and Zeckhauser, 2002), lending platforms (Burtch et al, 2014), healthcare provider reviews (Ubel et al, 2019), and local business evaluations (Luca, 2016). They create an environment of constant monitoring and evaluation, forming 'invisible cages' of control (Rahman, 2019). The belief in data-driven decision-making and real-time accountability reinforces this rating culture, underpinned by the notion that algorithmic systems offer objective and fair assessments (Citron and Pasquale, 2014). However, this perception obscures the biases embedded in these systems (Edelman and Luca, 2014; Christin, 2017), as seen in Uber's higher fares for passengers with African American-sounding names (Hannák et al, 2017) and manipulated reviews on Amazon (He et al, 2020).

Even with critical awareness, the everyday practice of mutual monitoring through rating systems grants individuals a perceived sense of control in an increasingly precarious society. Rating an Uber driver or reviewing a product on Amazon provides empowerment, especially where individuals have little control (Ticona and Mateescu, 2018a). Online feedback mechanisms serve as a 'digitized form of word-of-mouth', allowing consumers to influence and hold businesses accountable (Dellarocas, 2003). In a world where traditional sources of stability have eroded, these practices offer a sense of agency, however limited or illusory, responding to the broader crisis of social and economic insecurity. This sense of control can be understood through Lacanian psychoanalysis as a form of jouissance, the transgressive enjoyment from pursuing an unattainable fantasy (Lacan, 1966). The fantasy of total control promised by rating systems is always out of reach, as social and economic relations' complexity cannot be fully managed through data alone. Yet, engaging with these systems provides pleasure and empowerment, reinforcing the structures of control individuals seek to overcome. For Lacan, jouissance is a form of enjoyment tinged with pain, derived from pursuing an unattainable ideal. In rating systems, the fantasy of control and perfect information drives engagement, providing temporary mastery over complex social and economic relations.

Pursuing the fantasy of control paradoxically reinforces greater subjection to power structures these systems represent. The algorithmic construction of identity and internalization of datafied norms create a new form of power through shaping subjectivity (Cheney-Lippold, 2011). Individuals become 'desiring subjects' (Lacan, 1966) of self-control and personal colonization, investing psychic energy in pursuing an ideal that reinforces domination. This subjectivation process explains how rating systems and the culture of '360 management' become entrenched and often welcomed. As individuals invest in control and jouissance through these systems, they become complicit in their subjection to the power structures they seek to overcome. The proliferation of self-tracking technologies, from fitness apps to productivity tools, exemplifies how the desire for control and optimization leads to internalizing disciplinary norms (Lupton, 2016b). Constantly monitoring and quantifying behaviour, individuals become their own managers, striving for efficiency and performance ideals. Similarly, 'people analytics' in the workplace, where employees face granular monitoring and assessment (Kellogg et al, 2020), shows how data-driven control erodes worker autonomy and privacy. Digitally enabled rating systems have transformed social and economic interactions, central to personal identity and subjective security. Digital platforms, apps, and devices allowing constant self-tracking, quantification, and optimization have created a new subjectivity, actively engaging with control and surveillance processes, promising greater mastery over lives and environments.

Active participation in control processes gives individuals a sense of psychic security and personal empowerment. By tracking performance, comparing themselves to others, and optimizing behaviour according to metrics and standards, individuals feel in charge of their destiny in a complex, changing world. Monitoring and managing others through digital platforms and rating systems enhances this control and security. Evaluating others' performance – whether rating a ride-sharing driver, reviewing a product, or providing colleague feedback – allows individuals to feel they contribute to social order and stability. This empowerment is significant in contexts where they feel powerless or vulnerable, such as in the workplace or dealings with large corporations.

This shift from structural securitization to a subjective sense of security and empowerment is central to the AFC. By equipping individuals with tools to monitor and manage themselves and others, the system fosters a new form of governmentality, relying on individuals' willing participation in their subjugation. However, this sense of security is fragile, requiring constant digital profile maintenance, behaviour tracking, and evaluation of others. Any deviation from norms can lead to loss of status, reputation, or resource access. Despite this, the promise of security and empowerment offered by these technologies and techniques powerfully lures individuals seeking to navigate life's complexities and uncertainties within the AFC, making them feel in control of their destiny and securing their place in the social and economic order, thus transforming the structural need for securitization into a deeply personal and subjective experience of self-mastery and empowerment.

Unquenchable domination

The escalating use of digital technologies for tracking, monitoring, and control has created a novel extractivist economy driven by an insatiable demand for command-oriented digital technologies and the relentless pursuit of new extraction frontiers linked to fantasies of data-driven personal empowerment (Couldry and Mejias, 2019; Sadowski, 2019). This unending demand is illustrated by the Amazon Echo's production, which involves mining rare earth elements and exploiting workers in the global electronics supply chain, embodying the extractivist logic of the digital economy. This economy extends to the rapid growth of data processing centres, exemplified by the Utah Data Center's massive energy and water consumption, highlighting the environmental costs of the data economy (Hogan, 2015; Shehabi et al, 2016). Furthermore, the relationship between data centres and governments, as seen in Oregon's 'Silicon Forest', where substantial tax breaks and subsidies attract data centre investments, reinforces the extractivist logic, siphoning profits to corporate headquarters while local communities bear the environmental and social costs (Levenda and Mahmoudi, 2019).

The insatiable demand for control-based digital technologies is fuelled by a profound psycho-social complex, marked by an obsessive fixation on digital technology as a solution for personal and social issues (Gabrys, 2013; Fitzpatrick, 2015). The design of electronic gambling machines, which induce a state of 'flow', mirrors the design of digital technologies, both aimed at creating a sense of control and engagement to keep users entranced (Schüll, 2012). This desire for control and escape, rooted in contemporary anxieties, is exploited for profit, intertwined with the politico-economic complex driving the extractivist economy (Sadowski, 2019). Power and wealth concentration among a few technology giants allows them to shape technologies for their economic interests (Srnicek, 2017), with digital platforms extracting maximum value from users' data and attention. This extractivist logic leads to new forms of precarious and exploitative work (Scholz, 2012; Graham et al, 2017), exemplified by content moderators in the Philippines who face poor pay and psychological trauma while reviewing disturbing content. Additionally, the environmental consequences are severe, with resource depletion, toxic waste, and climate change acceleration (Parikka, 2015; Cubitt, 2017), as seen in the e-waste dumping in Agbogbloshie, Ghana, where workers are exposed to toxic chemicals while extracting metals from discarded electronics (Gabrys, 2013).

The mutually reinforcing relationship between the psycho-social complex of control and the politico-economic complex of extraction creates a powerful feedback loop, with the desire for control fuelling the expansion of the extractivist economy, which in turn reinforces the desire for control (Sadowski, 2019). The lithium mining boom in the 'Lithium Triangle' of Chile, Argentina, and Bolivia exemplifies this dynamic (Riofrancos, 2023). The demand for lithium-ion batteries, driven by smartphones, laptops, and electric vehicles, has sparked a scramble for control over this strategic resource, leading to a new form of 'green extractivism' that impacts local communities and ecosystems. This extractivist economy has broad political and social implications, as the desire for control-based technologies has led to vast data collection and analysis infrastructures (Pasquale, 2015; O'Neil, 2016). The psycho-social complex, marked by an obsession with digital technology as a solution for personal and social issues, fuels the demand for control-based technologies (Gabrys, 2013; Fitzpatrick, 2015). As users become dependent on these technologies, their data and attention are commodified, strengthening the political-economic complex. This feedback loop creates a repressive cycle of lucrative control, where the extractivist logic perpetuates itself by exploiting users' desires and anxieties. The more users engage with these technologies, the more data is extracted, empowering technology giants to further shape and reinforce the cycle of control and extraction. This personalization of control leads to a granular form of commodification, where users' private moments are monetized, and the dissemination of control-based technologies across various domains of life expands the reach and profitability of this commodified economy.

As more aspects of daily life are mediated by digital technologies, opportunities for data extraction and behaviour modification multiply, creating new markets for personalized control. Politicians increasingly promote smart data-driven decision-making as a solution for social issues, emphasizing efficiency and optimization. Communities, seeking economic opportunities, welcome data centres, often overlooking their environmental and social costs. At the individual level, empowerment has become linked to datafication, as people are encouraged to track, quantify, and analyse their lives through digital technologies. From fitness apps to social media platforms, individuals view personal data as a source of self-knowledge and control, reinforcing the commodified economy of control and normalizing value extraction from intimate aspects of existence. The AFC has made control synonymous with freedom by presenting digital technologies as empowering tools that enhance choice and autonomy. This obscures the dynamics of extraction and manipulation, as users embrace datafication and domination as self-expression and liberation.

Conclusion

The proliferation of digital control technologies, financialization of the economy, and the entanglement of state and corporate interests have profoundly transformed power, subjectivity, and desire in contemporary society. Embodied in the AFC, this new form of governmentality commodifies personal information through datafication, creating vast markets for behavioural control. By rendering individuals legible as data points, it erases the boundaries between private and public, personal and political. Surveillance capitalism exemplifies this process, transforming human experience into raw material for economic exploitation, shaping self and subjectivity in service of capital. The AFC cultivates insecurity and precarity, using these conditions to justify intrusive monitoring and control. It manufactures desire, encouraging self-tracking and self-optimization through digital technologies, as seen in the quantified self movement, appealing to the psychological need for control and mastery. This hyper-capitalist internal colonization transforms desires, beliefs, and behaviours into markets for profit, driven by neoliberal capitalism's logic of commodifying every aspect of life. Personal identity and self-worth are shaped to meet market standards of productivity and well-being, sustained by fantasies of control and technological solutionism. Behavioural modification tools, presented as solutions to social and political problems, become valuable commodities, driving the expansion of control and fuelling new industries. This dynamic alienates individuals from their own thoughts and desires, reducing the self to a project for optimization. As the AFC operates within everyday life, it subtly shapes desires and aspirations, posing profound challenges to traditional forms of political resistance and critique.

The next chapter will expand this analysis, illuminating how the personalized fantasy of control has evolved into a collective discourse that equates domination with progress. This collective narrative posits that the ability to monitor, quantify, and optimize every aspect of existence through digital technologies is not only desirable but a necessary prerequisite for societal advancement. Consequently, the relentless pursuit of control is framed as a collective imperative, obscuring the underlying dynamics of extraction and exploitation that underpin this extractivist digital economy.

8

Repressive Progress

Introduction

The preceding chapter examined how surveillance, datafication, and quantification have been paradoxically framed as vehicles for individual empowerment and self-mastery, tapping into fantasies of control over life circumstances. This chapter expands on this by exploring how this paradigm has become a potent global discourse linking societal progress to the authoritarian–financial complex (AFC). Central to this discourse is the rhetoric of 'smart progress', which rationalizes and legitimizes authoritarian governance strategies, such as China's Social Credit System (SCS) and Hong Kong's national security legislation, by portraying digital surveillance as essential for efficient administration, public safety, and development (Cheung and Chen, 2022). This framing obscures the coercive nature of such practices and has been embraced by repressive regimes and developmental states in the Global South, where digital surveillance is used under the guise of ensuring stability and optimizing aid distribution (Fisher and Anderson, 2015). The concept of 'smart progress' is also influential in urban governance, with 'smart city' initiatives promoting digital innovation and big data analytics while downplaying the expansion of state surveillance and invasive data extraction (Gruin and Knaack, 2020).

Utopian visions of hyper-efficient, sustainable, and integrated urban environments are closely tied to digital control and social engineering, embedded within market-driven agendas that emphasize scientific progress and economic competitiveness (Wong, 2005). The rhetoric of cutting-edge technologies driving national prosperity conceals the consolidation of state power and technocratic governance. The 'smart progress' discourse, appealing to global social aspirations, reflects the allure of the 'democratic developmental state' model, which once combined centralized planning with democratic norms (White, 1995; Kieh, 2015). However, today, 'smart progress' is deeply intertwined with neoliberal rationality and authoritarian capitalism, promoting an 'economic technocracy' that privileges policy elites over public deliberation, undermining democratic governance (Kiely, 2017). This convergence champions centralized control, data-driven decision-making, and civic subordination to constant surveillance, reinforcing an AFC where state power, digital platforms, and financial flows intersect (Gruin and Knaack, 2020). Quantifying and algorithmically processing vast data streams have become essential for attracting investment, spurring economic growth, and displaying technological sophistication. Transnational exchanges of expertise and policy frameworks have further entrenched this model, repackaging regional strategies into universal templates aligned with digital governance (Carroll and Jarvis, 2017). The paradox of liberation through control allows the 'smart progress' narrative to transcend national and ideological boundaries, linking technological mastery with population management, particularly targeting economically precarious and marginalized groups under the guise of 'inclusion' and 'accountability'.

This framing obscures the coercive and disempowering nature of digital surveillance and biometric systems, presenting them as benevolent interventions aimed at uplifting vulnerable communities and ensuring equitable access to resources. Proponents argue that granular data can streamline aid delivery, reduce corruption, and optimize resource allocation, yet this commitment to empowerment and equal opportunity conceals the underlying logic of control and normalization. Rather than liberating marginalized populations, data accumulation renders them more governable by centralized authorities and algorithms. The rhetoric of 'inclusion' and 'accountability' masks power asymmetries, subjecting vulnerable communities to invasive monitoring and behavioural modification while shielding the system's architects from such scrutiny. The spread of digital tracking technologies has become a powerful force in shaping individuals within the global capitalist order, yet this subjectification is often experienced as a source of enjoyment – jouissance – driven by the fantasy of participating in 'smart progress'. The constant gaze of algorithmic systems and the quantification of life are not perceived as invasive, but rather as empowering tools for self-optimization and personal growth. Framed as instruments of meritocracy and inclusion, these technologies promise to dismantle traditional barriers, resonating with aspirations for self-improvement and social mobility. This seductive promise of empowerment embeds individuals more deeply within the logics of global capitalist production, making the allure of these systems far more insidious than overt coercion.

This chapter will reveal how the discourses surrounding and informing digital surveillance, data extraction, and algorithmic governance as vital instruments of efficiency, security, and collective advancement has permitted the normalization and diffusion of authoritarian practices across diverse national contexts. Particular attention will be paid to the ways in which this rhetoric articulates and taps into enduring social aspirations, recasting mechanisms of control as vehicles for empowerment and self-optimization. These insights will allow for a broader critical examination on how the transnational circulation of expertise, policy frameworks, and technological infrastructures has accelerated the global entrenchment of the AFC. It will shed light, in this respect, on the insidious convergence of state power, digital platforms, and globally integrated financial flows, which has given rise to a self-perpetuating system predicated on the relentless expansion of datafication and quantification.

Repressive progress

Narratives of international development often promise empowerment and progress but actually embed countries into an exploitative, unequal global economic order. Beneath their benevolent rhetoric lies a complex power structure that reinforces asymmetrical North–South relations rooted in European expansionism and capitalist accumulation, as explored in critical development studies, postcolonial theory, world-systems analysis, and radical political economy. These narratives, rooted in colonial modernity, construct the 'Third World' as inherently deficient and in need of Western intervention and knowledge transfer (Escobar, 1984; Mignolo, 2011). The concept of 'development' reflects Western historical and epistemological frameworks (Lipton and Sachs, 1992), positioning Global South nations as subjugated subjects within systems that serve Western interests (Althusser, 1971; Hall, 1985; Butler, 1997). This structure connects to power hierarchies dominated by states, multilateral organizations, international non-governmental organizations (NGOs), and Northern corporations. Development's forms of governmentality reshape Southern societies through evolving expertise cultures, where scientific knowledge and bureaucratic planning exploit local populations (Foucault, 1977; Li, 2007), often disregarding local contexts and marginalizing other ways of knowing.

Development agendas are backed by disciplinary regimes that restructure the environments and populations of the Global South, enforcing Western conceptions of progress while suppressing local alternatives (Li, 2007). Infrastructure projects reshape landscapes, and public health campaigns regulate individual behaviours, all under the guise of improvement and poverty alleviation. These interventions in agriculture, health, and infrastructure depoliticize poverty, allowing state and international actors to consolidate bureaucratic control over territories and populations in the Global South (Ferguson, 1990; Scott, 1998). This dynamic aligns with capitalism's broader aim of controlling life, extracting value, and creating subjectivities amenable to domination under imperial biopower (Hardt and Negri, 2000). According to dependency and world-systems theory, the underdevelopment of the global periphery is essential for the capitalist development of the

European/Western core, achieved through colonial conquest, extraction, land appropriation, and slave labour (Frank, 1969; Rodney, 1972; Wallerstein, 2004). This process established a core–periphery divide within the world-capitalist system, perpetuating international inequalities between developing and developed nations (Amin, 1976). Capitalism's global expansion was predicated on the violent commodification of nature, transforming it into 'cheap things' for privatization and accumulation by capitalist entrepreneurs (Patel and Moore, 2017). This disrupted sustainable human–environment interactions across the Global South, where communities had cultivated symbiotic relationships with their ecosystems over centuries. The imposition of capitalist property regimes shattered these relationships, leading to socio-ecological crises such as deforestation, biodiversity loss, water shortages, and climate destabilization. These policies deepened environmental inequalities, as the Global South bore the costs while the Global North reaped the benefits. Instead of bringing prosperity, forced integration into the capitalist world-ecology eroded sustainable practices, weakened community resilience, and accelerated socio–ecological degradation, exposing the hollow promises of 'development'.

Neoliberal globalization since the 1970s and 1980s, driven by institutions like the World Bank, International Monetary Fund, World Trade Organization, and multinational corporations, has intensified land grabs, resource exploitation, and labour abuses in the Global South through structural adjustment programmes, free trade agreements, debt entrapment, privatization, and state restructuring, all aimed at sustaining Western capitalist dominance (Chomsky, 1999; Harvey, 2005). This model has deepened inequalities in income, wealth, public health, housing, education, and environmental stability between developed and developing nations (Hickel, 2017). Even progressive frameworks like sustainable development and participatory methods often legitimize interventions that co-opt local resistance and prioritize capital accumulation over social and environmental welfare (Cooke and Kothari, 2001; Banerjee, 2003). The developmentalist paradigm continues colonial racialized logics, treating the Global South as an object for Western corrective intervention (Said, 1978; Mohanty, 1984). Development narratives marginalize diverse experiences and cultural perspectives, imposing a universal developmentalist view that casts these societies as passive recipients of Northern expertise and capital (Escobar, 1995). This framework is reproduced through hegemonic processes that normalize Western capitalist modernity as the superior path (Gramsci, 1971), reinforced by educational institutions, media, state policies, and development agencies that maintain hierarchical binaries of developed versus underdeveloped. Even movements like food sovereignty, which challenge agribusiness, are rearticulated within dominant capitalist frameworks (McMichael, 2017). Despite rhetoric about empowerment and sustainability, these narratives function as regimes of governance, framing the Global South as perpetually in need of Western intervention (Ziai, 2007; Rist, 2014). This perpetuates an asymmetrical global order rooted in racialized knowledge–power hierarchies, marginalizing radical alternatives from the Global South while claiming to support diversity and participation (Ziai, 2007; Mignolo, 2011).

Discourses of development have, thus, historically served as a powerful ideological force that has paradoxically enabled and legitimized strategies of underdevelopment in many parts of the Global South. The notion of 'development' itself emerged as a post-Second World War project, couched in the benevolent rhetoric of progress, modernization, and the promise of economic prosperity. However, beneath this facade lay a deep-seated desire for control, extraction, and the perpetuation of unequal power relations between the Global North and South. The pathological desire for development thus reinforces in the present era the repressive cycle of finance, where each perceived failure or setback was met with ever more interventionist and, often, controlling solutions. Such evolving colonization is, moreover, sustained and strengthened through equally evolving fantasies of collective 'development'.

Extractive promises

The rise of 'digital authoritarianism' marks a significant global transformation of repressive state mechanisms, driven by the spread of digital technologies and data-driven techniques. Authoritarian regimes globally have effectively used these tools to consolidate power, monitor dissent, and exert comprehensive social control through new and pervasive means (Lai, 2016; Petry, 2020). This trend illustrates a symbiotic relationship between authoritarian governance and capitalist development, with the digital surveillance and control industries becoming profitable avenues for capital accumulation. Digital authoritarianism encompasses both overt tactics like internet shutdowns, online censorship, and pervasive digital surveillance to restrict freedom of expression (Grinberg, 2017; Mare, 2020; Ayalew, 2021), and subtle strategies that induce self-censorship by exploiting individuals' cognitive and emotional responses to the risks of online dissent (Dal et al, 2022). These chilling effects undermine the potential for collective resistance, instilling fear and fostering widespread self-imposed silence.

The co-optation of digital platforms and peer-to-peer networks into authoritarian governance frameworks exemplifies digital authoritarianism's networked dimensions (Jack et al, 2021). State actors have instrumentalized technologies like Telegram for control and surveillance, subverting spaces meant for free communication (Wijermars and Lokot, 2022). Online communities engage in 'participatory censorship' by aligning discourse with authoritarian narratives (Luo and Li, 2022). Additionally, peer-aid platforms, initially spaces for mutual support, have become sites of state monitoring and manipulation. The pervasive collection and exploitation of citizen data are critical facets of digital authoritarianism, with China's SCS epitomizing comprehensive monitoring through gamified rewards and punishments (Wong and Dobson, 2019). 'Communicative authoritarianism' in Turkey includes media repression and transnational information controls, curtailing free expression (Çelik, 2020). Moreover, religious populism across Asia leverages online spaces to propagate exclusionary ideologies, marginalize dissent, and reinforce social hierarchies (Yilmaz et al, 2022).

Paradoxically, frameworks designed to protect privacy and civil liberties have been co-opted by authoritarian regimes to expand digital authoritarianism. An insidious 'authoritarian liberalism' has emerged, where privacy laws purportedly safeguarding individual rights are subverted for state surveillance and social control under the guise of security (Lippert and Walby, 2016). 'Surveillance design communities' develop technologies enhancing monitoring, data extraction, and predictive analytics, driven by capitalist profit motives (Baird, 2016). Restrictive NGO legislations and coercive state actions suppress civil society organizations, disabling dissent and pre-empting democratization (Foster, 2001; Flikke, 2016; Gilbert, 2020). International NGOs face pressures from donors' neoliberal agendas and host governments' restrictions, compromising their autonomy (Heiss and Kelley, 2017). Digital authoritarianism is also entwined with the marketization and global restructuring of social reproduction processes like childcare and elder care (Rosenman and Narayan, 2024). As these domains become commodified and integrated into capitalist strategies via digital platforms and data-driven governance, they are subjected to authoritarian control and exploitation, disrupting traditional care networks and subordinating them to market imperatives (Miraftab, 2011). This dynamic illustrates the entanglement between authoritarian political projects, capitalist development, and the profit-driven expansion of digital surveillance.

Digital authoritarianism transcends traditional state repression, forming a multidimensional system of domination that employs advanced technologies like facial recognition, predictive policing algorithms, and biometric databases alongside sophisticated data analytics and behavioural manipulation tactics. These tools, developed in collaboration with private tech firms, allow for granular monitoring, profiling, and targeted suppression of dissent (Grinberg, 2017). Social media platforms are also incorporated into this system, enabling large-scale content moderation, account restrictions, and disinformation campaigns aligned with authoritarian agendas (Wijermars and Lokot, 2022). Authoritarian regimes further exploit online affective dynamics, such as fear and polarization, to divide societies and manufacture consent for repressive policies (Dal et al, 2022). The entanglement of authoritarian control with capitalist development has transformed digital surveillance into a lucrative industry, where surveillance capitalism and authoritarian rule reinforce each other. Private data brokers, security contractors, and tech monopolies profit from expanding control systems marketed as law enforcement, border security, and counter-terrorism (Baird, 2016). This fusion of political repression and economic exploitation underpins digital authoritarianism as a pervasive mode of social control. In China, artificial intelligence and surveillance technologies generate revenue while enabling the monitoring of vast populations (Wong and Dobson, 2019). Globally, companies from Israel and Europe provide digital surveillance tools to authoritarian regimes, aiding in tracking dissidents and suppressing independent media (Grinberg, 2017), while biometrics firms profit from centralized databases for population control in regions like Asia and Africa (Ayalew, 2021). Even social media giants like Facebook collaborate with repressive regimes, tailoring content moderation and sharing user data to bolster digital authoritarianism (Wijermars and Lokot, 2022). This integration of high-tech repression with capitalist development exemplifies how authoritarianism and financial profit extraction are now deeply intertwined.

Rebooting global authoritarianism

The global spread of digital authoritarianism has reshaped the developmental state model, merging repressive digital technologies with narratives of national progress and modernization. This AFC reframes traditional repressive state apparatuses (RSAs) into ideological state apparatuses (ISAs) (Althusser, 1971), justifying surveillance and control as necessary for economic and social development. In Guyana, flood control infrastructure reflects this dynamic, expanding state control while invoking colonial legacies (Mullenite, 2019), and China's Belt and Road Initiative, while promoting infrastructure, deepens inequalities and projects authoritarian governance beyond its borders (Apostolopoulou, 2021; Gurol and Schütze, 2022). Similar trends are evident in Cambodia's 'hydraulic despotism' (Blake, 2019), land grabs in Paraguay facilitated by road construction (Gonzalez et al, 2022), and the use of digital surveillance in Gulf states to monitor dissent (Shires, 2021). Authoritarian regimes have strategically used state-led development and infrastructure investment to legitimize their rule, as seen in South Korea's repression of protests and Russia's authoritarian state capitalism, evident in spatial planning and megaprojects (Kinossian and Morgan, 2023). China's wind energy market highlights how fragmented authoritarianism is coordinated to sustain both development and control (Lema and Ruby, 2007). Additionally, 'smart' infrastructures like India's e-governance initiatives erode democratic accountability while enhancing state surveillance (Yerramsetti, 2022), creating 'sentient cities' governed by pervasive computing technologies (Thrift, 2014). This hybrid model of state intervention, market reforms, and authoritarianism is mirrored in countries like Rwanda (Hasselskog, 2018), Ethiopia (Emmenegger, 2016), and Southeast Asia (Régnier, 2011). China's mix of state control and market-driven policies has facilitated its economic ascent while solidifying its authoritarian regime (Zhang, 2018; Hasmath et al, 2019). However, critiques highlight the contradictions of developmental authoritarianism, including its neoliberal aspects in Syria (Dahi and Munif, 2012) and the persistence of personalistic rule in Rwanda, Ethiopia, and East Asia (Matfess, 2015; Wong, 2020).

The concept of 'petro-masculinity' highlights how fossil fuel systems reinforce authoritarian, patriarchal power relations (Daggett, 2018), with the US 'energy security imaginary' linking energy development to nationalist and militaristic themes (Tidwell and Smith, 2015). Authoritarian regimes creating hybrid 'developmental states' face pressures to balance private actors, civil society, and democratic accountability (Lim, 2010). In Brazil, civil society and environmental politics have constrained hydroelectric dam projects (Burrier, 2016), while Nigeria's efforts to build a 'democratic developmental state' contend with governance, ethnic divisions, and rent-seeking behaviour (Basiru and Akinboye, 2018). Ethiopia's authoritarian developmental state navigates ethnic federalism, external intervention, and ideological contests over reforms (Abbink and Hagmann, 2016), showing the complex adaptations required. National development and progress are discursively tied to deploying repressive digital technologies and data-driven techniques. RSAs have become ISAs by framing these interventions as essential for development (Althusser, 1971). This rebranding co-opts societal desires for progress to entrench authoritarian control, positioning repressive digital infrastructures as necessary for economic growth, technological progress, and service delivery. Surveillance, social control, and centralized data systems are presented as ISAs facilitating prosperity (Kamra et al, 2023), marginalizing dissent as obstructive to national development and legitimizing repressive tactics as vital components of the development machine (Han, 2017).

Citizen monitoring and data extraction are framed as necessary sacrifices for national advancement, exemplified by Cambodia's 'hydraulic despotism' under the guise of flood control and water infrastructure (Blake, 2019) and Gulf states positioning digital surveillance as enhancing security and economic progress (Shires, 2021). China's social control mechanisms are similarly justified as ensuring stability crucial for growth and poverty alleviation (Heberer, 2016). Authoritarian regimes have rebranded their RSAs as ISAs, promoting their interventions as essential for national development and shared progress (Althusser, 1971). This manoeuvre co-opts societal aspirations for progress, entrenching authoritarian control under the guise of collective advancement. In the AFC, the imperatives of national development have become intertwined with repressive digital technologies and data-driven techniques, transforming RSAs into potent ISAs. This digitally driven authoritarianism has shifted the nature of developmental states, integrating authoritarian methods into the core notion of 'development' itself, permeating all economic activities deemed vital for national progress and prosperity.

This new paradigm departs from viewing authoritarianism as a temporary measure for creating an environment conducive to international loans and development projects. Repressive digital technologies, ubiquitous surveillance, and centralized data systems have evolved into indispensable drivers of economic growth, technological advancement, and optimized service delivery. By intertwining repressive practices with nation-building narratives and aspirations for modernity, authoritarian regimes have created a justificatory framework that legitimizes repression across all economic activities linked to national development goals. Economic imperatives fueling this shift include large-scale infrastructure projects financed by foreign capital, prioritizing profit extraction over equitable growth and necessitating mechanisms for suppressing dissent and maintaining social control. Additionally, safeguarding the profitability of foreign-financed projects drives the normalization of digital authoritarianism, reframed as necessary sacrifices for national advancement (Heberer, 2016; Blake, 2019; Shires, 2021).

This paradigm shift has transformed 'development' into an ideological state apparatus justifying repression, presenting centralized control over digital infrastructures, invasive surveillance, and curtailed freedoms as essential for advancing toward a modern society. Dissent is marginalized as an obstacle to prosperity, achievable only through high-tech control. Digital authoritarianism updates authoritarianism with technology-driven development, allowing regimes to exploit digital tools to tighten control and suppress civil liberties. Artificial intelligence-powered surveillance monitors citizens, chilling free expression, while social media platforms manipulate narratives and silence critics. Facial recognition, biometric data collection, and predictive policing become tools for social control, targeting marginalized groups and political opponents. This convergence of state power and private tech companies, driven by profit, enables digital oppression, showing how the rhetoric of technological development conceals strategies for entrenching authoritarianism through sophisticated control systems, transforming technologies initially seen as democratizing tools into apparatuses of repression and control.

Smart repression

The affective promise of 'smartness' symbolizes modernity, progress, and global prestige, driving the pursuit of smart city initiatives not only for urban development and economic growth but also for recognition and validation as technologically advanced societies. This desire fuels an ideological force that legitimizes sophisticated systems of control, surveillance, and social manipulation under techno-utopian rhetoric. The repression enabled by smart city technologies is thus demanded by a collective psycho-social complex of 'smartness', repackaging mechanisms of oppression as tools of progress, perpetuating the AFC. Discourses surrounding smart cities link digital authoritarianism's repressive technologies to empowering ideologies of techno-development, framing smart cities as modernizing projects that promise efficiency, sustainability, and improved quality of life through data-driven governance (Kitchin, 2014). However, this rhetoric conceals underlying control systems, as smart city policies in the Global South promote profitable surveillance by state and corporate actors (Sadowski, 2020). For instance, Dholera smart city in Gujarat, India, is shaped by private firms prioritizing data commodification (Datta, 2015), and Songdo in South Korea, developed through public–private partnerships and foreign capital, is critiqued as 'privatized urbanism' serving elite interests (Shwayri, 2013).

Under the guise of urban optimization, sensor networks, facial recognition systems, and predictive policing algorithms are being rolled out, often in partnership with private technology firms profiting from metadata streams (Firmino et al, 2019). In Brazil, these technologies have raised concerns about privacy violations and targeting marginalized communities (Headrick and Miraldi, 2022). Nigeria's smart city initiatives spark debates around transparency, accountability, and potential social control. Vietnam rapidly adopts smart city initiatives but lacks mechanisms for algorithmic transparency (Nguyen, 2019). In Nairobi, smart metering systems for utilities reinforce existing inequalities (Guma, 2019). The smart city fantasy drives policy makers, planners, and corporations, promising techno-utopian optimization and renaissance (Sadowski and Bendor, 2019). This fuels perpetual technological adoption and data extraction, as cities competitively implement 'smart' solutions to attract investment and project modernity (Shwayri, 2013). By reducing cities to technical, managerial problems, it forecloses more democratic, inclusive, and justice-oriented transformations (Watson, 2015; Odendaal, 2016). This psycho-social complex enables expansive 'surveillance capitalism', where daily life is datafied, commodified, and used to shape behaviour benefiting capital and authoritarians.

The smart city discourse embodies a contemporary fantasy of development, suggesting that the perceived lack of efficient, modern, and sustainable urban environments can be addressed through integrating smart technologies and data systems. This fantasy distorts and obscures socio-political antagonisms, power imbalances, and inherent contradictions in urban development. By framing cities as technical, managerial problems, it prevents democratic, inclusive, and justice-oriented transformations. The allure of smart cities legitimizes an AFC, merging digital authoritarianism with surveillance capitalism's profit-driven logics. This rhetoric masks oppressive systems of control and surveillance in the guise of techno-development and urban progress, obscuring the underlying inequalities and civil liberties erosion accompanying smart city initiatives. These projects often lead to gentrification and displacement of low-income residents, with urban spaces optimized for capital and the technocratic elite. The rhetoric of efficiency and data-driven decision-making depoliticizes dispossession, framing it as necessary for a rational urban environment (Datta, 2018). Despite being touted as eco-friendly solutions, the energy-intensive and environmentally damaging nature of massive data infrastructures and sensor networks required for these systems highlights their environmental impact (Sadowski, 2020; Upham et al, 2022).

The rise of 'technological citizenship' under the smart city paradigm exemplifies a depoliticizing trend that recasts citizens as data points to be managed by opaque urban operating systems controlled by private corporations and algorithmic decision-making frameworks, stripping them of political agency and self-determination (Vanolo, 2014). This shift erodes democratic governance and accountability, as public–private partnerships often operate without transparency or oversight (Marvin and Luque-Ayala, 2017; Nguyen, 2019). The smart city narrative legitimizes an AFC that merges digital authoritarianism's repressive technologies with surveillance capitalism's profit-driven logics. Developing nations are caught in a relentless pursuit of technological integration and data-driven governance, driven by the desire for 'smartness' that promises control and optimization but deepens systems of repression. This phenomenon aligns with the 'libidinal economy' of contemporary capitalism, where a cycle of desire and consumption fuels the constant demand for digital technologies, sensor networks, and algorithmic systems, each offering greater control and efficiency. This desire is not merely imposed but has become an internalized psycho-social complex, embedded within the collective psyche of developing countries and their populations, driving a perpetual thirst for the latest in smart technologies.

Inclusive repression

The fantasy of the 'smart' city and its promise of efficient, data-driven governance is closely linked to authoritarian tendencies and technologies of control (Thrift, 2014; Grossi and Pianezzi, 2017). This fantasy is reinforced by its association with progressive values like inclusion, empowerment, and accountability, despite perpetuating power asymmetries and surveillance. India's Aadhaar biometric identification system and China's SCS exemplify this fusion of emancipatory rhetoric and control mechanisms. Aadhaar, initially promoted to enable inclusive social protection through authenticated beneficiary identification (Bhatia and Bhabha, 2017), began taking shape in the late 1990s and early 2000s to address fraudulent welfare access. In 2009, the Congress-led government established the Unique Identification Authority of India to implement this biometric-based ID programme. Over the next decade, Aadhaar became the world's largest biometric system, collecting data from over 1.2 billion residents and assigning unique 12-digit identification numbers to serve as a digital authentication infrastructure.

Initially pitched as a voluntary programme to streamline subsidy delivery, Aadhaar has evolved into a de facto prerequisite for accessing various rights and services, from banking to healthcare, redefining the citizen–state relationship (Chaudhuri and König, 2018). Its centralized database has faced security breaches and reports of coerced enrolments, highlighting its surveillance potential and insufficient data protections (Orren, 2019). Despite these issues, Aadhaar persists, driven by narratives of modernization, anti-corruption, and a 'Digital India' fantasy promising transparent, tech-enabled governance (Rao and Nair, 2019; Raychaudhuri and D'Agostino, 2019). Meanwhile, China's SCS, launched as local pilots in 2014, aims to quantify and regulate citizen behaviour through big data and analytics. The SCS integrates records from various sources into a unified database, using algorithms to generate social credit scores that influence access to services, rewards, or punitive actions like travel restrictions and public shaming (Liang et al, 2018; Dai, 2020).

While promoted as fostering 'social sincerity' and moral governance through incentives and disincentives, the SCS functions as a potent tool for detailed population monitoring and social control, tracking everything from financial dealings to social media activities (Liang et al, 2018; Hoffman, 2018). It propagates narratives valorizing 'model citizens' engaged in loyalty and civic duty, while punishing acts coded as signs of 'untrustworthiness' like dissent or litigation against corporations (Chen and Grossklags, 2022). However, this techno-utopian vision of cultivating virtuousness by rendering individuals' reputations as auditable and behaviourally guidable metrics offers a perpetual jouissance – with the subject's desire for complete transparency and trustworthy reputation never fully satiated (Dai, 2018; Zhang, 2020).

These socio-technical systems of control like Aadhaar and the SCS operate not through overt repression but through the continual deferral of a utopian 'smart' future premised on values of inclusion, empowerment, efficiency and accountability. The allure of transparent, technology-enabled good governance becomes a commodified spectacle, obscuring the realities of asymmetrical power relations, discriminatory impacts, data injustices and the production of new urban risk-class inequalities (Curran and Smart, 2021; Hansen and Weiskopf, 2021). Citizens are seduced by the promise of being recognized as 'included' and 'accountable' subjects within these quantified regimes, even as they are subjected to ever-increasing granular surveillance, social scoring, behavioural modification and nudging tactics in the name of digital citizenship (Chong, 2019; Engelmann et al, 2021).

The paradoxical intertwining of progressive rhetoric and authoritarian control can be understood through the Lacanian notion of jouissance and Žižek's conceptualization of ideology as a fantasmatic narrative (Žižek, 1997). The promise of 'smart' urban–digital development perpetually defers complete satisfaction, sustaining desire and investment in systems that quantify, commodify, and render governable individual identities and behaviours. The fantasy of inclusion, empowerment, and accountability paradoxically becomes a site of affective reinvestment, further entrenching hierarchies and power asymmetries while producing new forms of data-driven marginalization and social control (Liang et al, 2018; Curran and Smart, 2021; Hansen and Weiskopf, 2021). This authoritarian–financial fantasy thrives on the deferral of its own fulfilment, with citizens complicit in their subjugation by deriving satisfaction from being interpellated as empowered digital subjects (Althusser, 1971; Žižek, 1997). The utopian vision of 'smart' cities becomes a site of continual investment, reinforcing power structures and exacerbating marginalization along social stratification lines (Chacko, 2020). The cases of Aadhaar and the SCS illustrate how this fantasy operates through linking technologies of population management to narratives of progressive change and efficient service delivery, sustaining jouissance by continuously deferring the ultimate promise of rationality and frictionless modernity (Thrift, 2014; Grossi and Pianezzi, 2017).

Central to this dynamic is the production of a 'data-driven society' (Liang et al, 2018) where individuals' identities and life chances are shaped by scoring, ranking, and social quantification, experienced not as repressive but as empowering and meritocratic. The SCS serves as an 'infrastructure of social quantification' (Liang and Chen, 2022), positioning individuals by their scores and reputational metrics, making this subjectification enjoyable through its paradoxical disappointment – desire is never fully satisfied but continually reinvested in the fantasy of transparency and accountability (Dai, 2018; Chen et al, 2022). Systems like Aadhaar and the SCS embody a new authoritarian desire, where control through quantification translates into perverse daily enjoyment linked to individual and collective progress. These 'smart' control infrastructures gain power from the jouissance – the tantalizing, never-fulfilled promise of total rationalization and transparency. Individuals derive pleasure from accumulating data points about their lives, feeling legible and auditable within these socio-technical matrices, experiencing their reality as intelligible and improvable.

This jouissance taps into deep desires for order, accountability, and self-optimization, central to contemporary narratives of 'smart' urban development and digital citizenship. The social credit score or Aadhaar number becomes a fetish object, representing aspirations for upward mobility, access to services, and recognition as a virtuous neoliberal subject. Self-governance, rather than an imposition, is pursued as individuals modulate their behaviour to achieve better ratings within these control regimes, which fuse collective repression with individual self-optimization. At a collective level, they serve as apparatuses for population monitoring and social sorting, while at an individual level, they channel desires for self-improvement and entrepreneurial self-fashioning. Citizens engage with these systems through narratives of personal empowerment and efficiency, finding enjoyment in measuring and auditing their behaviour to comply with desired metrics. Consequently, collective subjugation is reproduced through individual aspirations for digitally mediated self-advancement within these authoritarian matrices. Authoritarian desire flourishes under the guise of digital empowerment and data-driven inclusion, as individuals find enjoyment in subjugation by engaging in quantified self-improvement and self-tracking. This affective attachment to profitable repression reveals a deeper social fantasy of frictionless, controllable urban futures, where smart technologies promise to resolve issues of trust, disorder, and marginality, continually investing in the elusive 'smart' utopian horizon.

Oppressive development

The AFC thrives on the commodification and control of data, much like traditional extractivism thrives on the exploitation of natural resources (Pegg, 2006; Obi, 2010). This process is facilitated by the concentration of power and resources in the hands of multinational corporations and state actors, who wield immense influence over the production, circulation, and monetization of data (Watts, 2004). These entities have the capacity to extract and process vast amounts of data through sophisticated surveillance technologies and data mining techniques, leveraging this information for profit, social control, and the entrenchment of their own power and influence (Hogan, 2015; Parikka, 2015). The extractivist logic that underpins this AFC extends beyond the realm of digital data to encompass the physical infrastructure and global supply chains that support the digital economy (Tsing, 2009; Fuchs, 2021). The extraction of rare earth minerals, the assembly of electronic devices, and the maintenance of energy-intensive data centres all rely on exploitative labour practices, environmental degradation, and the perpetuation of global inequalities between the Global North and the Global South (Amnesty International, 2016; Sanderson, 2019). Moreover, the AFC perpetuates a form of data colonialism, wherein the extraction and control of data reinforce existing power imbalances and inequalities between the Global North and the Global South (Thatcher et al, 2016; Mejias and Couldry, 2019).

The extractivist economy, traditionally rooted in natural resource exploitation, is evolving to commodify and control human populations (Acosta, 2013; Svampa, 2019). Driven by a desire for data and the fantasy of 'smart development', this shift sustains a neo-colonial extractivist logic (Burchardt and Dietz, 2014; Veltmeyer and Petras, 2014). Central to this AFC is the commodification of data, akin to natural resources, traded as a valuable asset (Arsel et al, 2016; McKay, 2017). Data-driven extractivism targets digital traces and entire populations, treating them as 'human resources' for economic gain through surveillance (Bebbington, 2009). This mentality, reinforced by 'smart development' rhetoric, views data as an inexhaustible commodity to solve social, economic, and environmental challenges through advanced analytics (Frankel, 2010; Carmody, 2016). However, like natural resource extraction, data extraction causes privacy violations, autonomy loss, human rights issues, and exacerbates power imbalances (Lahiri-Dutt, 2018; Kinyondo and Huggins, 2019).

This process marginalizes indigenous epistemologies, reinforcing Western-centric knowledge systems and entrenching colonial legacies (Ricaurte, 2019). It exacerbates vulnerabilities and inequalities within marginalized communities in both the Global North and South through data exploitation, algorithmic discrimination, and privacy erosion, perpetuating systemic oppression (Andrejevic, 2007; Madden et al, 2017). The AFC merges extractivism, neoliberal capitalism, and authoritarian governance, facilitated by digital technologies and data commodification (Arora, 2016; Coleman, 2019). This convergence creates a new frontier of control, intertwining data extraction with surveillance expansion and digital authoritarianism, particularly in the Global South (Kukutai and Taylor, 2016; Mann, 2018). It reinforces power structures, privileges corporate interests, and perpetuates power imbalances between the Global North and South (Amar, 2013; Klauser and Pedrozo, 2015). As digital technologies permeate all aspects of life, this complex reshapes society, prioritizing profit and control over well-being (Feldstein, 2019; Mozur et al, 2019). It exports surveillance mechanisms from the Global North to the South, entrenching digital authoritarianism globally (Hawkins, 2018; Amnesty International, 2021a). This represents a high-tech iteration of colonial and imperialist exploitation, commodifying human populations and data, and prioritizing profit over human dignity (Murakami Wood, 2006; Dragu and Lupu, 2021).

This complex thrives on techno-utopian fantasies, shaping collective imaginaries and channelling the yearning for a better future into an insatiable demand for more data, sophisticated technologies, and invasive surveillance and control. Mirroring historical resource plunder, this external colonialism extends into the digital realm and links material exploitation to the internal colonization of the psyche. Through the rhetoric of 'smart development' and techno-utopian fantasies, it shapes aspirations and social desires, conditioning populations to embrace systems that enable their own domination and dispossession. This internal colonialism inscribes extraction logic deep within the psyche, naturalizing the compulsion for data accumulation and deflecting resistance through promises of technological salvation. By uniting these dimensions, the AFC forges new regimes of profitable control extending into human consciousness. Extracting material data and the desires and dreams of individuals, it erects a system that commodifies the entirety of human experience for the enrichment of a few.

Conclusion

This chapter critically analyaes the emergence of an AFC that fuses digital authoritarianism with the profit-driven mechanisms of surveillance capitalism. It delves into how the rhetoric of 'smart progress' – promising efficiency, sustainability, and collective advancement – has become a powerful ideological tool for legitimizing authoritarian governance across various national contexts. By framing digital surveillance, data extraction, and algorithmic governance as tools for security and efficiency, this narrative has normalized authoritarian practices globally. Particularly in African nations, securitized development initiatives are justified as means of stability and resource optimization, often masking state surveillance and control. The transnational spread of technological expertise has further entrenched this complex, transforming localized strategies into universal templates aligned with digital governance. Urban spaces increasingly adopt digital innovation and big data, concealing the intrusive data extraction and surveillance that accompany these initiatives. Moreover, the chapter explores how 'smart city' discourses, which connect repressive technologies to emancipatory development narratives, obscure the control and surveillance inherent in these projects. It investigates how the extractivist economy has shifted towards data commodification and population control, exacerbating vulnerabilities among marginalized groups and eroding indigenous knowledge systems. The chapter reveals that 'smart progress' recalibrates the 'democratic developmental state' to fit neoliberal and authoritarian capitalist imperatives, advocating centralized control and constant monitoring. Ultimately, this AFC perpetuates data colonialism, transforming aspirations for progress into demands for more data and surveillance, while repressive state apparatuses now serve as ideological state apparatuses, linking surveillance and privacy erosion to promises of national prosperity and sustainable urbanism.

Crucially, this discursive maneuver aligns the imperatives of authoritarian control with the prevailing capitalist fantasy of perpetual 'smart' development driven by data-centric solutions. Digital authoritarianism is repositioned not as an impediment to progress but as a vital catalyst, seamlessly integrating technologies of repression into the relentless pursuit of economic growth, technological sophistication, and the optimization of governance through quantification. In doing so, the AFC has successfully transmuted what were once reviled symbols of state repression into objects of desire, tapping into a 'libidinal economy' where individuals and societies actively seek out and consume the very mechanisms of their subjugation under the intoxicating promise of collective empowerment and betterment through cultures of high-tech control.

9

Perpetual Crisis

Introduction

The authoritarian–financial complex (AFC) thrives on manufacturing perpetual crises, which paradoxically fuel its expansion rather than dismantling it. Similar to how the military–industrial complex relies on armed conflicts under the guise of defence, this complex stokes precarity and insecurity to justify increasing population control. This cycle serves two purposes: it fosters a pervasive sense of fear, driving desires for security and order, and creates lucrative opportunities for economic and political elites. The demand for securitization spawns new markets for surveillance technologies, data-driven governance, and privatized security services, ensuring a constant supply of crises for profit and power consolidation. Consequently, the complex is self-perpetuating, as its contradictions necessitate its expansion, exacerbating societal fractures and undermining democratic norms. The consolidation of this complex has enabled authoritarian movements and leaders to capitalize on economic insecurities, cultural apprehensions, and political estrangement, challenging liberal democratic institutions. This backlash against globalization and progressive values is fuelled by the failure of elites to address inequality and social fragmentation, perceived erosion of national sovereignty, and populist scapegoating of immigrants and minorities. Ethno-nationalist populism resonates with those feeling marginalized by rapid transformations, offering a vision of reclaimed national grandeur and cultural homogeneity.

Authoritarian populism is driven by the erosion of democratic norms and institutions (Levitsky and Ziblatt, 2018), with leaders like Trump in the United States and Bolsonaro in Brazil weakening checks and balances, civil liberties, and electoral processes to consolidate power (Hunter and Power, 2019; Svolik, 2019). This decline is linked to a broader crisis of liberal democracy, characterized by declining trust in political elites, weakened party allegiances, and the spread of disinformation (Judis, 2016; Snyder, 2018). The AFC has facilitated transnational networks among far-right movements and regimes, enhancing the influence of authoritarian populists.

While populism can address democratic deficits (Mudde and Kaltwasser, 2012), the current wave threatens core democratic values by exploiting financialized technologies and societal disruptions for political gain. These movements attract support by channelling grievances against immigrants, minorities, and elites (Wodak, 2015; Bonikowski, 2017), tapping into fears of lost sovereignty and identity in an age of globalization and liberalism (Norris and Inglehart, 2019). Authoritarian populists undermine democratic norms through a playbook that vilifies out-groups and offers a seductive vision of empowerment (Mudde and Kaltwasser, 2012; Levitsky and Ziblatt, 2018), while transnational networks connect far-right movements and authoritarian regimes, amplifying their reach. Empowered by economic anxieties, cultural resentments, and political disillusionment (Eatwell and Goodwin, 2018; Norris and Inglehart, 2019), authoritarian leaders adeptly use financialized technologies for surveillance, propaganda, and control to subvert liberal democracy (Mudde and Kaltwasser, 2012).

The AFC entraps politics in a cycle of escalating demands for control and security, shaping the political arena into a false dichotomy between a repressive 'smart' democratic status quo and populist authoritarian calls for ethno-nationalist security. This complex promotes a fantasy of profitable securitization through digital technologies and data-driven governance, which promises empowerment but ultimately reinforces existing power structures and enables pervasive population control. Concurrently, authoritarian populists exploit societal anxieties, stoking fears of internal enemies and external threats, and calling for law and order, cultural homogeneity, and national greatness. Both technodiscourses of smart development and far-right populism, despite being competing political fantasies, converge in their endorsement of greater securitization and state power. This dynamic undermines democratic norms and frames political discourse within a cycle of escalating control and repression, constraining conventional avenues for dissent and reform. The AFC thus transforms the political arena into a zero-sum game between competing repressive visions, both inimical to genuine democratic pluralism and human freedom.

This chapter will highlight the paradoxical manner in which the AFC is fortified through fostering a perpetual sense of crisis stemming from its inherent economic and political contradictions. It will examine how the complex's reliance on exploiting societal fractures and stoking precarity ultimately breeds the very conditions that necessitate its expansion. The analysis will unveil the self-perpetuating cycle whereby the insecurities engendered by the complex fuel desires for securitization, which in turn create lucrative markets for surveillance technologies and data-driven governance. This symbiotic relationship between authoritarian states and financial elites ensures a constant supply of crises to be capitalized upon. Moreover, the chapter will explore how the manufactured state of crisis fuels competing psycho-social complexes rooted in contrasting political fantasies – the technocratic promise of profitable securitization and the authoritarian populist clamour for ethno-nationalist security. Despite their apparent opposition, both complexes converge in endorsing ever-greater state control and repression, further entrenching the elite beneficiaries of the authoritarian–financial nexus.

Perpetual crisis

The AFC has precipitated a resurgence of explicitly and implicitly authoritarian movements and leaders, reflecting a paradoxical dynamic where perpetual crises and dislocations serve to reinforce and legitimize the very system that spawns them (Kinnvall, 2018; Bonanno, 2020). This process is driven by the intensification of the repressive cycle of finance, whereby the insecurity and social costs of financialization create opportunities for expanded securitization and political control. Concurrently, there is a psycho-social complex at play, where the yearning for greater control emerges from a sense of precarity and instability in an increasingly volatile world (Kinnvall, 2018; Löfflmann, 2024). The AFC thrives, ironically, on crisis, desiring not to overcome it, but to perpetuate it and capitalize on the opportunities it presents for new digital technologies and data-driven techniques of profitable population control (Suarez-Villa, 2012; Mirowski, 2013).

In the wake of the 2008–2009 global financial crisis, the contradictions of neoliberal capitalism became starkly apparent (Harvey, 2010; Duménil and Lévy, 2011; Kotz, 2015). Instead of triggering systemic reforms, the crisis was leveraged to deepen neoliberal policies and strengthen the grip of financial elites (Crouch, 2011; Mirowski, 2013; Admati and Hellwig, 2014). Bailouts and austerity measures protected the interests of the financial oligarchy, while neglecting structural changes that could benefit the wider economy (Crouch, 2011; Wolfson and Epstein, 2013). Political institutions were captured by corporate interests, allowing elites to shape crisis narratives and policy responses for their own gain (Johnson and Kwak, 2010; Stiglitz, 2010; Taibbi, 2010; Prins, 2018). Central bankers colluded with these elites through mechanisms like quantitative easing and bailouts, prioritizing financial markets over broader economic needs (Prins, 2018). The crisis also heightened economic insecurities and social anxieties, fuelling the rise of populist movements and authoritarian leaders who capitalized on fears of cultural and economic displacement (Kinnvall, 2018; Bonanno, 2020). These leaders offered narratives of existential threat and security through nationalism and isolationism, tapping into emotional needs for belonging and protection (Davies and Blanco, 2017; Löfflmann, 2024). At the same time, austerity policies undermined public services, sparking grassroots movements that contested neoliberal urbanism and fought for social justice amid global challenges like climate change and inequality (Davies, 2021). Urban governance became a battleground between capital accumulation demands and the need for social stability and political legitimacy (Streeck, 2017).

The AFC thrives on a confluence of economic, political, and psychological factors, instrumentalizing the crises and contradictions of neoliberal capitalism to consolidate wealth and power in the hands of a few (Foster and Magdoff, 2009; Varoufakis, 2015). Instead of resolving these crises, the system perpetuates new forms of instability, enabling authoritarian movements and leaders to promise security and control in an increasingly precarious world, while entrenching the very structures that create insecurity (Brenner, 2006; Shaikh, 2016; Streeck, 2017). This complex is deeply entwined with the global expansion of finance capital and the integration of national economies into a unified global market, where technocapitalism – marked by the fusion of technological innovation and corporate power – exacerbates inequality and undermines democratic processes, setting the stage for authoritarian responses (Suarez-Villa, 2012; Panitch and Gindin, 2013). The dynamics of overaccumulation, speculation, and uneven geographical development inherent in capitalism have led to persistent stagnation and financial instability, fueling social tensions and political volatility (Brenner, 2006; Harvey, 2010). The 2008–2009 financial crisis, viewed through a Marxian lens, exposed the system's structural flaws, including the long-term decline in the rate of profit and tendencies towards overproduction (Kliman, 2012). Instead of addressing these deep-rooted issues, the post-crisis response only heightened risks and inequalities without achieving sustained growth (Brenner, 2006; Stiglitz, 2010). Authoritarian movements have strategically exploited these vulnerabilities, channelling economic grievances into nationalist narratives and scapegoating, offering a false sense of security while reinforcing the systemic instability they claim to combat (Kinnvall, 2018; Löfflmann, 2024).

The AFC thrives on a self-perpetuating cycle of crisis, repression, and control, driven by capitalism's inherent contradictions and crisis tendencies (Harvey, 2010; Shaikh, 2016). By exploiting crises and emotional insecurities, this complex fosters new authoritarian movements and leaders who promise security while reinforcing the structures that create instability and inequality. This crisis politics is bolstered by the symbiotic relationship between the US economy and the rest of the world, described as the 'Global Minotaur' by Varoufakis (2015), where the United States consumes surplus capital and goods while providing investment opportunities and a reserve currency. However, the 2008 financial crisis exposed the unsustainability of this model, highlighting the need for a more balanced global economic order. Neoliberal policies' failure to restore growth and profitability eroded confidence in established institutions, fuelling the appeal of authoritarian solutions. The AFC, thus, is a multifaceted phenomenon shaped by economic, political, psychological, and technological forces, representing both the contradictions of capitalism and a strategic response by elites to maintain power amid social and economic tensions.

The AFC survives and thrives on a politics of 'perpetual crisis', evolving from merely securing financial profits to exploiting constant unrest and insecurity as a lucrative market for commodified population control (Harvey, 2010; Shaikh, 2016). This shift reflects the complex's strategic adaptation, capitalizing on instability by perpetuating and managing crises rather than resolving them. The ongoing states of insecurity create a continuous demand for the complex's products and services, including surveillance technologies, private security firms, and data-driven predictive policing systems. By fostering a sense of pervasive threat, the complex justifies the expansion of securitization measures, presenting them as essential for maintaining order. This creates a self-perpetuating cycle where the consequences of the complex's actions – social unrest, economic insecurity, and political volatility – justify further interventions and profit-making opportunities. The industry of population control thus becomes both the cause and the solution to the crises it generates, ensuring its enduring relevance and profitability in an increasingly volatile world.

Populist security

The paradox of far-right populist movements lies in their portrayal as anti-establishment forces while being deeply entangled with the very systems they claim to oppose. These movements emerge from the crises and contradictions of neoliberal capitalism, which have fostered widespread insecurity, resentment, and cultural dislocation, particularly following events like the 2008 financial crisis (Saull, 2015; Patomäki, 2021). Globalization has exacerbated these feelings, leaving certain populations feeling marginalized or like the 'losers' in the global system (Mayer, 2014; Karner and Weicht, 2020). Far-right populism taps into these sentiments, offering conspiratorial narratives of national decline, and scapegoating immigrants, supranational institutions, and cosmopolitan elites as enemies (Streeck, 2017; Norris and Inglehart, 2019). These movements channel affective responses – anger, fear, and ressentiment – into myth-making that promises the symbolic regeneration of embattled national identities (Salmela and von Scheve, 2017). However, far from rejecting neoliberalism, far-right populist leaders embrace its tenets. Their rhetoric around nationalist retrenchment and authoritarian governance aligns with neoliberalism's disdain for democratic institutions and celebration of market hierarchies (Patomäki, 2017; Doval and Souroujon, 2021). Figures like Trump exemplify this, cloaking their conservative agendas in anti-establishment rhetoric while reinforcing entrenched financial and political power structures (Kiely, 2021). Digital platforms, products of the very globalizing forces these movements decry, have further fuelled the far-right's rise. Algorithm-driven social media ecosystems, prioritizing engagement over truth, foster extremist subcultures, enabling the spread of inflammatory rhetoric and coordinated online harassment (Pérez-Curiel et al, 2021; Marwick et al, 2022). Far-right groups exploit technologies of anonymity and minimal content moderation to build virtual communities centered on shared feelings of persecution, offering a powerful axis for collective identity and resistance against mainstream institutions (Jasser et al, 2023).

The pernicious synergy between these reactionary currents and their digital mediators illustrates how far-right populism remains fundamentally tethered to the power structures from which it claims emancipation. Indeed, far from a genuine grassroots insurrection, this phenomenon represents an authoritarian mutation engendered by – and continuously reconstituted through – the core contradictions of neoliberal capitalism itself (Edelman, 2020). Its rallying cries of anti-elitism and national resurgence obfuscate the enduring hierarchies and regressive politics it upholds; its fetishization of a unitary popular will cloak efforts to further entrench existing class, gender, and racial dispositions (Winlow et al, 2017). Ultimately, comprehending this authoritarian-populist resurgence mandates recognizing its recursive relationship with the very system it purports to overthrow. The digital sphere facilitating its proliferation remains beholden to the commercial imperatives of platform capitalism, while the solutions espoused by the far-right adhere to core neoliberal tenets of corporatist governance and market supremacy (Buštíková and Guasti, 2019; Devries et al, 2021). Confronting far-right ascendancy thus necessitates deconstructing the chimeric anti-establishment persona it projects – one which, upon closer examination, reveals itself as a reactionary vanguard for the rejuvenation and diffusion of authoritarian practices deeply consonant with the neoliberal paradigm (Fielitz and Marcks, 2019; Zhang and Davis, 2022).

Fundamental to this siege mentality is an authoritarian mindset that fetishizes strong, decisive leadership over liberal democratic norms. The mythic idea of a paternal statesman, unencumbered by bureaucratic restraints, able to take the tough choices necessary to protect the nation from its enemies, becomes a powerfully seductive vision. This cult of personality politics aligns strikingly with corporate leadership models prioritizing top-down control and profit maximization. Crucially then, rather than outward military campaigns, the battleground has shifted inwards – towards legislating draconian immigration policies, stoking moral panics around 'cultural Marxism', and consolidating power sufficient to neutralize domestic 'threats' to a unified national will. The techniques deployed evince the complex's embeddedness within digital domains – harnessing online disinformation, algorithmic radicalization, and surveillance capitalism. This intersectional dynamic between ethnic revanchism, authoritarian populism, and rapacious finance capital represents the crux of the AFC animating contemporary far-right politics. A potent brew of regressivism, tech-driven social control, and corporate sovereignty geared not towards foreign adventurism, but a perpetual war against the 'globalist' enemy within.

This symbiotic relation between ascendant far-right forces and their ostensible capitalist antagonists signals the perpetuation of a deeply entrenched and complex authoritarian–financial order. One propelled by technologies of remote, algorithmic control and undergirded by cross-pollinating currents of ultra-nationalism, ethnic chauvinism, and corporate authoritarianism (Higgott, 2021). To meaningfully disrupt this trajectory requires excavating its obscured foundations – recognizing how the resurgent far-right, for all its anti-globalist bluster, remains an appendage of the very structures enabling and profiting from its rise. The contemporary far-right populist movement reflects, in this respect, an AFC quite distinct from its historical antecedents. Rather than pursuing outward military expansionism or territorial conquest as the pathway to national renewal, this new strain is oriented inwards, obsessively fixated on securing borders and purging perceived internal threats. Central to this fixation is a profound fear of the 'globalist' agenda – an insidious, shadowy force seen as orchestrating the dilution of national sovereignty and traditional cultural heritages through open borders, multiculturalism, and progressive social values. This xenophobic obsession with security has become the *raison d'être* of the contemporary far-right, a perpetual rallying cry to marshal supporters against the creeping influence of cosmopolitan 'outsiders'.

Profitable polarization

The AFC fuelling contemporary far-right populism is deeply linked to a political-economic apparatus profiting from perpetual crisis and instability. Real or perceived existential threats, such as immigrant 'invasions', threats to traditional values, or globalist conspiracies, become lucrative ventures. Corporate titans and techno-elites exploit social unrest and reactionary backlash to consolidate power and accumulate capital. Far-right calls for security, order, and decisive leadership create markets for private military contractors, data analytics firms, digital surveillance, and 'law and order' platforms. Furthermore, digital infrastructures and information communication technologies that amplify far-right grievances have become indispensable assets for this regime. Social media algorithms maximize engagement through inflammatory content, spreading disinformation and radicalizing audiences, fragmenting online discourse into echo chambers. This benefits techno-oligopolies, turning mass data harvesting, behavioural monitoring, and predictive analytics into new modes of control under the guise of 'customization'. The authoritarian tendencies of the far-right thrive in these digitally mediated systems of oversight. As social fabrics fray, the demand for securitization and top-down governance grows, allowing the AFC to entrench its dominance further. Crisis becomes a strategic asset, stoked and commodified through the technologies it fosters, making upheaval a profitable industry.

The convergence of authoritarian politics and unbridled financial interests has birthed a nefarious force that exploits digital technologies to sow discord, erode democratic norms, and entrench societal divides. This AFC thrives on perpetual conflict and polarization, wielding online platforms and data-driven analytics as instruments of control and profit maximization. Its modus operandi rests on a paradox: the very tools heralded as harbingers of global connectivity have been co-opted to fragment communities and solidify existing power structures. Crucial to the survival and spread of this complex lies the monetization of conflict and division. Big Tech companies have leveraged tools of corporate financialization to consolidate their infrastructural dominance, enabling them to profit handsomely from the very divisions they perpetuate (Klinge et al, 2023).

For authoritarians and repressive authorities, more generally, the manipulation of online discourse serves as a potent mechanism for suppressing dissent, amplifying propaganda, and manufacturing a climate of fear and mistrust conducive to the consolidation of power (Curato, 2017). Simultaneously, tech companies profit immensely from the engagement and data generated by the virtual battles they enable, incentivizing the perpetuation of conflict and division (Lanier, 2018; Vaidhyanathan, 2018). This dynamic is not confined to overtly repressive regimes; ostensible democracies have proven equally susceptible to the corrosive forces of polarization fueled by digital echo chambers. The rise of Donald Trump's authoritarian populism, for instance, has been catalysed and reinforced by the tribalistic discourse cultivated on social media platforms (Smith, 2019). Likewise, the Tea Party movement's destructive tendencies found fertile ground in online spaces, eroding democratic norms and fostering ideological entrenchment (Lundskow, 2012).

The AFC has successfully monetized societal divisions, turning virtual conflicts into a profitable enterprise. Platforms like Twitter are designed to encourage simplification, polarization, and moral grandstanding, leading to phenomena such as 'cancel culture' that often devolve into digital spectacle rather than substantive change (Bouvier, 2020). Psychological drivers like blame-shifting and moral identity restoration perpetuate these cycles of division, especially affecting younger generations, whose social interactions are increasingly shaped by fear and conformity (Yar and Bromwich, 2019). Big Tech's financial growth thrives on the engagement generated by polarizing content and ideological echo chambers, fostering conflict to drive user activity and profit (Lanier, 2018; Vaidhyanathan, 2018). These companies wield immense global influence, shaping geopolitical dynamics and exerting leverage over nation-states (Liu, 2021; Tokat, 2022). As they reinvest profits into expanding their digital dominance, the intertwining of profit pursuit with the stoking of perpetual conflict erodes shared truths and societal cohesion (Klinge et al, 2023). Cancel culture, which aims for accountability, often becomes a performance of digital justice fuelled by moral grandstanding, blame-shifting, and fear, rather than a mechanism for real change (Bouvier, 2020; Bouvier and Machin, 2021).

The AFC functions as a self-reinforcing system, where authoritarian goals align with profit-driven motives through digital platforms. Authoritarian regimes use these platforms to suppress dissent, manipulate public opinion, and foster polarization, all while tech companies profit from the engagement and data these conflicts generate. Online platforms encourage simplification, polarization, and moral grandstanding, which deepens ideological divides and tribalism in democracies and fuels the spread of propaganda and fear in authoritarian regimes (Curato, 2017; Győrffy, 2020). This dynamic fosters real-world political rifts and allows authoritarians to justify repressive measures, vilifying marginalized groups and dissenting voices to consolidate power. The complex is not sustained solely by material interests but also by the psychological gratification, or jouissance, derived from the virtual policing and shaming of perceived enemies. Public shaming, or 'cancelling', within digital spaces becomes a spectacle of moral superiority, reinforcing in-group solidarity and providing a cathartic release for participants, who derive satisfaction from asserting moral dominance over others (Lundskow, 2012; Smith, 2019). This ritualistic denigration becomes a tool for reinforcing existing power structures, allowing both authoritarian regimes and populist movements to exploit these dynamics for control.

Here, the spectre of populist upheaval is conjured, with digital echo chambers amplifying fears of societal unravelling and the subversion of established norms. Elite interests coalesce around a narrative of preserving the integrity of democratic institutions, portraying grassroots movements as threats to the social fabric. In both contexts, the digital sphere serves as a crucible for the construction and dissemination of securitizing narratives. Online platforms become battlegrounds for crafting and amplifying threat perceptions, stoking collective anxieties, and mobilizing public sentiment in favour of authoritarian overreach or the suppression of dissent. The result is, once again, a repressive cycle of polarization and conflict, where the very existence of the 'other' – whether foreign, marginalized, or populist – is framed as an existential danger to be eradicated through extraordinary measures.

Lucrative resistance

The AFC represents a convergent assemblage of state agencies, private military contractors, technology firms, and financial interests, driven by the imperative to perpetuate social upheaval and political instability for profit. Instead of addressing the root causes of unrest, such as deepening inequalities and eroding democratic norms, these actors capitalize on crises and dissent. Central to this complex is the proliferation of surveillance technologies aimed at monitoring, predicting, and suppressing civil disobedience. Companies like Palantir exemplify this trend, providing data integration platforms that help governments collate data and identify threats through predictive analytics. Palantir's software played a crucial role in the Trump administration's harsh border enforcement measures, including family separations by Immigration and Customs Enforcement (Collins and Sullivan, 2018). Framed as essential security tools, these systems obscure their true purpose of criminalizing migrants and stifling dissent (Franco, 2020).

The tech sector's partnerships with state surveillance and policing agencies, involving companies like Amazon, Microsoft, and Google, have generated substantial profits through contracts for facial recognition, cloud services, and artificial intelligence (AI) analytics touted as essential for public safety (Hu, 2020; Lau, 2020). However, these collaborations enable over-policing of marginalized communities, suppression of protest movements, and expansion of biased carceral control systems (Browne, 2015; Summers, 2016). The resulting surveillance infrastructure fosters fear, self-censorship, and normalizes authoritarian governance, exacerbated by the opacity of tech companies' AI systems (Whittaker, 2020). This environment frames dissent as subversive, legitimizing state suppression of civil liberties under the guise of public safety. These systems, driven by financial incentives, provide substantial profits to private sector entities whose technologies are marketed as indispensable. Amnesty International (2023) found that at least 23 major firms producing 'less-lethal' crowd control munitions have facilitated violent crackdowns on protesters in over 50 countries, prioritizing profits over ethical concerns. Corporate malfeasance is further emboldened by the absence of binding international regulations and the revolving door between government, the military–industrial complex, and the private sector, which allows individuals to secure lucrative contracts that align state authoritarianism with corporate profit motives (Shorrock, 2008). Projects like the Intelligence Advanced Research Projects Activity's Project Mercury, which uses data intercepted from countries like Egypt and Syria to develop AI systems anticipating political crises and pandemics, exemplify how civil society groups are treated as subjects for surveillance and threat assessments. This dynamic underscores the deep entanglement of surveillance capitalism with the security state, as technologies initially developed for military and intelligence applications – like the internet, GPS, and algorithmic systems – now form the foundation of tech giants like Google, Facebook, and Amazon.

The growth of 'smart cities', as discussed previously, has significant implications for population control and authoritarian governance. The integration of sensor networks, machine learning systems, and predictive analytics into urban infrastructures facilitates extensive monitoring, behavioural regulation, and potential suppression of dissent, all under the guise of public safety and efficiency (Sadowski and Pasquale, 2015). Globally, projects developing AI surveillance systems for 'smart policing' are multiplying, forming strategic alliances between states, tech companies, and private military contractors to exert urban power (Lau et al, 2020). These initiatives quickly become entrenched infrastructures designed to be opaque and resistant to public accountability (Jaffe and Pilò, 2023). Justified through discourses of security and technological solutionism, they expand the carceral state's reach and privatize public services and spaces (Krivý, 2018). Implementation failures merely create opportunities for further trials and embedding control technologies into urban life. This AFC operates globally, not just in the Global North. In developing regions, privatized security networks safeguard multinational corporate investments, often operating in legal gray areas and committing human rights violations with impunity (Arduino, 2020; Ghiselli, 2021). Private military and security companies escalate conflicts and destabilize regions to protect economic interests, rooted in the dynamics of capital accumulation and resource extraction they support (Bures and Cusumano, 2021; Petersohn, 2021).

Contemporary capitalism, thus, depends upon and actively ferments political dislocation and civil unrest, opportunistically capitalizing on instability to consolidate its power and reap immense profits. Rather than existential threats, eruptions of social upheaval catalysed by structural inequities simply represent opportunities to be exploited. Civil disobedience is recast as a security risk to be managed through force multiplication and the expansion of carceral networks enmeshed with private sector profiteering. Unrest incites crackdowns that in turn breed more resistance – a cyclical dynamic perfectly symbiotic with the complex's own compulsions for relentless capital accumulation. In this paradoxical paradigm, authentic resolution of underlying grievances is anathema. Sustainable peace and stability would undermine the very pretexts and economic incentives animating the authoritarian–financial apparatus. Its perpetuity depends on the instrumentalization, commodification, and exploitation, in this respect, of ever new political conflicts.

Repressive improvements

The AFC sustains itself through a self-reinforcing cycle of manufacturing social conflicts and positioning its control mechanisms as solutions, creating a profitable and self-perpetuating system of crisis and commodified crisis response. This complex not only thrives on overt repression but also strategically frames issues to justify its 'progressive' interventions. For instance, public backlash against discriminatory policing and mass incarceration has been exploited as an opportunity to repackage surveillance technologies and mass supervision as ethically progressive reforms. Predictive policing and community supervision, initially presented as alternatives to incarceration, have extended carceral control over marginalized communities, perpetuating 'pervasive punishment' (Phelps, 2013; Miller and Stuart, 2017). Rather than dismantling these systems, the complex reinvents them through algorithmic and data-driven methods, presenting such tools as neutral, scientifically rigorous solutions (McNeill, 2018). Predictive policing technologies, which forecast potential criminal activity through advanced computation, exemplify this approach, where discriminatory practices are repackaged as impartial and fair (McDaniel and Pease, 2021). The complex creates a demand for its own interventions by framing its tools as necessary responses to the very problems it perpetuates, mirroring Foucault's (1997) theory of power operating through the construction of problems that require governance (Egbert and Leese, 2021).

Predictive algorithms in policing, though marketed as impartial reforms, risk perpetuating racial bias and disproportionately subject marginalized communities to pre-emptive surveillance and control (Yen and Hung, 2021; Susser, 2022). The proprietary nature of these technologies raises concerns about transparency, privacy violations, and the erosion of civil liberties (Miller, 2014). Predictive policing reduces police discretion and accountability while being framed as a scientifically valid solution to problems like biased enforcement (Sandhu and Fussey, 2021). This narrative, constructed by the AFC, manipulates public perception by presenting its interventions as solutions to crises it has helped generate. Public–private partnerships between law enforcement and tech corporations illustrate how the complex profits from both the creation of societal crises and the commodification of their supposed remedies. The collaboration between Amazon's Ring cameras and police departments exemplifies how privatized surveillance is normalized, fostering discriminatory policing while diverting public funds to corporate interests (Ongweso, 2020; Ferguson, 2024). This dynamic sustains a profitable cycle of surveillance and control disguised as reform, with little democratic oversight.

The AFC thrives on generating societal crises, such as over-policing, racial profiling, and mass incarceration, only to profit from providing solutions framed as scientifically validated and ethically progressive (Egbert and Leese, 2021). It manipulates public demands for reform by repackaging surveillance and control technologies as neutral tools for accountability. The complex's expansion into both public and private sectors is bolstered by consistent funding, such as the US Department of Justice's support for predictive policing programmes and real-time crime centres, despite their documented bias and questionable effectiveness (Ferguson, 2024). This ecosystem, involving police departments, tech vendors, and academic institutions, financially benefits from developing these surveillance tools with little scrutiny. Public resistance or criticism of such technologies becomes reabsorbed into the cycle, reinforcing the need for more advanced systems of control rather than dismantling them (McDaniel and Pease, 2021). Consequently, calls for reform lead to further institutionalization of the complex, as public–private partnerships distribute the risks and costs of these systems while solidifying the complex's dominance and ensuring its continual renewal (Ongweso, 2020).

Initiatives marketed as reform paradoxically become mechanisms for the AFC to preserve and expand its control through increasingly pervasive systems of algorithmic surveillance and monitoring. The more intrusive these technologies become, the more societal grievances they generate – grievances then repackaged as existential crises that only the complex's latest innovations can resolve. This cyclical dynamic produces a form of jouissance, where technological control systems perpetuate oppression under the guise of progress and reform. Instead of dismantling oppressive institutions, societal desires for transformation are co-opted into a neurotic fantasy of liberation, re-inscribed through sophisticated modes of digital subjugation. The complex positions its technological solutions as the progressive future of justice and security, converting genuine aspirations for institutional reform into investments in updated control mechanisms. Fantasies of impartial algorithms, scientifically validated crime forecasting, and frictionless accountability are celebrated as ideals, while in reality they entrench domination. Reform is subsumed into the apparatus of the complex, reinforcing totalizing surveillance infrastructures under the guise of accountability and insulating the complex from critique. This paradox allows the AFC to present its digitized control as a revolutionary break from its analogue past, while in truth it fortifies its power, granting it psychic legitimacy as a force for progress.

The AFC flourishes by creating and amplifying social grievances related to discrimination, civil liberties, and law enforcement accountability, while simultaneously redirecting calls for systemic change into technocratic solutions that necessitate ongoing enhancements. Outrage over police violence and prison abuses is repurposed to promote technological interventions like predictive policing and digital monitoring, framed as impartial remedies to the injustices causing dissent. This complex harnesses demands for radical change, commodifying them into profitable technologies that reinforce existing power structures. Societal upheavals are absorbed into cycles of computational refinement, ensuring problems remain embedded within the system, necessitating continuous upgrades that benefit private stakeholders and protect state institutions from transformative pressures. Systemic critiques are reduced to demands for more sophisticated versions of oppressive structures, perpetuating a cycle of technocratic solutionism that solidifies the complex's dominance and insulates it from genuine reform.

Reinforcing contradictions

The AFC exhibits a perpetual opportunism, exploiting crises to expand its influence and accumulate profits through the deployment of digital technologies and data-driven techniques for population control. This insidious modus operandi involves cultivating a political culture of perpetual conflict that obscures and delegitimizes the complex's core motives – profiting from real material and public crises through the proliferation of surveillance systems under the guise of management, security and optimization. Consequently, this strategy undermines and delegitimizes more democratic and public-oriented applications of these technologies that could empower citizens and communities for the greater social good.

The COVID-19 pandemic exposed the opportunism of the AFC, as misinformation and digital technologies were manipulated to undermine public health efforts and democratic governance (Bernard et al, 2020; Gruzd and Mai, 2020; Darius and Urquhart, 2021). Social media platforms and fringe websites became conduits for conspiracy theories that eroded trust in science and democracy (Zeng and Schäfer, 2021; McNeil-Willson, 2022), exploiting public fears about control and freedom (Chapelan, 2021; Eberl et al, 2021). In Brazil, President Bolsonaro weaponized disinformation to downplay the virus and promote unproven treatments, using the crisis to prioritize economic interests and consolidate authoritarian power (Zimmermann, 2020). His administration spread conspiracy theories to erode institutional trust and strengthen far-right support, amplifying a 'politics of fear' through social media (Kalil et al, 2021). The Brazilian case exemplifies how authoritarian regimes exploited COVID-19 misinformation to justify overreach and weaken democratic checks (Zimmermann, 2020). Even in democratic contexts, corporations reframed centralized surveillance tools like contact tracing as forms of 'empowerment' (Bernard et al, 2020). Tech giants like Apple and Google promoted decentralized protocols that preserved their data-extractive models, circumventing democratic oversight and weakening public health systems' ability to protect privacy.

The COVID-19 conspiracy landscape, fuelled by distrust in democratic institutions and fears of control, was strategically exploited by corporate and authoritarian actors to undermine egalitarian technology applications while promoting privatized population control systems framed as individual empowerment (Zeng and Schäfer, 2021). Technological 'solutionism' narratives normalized self-surveillance and behavioural tracking (Teräs et al, 2020; Sturm and Albrecht, 2021), while intrusive digital ID systems were introduced, especially in the Global South, under the pretext of development

(Privacy International, 2021). Anti-institutional distrust provided cover for embedding surveillance capitalism deeper into societal infrastructures, inhibiting civil society's influence and positioning 'freedom' in opposition to public health and democratic governance (Akbari, 2021; Richards, 2022). This dynamic allowed authoritarians and corporations to bypass democratic principles, erode scientific expertise, and prioritize reactionary fears that enabled unaccountable private sector control. The commercialization of 'technologies of crisis' restructured mass psychology around security and vulnerability, fostering acquiescence to algorithmic governance driven by corporate and authoritarian interests (Kampmark, 2020; Vicdan, 2020). Consequently, the pandemic hastened a power consolidation that imposed technologies undermining democratic accountability, with COVID-19 misinformation expressing disempowerment from technocratic policies prioritizing market fundamentalism over the public good (Curley et al, 2022; Schulze et al, 2022).

Within this context, the AFC adeptly harnessed the legitimate societal angst surrounding the pandemic to reaffirm its political-economic hegemony by further subsuming human experience into paradigms of digitized social control marketized for private profit accumulation. The very notion of democratic accountability and participatory technological development oriented towards benefiting all people was undermined as systems of monitoring, prediction, and behavioural modification attained self-perpetuating logics optimized for capitalist valorization and authoritarian supervision rather than maximal social utility. The COVID-19 pandemic represented an evolutionary leap in the Deleuzian societies of control, where the viral dynamics of opportunistic capitalism blended with commodified techniques of social repression. Rather than static modes of disciplinary control confined to enclosed spaces, the perpetual crisis-making of the AFC unleashed a proactive, endlessly mutating politics of division.

Public health became a battleground for fostering insecurities that could be manipulated into factional resentments, with digital infrastructures of misinformation fuelling a disorienting cycle where conspiratorial narratives redirected collective energies from empirical realities. Institutional trust and rational governance were eroded through marketing strategies designed to maintain populations in a state of panic, creating lucrative opportunities for privatized solutions framed as protection from risk. These corporatized technologies of control redefined everyday life, embedding surveillance into citizenship and optimizing human needs for profit and social control. Rather than enforcing a singular authoritarian rule, the crisis prompted a cybernetic reorganization of society, fragmenting lived experiences and commodifying basic necessities. This opportunistic use of a public health emergency extended systems of control, where power and resistance worked in tandem to reproduce cycles of domination. The pandemic enabled a planetary reconfiguration of biosocial life, embedding fear and security into the very fabric of social interactions. The AFC thrives on this culture, exploiting the anxieties it cultivates to reinforce a state of perpetual emergency, turning both public and private spaces into arenas of vulnerability. In this environment, human activity is framed as a risk to be managed, generating an economy of security consumption driven by technological solutions that promise protection but ultimately extend surveillance and control.

Yet the very purveyors fuelling these existential anxieties through crisis narratives are positioned to profiteer from peddling protocols, infrastructures, and data-driven systems that reconstitute human experience as a domain of surveillance citizenship. Digital enclosures and governance technologies branded as empowerment are seamlessly integrated into the social terrain transformed into a permaculture of mistrust. The security–control paradox manifests a mutated politics where subjects actively comply with their own dispossession, perpetually investing psychic energies into system preservations rather than emancipatory social horizons. Elites harness these pathologies through speculative opportunism, reifying the public's attentiveness to imaginary menaces while accruing influence from their presumed ability to deliver freedom from future contingencies through regimes of cybernetic discipline. Collectively, subjective experience becomes a commodified frontier where the irrational compulsions of control mania and its conjoined terror of ever-present threats serve as the axiomatic conditions for elite accumulation and social reproduction within the constrictive architectures of secured societies.

Conclusion

The AFC thrives through a cycle of crisis generation and commodification, strategically cultivating instability and societal rupture to present its own securitized, data-driven solutions as indispensable. This model leverages the anxieties it foments, framing dislocations as existential threats that demand intervention, thereby entrenching its power and generating profit. By amplifying social divisions and undermining democratic norms, the complex manufactures a landscape rife with perceived threats, legitimizing the expansion of surveillance infrastructures, population control mechanisms, and privatized security regimes. These interventions are presented as impartial, scientifically validated solutions, masking their role in perpetuating civil liberty erosions and marginalization. Predictive policing technologies exemplify this paradox, where discriminatory enforcement practices are repackaged to justify the adoption of algorithmic control systems, touted as tools of fairness and transparency. Public–private partnerships further entrench this dynamic, as law enforcement's reliance on proprietary surveillance systems cements the carceral logic embedded in these tools, despite public criticism. Resistance is absorbed into discourses that continually promote 'improved' technological solutions, diverting attention from meaningful systemic reform while benefiting the complex's stakeholders.

The rise of far-right populist movements exemplifies the AFC's capacity to exploit economic insecurities, cultural grievances, and political disillusionment, reinforcing the very power structures these movements claim to resist. Though outwardly rejecting globalization and progressive values, these movements are deeply rooted in the neoliberal paradigm, advocating for nationalist retrenchment, authoritarianism, and hierarchical leadership – values aligned with market fundamentalism and elite control. The digital infrastructures that enable the spread of far-right ideologies, disinformation, and conspiracy theories are products of the global techno-economic system these movements purport to oppose. This further entrenches existing power dynamics while obscuring their role in exacerbating societal divisions. The AFC thrives on perpetual instability, capitalizing on crises to expand control technologies, surveillance systems, and security markets. Its collaboration with financial elites, coupled with the erosion of democratic safeguards, enables a continuous cycle of crisis exploitation for profit and control. By amplifying collective fears and insecurities, the complex cultivates a fixation on security that justifies widespread surveillance and algorithmic management, transforming human activity into a potential risk factor to be monitored and modified, thus reinforcing a system of control masked as protection.

The survival and spread of the AFC relies, for this reason, on the fostering of perpetual complexes rooted in ontological insecurities and psycho-social anxieties surrounding control, autonomy, and the desire for security. By manufacturing perpetual crises and stoking pervasive fears around existential threats, the complex cultivates a social environment where its interventions – surveillance systems, data-driven population control mechanisms, and privatized security regimes – become positioned as necessary and rational solutions. These 'solutions' are then strategically framed as impartial, scientifically validated, and progressive, obscuring their role in perpetuating marginalization, eroding civil liberties, and reinforcing existing power structures. This allows the complex to co-opt resistance and reform movements, subsuming their emancipatory aspirations into investments in ever-more sophisticated modes of technological subjugation marketed as empowering and accountable. The complex's power lies in its ability to tap into widespread anxieties and channel them towards a pathological fixation on security, control, and the constant need for its commodified interventions.

Breaking Free from the Authoritarian–Financial Complex

Introduction

The authoritarian–financial complex (AFC) represents the powerful nexus between large corporations/financial institutions and centralized state power in the contemporary era. As this book has explored, it represents an evolution from the earlier military–industrial complex, reflecting how political-economic dominance has shifted from the military–industrial bases of the mid-20th century towards the new epicentres of global financial capitalism and digital techno-utopian corporatism. At its core, the AFC is an interlocking system that concentrates wealth and power in the hands of mutually reinforcing political, corporate, and financial elites. Crucially, this book has revealed how the perpetuation of this complex relies not just on structural economic advantages or monopolization of coercive force, but on the production and normalization of pathological psycho-social fantasies that instil desire for its valorization circuits. Through potent ideological narratives celebrating capitalist individualism, consumerism, market fundamentalism, and techno-solutionism, the AFC culls popular allegiance to its hierarchical command. It conditions the popular imagination and circumscribes the horizons of reported possibilities, ensuring the perpetuation of elite dominance despite the flagrant contradictions and exploitations intrinsic to its model.

The AFC capitalizes on crises and structural contradictions, strategically leveraging social unrest, economic instability, and political conflicts to consolidate and expand its control. Rather than being destabilized by upheavals, it uses them as opportunities to entrench its power, profiting from the volatility it helps create. Surveillance technologies, carceral systems, and exploitative debt structures are employed to reinforce its dominance, framing each cycle of instability as further justification for its existence. In response, grassroots movements and radical theoretical currents have emerged to challenge this complex and the neoliberal capitalist system it supports. Drawing from anarchism, ecosocialism, feminism, and indigenous traditions, these movements emphasize economic democracy, worker self-management, and the decommodification of resources, focusing on social and ecological well-being rather than profit. Innovative economic models such as worker-owned cooperatives and peer production networks seek to democratize the governance of resources, redirecting value creation towards community needs. Politically, radical municipalist projects and direct democracy practices – like the neighbourhood assemblies in Buenos Aires and the democratic confederations in Rojava – are constructing horizontal systems of self-rule that offer a compelling alternative to centralized authority and corporate domination.

While the emergence of alternative economic and political movements offers hope, their potential to truly dismantle the AFC demands a deeper understanding of how complex power functions within modern capital–state structures. The system's hegemony transcends control of institutions and permeates the social, cultural, and psychological fabric of life. Capitalism's narratives of individualism, competition, and commodification have become so entrenched within collective consciousness that they are perceived as natural and inevitable (Scott, 2012; Arvidsson and Peitersen, 2013). To create lasting alternatives, it is crucial to challenge and dismantle these deeply rooted ideological constructs that uphold the authoritarian–financial system. This requires not only confronting economic and political power but also engaging in a prolonged struggle to delegitimize the dominant narratives and values that perpetuate atomized identities and desires (Sitrin and Azzellini, 2014). Only by disrupting these internalized norms can cooperative, sustainable, and collectively empowering practices genuinely thrive and displace the current order.

This final chapter examines the diverse avenues for escaping the AFC's grip. Despite the immense obstacles, it outlines how repurposing digital technologies and data-driven tools can shift them from instruments of control to catalysts for collective empowerment and liberation. The chapter argues that the security promised by the current capitalist system is a fragile illusion, masking deep systemic insecurities, inequalities, and ecological vulnerabilities. Instead, it advocates for bold policies and new institutional structures aimed at providing genuine material security and psychological emancipation for all. Central to this vision is the democratization and decommodification of essential services, the implementation of universal basic provisions, and a transition towards ecologically regenerative, commons-based models of production and social organization. Through the integration of emerging technological potentials with political-economic reorganization, the chapter charts a path towards genuine societal transformation, emphasizing the necessity of dismantling the AFC to preserve freedom and foster true emancipation.

Democratizing technology

The AFC exerts a hegemonic influence over the production and dissemination of knowledge, effectively circumscribing the boundaries of what is perceived as socially and politically possible. Through its control over dominant narratives, media platforms, and educational institutions, it perpetuates a neoliberal orthodoxy that naturalizes the primacy of market forces, individualism, and profit maximization. Alternatives that challenge the fundamental tenets of capitalism are often marginalized, dismissed as utopian fantasies, or actively suppressed through coercive means. This epistemic foreclosure serves to reinforce existing power structures and insulate them from radical critique, thereby perpetuating a cycle of ideological reproduction that sustains the status quo. However, the emergence of digital technologies and the growing recognition of the social, ecological, and economic crises wrought by unfettered capitalism have created fissures in this hegemonic order. Scholars and activists across various disciplines are seizing upon these openings to radically reimagine the social, political, and economic possibilities of technology, offering visions that transcend the narrow confines of the AFC.

Digital socialists envision repurposing technologies developed under capitalism as a central part of the transition to a socialist society. They advocate for democratizing ownership and control over digital infrastructure like online platforms, computer networks, data systems, and artificial intelligence (Fuchs, 2020). Rather than these core technologies remaining proprietary resources centralized under corporate control, the 'means of digital production' would become socially owned and directly governed by workers and communities themselves. This decentralized, participatory model of democratic ownership could enable a radical restructuring of how societies organize their economic activities. With access to open data and advanced analytics capabilities, democratic institutions and collectives could make informed decisions over investment priorities and resource allocation based on social needs rather than profit motives (Morozov, 2019). Transparent digital platforms could coordinate collaborative production across decentralized networks while enabling new forms of non-capitalist value flows and exchange (Cockshott et al, 2010).

Commonly owned technological capabilities could also be leveraged to systematically reduce necessary labour time and democratize the benefits of automation across societies (Cox, 2020). This could free communities to prioritize human development, self-actualization, and ecological sustainability over the capitalist compulsion for endless capital accumulation. Moreover, digital socialists theorize how technologies can be instrumental in restructuring social reproduction and care work, which capitalism has systematically devalued and externalized as responsibilities for the unpaid labour of women and families (Tronto, 2017; Della Ratta, 2020). Smart technologies, sharing economy platforms, and open design systems could enable more localized self-sufficiency and sustainable provisioning of basic needs like food, housing, and caregiving. This recentring of collective organization around social reproduction could fundamentally shift how societies provision and distribute resources, caring labour, and emotional services.

Post-capitalist theorists and activists take these ideas even further by envisioning technologies as opening a transition beyond capitalist commodity production and market valuation entirely. They posit that advanced digital technologies, automation capabilities, and networked coordination systems could become so productive that societies could superabundantly provide for basic material needs with very little human labour input required (Srnicek and Williams, 2015; Bastani, 2019). This could enable a historic possibility of a 'post-work' society where the pressures and incentive systems of production for market consumption dissolve. In such a world, digital platforms and automated production systems could allow societies to collectively and democratically govern the provisioning of needs through decentralized, participatory planning mechanisms rather than market pricing (Cockshott et al, 2010). With a guaranteed material foundation of abundance, the bulk of human effort and activities could be freed to pursue creative, intellectual, and collaborative endeavors ungoverned by capitalist work disciplines or income constraints.

Crucially, post-capitalists depict potential future scenarios where the central purpose of technology enables societies to reprioritize non-alienated activities aimed at developing broad human capacities and potentials to their fullest (Frase, 2016). Intelligent automation systems could assume the roles of basic provisioning labour, while communities could self-organize culturally vibrant, ecologically sustainable ways of 'post-work' living enriched by flows of unalienated experimentation, crafting, skilled making, and artistry. Some theorists outline distinct transitional phases through which such scenarios could gradually emerge (Srnicek and Williams, 2015). An initial 'socialist' stage could expand public luxuries while dramatically compressing necessary labour time, providing breathing room for communities to cultivate collective socio-technical literacy and democratic planning capacities. An educated, networked post-work class could then leverage maturing technologies to automate a maximized provision of goods and services through democratic coordination. This could set a foundation for progressing into a 'post-capitalist' society where scarcity constraints dissolve and societies re-orient towards realizing the fullest possibilities for non-alienated individuality and social self-actualization.

What fundamentally unites digital socialism and post-capitalism theoretically is their radical reconceptualization of technology's role and ideal relationship to society. Rather than profitability and capital accumulation determining the directions of innovation in alienating and destructive ways, technological development could instead prioritize maximal collective social empowerment, free human development, and ecological integrity as first principle ends. These visions reimagine integrating productive technologies back into society in harmonized ways – as catalysing forces for decommodifying material provision, reducing necessary toil, and democratically opening new spaces for joyful individuality, community self-actualization, and diverse flourishing.

Ultimately, both digital socialism and post-capitalism position emerging technologies as potent emancipatory toolsets that could open productive possibilities for transcending capitalism's core drives and value hierarchies. If democratically controlled and consciously guided by societies themselves, technological systems could become means for remaking how we provide for our needs and what we understand as the purpose of material production and economic activity. Rather than intrinsically being instruments of domination, enclosure, and extractive exploitation, these perspectives theorize how technologies could catalyse remaking society based on substantive equality, sustainability, solidarity, and the full realization of human potentials.

These theorizations of digital socialism and techno-utopian post-capitalism represent a radical departure from the constrictive paradigms that have traditionally circumscribed how technology's societal role is conceptualized. Dominant framings have largely oscillated between two poles – technology as an instrument for enhancing security, efficiency, and social control to be embraced, or as an existential threat to human autonomy to be rejected. Both perspectives remain trapped within the reductive logic of capitalism, which valorizes technological development primarily as a means for economic competitiveness and capital accumulation. In contrast, these emerging perspectives decouple technology from such instrumental rationalities, reconceptualizing it as a transformative force that can fundamentally restructure and transcend capitalist social relations themselves. They position technological systems not as tools subordinated to the profit motives of capital, but as potentially emancipatory means of production that can facilitate democratic self-mastery over how societies reproduce their material conditions of existence.

This reframing catalyses a recuperation of technology's radical, world-making possibilities that had been foreclosed by capitalism's hegemonic frames. It re-enchants technological development with emancipatory fantasies – of collectively harnessing machines' productive capacities to institutionalize economic democracy, overcome alienated labour, decommodify social reproduction, and actualize new post-capitalist cultures of sustainable human flourishing. Rather than resigning technology's fate to either reifying domination or necessitating its rejection, these perspectives theorize it as a crucial terrain of social struggle and site for manifesting liberatory transformation. They discursively reclaim technological infrastructures as communal loci of potential empowerment over which to wage battles for democratic governance and realization of alternative political-economic models.

From (in)security to possibility

The AFC depends upon the perpetuation of insecurity and precarity. By fostering a pervasive sense of economic instability and social vulnerability, this apparatus sustains its power through the allure of capitalist securitization – the false promise of security through adherence to the dictates of the market and the capitalist state (Selbin, 2019). However, this chimeric pursuit of security through capitalist means ultimately reinforces the very conditions of insecurity and exploitation that the AFC requires to maintain its hegemony. Amidst this dismal landscape, progressive perspectives such as universal basic income (UBI), regenerative economics, and the caring economy offer emancipatory alternatives that disrupt the narratives and practices underpinning the authoritarian–financial nexus. By centring human dignity, ecological sustainability, and equitable provisioning, these frameworks reveal the precarity intrinsic to capitalism and catalyse new discourses that affectively link genuine security to the transcendence of capitalist relations (Fraser, 2016).

The concept of UBI represents a direct challenge to the economic insecurity perpetuated by the AFC. By decoupling subsistence from wage labour, UBI mitigates the coercive power of capital over workers and fosters greater individual autonomy (Van Parijs and Vanderborght, 2017). As automation and technological disruption render increasing swaths of the population economically redundant, UBI offers a means of ensuring basic economic security and dignity without reliance on exploitative wage relations (Stern, 2016; Lowrey, 2018). Moreover, by alleviating poverty and reducing inequality, UBI has the potential to diminish the social tensions and political instability upon which authoritarian forces often prey (Hoynes and Rothstein, 2019). Beyond its immediate economic impacts, UBI also holds transformative potential by decoupling access to resources from the capitalist imperative of endless growth and valorization. By providing a guaranteed baseline of material security, UBI creates space for individuals to engage in socially reproductive activities – caring labour, community building, artistic expression – that are essential to human flourishing yet systematically devalued under capitalism. In this way, UBI opens up possibilities for alternative economic imaginaries and practices to take root, challenging the hegemony of the capitalist paradigm and its authoritarian corollaries.

The perspective of regenerative economics represents a further rupture from the extractive and exploitative logic of the AFC. Rooted in ecological principles and indigenous knowledge systems, regenerative economics envisions economic activity as deeply embedded within, and dependent upon, the regenerative capacities of the biosphere (Wahl, 2016; Raworth, 2017). Rather than pursuing endless growth at the expense of ecological and social systems, regenerative economics prioritizes the maintenance and restoration of the natural and social capital upon which all economic activity ultimately relies (Lovins et al, 2018). Through emphasizing holistic, place-based approaches to economic development, regenerative economics challenges the homogenizing and disruptive forces of global capitalism, which relentlessly disembed economic activity from local ecological and social contexts (Mang and Reed, 2012). Practices such as regenerative agriculture, circular production systems, and renewable energy, regenerative economics offers pathways for communities to assert greater economic self-determination and resilience in the face of the AFC's drive towards centralization and control (Fullerton, 2015). Moreover, regenerative economics recasts traditional conceptions of growth and development, centering indicators of holistic well-being – social equity, ecological integrity, cultural vitality – over narrow metrics of financial accumulation (Fath et al, 2019). In doing so, it subverts the ideological foundations of the AFC, which relies on the sacrosanct pursuit of gross domestic product growth to justify its extractive and exploitative practices.

The care economy, likewise, calls for a radical revaluation of this work, arguing that it should be recognized as a core economic activity and supported through robust public policies and institutional frameworks (Gibson-Graham et al, 2013). By reconfiguring economic priorities around the essential work of care, it subverts the AFC's fixation on profit maximization and capital accumulation. It redirects economic resources towards the nurturing and sustaining of human lives and communities, fostering resilience and solidarity in the face of capitalist precarity and authoritarian control (Hester, 2018). Additionally, by challenging the gendered division of labour and promoting more equitable distributions of care work, the caring economy undermines the patriarchal power structures that commonly undergird authoritarian regimes (Elson, 2017).

Crucially, the caring economy frames care not merely as a set of individual activities, but as a relational ethic that emphasizes interdependence, empathy, and responsibility towards others (Himmelweit, 2007). It nurtures, in this respect, an ethos of mutuality and collective well-being that stands in direct opposition to the atomizing and alienating forces of the AFC. By affirming the inherent dignity and worth of all human lives, the caring economy fortifies resistance to authoritarian ideologies of exploitation and dehumanization. Collectively, the perspectives of UBI, regenerative economics, and the caring economy represent powerful counter-narratives to the AFC's ideology of capitalist securitization. Rather than chasing the mirage of security through acquiescence to oppressive economic and political systems, these frameworks locate genuine security in the transcendence of capitalist relations and the embrace of more equitable, sustainable, and humane modes of collective provisioning. By revealing the intrinsic precarity and unsustainability of capitalism, these perspectives nurture revolutionary economic imaginaries that envision post-capitalist futures grounded in principles of universal dignity, ecological regeneration, and an ethic of care (Beltramini, 2021).

The progressive perspectives of UBI, regenerative economics, and the caring economy represent a dialectical movement in response to the precarity and insecurity perpetuated by the AFC. This movement arises from the fundamental human desire for security and stability, which the current capitalist order claims to provide through its narratives of securitization. However, the inherent contradictions and unsustainability of capitalism inevitably result in the very insecurity and exploitation that it purports to resolve. This dialectical tension between the promise of capitalist security and the reality of pervasive precarity generates a revolutionary impulse – a drive to imagine and construct alternative social and economic arrangements capable of fulfilling the genuine human need for security.

As such, these perspectives combine to individually and collectively challenge the material and discursive foundations of the AFC, eroding its legitimacy and catalysing new practices of resistance and solidarity. Ultimately, the struggle against the AFC is a struggle over the very paradigms and narratives that shape our collective understanding of security, prosperity, and the parameters of the possible. They perspectives emerge from the yearning for security and stability yet challenge the capitalist foundations that generate insecurity. By centring universal provisioning, ecological regeneration, and an ethic of care, these frameworks represent a synthesis – a revolutionary reconfiguration of economic relations and priorities aimed at transcending the precarity intrinsic to capitalism. In this dialectical process, the hegemonic investment in capitalist securitization is transformed into a search for new, emancipatory modes of collective security and well-being. The desire for security that once anchored capitalist hegemony is, thus, radically sublimated into a revolutionary force, catalysing the imagination and construction of post-capitalist, post-authoritarian social orders oriented towards genuine human flourishing.

Monitoring power

Sousveillance, a form of inverse surveillance, enables citizens to monitor and expose elites using digital technologies (Mann and Ferenbok, 2003). This bottom-up approach inverts the traditional panoptic gaze, undermining the plausible deniability of those in power and forcing them to confront their oppressive positions (Althusser, 1971). The widespread adoption of smartphones and wearable technologies has facilitated a 'generalized sousveillance society' (Ganascia, 2010), challenging traditional surveillance monopolies. Notable examples include viral videos of police brutality fuelling the Black Lives Matter movement (Boyd et al, 2021) and citizen journalists documenting human rights violations in authoritarian regimes, as seen during the 2009 Iranian Green Movement protests (Yesil, 2011).

Beyond simply recording injustices, sousveillance enables the crowdsourced compilation and analysis of data that can reveal systemic patterns of oppression and exploitation. For instance, abolitionist feminist scholars have utilized sousveillance tactics to expose the racist and sexist surveillance practices of the child welfare system, which disproportionately polices and separates families of colour under the guise of 'protection' (Michalsen, 2019). By aggregating multiple data points, sousveillance can render visible the invisible structures and networks underpinning intersecting systems of domination. Moreover, sousveillance provides a means of fostering collective resistance and mobilization around these uncovered injustices.

The dissemination of sousveillance footage and data via social media and online platforms allows, in turn, for the rapid sharing of information, coordination of protest actions, and construction of counter-narratives that challenge hegemonic discourses (Castells, 2012; Gerbaudo, 2012). Platforms like Twitter and Facebook, despite their own capitalistic motives, have been pivotal in allowing dispersed individuals and communities to coalesce into 'networked social movements' capable of exerting disruptive pressure on power structures (Juris, 2012; Kavada, 2015). This harnessing of 'hybrid spaces' that blend digital networks with physical activism has proven essential for movements like Occupy Wall Street and Black Lives Matter in amplifying their messages, garnering solidarity, and enacting forms of 'cloud protesting' that transcend geographical boundaries (Milan, 2013; Tufekci, 2017). The viral spread of hashtags like #BlackLivesMatter has enabled these movements to assert narrative agency and engage in 'storytelling' that counters dominant framings of racism and police violence (Yang, 2016).

However, it is crucial to recognize that sousveillance and digital activism are not inherently emancipatory or immune to co-optation and repression. The rise of 'lateral surveillance' – where citizens monitor and report on each other's behaviour – can reinforce, for instance, existing power structures and sow cultures of suspicion that undermine solidarity (Reeves, 2012). Additionally, state and corporate actors have rapidly adapted to the threat posed by sousveillance, employing tactics like surveillance of social media, data mining, and algorithmic suppression to neutralize online dissent and manage public discourse (Tufekci, 2017). Furthermore, the increasing corporate control and commercialization of digital platforms pose significant challenges for movements seeking to leverage these spaces for resistance (Cammaerts, 2012).

The profit-driven logics and opaque algorithms of platform companies can, furthermore, inhibit the spread of counter-narratives and reinforce dominant ideological framings. While populations are subject to intensifying surveillance and monitoring, the activities of powerful elites often remain obscured and unaccountable. Nonetheless, the potential of sousveillance and digital activism to expose injustice, cultivate critical consciousness, and mobilize collective action remains formidable. By inverting the traditional flows of surveillance and rendering power visible, sousveillance subverts the AFC's efforts to naturalize and obscure systems of domination. It represents a crucial tactic in the broader struggle to build more equitable, democratic, and transparent societies. Realizing this emancipatory potential, however, requires developing robust strategies for resistance that circumvent corporate and state control over digital infrastructures. This may entail constructing decentralized, community-governed platforms and communication networks, as well as fostering digital literacy and data sovereignty among marginalized communities.

Additionally, sousveillance must be coupled with sustained on-the-ground organizing, direct action, and the construction of alternative institutions capable of enacting substantive social and political transformations. The revolutionary implications of sousveillance lie not merely in its ability to document and expose wrongdoing, but in its capacity to catalyse processes of radical subject formation. It opens a space for the emergence of new, emancipated subjectivities premised on principles of collective liberation, autonomy, and radical democracy. In this sense, sousveillance exists as a crucial front in the broader struggle against the alienating and dehumanizing forces of capital, state oppression, and intersecting matrices of domination. By rendering visible the invisible, sousveillance lays bare the contradictions and injustices inherent to these systems, creating opportunities for marginalized populations to reclaim their agency, assert their voices, and mobilize towards alternative social arrangements rooted in equity, accountability, and self-determination.

Through facilitating processes of critical consciousness-raising and collective narrative construction, digital activism enables marginalized populations to mount a direct challenge to the AFC's hegemony over meaning-making. Hashtag mobilizations and viral audiovisual materials assert counter-narratives that reject the dehumanizing interpellations imposed by regimes of power. They reframe technological 'progress' not as an inexorable, universally beneficial phenomenon, but as a site of contestation over society's fundamental social, political, and economic configurations. Through this process, sousveillance and digital resistance nurture the germination of new political subjectivities premised on values of autonomy, horizontal solidarity, and collective self-determination. They provide the necessary preconditions for envisaging and actualizing radically divergent socio-technical assemblages that prioritize liberatory ends over the perpetuation of alienated production and consumption. By transforming instruments of oppression into implements of liberation, these practices bear revolutionary implications – not merely in their capacity to reform extant systems, but in their ability to catalyse the transcendence of the ideological foundations upholding the AFC itself.

Viral democracy

Digital technologies have reshaped democracy and civic engagement, often reinforcing surveillance and control by the AFC (Tang, 2020) while also harbouring emancipatory potential. This complex of state and market actors uses digital infrastructures to entrench power hierarchies and securitize populations (Pohle and Thiel, 2020; Stoycheff et al, 2020). However, the decentralized nature of digital networks offers opportunities for more direct forms of democracy (Boyte, 2020; Skaržauskienė and Mačiulienė, 2020), enabling collaborative problem-solving and grassroots mobilization (Aichholzer and Rose, 2020; Artyushina, 2020). This potential requires a shift from 'deliberative democracy' to a vision empowering citizens as active co-creators in policy design and implementation (Franks, 2021).

Initiatives like the WeBuildAI framework embody efforts to democratize artificial intelligence governance through stakeholder involvement, challenging the centralization of control over digital infrastructures (Hintz, 2021). Citizen assemblies for algorithmic governance offer forums for deliberation on data and artificial intelligence ethics issues, though they face challenges in ensuring inclusive participation (Hintz, 2021). Digital democracy also enables new forms of worker resistance against workplace surveillance and datafication (Moore, 2019; Taylor and Dobbins, 2021). Workers can use social media and sousveillance tactics to counter employer surveillance and assert agency (Webb, 2020), while trade unions must develop strategies to resist surveillance technologies and promote accountability through collective bargaining and worker privacy advocacy (Moore, 2019).

The hacker culture's emphasis on transparency and decentralization offers a framework for advancing digital democracy (Webb, 2020), with tactics like encryption and data leaks challenging surveillance systems (Ulbricht, 2020). However, limitations and risks of hacker activism necessitate building bridges with broader social movements (Webb, 2020). Realizing this emancipatory potential requires addressing digital divides (Gauja, 2021; Papacharissi, 2021) and interrogating biases in digital platforms (Ford et al, 2021a). A 'new materialist' perspective (Asenbaum, 2021) emphasizes corporeal experiences in shaping online political subjectivities, illuminating how digital technologies influence political agency and participation (Deseriis, 2021).

Realizing robust digital democracy requires integrating technological innovation with broader societal transformations (Berg and Hofmann, 2021; Wilson and Tewdwr-Jones, 2021), developing digital literacy and civic engagement (White, 2020; Kwon et al, 2021), and fostering understanding of digital rights and citizenship (Pangrazio and Sefton-Green, 2021). This holistic approach can challenge the AFC, creating a more participatory democratic order where citizens are active co-creators of society (Mačiulienė and Skaržauskienė, 2020; Saud and Margono, 2021). Examples include digital participatory planning in urban governance (Wilson and Tewdwr-Jones, 2021) and platforms in Madrid and Barcelona enabling citizens to influence municipal policies and budgets through open-source, commons-based approaches (Smith and Martín, 2022).

Digital democracy platforms reflect tensions between governability and demands for equality, with tools like Decidim.viz aiming to democratize data and enable community-driven improvements. These technologies expand democracy's scope, fostering collective decision-making and cooperative action beyond passive deliberation. Data analytics and civic tech could enable evidence-based decision-making and equitable resource allocation, redefining the demos as an interconnected collective committed to participatory self-determination. This vision transcends national boundaries, empowering marginalized populations and renegotiating power relations, shifting from profitable policing to shared stewardship of our collective future.

Digital infrastructures enabling 'societies of control' also contain potential for transition to 'societies of collective freedom' by inscribing democratic principles into daily life. Rather than concentrating power in elite bodies, digital networks can disperse it among an interconnected multitude, embedding democracy into mundane routines and tools. Apps, platforms, and data streams could become catalysts for decentralized coordination and value creation, with automated systems open to collective scrutiny and participatory refinement. This evolution transforms democracy from a stagnant framework into a dynamic culture of empowerment, rooted in recursive dialogue and cooperative world-building, perpetually reinventing modalities of shared governance for collective benefit and greater freedom.

Radicalizing finance

Decentralized finance and cryptocurrencies have offered a catalyst for reimagining finance and exchange beyond traditional systems, in ways that both reinforce existing hyper-capitalist ideologies and can potentially radically challenge them. Blockchain-based financial instruments like tokenized securities enable increased transparency, liquidity, and accessibility, mobilizing private capital for sustainable development projects (Schletz et al, 2020). Initiatives such as the Bank of Bob represent 'anticipatory infrastructures' that prefigure a post-capitalist future by enabling peer-to-peer transactions and challenging the dominance of traditional financial institutions (Ulfstjerne, 2020). However, while cryptocurrencies hold the potential to promote individual autonomy, they also risk reinforcing existing power structures and enabling new forms of surveillance and control (Malabou, 2020).

These diverse efforts at decentralizing and democratizing finance through new digital technologies, the sharing economy, and solidarity economy movements represent processes of 'decomplexification' – counter-processes that seek to undo the socially manufactured pathological fixations perpetuated by the AFC. While capitalist finance has sought to represent itself as the sole means to 'fund' individual and collective desires, these alternative perspectives and initiatives demonstrate alternative routes through which to materially realize shared and diverse aspirations. The modern state serves as an 'operating system' enabling the functioning of capitalism and domination, perpetuating inequality and oppression (Laursen, 2021). In contrast, these initiatives challenge the notion that capitalist finance is the only way to 'fund' our desires, offering alternative routes for realizing our shared and diverse aspirations.

Scholars have engaged critically with these emerging technologies, analysing their limitations and risks while exploring their transformative potential. A framework has been developed for evaluating blockchain applications' capacity to reduce resource consumption, promote social equity, and enable democratic participation (Howson, 2021). The intersection of blockchain and data justice has been examined, underscoring the challenges of ensuring privacy, security, and equity in system design and governance (Semenzin, 2021). These analyses underscore the need for continual innovation and adaptation across diverse cultural and political contexts to realize the emancipatory potential of these technologies.

The sharing economy has similarly been posited as a potential avenue for promoting more sustainable consumption patterns and community empowerment. Its potential for reducing overconsumption has been analysed, while acknowledging risks such as reinforcing inequalities and negative environmental impacts (Lai and Ho, 2020). Leveraging the sharing economy to improve public services and social inclusion has been explored, emphasizing the importance of appropriate regulation and governance frameworks (Pallesen and Aakjær, 2020). However, critical perspectives have emerged, questioning the emancipatory potential of the sharing economy. The paradox of sharing platforms disrupting traditional economic relations while simultaneously reproducing capitalist power structures has been highlighted (Acquier et al, 2017). The notion of the digital commons has been critiqued, arguing that online alternative economies often obscure underlying capitalist relations of production, perpetuating a form of 'false consciousness' (Ossewaarde and Reijers, 2017).

The solidarity economy, grounded in principles of cooperation, reciprocity, and collective ownership, represents another pathway for challenging capitalist economic relations. The solidarity economy in Bolivia and its potential for promoting women's emancipation and development as a viable alternative to capitalist development models has been examined (Hillenkamp, 2015). The social and solidarity economy has been explored as a means of emancipation from capitalist relations, while acknowledging the risk of reproducing those relations in different forms (Marques, 2014). Initiatives like FairCoop demonstrate the possibilities and challenges of building digital commons and post-capitalist alternatives through practices such as developing their own cryptocurrency and alternative digital banking infrastructures (Rasillo, 2023). Engaging with tensions, hierarchies, and democratic deficits is crucial when studying the present and future of digital commoning.

While offering alternative routes for realizing shared aspirations, scholars have critically examined the limitations and contradictions of these initiatives. Argentina's barter network has been critiqued as representing a form of petty capitalism rather than a true alternative to capitalist relations. The critique has been extended to the digital commons, asserting that online alternative economies often reproduce capitalist production relations, obscuring underlying structures of power and oppression (Ossewaarde and Reijers, 2017). The emergence of 'cryptoeconomics' and the rise of 'hacker-engineers' building decentralized economic systems based on principles of transparency and self-sovereignty carry vulnerabilities such as susceptibility to speculative bubbles, market manipulation, and risks of co-optation by capitalist interests (Brekke, 2021). The need to re-examine the respective roles of markets and institutions in pursuing broader normative goals beyond mere efficiency has been emphasized when evaluating the purported 'democratization' of finance through decentralized finance and fintech platforms (White, 2023).

A 'counter-hegemonic computing' framework centring marginalized communities' experiences and prioritizing social value creation over profit maximization may offer a path towards more equitable and emancipatory forms of technological development (Eglash et al, 2021). Initiatives like FairCoop, and the broader decentralization and democratization of finance, represent multifaceted landscapes where the potential for emancipation and the creation of alternative economic models coexist with the risks of reproducing power structures and new forms of oppression. Continual innovation and adaptation across diverse contexts are needed for these 'decomplexification' processes challenging the AFC.

These different strategies at decentralizing and democratizing finance represent a direct challenge to the AFC that has long dominated economic and political systems. The AFC refers to the intricate web of powerful institutions, vested interests, and entrenched hierarchies that have perpetuated a system of economic exploitation, social control, and concentrated power. Traditional finance, with its centralized banking systems, opaque decision-making processes, and prioritization of profit over societal well-being, has served as a key pillar of this complex, enabling the accumulation of wealth and influence in the hands of a few while marginalizing the needs and aspirations of the broader populace. The decentralization of finance through technologies like blockchain and cryptocurrencies challenges this concentration of power by enabling peer-to-peer transactions, transparent record-keeping, and decentralized governance models.

The sharing economy and solidarity economy movements disrupt the AFC by promoting alternative economic relations rooted in principles of cooperation, reciprocity, and collective ownership. By rejecting the profit-driven logic of capitalism, these movements seek to dismantle the systemic exploitation and inequalities perpetuated by the AFC. Reflected, in turn, is a growing recognition that the current economic and political order, dominated by the AFC, is unsustainable and unjust. They embody a collective yearning for a more equitable, democratic, and ecologically sustainable future, one in which economic power is decentralized, decision-making processes are transparent, and the well-being of communities and the planet takes precedence over the accumulation of wealth and power.

However, the process of dismantling this entrenched complex cannot be reduced to a monolithic or linear trajectory. Instead, it necessitates a continual process of 'decomplexification' – a counter-movement aimed at unravelling the socially manufactured pathological fixations that have become deeply ingrained within our economic and political systems. This 'decomplexification' is inherently dynamic, requiring constant innovation and adaptation to navigate the diverse cultural and political contexts in which these alternative initiatives operate. The sharing economy, for instance, may hold emancipatory potential in certain socio-cultural contexts, yet risk reinforcing existing inequalities and power asymmetries in others. Cryptocurrencies, while offering a path towards financial inclusion in regions with underdeveloped banking infrastructure, could simultaneously enable new forms of surveillance and control in societies with authoritarian tendencies. The solidarity economy's emphasis on cooperation and collective ownership may resonate profoundly in communities with strong traditions of mutual aid, while facing resistance in contexts where individualistic values predominate.

This diversity of contexts necessitates a continuous process of innovation and adaptation, as initiatives like FairCoop and others confront the tensions, hierarchies, and democratic deficits that inevitably emerge within their alternative economic models. Sustained engagement with local communities, critical self-reflection, and a willingness to modify practices and governance structures are essential for these 'decomplexification' processes to effectively challenge the AFC in a meaningful and enduring manner. Moreover, the AFC itself is not a static monolith, but rather a dynamic and ever-evolving system that adapts to new challenges and co-opts potential threats. Consequently, the processes of 'decomplexification' must also evolve, constantly seeking new avenues for resistance and liberation, and remaining vigilant against the insidious ways in which the complex can reassert its dominance through co-optation or subversion. In this ongoing struggle, the sharing of knowledge, experiences, and best practices across diverse cultural and political contexts becomes crucial. By fostering global networks of collaboration and mutual learning, these initiatives can collectively innovate and adapt, drawing strength from their diversity while remaining unified in their commitment to building a more just, equitable, and sustainable economic order that challenges the AFC.

Breaking free from the authoritarian–financial complex

Societies today face a formidable challenge in confronting the AFC, a system that wields immense power through the consolidation of state authority and capitalist exploitation. However, a diverse array of emancipatory movements and practices have emerged, offering radical alternatives and envisioning a world beyond the confines of this oppressive order. These movements not only articulate a compelling vision for the future but also provide concrete pathways for individuals and communities to actively participate in the dismantling of authoritarian and capitalist structures.

At the forefront of these struggles is the resurgence of abolitionist perspectives, which have begun to open up new possibilities for a society without the coercive institutions of policing and incarceration (Walcott, 2021). Rooted in a rich historical legacy of resistance against slavery and oppression, contemporary abolitionist movements are reclaiming the radical potential of abolition as a transformative project that challenges the very foundations of racial capitalism and the carceral state (Walcott, 2021). By exposing the entangled histories of property, policing, and incarceration, abolitionists are imagining alternative forms of social and economic relations that transcend the violence and dispossession inherent in the current system.

Abolitionists recognize that the dismantling of oppressive institutions cannot be achieved through mere reform or piecemeal change; rather, it demands a fundamental restructuring of society itself. Traditional approaches to abolition are insufficient for addressing the complex and global nature of contemporary forms of exploitation, necessitating a new framework of 'neo-abolitionism' that encompasses legal and policy reforms, economic empowerment, and cultural transformations (Ellerman, 2021). This holistic vision reflects a novel theory and practice of abolition in the context of decarceration and social justice focusing on the need not just for dismantling the prison–industrial complex but about building new forms of community safety, well-being, and collective liberation (Montford and Taylor, 2021).

Parallel to the abolitionist movement, community wealth building strategies have emerged as a powerful force for transitioning beyond the exploitative logic of capitalism (Lizárraga, 2020). These initiatives prioritize local ownership, community control, and the equitable distribution of economic benefits, offering a concrete alternative to the extractive models of traditional economic development. By fostering democratic ownership and redirecting resources towards local communities, community wealth building has the potential to create a more just and sustainable economy rooted in the principles of economic democracy and self-determination.

Community wealth building, to this end, has the potential to repair the harms of systemic racism and address long-standing inequalities (see Hanna and Kelly, 2021). Through case studies like the 'Preston model' in the UK, they demonstrate how community-led initiatives can revitalize local economies, promote inclusive decision-making, and challenge the concentration of wealth and power in the hands of global corporations (Manley and Whyman, 2021). Crucially, these strategies not only offer economic empowerment but also a profound shift in values and priorities, centering the well-being of communities over the relentless pursuit of profit.

In a different yet complementary vein, the emergence of hacktivism and digital activism has revealed the transformative potential of technology as a tool for subverting and exposing the forces that control and exploit populations (Romagna, 2020; Yonita and Darmawan, 2021). Hacktivists and digital activists have leveraged the power of the internet and digital tools to challenge authoritarian regimes, expose corporate malpractice, and amplify the voices of marginalized communities. From the decentralized collective Anonymous to the Ukrainian IT Army's efforts against Russian aggression, these movements have demonstrated the capacity of digital activism to disrupt and undermine the structures of economic and political power.

However, the role of hacktivism and digital activism in emancipatory struggles is complex and multifaceted (Cornelius, 2022; Conduit, 2023). While these movements have the potential to catalyse social and political change, they also raise ethical and legal questions around anonymity, accountability, and the potential for misuse or co-optation by authoritarian forces. Nonetheless, the subversive power of digital technologies cannot be ignored, as they offer new avenues for challenging the hegemony of the AFC and undermining the mechanisms of control and exploitation.

It is important to acknowledge, however, that these emancipatory movements are not monolithic or without their own internal contradictions and challenges. Alternative economic projects and digital commoning initiatives often grapple with issues of governance, transparency, and the reproduction of hierarchies and inequalities (Atarah et al, 2023; Rasillo, 2023). Similarly, the decentralized and grassroots nature of abolitionist organizing can pose challenges in terms of coalition-building, longevity, and accessibility (Carrera et al, 2023). These tensions and limitations underscore the need for ongoing critical reflection and a willingness to confront the complexities of building truly emancipatory alternatives.

Critically, what unites these diverse movements, though, is not merely their shared opposition to oppressive systems but their ability to offer tangible practices and experiences that allow individuals and communities to affectively invest in new identities and modes of being directly aimed at dismantling the authoritarian–financial order. Through their engagement in abolitionist organizing, community wealth building initiatives, and digital activism, people are given the opportunity to embody and enact alternative forms of social, economic, and political relations (Dowin Kennedy, 2021; Phelps et al, 2021). These movements provide spaces for collective jouissance, to invoke Lacanian terminology, where individuals can derive pleasure and satisfaction from actively participating in the subversion of the dominant order and the construction of emancipatory alternatives. By fostering a sense of agency, solidarity, and collective empowerment, these practices enable a profound shift in subjective identifications, challenging the internalized narratives of individualism, competition, and security that underpin the AFC (Chua, 2020; Nunnally, 2020).

In this regard, the emancipatory potential of these movements lies not only in their ability to envision a world beyond authoritarian control and capitalist exploitation but also in their capacity to create lived experiences that challenge the psychic and material investments in the current order. Through their engagement in abolitionist struggles, community wealth building, and digital activism, individuals and communities are afforded the opportunity to construct new subjectivities and forms of collective life that directly undermine the AFC's grip on their psyches and material realities. Rather than being interpellated as passive consumers, surveilled subjects, or sources of exploitable labour-power, these movements enable people to embrace new subjected positions as liberators, community builders, and digital dissidents. In this process, the seductive fantasies peddled by the AFC – of security through control, fulfillment through consumption, freedom through wage labour – are actively subverted and resignified.

Through materially embodying and enacting alternative social, economic, and technological relations, individuals and communities can derive immense psychic gratification from the very act of refusing and dismantling the systems of oppression that previously governed their existence. The abolitionist rejecting the violence of the carceral state, the community wealth builder redistributing resources and power at a local level, the hacktivist breaching digital enclosures – each represents a direct affront to the ideological and libidinal economy of the status quo. Consequently, these movements do not merely offer compelling counter-narratives, but provide the practical means for individuals to invest their desires, energies, and identities into tangible emancipatory praxis. The alienation, precarity and disempowerment engendered by commodified technological control finds its antithesis in the experiences of solidarity, self-determination, and jouissance enabled by these new modes of collective political subjectivation.

Paradoxically, it is in this act of challenging control and imagining a world without the false promises of security and stability that true emancipation becomes possible. By actively participating in the dismantling of oppressive systems and the construction of alternative institutions and social relations, individuals and communities can find a sense of security and well-being that transcends the limited horizons of the AFC (Guinan and O'Neill, 2019). The collective efforts of these diverse movements represent a profound challenge to the AFC and its mechanisms of control and exploitation. By offering not just a compelling vision for the future but also concrete practices and experiences that allow individuals and communities to actively participate in the subversion of oppressive systems, these movements hold the promise of a radical transformation of social, economic, and political relations.

The struggles to break free from this complex are multifaceted and ongoing, but the resurgence of abolitionist perspectives, community wealth building strategies, and hacktivism has opened up new possibilities for emancipation. By offering tangible pathways for individuals and communities to invest in new identities and modes of being, these movements have the potential to unleash a profound shift in subjective and material realities, challenging the very foundations of authoritarian control and capitalist exploitation. They represent a powerful force for imagining and creating a world beyond the confines of ever-expanding control.

The AFC perpetuates itself through a seductive narrative that equates security with control – the more comprehensively we surveil, regulate, and dominate social and technological systems, the greater our supposed safety. Yet the emancipatory movements challenging this order reveal a profound paradox: true psychic and material security can only be achieved by dismantling, rather than fortifying, the regimes of control that strive to render the world predictable and containable. By opening spaces to imagine radical alternatives that transcend the stultifying logic of commodification and enclosure, these movements unlock new subjective and existential possibilities foreclosed by the financial-authoritarian paradigm. The abolitionist's recognition that police and prisons are sources of terror rather than public safety; the community wealth builder's faith in the regenerative capacities of the local commons over globalized extractivism; the hacktivist's defiance of proprietary digital hierarchies – each of these represents a shift towards an epistemology of security-through-openness.

Hence, the new revolutionary movements of our time must directly challenge and replace the pathological and insatiable desire for capitalist repression. Rather, they must transform psychic and material security so that it stems not from tightening one's grip, but from loosening it; not from the illusion of total security, but from an embrace of contingency, interdependence, and becoming. The more individuals and communities can release their attachments to the authoritarian fantasy of absolute knowledge and control, the more capacity they cultivate for authentic self-determination, mutual care, and worldly co-flourishing. In doing so, we can abolish the underlying economic, social, and political precarity that perpetuates these profitable systems for a world of genuine security and possibility.

References

Aalbers, M.B., Rolnik, R., and Krijnen, M. (2020). The financialization of housing in capitalism's peripheries. *Housing Policy Debate*, 30(4), 481–485.

Abbink, J. and Hagmann, T. (2016). *Reconfiguring Ethiopia: The politics of authoritarian reform*. Routledge.

Abbott, D.P. (1996). *Rhetoric in the New World: Rhetorical theory and practice in colonial Spanish America*. University of South Carolina Press.

Abdolali, N. and Ward, D.S. (1998). The Senate Armed Services Committee and defense budget making: The role of deference, dollars, and ideology. *Journal of Political & Military Sociology*, 26(2), 229–252.

Abdukadirov, S. (ed) (2016). *Nudge theory in action: Behavioral design in policy and markets*. Springer.

Acosta, A. (2013). Extractivism and neoextractivism: Two sides of the same curse. In M. Lang and D. Mokrani (eds), *Beyond development* (pp 61–86). Routledge.

Acquier, A., Daudigeos, T., and Pinkse, J. (2017). Promises and paradoxes of the sharing economy: An organizing framework. *Technological Forecasting and Social Change*, 125, 1–10.

Adams, W. (1968). The military-industrial complex and the new industrial state. *The American Economic Review*, 58(2), 652–665.

Adams, W. and Adams, W.J. (1972). The military-industrial complex: A market structure analysis. *The American Economic Review*, 62(1/2), 279–287.

Adeney, M. and Lloyd, D. (1986). *Loss without limit: The miners' strike of 1984–5*. RKP.

Adkins, L. and Dever, M. (2018). Gender and labour in new times: An introduction. In L. Adkins and M. Dever (eds), *Gender and labour in new times* (pp 1–11). Routledge.

Admati, A. and Hellwig, M. (2014). *The bankers' new clothes: What's wrong with banking and what to do about it*. Princeton University Press.

Aichholzer, G. and Rose, G. (2020). Experience with digital tools in different types of e-participation. In L. Hennen, I. Van Keulen, I. Korthagen, G. Aichholzer, R. Lindner, and R.Ø. Nielsen (eds), *European e-democracy in practice* (pp 93–140). Springer.

"

Aitken, R. (2011). Financializing security: Political prediction markets and the commodification of uncertainty. *Security Dialogue*, 42(2), 123–141.

Ajana, B. (2018). Communal self-tracking: Data philanthropy, solidarity and privacy. In B. Ajana (eds), *Self-tracking* (pp 125–141). Palgrave Macmillan, Cham.

Akbari, A. (2021). Authoritarian surveillance: A corona test. *Surveillance & Society*, 19(1), 98–103.

Akesson, B. and Badawi, D. (2020). 'My heart feels chained': The effects of economic precarity on Syrian refugee parents living in Lebanon. In C.W. Greenbaum, M.M. Haj-Yahia, and C. Hamilton (eds), *Political violence toward children: Psychological effects, intervention and prevention policy* (pp 301–322). Oxford University Press.

Alberti, G., Bessa, I., Hardy, K., Trappmann, V., and Umney, C. (2018). In, against and beyond precarity: Work in insecure times. *Work, Employment and Society*, 32(3), 447–457.

Albertus, M. and Menaldo, V. (2018). *Authoritarianism and the elite origins of democracy*. Cambridge University Press.

Alho, P.M. (2006). Collective complexes: Total perspectives. *Journal of Analytical Psychology*, 51(5), 661–680.

Allen, J.A. (2019). The color of algorithms: An analysis and proposed research agenda for deterring algorithmic redlining. *Fordham Urban Law Journal*, 46, 219.

Aloisi, A. and Gramano, E. (2020). Workers without workplaces and unions without unity: Non-standard forms of employment, platform work and collective bargaining. In *Employment relations for the 21st century* (pp 37–59).

Alschuler, L. (2009). The politics of complexes. *Psychotherapy and Politics International*, 7(2), 108–121.

Althusser, L. (1969). *For Marx* (B. Brewster, trans). Vintage.

Althusser, L. (1971). Ideology and ideological state apparatuses (notes towards an investigation). In *Lenin and philosophy and other essays* (pp 127–186). Monthly Review Press.

Althusser, L. (2000). Ideology interpellates individuals as subjects. *Identity: A Reader*, 31–38.

Althusser, L. (2012). *Ideology & ideological state apparatuses: Notes towards an investigation*. Critical Quest.

Althusser, L. (2014). *On the reproduction of capitalism: Ideology and ideological state apparatuses*. Verso Books.

Amar, P. (2013). *The security archipelago: Human-security states, sexuality politics, and the end of neoliberalism*. Duke University Press.

Amicelle, A. (2017). When finance met security: Back to the war on drugs and the problem of dirty money. *Finance and Society*, 3(2), 106–123.

Amicelle, A. and Favarel-Garrigues, G. (2012). Financial surveillance: Who cares? *Journal of Cultural Economy*, 5(1), 105–124.

Amin, G.A. (1976). Dependent development. *Alternatives*, 2(4), 379–403.

Amnesty International (2016). This is what we die for: Human rights abuses in the Democratic Republic of the Congo power the global trade in cobalt.

Amnesty International (2021a). The repression trade: Investigating the transfer of weapons used to crush dissent.

Amnesty International (2021b). Surveillance giants: How the business model of Google and Facebook threatens human rights.

Amnesty International (2023). The repression trade: Investigating the transfer of weapons used to crush dissent. 11 October. https://www.amnesty.org/en/latest/research/2023/10/repression-trade/

Amott, T. and Krieger, J. (1982). Thatcher and Reagan: State theory and the 'hyper-capitalist' regime. *New Political Science*, 2(4), 9–37.

Andrejevic, M. (2007). Surveillance in the digital enclosure. *The Communication Review*, 10(4), 295–317.

Anwar, M.A. and Graham, M. (2021). Between a rock and a hard place: Freedom, flexibility, precarity and vulnerability in the gig economy in Africa. *Competition & Change*, 25(2), 237–258.

Apaydin, F. and Çoban, M.K. (2023). The political consequences of dependent financialization: Capital flows, crisis and the authoritarian turn in Turkey. *Review of International Political Economy*, 30(3), 1046–1072.

Apostolopoulou, E. (2021). A novel geographical research agenda on Silk Road urbanisation. *The Geographical Journal*, 187(4), 386–393.

Appleyard, L., Rowlingson, K., and Gardner, J. (2016). The variegated financialization of sub-prime credit markets. *Competition & Change*, 20(5), 297–313.

Arduino, A. (2020). The footprint of Chinese private security companies in Africa (No. 2020/35). Working Paper.

Arora, P. (2016). Bottom of the data pyramid: Big data and the global south. *International Journal of Communication*, 10, 19.

Arrighi, G. (1994). *The long twentieth century: Money, power, and the origins of our times.* Verso.

Arrigo, B.A. (2001). Transcarceration: A constitutive ethnography of mentally ill 'offenders'. *The Prison Journal*, 81(2), 162–186.

Arsel, M., Hogenboom, B., and Pellegrini, L. (2016). The extractive imperative in Latin America. *The Extractive Industries and Society*, 3(4), 880–887.

Artyushina, A. (2020). Is civic data governance the key to democratic smart cities? The role of the urban data trust in Sidewalk Toronto. *Telematics and Informatics*, 55, 101456.

Arvidsson, A. and Peitersen, N. (2013). *The ethical economy: Rebuilding value after the crisis.* Columbia University Press.

Ascher, I., Hardin, C., Klein, S., Montgomerie, J., and Rosamond, E. (2022). Finance and the financialization of capitalism. In A. Azmanova and J. Chamberlain (eds), *Capitalism, democracy, socialism: Critical debates* (pp 71–97). Springer International Publishing.

Asenbaum, H. (2021). The politics of becoming: Disidentification as radical democratic practice. *European Journal of Social Theory*, 24(1), 86–104.

Ashiagbor, D. (2021). From digital authoritarianism to platforms' Leviathan power: Freedom of expression in the digital age under siege in Africa. *Mizan Law Review*, 15(2), 455–492.

Aspaturian, V.V. (1972). The Soviet military-industrial complex: Does it exist? *Journal of International Affairs*, 26(1), 1–28.

Atarah, B.A., Finotto, V., Nolan, E., and van Stel, A. (2023). Entrepreneurship as emancipation: A process framework for female entrepreneurs in resource-constrained environments. *Journal of Small Business and Enterprise Development*, 30(4), 734–758.

Ayalew, Y.E. (2021). From digital authoritarianism to platforms' leviathan power: Freedom of expression in the digital age under siege in Africa. *Mizan Law Review*, 15(2), 455–492.

Baack, B. and Ray, E. (1985). The political economy of the origins of the military-industrial complex in the United States. *The Journal of Economic History*, 45(2), 369–375.

Bagley, B.M. (1988). The new hundred years war? US national security and the war on drugs in Latin America. *Journal of Interamerican Studies and World Affairs*, 30(1), 161–182.

Baines, G. (2019). The arsenal of securocracy: Pretoria's provision of arms and aid to Salisbury, c. 1974–1980. *South African Historical Journal*, 71(3), 423–441.

Baird, T. (2016). Surveillance design communities in Europe: A network analysis. *Surveillance & Society*, 14(1), 34–58.

Bak, D., Sriyai, S., and Meserve, S.A. (2018). The internet and state repression: A cross-national analysis of the limits of digital constraint. *Journal of Human Rights*, 17(5), 642–659.

Bakker, I. and Gill, S. (2019). Rethinking power, production, and social reproduction: Toward variegated social reproduction. *Capital & Class*, 43(4), 503–523.

Ball, K. (2017). All consuming surveillance: Surveillance as marketplace icon. *Consumption Markets & Culture*, 20(2), 95–100.

Ball, K. (2021). *Electronic monitoring and surveillance in the workplace*. European Commission Joint Research Centre.

Banaji, J. (1977). Modes of production in a materialist conception of history. *Capital & Class*, 1(3), 1–44.

Banerjee, S.B. (2003). Who sustains whose development? Sustainable development and the reinvention of nature. *Organization Studies*, 24(1), 143–180.

Banki, S. (2016). Precarity of place: A complement to the growing precariat literature. In M. Johnson (ed), *Precariat: Labour, work and politics* (pp 66–79). Routledge.

Baran, P.A. (1968). *Political economy of growth* (vol 76). New York University Press.

Bargu, B. (ed) (2019). *Turkey's necropolitical laboratory: Democracy, violence and resistance.* Edinburgh University Press.

Barnes, T.J. (2008). Geography's underworld: The military–industrial complex, mathematical modelling and the quantitative revolution. *Geoforum*, 39(1), 3–16.

Basiru, A.A. and Akinboye, S.O. (2018). A democratic developmental state in post-authoritarian Nigeria? Issues and prospects. *Jebat: Malaysian Journal of History, Politics & Strategic Studies*, 45(1), 34–55.

Bastani, A. (2019). *Fully automated luxury communism: A manifesto.* Verso Books.

Bautista, V.F. (2018). The pervert's guide to historical revisionism: Traversing the Marcos fantasy. *Philippine Studies: Historical & Ethnographic Viewpoints*, 66(3), 273–300.

Bebbington, A. (2009). The new extraction: Rewriting the political ecology of the Andes? *NACLA Report on the Americas*, 42(5), 12–20.

Beckett, K. (1999). *Making crime pay: Law and order in contemporary American politics.* Oxford University Press.

Beer, A., Bentley, R., Baker, E., Mason, K., Mallett, S., Kavanagh, A., et al (2016). Neoliberalism, economic restructuring and policy change: Precarious housing and precarious employment in Australia. *Urban Studies*, 53(8), 1542–1558.

Beltramini, E. (2021). The cryptoanarchist character of Bitcoin's digital governance. *Anarchist Studies*, 29(2), 75–99.

Bennett, D. (2017). Metaphors of desire: Neoliberalism and libidinal economy. *English Language and Literature*, 63(1), 3–21.

Berberoglu, B. (ed) (2020). *The global rise of authoritarianism in the 21st century: Crisis of neoliberal globalization and the nationalist response.* Routledge.

Berg, S. and Hofmann, J. (2021). Digital democracy. *Internet Policy Review*, 10(4).

Berlant, L. (2011). *Cruel optimism.* Duke University Press.

Berman, B.J. and Tettey, W.J. (2001). African states, bureaucratic culture and computer fixes. *Public Administration and Development: The International Journal of Management Research and Practice*, 21(1), 1–13.

Bernard, R., Bowsher, G., and Sullivan, R. (2020). COVID-19 and the rise of participatory SIGINT: An examination of the rise in government surveillance through mobile applications. *American Journal of Public Health*, 110(12), 1780–1785.

Bernards, N. (2019). The poverty of fintech? Psychometrics, credit infrastructures, and the limits of financialization. *Review of International Political Economy*, 26(5), 815–838.

Bernards, N. (2020). Centring labour in financialization. *Globalizations*, 17(4), 714–729.

Bernstein, M.A. and Wilson, M.R. (2011). New perspectives on the history of the military–industrial complex. *Enterprise & Society*, 12(1), 1–9.

Berson, I.R. (2015). *Computable bodies: Instrumented life and the human somatic niche*. Bloomsbury Publishing.

Bhatia, A. and Bhabha, J. (2017). India's Aadhaar scheme and the promise of inclusive social protection. *Oxford Development Studies*, 45(1), 64–79.

Biebricher, T. (2020). Neoliberalism and authoritarianism. *Global Perspectives*, 1(1), 11872.

Bielefeld, S., Harb, J., and Henne, K. (2021). Financialization and welfare surveillance: Regulating the poor in technological times. *Critical Social Policy*, 41(3), 445–465.

Birch, K. (2017). Financing technoscience: Finance, assetization and rentiership. In D. Tyfield, R. Lave, S. Randalls, and C. Thorpe (eds), *The Routledge handbook of the political economy of science* (pp 169–181). Routledge.

Birch, K. and Bronson, K. (2022). Big tech. *Science as Culture*, 31(1), 1–14.

Blake, D.J. (2019). Recalling hydraulic despotism: Hun Sen's Cambodia and the return of strict authoritarianism. *ASEAS-Austrian Journal of South-East Asian Studies*, 12(1), 69–89.

Blomqvist, P. (2004). The choice revolution: Privatization of Swedish welfare services in the 1990s. *Social Policy & Administration*, 38(2), 139–155.

Bloom, P. (2023). *Authoritarian capitalism in the age of globalization*. Edward Elgar.

Bloom, P. and Cederstrom, C. (2009). 'The sky's the limit': Fantasy in the age of market rationality. *Journal of Organizational Change Management*, 22(2), 159–180.

Bloom, P., Smolović Jones, O., and Woodcock, J. (2021). *Guerrilla democracy: Mobile power and revolution in the 21st century*. Policy Press.

Boaz, D. (2015). Maoist shaming tactics spread from Shanghai to Santa Monica and Silicon Valley. *Reason*, 46(8), 20.

Boffo, M., Saad-Filho, A., and Fine, B. (2019). Neoliberal capitalism: The authoritarian turn. *Socialist Register*, 55, 312–320.

Bogliaccini, J.A., Geymonat, J., and Opertti, M. (2021). Big business and bureaucratic authoritarianism in Uruguay: A network-based story of policy infiltration for self-preservation. In V. Basualdo, H. Berghoff, and M. Buchell (eds), *Big business and dictatorships in Latin America: A transnational history of profits and repression* (pp 127–156). Routledge.

Bonanno, A. (2020). The crisis of neoliberalism, populist reaction, and the rise of authoritarian capitalism. In B. Berberoglu (ed), *The global rise of authoritarianism in the 21st century: Crisis of neoliberal globalization and the nationalist response* (pp 15–29). Routledge.

Bonefeld, W. (2017a). Authoritarian liberalism: From Schmitt via ordoliberalism to the Euro. *Critical Sociology*, 43(4–5), 747–761.

Bonefeld, W. (2017b). Authoritarian liberalism, class and rackets. *Logos: A Journal of Modern Society and Culture*, 12(1–2).

Bonikowski, B. (2017). Ethno-nationalist populism and the mobilization of collective resentment. *The British Journal of Sociology*, 68(S1), S181–S213.

Boukalas, C. (2014). No exceptions: Authoritarian statism. Agamben, Poulantzas and homeland security. *Critical Studies on Terrorism*, 7(1), 112–130.

Bourgois, P. (2018). Decolonising drug studies in an era of predatory accumulation. *Third World Quarterly*, 39(2), 385–398.

Bouvier, G. (2020). Racist call-outs and cancel culture on Twitter: The limitations of the platform's ability to define issues of social justice. *Discourse, Context & Media*, 38, 100431.

Bouvier, G. and Machin, D. (2021). What gets lost in Twitter 'cancel culture' hashtags? Calling out racists reveals some limitations of social justice campaigns. *Discourse & Society*, 32(3), 307–327.

Bowers, C. (2016). Digital colonization. In C. Bowers, *Digital detachment* (pp 35–45). Routledge.

Boyd, M.J., Sullivan Jr, J.L., Chetty, M., and Ur, B. (2021). Understanding the security and privacy advice given to black lives matter protesters. In *Proceedings of the 2021 CHI conference on human factors in computing systems* (pp 1–18).

Boyte, H.C. (2020). Civic-driven change and developmental democracy. In A. Fowler and C. Malunga (eds), *NGO management* (pp 81–97). Routledge.

Breen, M. and Doak, E. (2023). The IMF as a global monitor: Surveillance, information, and financial markets. *Review of International Political Economy*, 30(1), 307–331.

Brekke, J.K. (2021). Hacker-engineers and their economies: The political economy of decentralised networks and 'cryptoeconomics'. *New Political Economy*, 26(4), 646–659.

Brenner, N. and Theodore, N. (2002). Preface: From the 'new localism' to the spaces of neoliberalism. *Antipode*, 34(3).

Brenner, R. (2006). *The economics of global turbulence: The advanced capitalist economies from long boom to long downturn, 1945–2005*. Verso.

Brewer, R.M. and Heitzeg, N.A. (2008). The racialization of crime and punishment: Criminal justice, color-blind racism, and the political economy of the prison industrial complex. *American Behavioral Scientist*, 51(5), 625–644.

Bria, F. (2009). A crisis of finance: Financialisation as a crisis of accumulation of new capitalism. *Ephemera*, 9(4), 388–395.

Broomhill, R. and Sharp, R. (2007). The problem of social reproduction under neoliberalism: Reconfiguring the male-breadwinner model in Australia. In M. Griffin-Cohen and J. Brodie (eds), *Remapping gender in the new global order* (pp 99–122). Routledge.

Brown, O. (2014). From the Philadelphia Negro to the prison industrial complex: Crime and the marginalization of African American males in contemporary America. *Spectrum: A Journal on Black Men*, 3(1), 71–96.

Browne, S. (2015). *Dark matters: On the surveillance of blackness*. Duke University Press.

Bruff, I. (2014). The rise of authoritarian neoliberalism. *Rethinking Marxism*, 26(1), 113–129.

Bruff, I. and Tansel, C.B. (2020). Authoritarian neoliberalism: Trajectories of knowledge production and praxis. In I. Bruff and C.B. Tansel (eds), *Authoritarian neoliberalism* (pp 1–12). Routledge.

Brunton, B.G. (1988). Institutional origins of the military-industrial complex. *Journal of Economic Issues*, 22(2), 599–606.

Bucher, E.L., Schou, P.K., and Waldkirch, M. (2021). Pacifying the algorithm: Anticipatory compliance in the face of algorithmic management in the gig economy. *Organization*, 28(1), 44–67.

Bulut, E. (2015). Glamor above, precarity below: Immaterial labor in the video game industry. *Critical Studies in Media Communication*, 32(3), 193–207.

Burawoy, M. (1990). *The politics of production*. Verso.

Burchardt, H.J. and Dietz, K. (2014). (Neo-) extractivism: A new challenge for development theory from Latin America. *Third World Quarterly*, 35(3), 468–486.

Bures, O. and Cusumano, E. (2021). The anti-mercenary norm and United Nations' use of private military and security companies: From norm entrepreneurship to organized hypocrisy. *International Peacekeeping*, 28(4), 579–605.

Burrier, G. (2016). The developmental state, civil society, and hydroelectric politics in Brazil. *The Journal of Environment & Development*, 25(3), 332–358.

Burtch, G., Ghose, A., and Wattal, S. (2014). Cultural differences and geography as determinants of online prosocial lending. *MIS Quarterly*, 38(3), 773–794.

Buštíková, L. and Guasti, P. (2019). The state as a firm: Understanding the autocratic roots of religious persecution. *British Journal of Political Science*, 49(1), 143–162.

Butler, J. (1997). *The psychic life of power: Theories in subjection*. Stanford University Press.

Butler, J.C. (2000). Personality and emotional correlates of right-wing authoritarianism. *Social Behavior and Personality: An International Journal*, 28(1), 1–14.

Butler, J., Laclau, E., and Žižek, S. (2000). *Contingency, hegemony, universality: Contemporary dialogues on the left*. Verso.

Byrne, E.F. (2010). The US military-industrial complex is circumstantially unethical. *Journal of Business Ethics*, 95, 153–165.

Calderón, F.H. and Cedillo, A. (eds) (2012). *Challenging authoritarianism in Mexico: Revolutionary struggles and the dirty war, 1964–1982*. Routledge.

Cammack, P. (1982). Bureaucratic authoritarianism and Brazil: A dissenting note. *Politics*, 2(1), 9–13.

Cammaerts, B. (2012). Protest logics and the mediation opportunity structure. *European Journal of Communication*, 27(2), 117–134.

Campesi, G. (2009). Neoliberal and neoconservative discourses on crime and punishment. *Sortuz: Oñati Journal of Emergent Socio-Legal Studies*, 3(1), 33–52.

Carl, J. (2024). Mass incarceration and for-profit prisons. In A.P. (ed), *Handbook of forensic social work: Theory, policy, and fields of practice* (pp 205–223). University Press.

Carmody, P. (2016). *The new scramble for Africa*. John Wiley & Sons.

Carrera, D., Ovienmhada, U., Hussein, S., and Soden, R. (2023). The unseen landscape of abolitionism: Examining the role of digital maps in grassroots organizing. *Proceedings of the ACM on Human-Computer Interaction*, 7(CSCW2), 1–29.

Carroll, T. and Jarvis, D.S. (eds) (2017). *Asia after the developmental state: Disembedding autonomy*. Cambridge University Press.

Castells, M. (2012). *Networks of outrage and hope: Social movements in the internet age*. John Wiley & Sons.

Çelik, N.B. (2020). Turkey's communicative authoritarianism. *Global Media and Communication*, 16(1), 102–120.

Chacko, P. (2020). Gender and authoritarian populism: Empowerment, protection, and the politics of resentful aspiration in India. *Critical Asian Studies*, 52(2), 204–225.

Chan, M., Yi, J., and Kuznetsov, D. (2022). Government digital repression and political engagement: A cross-national multilevel analysis examining the roles of online surveillance and censorship. *The International Journal of Press/Politics*, 19401612221117106.

Chan, S. (2013). 'I am king': Financialisation and the paradox of precarious work. *The Economic and Labour Relations Review*, 24(3), 362–379.

Chapelan, A. (2021). 'Swallowing the red pill': The coronavirus pandemic and the political imaginary of stigmatized knowledge in the discourse of the far-right. *Journal of Transatlantic Studies*, 19(3), 282–312.

Chaudhuri, B. and König, L. (2018). The Aadhaar scheme: A cornerstone of a new citizenship regime in India? *Contemporary South Asia*, 26(2), 127–142.

Chen, M. and Grossklags, J. (2022). Social control in the digital transformation of society: A case study of the Chinese Social Credit System. *Social Sciences*, 11(6), 229.

Cheney-Lippold, J. (2011). A new algorithmic identity: Soft biopolitics and the modulation of control. *Theory, Culture & Society*, 28(6), 164–181.

Chesterman, S. and Lehnardt, C. (eds) (2007). *From mercenaries to market: The rise and regulation of private military companies.* Oxford University Press.

Cheung, A.S. and Chen, Y. (2022). From datafication to data state: Making sense of China's social credit system and its implications. *Law & Social Inquiry*, 47(4), 1137–1171.

Chimisso, C. (2015). Narrative and epistemology: Georges Canguilhem's concept of scientific ideology. *Studies in History and Philosophy of Science Part A*, 54, 64–73.

Chomsky, N. (1999). *Profit over people: Neoliberalism and global order.* Seven Stories Press.

Chong, G.P.L. (2019). Cashless China: Securitization of everyday life through Alipay's social credit system – Sesame Credit. *Chinese Journal of Communication*, 12(3), 290–307.

Christin, A. (2017). Algorithms in practice: Comparing web journalism and criminal justice. *Big Data & Society*, 4(2).

Christophers, B., Fine, B., Mader, P., Mertens, D., and van der Zwan, N. (2020). The value of financialization and the financialization of value. In P. Mader, D. Mertens, and N. van der Zwan (eds), *The Routledge international handbook of financialization* (pp 19–30). Routledge.

Chua, C. (2020). Abolition is a constant struggle: Five lessons from Minneapolis. *Theory & Event*, 23(5), S-127.

Citron, D.K. and Pasquale, F. (2014). The scored society: Due process for automated predictions. *Washington Law Review*, 89, 1.

Clifton, J.A. (1977). Competition and the evolution of the capitalist mode of production. *Cambridge Journal of Economics*, 1(2), 137–151.

Cockshott, P., Cottrell, A., and Dieterich, H. (2010). *Transition to 21st century socialism in the European Union.* Lulu.com.

Colaguori, C. (2005). The prison industrial complex and social division in market societies: The hyper-security state, crime and expendable populations. In L.A. Visano (ed), *Law and criminal justice: A critical inquiry.* Athenian Policy.

Coleman, D. (2019). Digital colonialism: The 21st century scramble for Africa through the extraction and control of user data and the limitations of data protection laws. *Michigan Journal of Race & Law*, 24(2), 417–439.

Coleman, M. (2007). A geopolitics of engagement: Neoliberalism, the war on terrorism, and the reconfiguration of US immigration enforcement. *Geopolitics*, 12(4), 607–634.

Collier, D. and Cardoso, F.H. (1979). *The new authoritarianism in Latin America.* Princeton University Press.

Collins, B. and Sullivan, M.T. (2018). Companies quietly work with ICE as border crisis persists. *NBC News*, 20 June.

Conca, K. (1997). *Manufacturing insecurity: The rise and fall of Brazil's military-industrial complex.* Lynne Rienner Publishers.

Conduit, D. (2023). Digital authoritarianism and the devolution of authoritarian rule: examining Syria's patriotic hackers. *Democratization*, 1–19.

Cook, I.R. (2010). Policing, partnerships, and profits: The operations of business improvement districts and town center management schemes in England. *Urban Geography*, 31(4), 453–478.

Cooke, B. and Kothari, U. (eds) (2001). *Participation: The new tyranny?* Zed Books.

Cooley, A. (2015). Authoritarianism goes global: Countering democratic norms. *Journal of Democracy*, 26(3), 49–63.

Cornelius, E. (2022). Anonymous hacktivism: Flying the flag of feminist ethics for the Ukraine IT army. https://digitalcommons.law.umaryland. edu/cgi/viewcontent.cgi?article=1019&context=home_sec_fac_pubs

Corva, D. (2008). Neoliberal globalization and the war on drugs: Transnationalizing illiberal governance in the Americas. *Political Geography*, 27(2), 176–193.

Cottam, M. and Marenin, O. (1989). Predicting the past: Reagan administration assistance to police forces in Central America. *Justice Quarterly*, 6(4), 589–618.

Couldry, N. and Mejias, U.A. (2019). Data colonialism: Rethinking big data's relation to the contemporary subject. *Television & New Media*, 20(4), 336–349.

Cousineau, M. (2011). The surveillant simulation of war: Entertainment and surveillance in the 21st century. *Surveillance & Society*, 8(4), 517–522.

Cousins, M. and Hussain, A. (1984). The question of ideology: Althusser, Pêcheux and Foucault. *The Sociological Review*, 32(S1), 158–179.

Cowen, D. (2014). *The deadly life of logistics: Mapping violence in global trade.* University of Minnesota Press.

Cox, C. (2020). Rising with the robots: Towards a human-machine autonomy for digital socialism. *TripleC: Communication, Capitalism & Critique*, 18(1), 67–83.

Crain, M. (2021). *Profit over privacy: How surveillance advertising conquered the internet.* University of Minnesota Press.

Cribb, R. (1990). Genocide in Indonesia, 1965–1966. *Journal of Genocide Research*, 3(2), 219–239.

Crouch, C. (2011). *The strange non-death of neo-liberalism.* Polity Press.

Cubitt, S. (2017). *Finite media: Environmental implications of digital technologies.* Duke University Press.

Cuff, R.D. (1978). An organizational perspective on the military-industrial complex. *Business History Review*, 52(2), 250–267.

Cumings, B. (2016). The Obama 'pivot' to Asia in a historical context of American hegemony. In D. Huang (ed), *Asia Pacific countries and the US rebalancing strategy* (pp 11–30). Palgrave Macmillan.

Curato, N. (2017). Flammable societies and the pandemic. *Journal of Contemporary Asia*, 51(1), 203–207.

Curley, C., Siapera, E., and Carthy, J. (2022). Covid-19 protesters and the far right on Telegram: Co-conspirators or accidental bedfellows? *Social Media+ Society*, 8(4), 20563051221129187.

Curran, D. and Smart, A. (2021). Data-driven governance, smart urbanism and risk-class inequalities: Security and social credit in China. *Urban Studies*, 58(3), 487–506.

Cushen, J. (2013). Financialization in the workplace: Hegemonic narratives, performative interventions and the angry knowledge worker. *Accounting, Organizations and Society*, 38(4), 314–331.

Da Costa Vieira, T. (2023). 'In time, every worker a capitalist': Accumulation by legitimation and authoritarian neoliberalism in Thatcher's Britain. *Competition & Change*, 10245294231153028.

Daggett, C. (2018). Petro-masculinity: Fossil fuels and authoritarian desire. *Millennium*, 47(1), 25–44.

Dahi, O.S. and Munif, Y. (2012). Revolts in Syria: Tracking the convergence between authoritarianism and neoliberalism. *Journal of Asian and African Studies*, 47(4), 323–332.

Dai, X. (2018). Toward a reputation state: The social credit system project of China. Working Paper. https://ssrn.com/abstract=3193577

Dai, X. (2020). Enforcing law and norms for good citizens: One view of China's social credit system project. *Development*, 63(1), 38–43.

Dal, A., Nisbet, E.C., and Kamenchuk, O. (2022). Signaling silence: Affective and cognitive responses to risks of online activism about corruption in an authoritarian context. *New Media & Society*, 14614448221135861.

Daldal, A. (2014). Power and ideology in Michel Foucault and Antonio Gramsci: A comparative analysis. *Review of History and Political Science*, 2(2), 149–167.

Darius, P. and Urquhart, M. (2021). Disinformed social movements: A large-scale mapping of conspiracy narratives as online harms during the COVID-19 pandemic. *Online Social Networks and Media*, 26, 100174.

Darmody, A. and Zwick, D. (2020). Manipulate to empower: Hyper-relevance and the contradictions of marketing in the age of surveillance capitalism. *Big Data & Society*, 7(1), 2053951720904112.

Datta, A. (2015). New urban utopias of postcolonial India: 'Entrepreneurial urbanization' in Dholera smart city, Gujarat. *Dialogues in Human Geography*, 5(1), 3–22.

Datta, A. (2018). The digital turn in postcolonial urbanism: Smart citizenship in the making of India's 100 smart cities. *Transactions of the Institute of British Geographers*, 43(3), 405–419.

Davies, J.S. (2021). *Between Realism and Revolt*. Bristol University Press.

Davies, J.S. and Blanco, I. (2017). Austerity urbanism: Patterns of neo-liberalisation and resistance in six cities of Spain and the UK. *Environment and Planning A*, 49(7), 1517–1536.

Davis, A. and Walsh, C. (2016). The role of the state in the financialisation of the UK economy. *Political Studies*, 64(3), 666–682.

Davis, C. (2019). Economic and political aspects of the military–industrial complex in the USSR. In H.-H. Hohmann (ed), *Economics and politics in the USSR* (pp 92–124). Routledge.

Davis, K. (2022). Vengeance is mine: How religious southern white supremacy shaped the prison industrial complex. *Venture: The University of Mississippi Undergraduate Research Journal*, 4(1), 8.

Dean, M. (2002). Liberal government and authoritarianism. *Economy and Society*, 31(1), 37–61.

De Goede, M. (2017). Chains of securitization. *Finance and Society*, 3(2), 197–207.

Deleuze, G. (1992). Postscript on the societies of control. In I. Szeman and T. Kaposy (eds), *Cultural Theory: An Anthology* (pp 139–142). Wiley.

Deleuze, G. and Guattari, F. (1987). *A thousand plateaus*. University of Minnesota Press.

De Lima, I.V. (2010). *Foucault's archaeology of political economy*. Palgrave.

Della Ratta, D. (2020). Digital socialism beyond the digital social: Confronting communicative capitalism with ethics of care. *tripleC: Communication, Capitalism & Critique. Open Access Journal for a Global Sustainable Information Society*, 18(1), 101–115.

Dellarocas, C. (2003). The digitization of word of mouth: Promise and challenges of online feedback mechanisms. *Management Science*, 49(10), 1407–1424.

De Peuter, G. (2011). Creative economy and labor precarity: A contested convergence. *Journal of Communication Inquiry*, 35(4), 417–425.

Der Derian, J. (2009). *Virtuous war: Mapping the military-industrial-media-entertainment-network*. Routledge.

Deseriis, M. (2021). Rethinking the digital democratic affordance and its impact on political representation: Toward a new framework. *New Media & Society*, 23(8), 2452–2473.

De Stefano, V.M. (2016). The rise of the 'just-in-time workforce': On–demand work, crowd work and labour protection in the 'gig-economy'. *Comparative Labor Law and Policy Journal*, 37(3), 471–504.

Devries, L., Attaran, A., Aylward, B., and Downey, L. (2021). *The binding force of precedent*. Available at SSRN 3837612.

Díaz, J. (2011). Immigration policy, criminalization and the growth of the immigration industrial complex: Restriction, expulsion, and eradication of the undocumented in the US. *Western Criminology Review*, 12(2), 35–54.

Dixon, A.D. (2011). Variegated capitalism and the geography of finance: Towards a common agenda. *Progress in Human Geography*, 35(2), 193–210.

Doctorow, C. and Giblin, R. (2022). *Chokepoint capitalism: How big tech and big content captured creative labor markets and how we'll win them back*. Beacon Press.

Donziger, S. and Fine, G.W. (1989). Police aid and Central America: The Reagan Years. *Harvard Human Rights Journal*, 2, 197–208.

Dormehl, L. (2014). *The formula: How algorithms solve all our problems – and create more*. Penguin.

Doty, R.M., Peterson, B.E., and Winter, D.G. (1991). Threat and authoritarianism in the United States, 1978–1987. *Journal of Personality and Social Psychology*, 61(4), 629–640.

Dourish, P. and Gómez Cruz, E. (2018). Datafication and data fiction: Narrating data and narrating with data. *Big Data & Society*, 5(2), 2053951718784083.

Doval, G.P. and Souroujon, G. (eds) (2021). *Global resurgence of the right: Conceptual and regional perspectives*. Routledge.

Dowin Kennedy, E. (2021). Creating community: The process of entrepreneurial community building for civic wealth creation. *Entrepreneurship & Regional Development*, 33(9–10), 816–836.

Dowling, E. (2017). In the wake of austerity: Social impact bonds and the financialisation of the welfare state in Britain. *New Political Economy*, 22(3), 294–310.

Dow Schüll, N. (2016). Data for life: Wearable technology and the design of self-care. *BioSocieties*, 11(3), 317–333.

Dragu, T. and Lupu, Y. (2021). Digital authoritarianism and the future of human rights. *International Organization*, 75(4), 991–1017.

Duckett, J. (2020). Neoliberalism, authoritarian politics and social policy in China. *Development and Change*, 51(2), 523–539.

Duggan, J., Sherman, U., Carbery, R., and McDonnell, A. (2020). Algorithmic management and app-work in the gig economy: A research agenda for employment relations and HRM. *Human Resource Management Journal*, 30(1), 114–132.

Duménil, G. and Lévy, D. (2004). *Capital resurgent: Roots of the neoliberal revolution*. Harvard University Press.

Duménil, G. and Lévy, D. (2011). The crisis of the early 21st century: General interpretation, recent developments, and perspectives. *World Review of Political Economy*, 562–580.

Dunigan, M. and Petersohn, U. (eds) (2015). *The markets for force: Privatization of security across world regions*. University of Pennsylvania Press.

Dunlap Jr, C.J. (2011). The military-industrial complex. *Daedalus*, 140(3), 135–147.

Dunleavy, P. (2006). *Digital era governance: IT corporations, the state, and e-government*. Oxford University Press.

Dunne, J.P. (1993). The changing military industrial complex in the UK. *Defence and Peace Economics*, 4(2), 91–111.

Dunne, J.P. and Sköns, E. (2010). The military industrial complex. In P. Levine and R. Smith (eds), *The global arms trade: A handbook* (pp 281–292). Routledge.

Durham, K.H. (2013). Accounting for precarity: Recent studies of labor market uncertainty. *Contemporary Sociology*, 44(4), 463–469.

Durkin, P. (2022). The invisible networks that bind the 'directors' club'. *Boss*, 3 June.

Eagleton, T. (1991). *Ideology: An introduction*. Verso.

Eatwell, R. and Goodwin, M. (2018). *National populism: The revolt against liberal democracy*. Penguin UK.

Ebeling, M.F. (2021). Mining the data oceans, profiting on the margins. *Global Policy*, 12, 85–89.

Eberl, J.M., Huber, R.A., and Greussing, E. (2021). From populism to the 'plandemic': Why populists believe in COVID-19 conspiracies. *Journal of Elections, Public Opinion and Parties*, 31(sup1), 272–284.

Eckert, C.J. (2000). Korea's transition to modernity: A will to greatness. In M. Goldman and A. Gordon (eds), *Historical perspectives on contemporary East Asia* (pp 119–154). Harvard University Press.

Edelman, B. and Luca, M. (2014). Digital discrimination: The case of Airbnb. com. Harvard Business School NOM Unit Working Paper (14–054), 1–16.

Edelman, L.B. (2020). The racial re-production of dissent. *Berkeley Journal of Gender, Law & Justice*, 35, 74.

Egbert, S. and Leese, M. (2021). *Criminal futures: Predictive policing and everyday police work*. Taylor & Francis.

Egels-Zandén, N. and Hansson, N. (2016). Supply chain transparency as a consumer or corporate tool: The case of Nudie Jeans Co. *Journal of Consumer Policy*, 39, 377–395.

Eglash, R., Bennett, A., Cooke, L., Babbitt, W., and Lachney, M. (2021). Counter-hegemonic computing: Toward computer science education for value generation and emancipation. *ACM Transactions on Computing Education (TOCE)*, 21(4), 1–30.

Eisenhower, D. (1961). Farewell address. National Archives. https://www. archives.gov/milestone-documents/president-dwight-d-eisenhowers-farew ell-address

Eitches, E.R. (2010). Coerced prison labor without union protection: The exploitation of the prison industrial complex. Columbia University Academic Commons. https://core.ac.uk/download/pdf/161444566.pdf

Ellerman, D. (2021). *Neo-abolitionism*. Springer International Publishing.

Ellis, A.R. (2015). Economic precarity, race, and voting structures. *Kentucky Law Journal*, 104(4), Article 5.

Elson, D. (2017). Recognize, reduce, and redistribute unpaid care work: How to close the gender gap. *New Labor Forum*, 26(2), 52–61.

Emmenegger, R. (2016). Decentralization and the local developmental state: Peasant mobilization in Oromiya, Ethiopia. *Africa*, 86(2), 263–287.

Engelmann, S., Chen, M., Dang, L., and Grossklags, J. (2021). Blacklists and redlists in the Chinese social credit system: Diversity, flexibility, and comprehensiveness. In *Proceedings of the 2021 AAAI/ACM Conference on AI, Ethics, and Society* (pp 78–88), July.

Epstein, G.A. (ed) (2005). *Financialization and the world economy*. Edward Elgar.

Epstein, K.C. (2014). *Torpedo: Inventing the military-industrial complex in the United States and Great Britain*. Harvard University Press.

Escobar, A. (1984). Discourse and power in development: Michel Foucault and the relevance of his work to the third world. *Alternatives*, 10(3), 377–400.

Escobar, A. (1995). *Encountering development: The making and unmaking of the third world*. Princeton University Press.

Ettlinger, N. (2007). Precarity unbound. *Alternatives*, 32(3), 319–340.

Eubanks, V. (2018). *Automating inequality: How high-tech tools profile, police, and punish the poor*. St. Martin's Press.

Evans, P. and Sewell, W.H. (2013). Neoliberalism: Policy regimes, international regimes, and social effects. In P.A. Hall and M. Lamont (eds), *Social resilience in the neoliberal era* (pp 35–68). Cambridge University Press.

Evans, R.G. (1997). Going for the gold: The redistributive agenda behind market-based health care reform. *Journal of Health Politics, Policy and Law*, 22(2), 427–465.

Fairclough, N. (2013). Language and ideology. In N. Fairclough, *Critical discourse analysis* (pp 56–68). Routledge.

Farber, H.S. and Western, B. (2002). Ronald Reagan and the politics of declining union organization. *British Journal of Industrial Relations*, 40(3), 385–401.

Fath, B.D., Fiscus, D.A., Goerner, S.J., Berea, A., and Ulanowicz, R.E. (2019). Measuring regenerative economics: 10 principles and measures undergirding systemic economic health. *Global Transitions*, 1, 15–27.

Feldman, A. (2004). Securocratic wars of public safety: Globalized policing as scopic regime. *Interventions*, 6(3), 330–350.

Feldman, J. (1989). *Universities in the business of repression: The academic-military-industrial complex and Central America*. South End Press.

Feldman, S., Mérola, V., and Dollman, J. (2021). The psychology of authoritarianism and support for illiberal policies and parties. In A. Sajó, R. Uitz, and S. Holmes (eds), *Routledge handbook of illiberalism* (pp 635–654). Routledge.

Feldstein, S. (2019). *The global expansion of AI surveillance*. Carnegie Endowment for International Peace.

Feldstein, S. (2021). *The rise of digital repression: How technology is reshaping power, politics, and resistance*. Oxford University Press.

Felix, D. (2019). On financial blowups and authoritarian regimes in Latin America. In J. Hartlyn and S.A. Morley (eds), *Latin American political economy* (pp 85–125). Routledge.

Felix, G. (2020). Super-circulation: Towards a political economy of platformisation. *Critical Sociology*, 46(7–8), 1221–1232.

Ferguson, A. (2017). *The Rise of Big Data Policing: Surveillance, race, and the future of law enforcement*. New York University Press.

Ferguson, A. (2024). DOJ funding pipeline subsidizes questionable big data surveillance technologies. *The Conversation*, 7 February.

Ferguson, J. (1990). *The anti-politics machine: 'Development', depoliticization, and bureaucratic power in Lesotho*. University of Minnesota Press.

Ferreri, M. and Sanyal, R. (2022). Digital informalisation: Rental housing, platforms, and the management of risk. *Housing Studies*, 37(6), 1035–1053.

Ferreri, M. and Vasudevan, A. (2019). Vacancy at the edges of the precarious city. *Geoforum*, 101, 165–173.

Fields, D. (2017). Unwilling subjects of financialization. *International Journal of Urban and Regional Research*, 41(4), 588–603.

Fields, D. and Raymond, E.L. (2021). Racialized geographies of housing financialization. *Progress in Human Geography*, 45(6), 1625–1645.

Fielitz, M. and Marcks, H. (2019). Transcultural narrations: Silk Road imaginaries and their counterdiscursive interpretations. *Europe Now Journal*.

Fink, B. (1995). *The Lacanian subject: Between language and jouissance*. Princeton University Press.

Firmino, R.J., de Vasconcelos Cardoso, B., and Evangelista, R. (2019). Hyperconnectivity and (im) mobility: Uber and surveillance capitalism by the Global South. *Surveillance & Society*, 17(1/2), 205–212.

Fisher, J. and Anderson, D.M. (2015). Authoritarianism and the securitization of development in Africa. *International Affairs*, 91(1), 131–151.

Fitzpatrick, M. (2015). *The pedagogy of anxiety: Ontological insecurity and psychoanalytic readings of Moby-Dick*. Palgrave Macmillan.

Flew, T. (2014). Six theories of neoliberalism. *Thesis Eleven*, 122(1), 49–71.

Flikke, R. (2016). Explaining Russian policy toward NGOs: Two theory-guided empirical accounts. *Post-Soviet Affairs*, 32(3), 197–215.

Flores, N. (2012). *From nation-states to neoliberalism: Language ideologies and governmentality*. City University of New York.

Fogg, B.J. (2002). Persuasive technology: Using computers to change what we think and do. *Ubiquity*, December, 2.

Ford, A., De Togni, G., and Miller, L. (2021a). Hormonal health: Period tracking apps, wellness, and self-management in the era of surveillance capitalism. *Engaging Science, Technology, and Society*, 7(1), 48–66.

Ford, B., Bernholz, L., Landemore, H., and Reich, R. (2021b). Technologizing democracy or democratizing technology? A layered-architecture perspective on potentials and challenges. In L. Bernholz, H. Landemore, and R. Reich (eds), *Digital technology and democratic theory* (pp 274–321). University of Chicago Press.

Forst, B. (2000). The privatization and civilianization of policing. *Criminal Justice*, 2(24), 19–78.

Foster, J.B. and Magdoff, F. (2009). *The great financial crisis: Causes and consequences*. Monthly Review Press.

Foster, J.B. and Holleman, H. (2010a). The financialization of the capitalist class: Monopoly-finance capital and the new contradictory relations of ruling class power. In H. Veltmeyer (ed), *Imperialism, crisis and class struggle* (pp 191–201). Brill.

Foster, J.B. and Holleman, H. (2010b). The financial power elite. *Monthly Review*, 62(1), 1.

Foster, J.B. and McChesney, R. (2014). Surveillance capitalism. *Monthly Review*, 66(3), 1–31.

Foster, K.W. (2001). Associations in the embrace of an authoritarian state: State domination of society? *Studies in Comparative International Development*, 35, 84–109.

Fotopoulou, A. and O'Riordan, K. (2017). Training to self-care: Fitness tracking, biopedagogy and the healthy consumer. In D. Lupton (ed), *Self-tracking, health and medicine* (pp 54–68). Routledge.

Foucault, M. (1977). *Discipline and punish: The birth of the prison*. Vintage Books.

Foucault, M. (1978). *The history of sexuality volume I: An introduction*. Pantheon Books.

Foucault, M. (1982). The subject and power. *Critical Inquiry*, 8(4), 777–795.

Foucault, M. (1997). What is critique. In S. Lotringer and L. Hochroth (eds), *The politics of truth* (pp 23–82). Semiotext(e).

Franco, M. (2020). Palantir filed to go public: The firm's unethical technology should horrify us. *The Guardian*, 4 September.

Frank, A.G. (1969). The development of underdevelopment. *Monthly Review*, 18(4), 17–31.

Frankel, J. (2022). The narcissistic dynamics of submission: The attraction of the powerless to authoritarian leaders. *American Journal of Psychoanalysis*, 82(3), 384.

Frankel, J.A. (2010). *The natural resource curse: A survey* (vol 15836, pp 1–55). National Bureau of Economic Research.

Franks, M.A. (2021). Beyond the public square: Imagining digital democracy. *Yale Law Journal*, 131, 427.

Frase, P. (2016). *Four futures: Life after capitalism*. Verso Books.

Fraser, N. (2016). Contradictions of capital and care. *New Left Review*, 100, 99–117.

Freeman, C. (2020). Feeling neoliberal. *Feminist Anthropology*, 1(1), 71–88.

Frieden, J.A. (1991a). *Debt, development, and democracy: Modern political economy and Latin America, 1965–1985*. Princeton University Press.

Frieden, J.A. (1991b). Invested interests: The politics of national economic policies in a world of global finance. *International Organization*, 45(4), 425–451.

Frumkin, P. and Andre-Clark, A. (1999). The rise of the corporate social worker. *Society*, 36(6), 46–52.

Fuchs, C. (2020). Communicative socialism/digital socialism. *tripleC: Communication, Capitalism & Critique. Open Access Journal for a Global Sustainable Information Society*, 18(1), 1–31.

Fuchs, C. (2021). The digital commons and the digital public sphere: How to advance digital democracy today. *Westminster Papers in Communication and Culture*, 16(1), 9–26.

Fuchs, C. and Trottier, D. (2017). Internet surveillance after Snowden: A critical empirical study of computer experts' attitudes on commercial and state surveillance of the Internet and social media post-Edward Snowden. *Journal of Information, Communication and Ethics in Society*, 15(4), 412–444.

Fullerton, J. (2015). *Regenerative capitalism: How universal principles and patterns will shape our new economy*. Capital Institute.

Gabrys, J. (2013). *Digital rubbish: A natural history of electronics*. University of Michigan Press.

Galič, M., Timan, T., and Koops, B.J. (2017). Bentham, Deleuze and beyond: An overview of surveillance theories from the panopticon to participation. *Philosophy & Technology*, 30, 9–37.

Ganascia, J.G. (2010). The generalized sousveillance society. *Social Science Information*, 49(3), 489–507.

Gandini, A. (2019). Labour process theory and the gig economy. *Human Relations*, 72(6), 1039–1056.

Gandy Jr, O.H. and Nemorin, S. (2019). Toward a political economy of nudge: Smart city variations. *Information, Communication & Society*, 22(14), 2112–2126.

García-Lamarca, M. and Kaika, M. (2016). 'Mortgaged lives': The biopolitics of debt and housing financialisation. *Transactions of the Institute of British Geographers*, 41(3), 313–327.

Garrett, T.M. (2023). Border securocracy: Global expansion of the US Department of Homeland Security bureaucratic apparatus before, during and beyond covid-19. *Administrative Theory & Praxis*, 45(3), 230–246.

Gauja, A. (2021). Digital democracy: Big technology and the regulation of politics. *The University of New South Wales Law Journal*, 44(3), 959–982.

Gautreau, G.L. (2012). To rid the world of the drug scourge: A human security perspective on the war on drugs in Colombia and Mexico. *Paterson Review of International Affairs*, 12, 61–83.

Geller, D.S. (1982). Economic modernization and political instability in Latin America: A causal analysis of bureaucratic-authoritarianism. *Western Political Quarterly*, 35(1), 33–49.

Gerbaudo, P. (2012). *Tweets and the streets: Social media and contemporary activism*. Pluto Press.

Gertel, J. (2019). Spatialities of precarity. In B. Sommer and S. Schmalz (eds), *Confronting crisis and precariousness: Organised labour and social unrest in the European Union* (pp 129–150). Rowman and Littlefield.

Gest, T. (2001). *Crime & politics: Big government's erratic campaign for law and order*. Oxford University Press.

Ghiselli, A. (2021). *Protecting China's interests overseas: Securitization and foreign policy*. Oxford University Press.

Gibbon, P., Bangura, Y., and Ofstad, A. (eds) (1992). *Authoritarianism, democracy, and adjustment: The politics of economic reform in Africa* (vol 26). Nordic Africa Institute.

Gibson-Graham, J.K., Cameron, J., and Healy, S. (2013). *Take back the economy: An ethical guide for transforming our communities*. University of Minnesota Press.

Gilbert, J. (2013). What kind of thing is 'neoliberalism'? *New Formations*, 80, 7–22.

Gilbert, J. (2017). Modes of anti-neoliberalism: Moralism, Marxism and 21st century socialism. In B. Jones and M. O'Donnell (eds), *Alternatives to neoliberalism* (pp 27–40). Policy Press.

Gilbert, L. (2020). Regulating society after the color revolutions: A comparative analysis of NGO laws in Belarus, Russia, and Armenia. *Demokratizatsiya: The Journal of Post-Soviet Democratization*, 28(2), 305–332.

Gill, R. and Pratt, A. (2008). Precarity and cultural work in the social factory? Immaterial labour, precariousness and cultural work. *Theory, Culture & Society*, 25(7–8), 1–30.

Gill, S. (1995). Globalisation, market civilisation, and disciplinary neoliberalism. *Millennium*, 24(3), 399–423.

Gilmore, J. (2011). A kinder, gentler counter-terrorism: Counterinsurgency, human security and the War on Terror. *Security Dialogue*, 42(1), 21–37.

Glassman, J. (2020). Lineages of the authoritarian state in Thailand: Military dictatorship, lazy capitalism and the cold war past as post-cold war prologue. *Journal of Contemporary Asia*, 50(4), 571–592.

Glassman, J. and Choi, Y.J. (2014). The Chaebol and the US military–industrial complex: Cold War geopolitical economy and South Korean industrialization. *Environment and Planning A*, 46(5), 1160–1180.

Glynos, J. (2001). The grip of ideology: A Lacanian approach to the theory of ideology. *Journal of Political Ideologies*, 6(2), 191–214.

Glynos, J. and Howarth, D. (2007). *Logics of critical explanation in social and political theory*. Routledge.

Glynos, J. and Howarth, D. (2008). Structure, agency and power in political analysis: Beyond contextualised self-interpretations. *Political Studies Review*, 6(2), 155–169.

Glynos, J. and Stavrakakis, Y. (2008). Lacan and political subjectivity: Fantasy and enjoyment in psychoanalysis and political theory. *Subjectivity*, 24, 256–274.

Gohdes, A.R. (2020). Repression technology: Internet accessibility and state violence. *American Journal of Political Science*, 64(3), 488–503.

Golash-Boza, T. (2009). The immigration industrial complex: Why we enforce immigration policies destined to fail. *Sociology Compass*, 3(2), 295–309.

Golka, P. (2023). The allure of finance: Social impact investing and the challenges of assetization in financialized capitalism. *Economy and Society*, 52(1), 62–86.

González, F.E.G. (2008). *Dual transitions from authoritarian rule: Institutionalized regimes in Chile and Mexico, 1970–2000*. Johns Hopkins University Press.

Gonzalez, F., Miquel-Florensa, J., Prem, M., and Straub, S. (2022). The Dark Side of Infrastructure: Roads, Repression, and Land in Authoritarian Paraguay. Repression, and Land in Authoritarian Paraguay (December 10, 2022).

Gonzalez Reyes, A. (2016). *Searching for growth and development in authoritarian Mexico*. World Bank.

Goodwin, M. and Duncan, S. (1989). The crisis of local government: Uneven development and the Thatcher administrations. In J. Mohan (eds), *The political geography of contemporary Britain* (pp 69–86). Palgrave.

Gordon, A.F. (1999). Globalism and the prison industrial complex: an interview with Angela Davis. *Race & Class*, 40(2–3), 145–157.

Gordon, T. (2005). The political economy of law-and-order policies: Policing, class struggle, and neoliberal restructuring. *Studies in Political Economy*, 75(1), 53–77.

Gordon, T. (2006). Neoliberalism, racism, and the war on drugs in Canada. *Social Justice*, 33(103), 59–78.

Graham, J. and Papadopoulos, D. (2023). Organizing the precarious: Autonomous work, real democracy and ecological precarity. *Organization*, 30(4), 649–667.

Graham, M. and Anwar, M.A. (2019). The global gig economy: Toward a planetary labor market. In A. Larsson and R. Teigland (eds), *The digital transformation of labor* (pp 213–234). Routledge.

Graham, M., Hjorth, I., and Lehdonvirta, V. (2017). Digital labour and development: Impacts of global digital labour platforms and the gig economy on worker livelihoods. *Transfer: European Review of Labour and Research*, 23(2), 135–162.

Gramsci, A. (1971). *Selections from the prison notebooks*. International.

Grasso, M.T., Farrall, S., Gray, E., Hay, C., and Jennings, W. (2019). Thatcher's children, Blair's babies, political socialization and trickle-down value change: An age, period and cohort analysis. *British Journal of Political Science*, 49(1), 17–36.

Greene, L. (2019). *Silicon states: The power and politics of big tech and what it means for our future*. Catapult.

Greer, I. (2016). Welfare reform, precarity and the re-commodification of labour. *Work, Employment and Society*, 30(1), 162–173.

Gregory, K. (2021). Labour process contradictions amid 'disruptive' technologies at food delivery platforms. *The Indian Journal of Labour Economics*, 64(3), 603–628.

Greitens, S.C. (2020). Dealing with demand for China's global surveillance exports. *Brookings Institution Global China Report*.

Griesbach, K., Reich, A., Elliott-Negri, L., and Milkman, R. (2019). Algorithmic control in platform food delivery work. *Socius*, 5, 2378023119867594.

Grinberg, D. (2017). Chilling developments: Digital access, surveillance, and the authoritarian dilemma in Ethiopia. *Surveillance & Society*, 15(3/4), 432–438.

Grossi, G. and Pianezzi, D. (2017). Smart cities: Utopia or neoliberal ideology? *Cities*, 69, 79–85.

Gruin, J. (2019). Financializing authoritarian capitalism: Chinese fintech and the institutional foundations of algorithmic governance. *Finance and Society*, 5(2), 84–104.

Gruin, J. and Knaack, P. (2020). Not just another shadow bank: Chinese authoritarian capitalism and the 'developmental' promise of digital financial innovation. *New Political Economy*, 25(3), 370–387.

Gruzd, A. and Mai, P. (2020). Going viral: How a single tweet spawned a COVID-19 conspiracy theory on Twitter. *Big Data & Society*, 7(2), 2053951720938405.

Guinan, J. and O'Neill, M. (2019). From community wealth-building to system change. *IPPR Progressive Review*, 25(4), 382–392.

Guizzo, D. (2021). Reassessing Foucault: Power in the history of political economy. *International Journal of Political Economy*, 50(1), 60–74.

Guma, P.K. (2019). Smart urbanism? ICTs for water and electricity supply in Nairobi. *Urban Studies*, 56(11), 2333–2352.

Gunder, M. (2010). Planning as the ideology of (neoliberal) space. *Planning Theory*, 9(4), 298–314.

Gunder, M. (2014). The role of fantasy in public policy formation. In R. Beunen, K. Van Assche, and M. Duineveld (eds), *Evolutionary governance theory: Theory and applications* (pp 143–154). Springer International Publishing.

Gurol, J. and Schütze, B. (2022). Infrastructuring authoritarian power: Arab-Chinese transregional collaboration beyond the state. *International Quarterly for Asian Studies*, 53(2), 231–249.

Guzzini, S. and Neumann, I. (eds) (2012). *The diffusion of power in global governance: International political economy meets Foucault*. Springer.

Győrffy, D. (2020). Financial crisis management and the rise of authoritarian populism: What makes Hungary different from Latvia and Romania?. *Europe-Asia Studies*, 72(5), 792–814.

Haiven, M. (2013). Walmart, financialization, and the cultural politics of securitization. *Cultural Politics*, 9(3), 239–262.

Haiven, M. (2023). From financialization to derivative fascisms: Some cultural politics of far-right authoritarianism in an era of unmanageable risk. *Social Text*, 41(2), 45–73.

Hall, S. (1985). Signification, representation, ideology: Althusser and the post-structuralist debates. *Critical Studies in Media Communication*, 2(2), 91–114.

Hall, S. (1986). Gramsci's relevance for the study of race and ethnicity. *The Journal of Communication Inquiry*, 10(2), 5–27.

Hall, S. (2012). Geographies of money and finance II: Financialization and financial subjects. *Progress in Human Geography*, 36(3), 403–411.

Hall, S.M. (2020). Social reproduction as social infrastructure. *Soundings*, 76(76), 82–94.

Halpern, D. and Sanders, M. (2016). Nudging by government: Progress, impact, & lessons learned. *Behavioral Science & Policy*, 2(2), 53–65.

Han, C. (2018). Precarity, precariousness, and vulnerability. *Annual Review of Anthropology*, 47, 331–343.

Han, H. (2017). Singapore, a garden city: Authoritarian environmentalism in a developmental state. *The Journal of Environment & Development*, 26(1), 3–24.

Hancock, J.T. and Guillory, J. (2015). Deception with technology. In S.S. Sundar (ed), *The handbook of the psychology of communication technology* (pp 270–289). Wiley.

Hanna, T. and Kelly, M. (2021). Community wealth building: The path towards a democratic and reparative political economic system. Democracy Collaborative. https://www.democracycollaborative.org/whatwethink/community-wealth-building-the-path-towards-a-democratic-and-reparative-political-economic-system

Hannák, A., Wagner, C., Garcia, D., Mislove, A., Strohmaier, M., and Wilson, C. (2017, February). Bias in online freelance marketplaces: Evidence from taskrabbit and fiverr. In *Proceedings of the 2017 ACM conference on computer supported cooperative work and social computing* (pp 1914–1933).

Hansen, H.K. and Weiskopf, R. (2021). From universalizing transparency to the interplay of transparency matrices: Critical insights from the emerging social credit system in China. *Organization Studies*, 42(1), 109–128.

Haque, A., Daniel, S., Maxwell, T., and Boerstoel, M. (2017). Postmarketing surveillance studies: An industry perspective on changing global requirements and implications. *Clinical Therapeutics*, 39(4), 675–685.

Hardt, M. (1998). The global society of control. *Discourse*, 20(3), 139–152.

Hardt, M. and Negri, A. (2000). *Empire*. Harvard University Press.

Harris, C. (2018). The Black Panther Party's War of Position, Neoliberal Passive Revolution, and the Origin of the Prison Industrial Complex in the US and Canada. *Groundings: Development, Pan-Africanism and Critical Theory*, 3(1), 17–49.

Harris, K.R. (2023). Beyond belief: On disinformation and manipulation. *Erkenntnis*, 1–21.

Harrison, G. (2020). Authoritarian neoliberalism and capitalist transformation in Africa: All pain, no gain. In I. Bruff and C.B. Tansel (eds), *Authoritarian neoliberalism* (pp 42–56). Routledge.

Hartnett, S.J. (2008). The annihilating public policies of the prison-industrial complex; or, crime, violence, and punishment in an age of neoliberalism. *Rhetoric & Public Affairs*, 11(3), 491–515.

Hartung, W.D. (2001). Eisenhower's warning: The military-industrial complex forty years later. *World Policy Journal*, 18(1), 39–44.

Hartung, W.D. (2010). *Prophets of war: Lockheed Martin and the making of the military-industrial complex*. ReadHowYouWant.com.

Hartung, W.D. and Washburn, J. (1998). Lockheed Martin: From warfare to welfare. *Nation*, 266(7), 11–15.

Harvey, D. (2005). *A brief history of neoliberalism*. Oxford University Press.

Harvey, D. (2010). *The enigma of capital and the crises of capitalism*. Oxford University Press.

Hasmath, R., Teets, J.C., and Lewis, O.A. (2019). The innovative personality? Policy making and experimentation in an authoritarian bureaucracy. *Public Administration and Development*, 39(3), 154–162.

Hasselskog, M. (2018). Rwandan 'home grown initiatives': Illustrating inherent contradictions of the democratic developmental state. *Development Policy Review*, 36(3), 309–328.

Hawkins, A. (2018). Beijing's big brother tech needs African faces. *Foreign Policy*, 24.

Hawley, J. (2021). *The tyranny of big tech*. Simon & Schuster.

Hayes, B. (2012). The surveillance-industrial complex. In K. Ball, K. Haggerty, and D. Lyo (eds), *Routledge handbook of surveillance studies* (pp 167–175). Routledge.

He, S., Hollenbeck, B., and Proserpio, D. (2020). The market for fake reviews. NET Institute Working Paper, 20(02).

Headrick, Z. and Miraldi, L.R. (2022). Smart city surveillance in Brazil: Big Brother is watching you. *Journal of Urban Affairs*, 44(2), 165–184.

Heberer, T. (2016). The Chinese 'developmental state 3.0' and the resilience of authoritarianism. *Journal of Chinese Governance*, 1(4), 611–632.

Hee-Yeon, C. (2000). The structure of the South Korean developmental regime and its transformation—statist mobilization and authoritarian integration in the anticommunist regimentation. *Inter-Asia Cultural Studies*, 1(3), 408–426.

Heidkamp, B. and Kergel, D. (eds) (2017). *Precarity within the digital age: Media change and social insecurity*. Springer.

Heiss, A. and Kelley, J. (2017). Between a shattered monolith and the acknowledgement of pluralism: Civil society and the negotiation of domestic normative change in the OSCE region. *International Negotiation*, 22(1), 49–72.

Heitzeg, N.A. (2016). *The school-to-prison pipeline: Education, discipline, and racialized double standards*. Bloomsbury Publishing USA.

Hellmann, O. (2018). High capacity, low resilience: The 'developmental' state and military–bureaucratic authoritarianism in South Korea. *International Political Science Review*, 39(1), 67–82.

Heng, Y.K. and McDonagh, K. (2009). *Risk, global governance and security: The other war on terror*. Routledge.

Henman, P. and Fenger, M. (eds) (2006). *Administering welfare reform: International transformations in welfare governance*. Policy Press.

Hepp, A., Alpen, S., and Simon, P. (2021). Beyond empowerment, experimentation and reasoning: The public discourse around the Quantified Self movement. *Communications*, 46(1), 27–51.

Hester, H. (2018). Care under capitalism: The crisis of 'women's work'. *IPPR Progressive Review*, 24(4), 343–352.

Hester, R.J. and Williams, O.D. (2020). The somatic-security industrial complex: Theorizing the political economy of informationalized biology. *Review of International Political Economy*, 27(1), 98–124.

Hickel, J. (2017). *The divide: A brief guide to global inequality and its solutions*. Windmill Books.

Higgott, R. (2021). Globalism, anti-globalism and individual security. *Critical Studies on Security*, 9(3), 256–258.

Hillenkamp, I. (2015). Solidarity economy for development and women's emancipation: Lessons from Bolivia. *Development and Change*, 46(5), 1133–1158.

Hiltzik, M. (2015). *Big science: Ernest Lawrence and the invention that launched the military-industrial complex*. Simon & Schuster.

Himmelweit, S. (2007). The prospects for caring: Economic theory and policy analysis. *Cambridge Journal of Economics*, 31(4), 581–599.

Hintz, A. (2021). Towards civic participation in the datafied society: Can citizen assemblies democratize algorithmic governance? *AoIR Selected Papers of Internet Research*. https://spir.aoir.org/ojs/index.php/spir/article/view/11943

Hirschman, A.O. (1965). Obstacles to development: A classification and a quasi-vanishing act. *Economic Development and Cultural Change*, 13(4, Part 1), 385–393.

Hirst, P.Q. (1976). Althusser and the theory of ideology. *Economy and Society*, 5(4), 385–412.

Hobson, C. (2014). Privatising the war on drugs. *Third World Quarterly*, 35(8), 1441–1456.

Hoffman, S. (2018). Managing the state: Social credit, surveillance and the CCP's plan for China. In N.D. Wright (ed), *AI, China, Russia, and the global order: Technological, political, global, and creative* (pp 42–27). Periodic Publication.

Hogan, M. (2015). Data flows and water woes: The Utah Data Center. *Big Data & Society*, 2(2), 2053951715592429.

Höglund, J. and Willander, M. (2017). Black hawk-down: Adaptation and the military-entertainment complex. *Culture Unbound*, 9(3), 365–389.

Holborow, M. (2007). Language, ideology and neoliberalism. *Journal of Language and Politics*, 6(1), 51–73.

Horwitz, A.V. (1984). The economy and social pathology. *Annual Review of Sociology*, 10(1), 95–119.

Howarth, D. (2010). Power, discourse, and policy: Articulating a hegemony approach to critical policy studies. *Critical Policy Studies*, 3(3–4), 309–335.

Howson, P. (2021). Distributed degrowth technology: Challenges for blockchain beyond the green economy. *Ecological Economics*, 184, 107020.

Hoynes, H. and Rothstein, J. (2019). Universal basic income in the United States and advanced countries. *Annual Review of Economics*, 11, 929–958.

Hu, M. (2020). Bulk biometric surveillance and big tech. *Hastings Law Journal*, 71(4), 1097–1142.

Hudson, R. (2020). The illegal, the illicit and new geographies of uneven development. *Territory, Politics, Governance*, 8(2), 161–176.

Huggins, C. (2017). *Agricultural reform in Rwanda: Authoritarianism, markets and zones of governance.* Bloomsbury Publishing.

Huggins, M.K. (1987). US-supported state terror: A history of police training in Latin America. *Crime and Social Justice*, 27/28, 149–171.

Humphrey, D. (2022). Sensing the human: Biometric surveillance and the Japanese technology industry. *Media, Culture & Society*, 44(1), 72–87.

Huneeus, C. and Undurraga, T. (2021). Authoritarian rule and economic groups in Chile: A case of winner-takes-all politics. In V. Basualdo, H. Berghoff, and M. Bucheli (eds), *Big business and dictatorships in Latin America: A transnational history of profits and repression* (pp 91–125). Routledge.

Hunt, A. (1985). The ideology of law: Advances and problems in recent applications of the concept of ideology to the analysis of law. *Law & Society Review*, 19, 11.

Hunt, C.J. (2019). Feeding the machine: The commodification of black bodies from slavery to mass incarceration. *University of Baltimore Law Review*, 49(3), Article 3.

Hunter, W. and Power, T.J. (2019). Bolsonaro and Brazil's illiberal backlash. *Journal of Democracy*, 30(1), 68–82.

Hürtgen, S. (2021). Precarization of work and employment in the light of competitive Europeanization and the fragmented and flexible regime of European production. *Capital & Class*, 45(1), 71–91.

Im, H.B. (1987). The rise of bureaucratic authoritarianism in South Korea. *World Politics*, 39(2), 231–257.

Ingram, A. and Dodds, K. (2016). *Spaces of security and insecurity: Geographies of the war on terror*. Routledge.

Jack, M.C., Chann, S., Jackson, S.J., and Dell, N. (2021). Networked authoritarianism at the edge: The digital and political transitions of Cambodian village officials. *Proceedings of the ACM on Human-Computer Interaction*, 5(CSCW1), 1–25.

Jaffe, R. and Pilò, F. (2023). Security technology, urban prototyping, and the politics of failure. *Security Dialogue*, 54(1), 76–93.

Jago, E. (2022). Algorithmic manipulation: How social media is shaping our theology. *Eleutheria*, 6(1), 9.

Jain, S. and Gabor, D. (2020). The rise of digital financialisation: The case of India. *New Political Economy*, 25(5), 813–828.

Jameson, F. (1981). *The political unconscious: Narrative as a socially symbolic act*. Cornell University Press.

Jamil, S. (2021). The rise of digital authoritarianism: Evolving threats to media and Internet freedoms in Pakistan. *World of Media. Journal of Russian Media and Journalism Studies*, 3.

Jarrahi, M.H., Newlands, G., Lee, M.K., Wolf, C.T., Kinder, E., and Sutherland, W. (2021). Algorithmic management in a work context. *Big Data & Society*, 8(2), 20539517211020332.

Jasser, G., McSwiney, J., Pertwee, E., and Zannettou, S. (2023). 'Welcome to# GabFam': Far-right virtual community on Gab. *New Media & Society*, 25(7), 1728–1745.

Jencks, H.W. (1980). The Chinese 'military-industrial complex' and defense modernization. *Asian Survey*, 20(10), 965–989.

Jenss, A. (2023). *Selective security in the war on drugs: The coloniality of state power in Colombia and Mexico*. Rowman & Littlefield.

Jessop, B. (1990). Mode of production. In J. Eatwell, M. Milgate, and P. Newman (eds), *Marxian economics* (pp 289–296). Palgrave Macmillan.

Jessop, B. (2010). Constituting another Foucault effect: Foucault on states and statecraft. In U. Bröckling, S. Krasmann, and T. Lemke (eds), *Governmentality* (pp 64–81). Routledge.

Jessop, B. (2013). Finance-dominated accumulation and post-democratic capitalism. In S. Fadda and P. Tridico (eds), *Institutions and development after the financial crisis* (pp 83–105). Routledge.

Jessop, B. (2019). Authoritarian neoliberalism: Periodization and critique. *South Atlantic Quarterly*, 118(2), 343–361.

Jili, B. (2022). The spread of Chinese surveillance tools in Africa: A focus on Ethiopia and Kenya. In C. Daniels, B. Erforth, and C. Teevan (eds), *Africa–Europe cooperation and digital transformation* (pp 32–49). Routledge.

Johanssen, J. (2021). Data perversion: A psychoanalytic perspective on datafication. *Journal of Digital Social Research*, 3(1), 88–105.

Johnson, S. and Kwak, J. (2010). *13 bankers: The Wall Street takeover and the next financial meltdown*. Pantheon Books.

Jones, M.O. (2022). *Digital authoritarianism in the Middle East: Deception, disinformation and social media*. Hurst Publishers.

Jordan, L.P. (2017). Introduction: Understanding migrants' economic precarity in global cities. *Urban Geography*, 38(10), 1455–1458.

Jørgensen, M.B. and Schierup, C.U. (2016). *Politics of precarity: Migrant conditions, struggles and experiences* (vol 97). Brill.

Jorgenson, D.O. (1975). Economic threat and authoritarianism in television programs: 1950–1974. *Psychological Reports*, 37(3_suppl), 1153–1154.

Judis, J.B. (2016). *The populist explosion: How the great recession transformed American and European politics*. Columbia Global Reports.

Juris, J.S. (2012). Reflections on #Occupy Everywhere: Social media, public space, and emerging logics of aggregation. *American Ethnologist*, 39(2), 259–279.

Kaempf, S. (2019). 'A relationship of mutual exploitation': The evolving ties between the Pentagon, Hollywood, and the commercial gaming sector. *Social Identities*, 25(4), 542–558.

Kalil, I., Silveira, S.C., Pinheiro, W., Kalil, Á., Pereira, J.V., Azarias, W., et al (2021). Politics of fear in Brazil: Far-right conspiracy theories on COVID-19. *Global Discourse*, 11(3), 409–425.

Kampmark, B. (2020). The pandemic surveillance state: An enduring legacy of COVID-19. *Journal of Global Faultlines*, 7(1), 59–70.

Kamra, L., Williams, P., and Johar, P. (2023). Grassroots authoritarianism: WhatsApp, middle-class boundary-making and pandemic governance in New Delhi's neighbourhoods. *Territory, Politics, Governance*, 1–20.

Karatani, K. (2014). *The structure of world history: From modes of production to modes of exchange*. Duke University Press.

Karner, C. and Weicht, B. (eds) (2020). *The populist radical right in Central and Eastern Europe: Ideology, impact, and electoral performance*. Routledge.

Katzenstein, P.J. and Seybert, L.A. (2018). Protean power and uncertainty: Exploring the unexpected in world politics. *International Studies Quarterly*, 62(1), 80–93.

Kaufman, R.R. (1985). Democratic and authoritarian responses to the debt issue: Argentina, Brazil, Mexico. *International Organization*, 39(3), 473–503.

Kavada, A. (2015). Social media as conversation: A manifesto. *Social Media+ Society*, 1(1), 1–2.

Kawachi, K. (2018). Safety and security management for international volunteers: A case study of Japan Overseas Cooperation Volunteers in Colombia during the war on drugs. *JICA Research Institute Working Paper*, 171, 1–44.

Keenan, L., Monteath, T., and Wójcik, D. (2023). Hungry for power: Financialization and the concentration of corporate control in the global food system. *Geoforum*, 147, 103909.

Kellogg, K.C., Valentine, M.A., and Christin, A. (2020). Algorithms at work: The new contested terrain of control. *Academy of Management Annals*, 14(1), 366–410.

Kelly, M.G. (2015). Discipline is control: Foucault contra Deleuze. *New Formations*, 84(84–85), 148–162.

Kieh, G.K. (2015). Constructing the social democratic developmental state in Africa: Lessons from the 'Global South'. *Bandung: Journal of the Global South*, 2, 1–14.

Kiely, R. (2017). From authoritarian liberalism to economic technocracy: Neoliberalism, politics and 'de-democratization'. *Critical Sociology*, 43(4–5), 725–745.

Kiely, R. (2021). The populism of the privileged and the perseverance of neoliberal hegemony. *Globalizations*, 1–16.

Kilty, J. and DeVellis, L. (2010). Transcarceration and the production of 'grey space': How frontline workers exercise spatial practices in a halfway house for women. In V. Strimelle and F. Vanhamme (eds), *Droits et voix: La criminologie à l'Université d'Ottawa/Rights and Voice: Criminology at the University of Ottawa*, (pp 137–158). University of Ottawa Press.

Kim, E.M., Kim, P.H., and Kim, J. (2013). From development to development cooperation: Foreign aid, country ownership, and the developmental state in South Korea. *The Pacific Review*, 26(3), 313–336.

Kim, S.Y. (2007a). Consolidating the authoritarian developmental state in the 1970s Korea: Chosen strategies. *International Review of Public Administration*, 12(1), 119–132.

Kim, S.Y. (2007b). The East Asian developmental state and its economic and social policies: The case of Korea. *International Review of Public Administration*, 12(2), 69–87.

Kimbles, S.L. (2006). Cultural complexes and the transmission of group traumas in everyday life. *Psychological Perspectives*, 49(1), 96–110.

Kinnvall, C. (2018). Ontological insecurities and postcolonial imaginaries: The emotional appeal of populism. *Humanity & Society*, 42(4), 523–543.

Kinossian, N. and Morgan, K. (2023). Authoritarian state capitalism: Spatial planning and the megaproject in Russia. *Environment and Planning A: Economy and Space*, 55(3), 655–672.

Kinyondo, A. and Huggins, C. (2019). Resource nationalism in Tanzania: Implications for artisanal and small-scale mining. *Resources Policy*, 63, 101436.

Kirshner, L.A. (2005). Rethinking desire: The objet petit a in Lacanian theory. *Journal of the American Psychoanalytic Association*, 53(1), 83–102.

Kisangani, E.N. (1987). Implementation of stabilization policies in an authoritarian setting: Zaire, 1970–1980. *Canadian Journal of African Studies/ La Revue canadienne des études africaines*, 21(2), 175–200.

Kitchin, R. (2014). The real-time city? Big data and smart urbanism. *GeoJournal*, 79(1), 1–14.

Klauser, F.R. and Pedrozo, S. (2015). Power and space in the drone age: A literature review and politico-geographical research agenda. *Geographica Helvetica*, 70(4), 285–293.

Klein, N. (2007a). Disaster capitalism. *Harper's Magazine*, 315, 47–58.

Klein, N. (2007b). *The shock doctrine: The rise of disaster capitalism*. Macmillan.

Kliman, D.M. (2012). The west and global swing states. *The International Spectator*, 47(3), 53–64.

Klinge, T.J., Hendrikse, R., Fernandez, R., and Adriaans, I. (2023). Augmenting digital monopolies: A corporate financialization perspective on the rise of Big Tech. *Competition & Change*, 27(2), 332–353.

Kofas, J.V. (1995). The politics of austerity: The IMF and US foreign policy in Bolivia, 1956–1964. *The Journal of Developing Areas*, 29(2), 213–236.

Kohl, B. and Farthing, L.C. (2006). *Impasse in Bolivia: Neoliberal hegemony and popular resistance*. Zed Books.

Kotz, D.M. (2015). *The rise and fall of neoliberal capitalism*. Harvard University Press.

Kramer, A.D., Guillory, J.E., and Hancock, J.T. (2014). Experimental evidence of massive-scale emotional contagion through social networks. *Proceedings of the National Academy of Sciences*, 111(24), 8788–8790.

Kraska, P.B. and Cubellis, L.J. (1997). Militarizing Mayberry and beyond: Making sense of American paramilitary policing. *Justice Quarterly*, 14(4), 607–629.

Krippner, G.R. (2012). *Capitalizing on crisis: The political origins of the rise of finance*. Harvard University Press.

Kristensen, D.B. and Ruckenstein, M. (2018). Co-evolving with self-tracking technologies. *New Media & Society*, 20(10), 3624–3640.

Krivý, M. (2018). Towards a critique of cybernetic urbanism: The smart city and the society of control. *Planning Theory*, 17(1), 8–30.

Krüger, S. (2019). The authoritarian dimension in digital self-tracking: Containment, commodification, subjugation. In V. King, B. Gerisch, and H. Rosa (eds), *Lost in perfection* (pp 85–104). Routledge.

Kuehn, K. (2019). Surveillance and South Africa. *The Political Economy of Communication*, 6(2).

Kukutai, T. and Taylor, J. (eds) (2016). *Indigenous data sovereignty: Toward an agenda*. ANU Press.

Kuldova, T.Ø. (2022). *Compliance-industrial complex: The operating system of a pre-crime society*. Springer Nature.

Kwon, K.H., Shao, C., and Nah, S. (2021). Localized social media and civic life: Motivations, trust, and civic participation in local community contexts. *Journal of Information Technology & Politics*, 18(1), 55–69.

Lacan, J. (1966). *Écrits*. Seuil.

Lacan, J. (1977). *The four fundamental concepts of psychoanalysis*. Hogarth Press.

Lacity, M.C. and Willcocks, L. (1997). Information systems sourcing: Examining the privatization option in USA public administration. *Information Systems Journal*, 7(2), 85–108.

Lacković, N. (2021). Postdigital living and algorithms of desire. *Postdigital Science and Education*, 3, 280–282.

Laclau, E. (1990). *New reflections on the revolution of our time*. Verso.

Laclau, E. (2003). Deconstruction, pragmatism, hegemony. In S. Critchley, J., Derrida, E., Laclau, and R. Rorty (eds), *Deconstruction and pragmatism* (pp 47–67). Routledge.

Laclau, E. and Mouffe, C. (1986). *Hegemony and Socialist Strategy: Towards a radical democratic politics*. Verso Books.

Lafer, G. (2020). Neoliberalism by other means: The 'War on Terror' at home and abroad. *New Political Science*, 26(3), 323–346.

Lahiri-Dutt, K. (2018). Extractive peasants: Reframing informal artisanal and small-scale mining debates. *Third World Quarterly*, 39(8), 1561–1582.

Lai, H. (2016). *China's governance model: Flexibility and durability of pragmatic authoritarianism*. Routledge.

Lai, M.K. and Ho, A.P. (2020). Unravelling potentials and limitations of sharing economy in reducing unnecessary consumption: A social science perspective. *Resources, Conservation and Recycling*, 153, 104546.

Laitinen, A. and Särkelä, A. (2019). Four conceptions of social pathology. *European Journal of Social Theory*, 22(1), 80–102.

Langley, P. (2008). *The everyday life of global finance: Saving and borrowing in Anglo-America*. Oxford University Press.

Langley, P. (2020). The financialization of life. In N. Van der Zwan, D. Mertens, and P. Mader (eds), *The Routledge international handbook of financialization* (pp 68–78). Routledge.

Lanier, J. (2018). *Ten arguments for deleting your social media accounts right now*. Random House.

Lapavitsas, C. (2009). Financialised capitalism: Crisis and financial expropriation. *Historical Materialism*, 17(2), 114–148.

Lapavitsas, C. (2013). The financialization of capitalism: 'Profiting without producing'. *City*, 17(6), 792–805.

Lau, E. (2020). Cybertruth or Cyberbunk? A reassessment of the militarization of the information age. *Philosophy & Technology*, 33(3), 347–358.

Lau, E. O., Jimenez, L., Carrion, S., and Vidarte, M. (2020). Smart cities and urban policing: Towards an ethical framework for preemptive technologies. In *IFIP international conference on artificial intelligence applications and innovations* (pp 313–320). Springer.

Laursen, E. (2021). *The operating system: An anarchist theory of the modern state*. AK Press.

Lavoie, M. (2012). Financialization, neo-liberalism, and securitization. *Journal of Post Keynesian Economics*, 35(2), 215–233.

Lazar, S. and Sanchez, A. (2019). Understanding labour politics in an age of precarity. *Dialectical Anthropology*, 43, 3–14.

Lazzarato, M. (2006). The concepts of life and the living in the societies of control. In B.M. Sørensen and M. Fuglsang (eds), *Deleuze and the social* (pp 171–190). Edinburgh University Press.

Lazzarato, M. (2012). *The making of the indebted man*. Semiotext(e).

Leal, C.C. and Oliveira, B. (2021). Choice architecture: Nudging for sustainable behavior. In C.F. Machado and J.P. Davim (eds), *Sustainable management for managers and engineers* (pp 1–17). Wiley.

Lear, J. and Collins, J. (1995). Working in Chile's free market. *Latin American Perspectives*, 22(1), 10–29.

Ledbetter, J. (2011). *Unwarranted influence: Dwight D. Eisenhower and the military industrial complex*. Yale University Press.

Lee, C.K. and Kofman, Y. (2012). The politics of precarity: Views beyond the United States. *Work and Occupations*, 39(4), 388–408.

Lee, D., Hampton, M., and Jeyacheya, J. (2015). The political economy of precarious work in the tourism industry in small island developing states. *Review of International Political Economy*, 22(1), 194–223.

Leftwich, A. (1995). Bringing politics back in: Towards a model of the developmental state. *The Journal of Development Studies*, 31(3), 400–427.

Leggett, W. (2014). The politics of behaviour change: Nudge, neoliberalism and the state. *Policy & Politics*, 42(1), 3–19.

Lehdonvirta, V. (2018). Flexibility in the gig economy: Managing time on three online piecework platforms. *New Technology, Work and Employment*, 33(1), 13–29.

Lema, A. and Ruby, K. (2007). Between fragmented authoritarianism and policy coordination: Creating a Chinese market for wind energy. *Energy Policy*, 35(7), 3879–3890.

Lemert, E. (2014). Social pathology. In T.L. Anderson (ed), *Understanding deviance* (pp 173–179). Routledge.

Leopold, L. (2009). *The looting of America: How Wall Street's game of fantasy finance destroyed our jobs, pensions, and prosperity – and what we can do about it*. Chelsea Green Publishing.

Lesutis, G. (2021). *The politics of precarity: Spaces of extractivism, violence, and suffering*. Routledge.

Levenda, A. and Mahmoudi, D. (2019). Silicon wildfire: Accumulation in the datafied wildland. *Society and Space*.

Levitsky, S. and Ziblatt, D. (2018). How wobbly is our democracy. *New York Times*, 27 January. https://www.nytimes.com/2018/01/27/opinion/sun day/democracy-polarization.html

Levy, D.L. (2008). Political contestation in global production networks. *Academy of Management Review*, 33(4), 943–963.

Li, T.M. (2007). *The will to improve: Governmentality, development, and the practice of politics*. Duke University Press.

Liang, F. and Chen, Y. (2022). The making of "good" citizens: China's Social Credit Systems and infrastructures of social quantification. *Policy & Internet*, 14(1), 114–135.

Liang, F., Das, V., Kostyuk, N., and Hussain, M.M. (2018). Constructing a data-driven society: China's social credit system as a state surveillance infrastructure. *Policy & Internet*, 10(4), 415–453.

Liang, X., Yuan, Q., Guo, Y., and Lu, J. (2023). Struggling with inequality and the uncertain reterritorialization of migrants: A case study of Guangzhou. *Transactions in Planning and Urban Research*, 2(4), 349–373.

Lim, H. (2010). The transformation of the developmental state and economic reform in Korea. *Journal of Contemporary Asia*, 40(2), 188–210.

Lim, T.C. (1998). Power, capitalism, and the authoritarian state in South Korea. *Journal of Contemporary Asia*, 28(4), 457–483.

Lindsay-Poland, J. (2016). A flexible war: Despite changing discourses, industries and agencies that have long profited off the drug wars are adapting to find new opportunities. *NACLA Report on the Americas*, 48(2), 167–172.

Linke, U. (2010). Fortress Europe: Globalization, militarization and the policing of interior borderlands. *TOPIA: Canadian Journal of Cultural Studies*, 23, 100–120.

Lippert, R.K. and Walby, K. (2016). Governing through privacy: Authoritarian liberalism, law, and privacy knowledge. *Law, Culture and the Humanities*, 12(2), 329–352.

Lipton, D. and Sachs, J. (1992). Privatization in Eastern Europe: The case of Poland. *Brookings Papers on Economic Activity*, 2, 293–341.

Liu, H.Y. (2021). Tech self-governance: The digital platform as private infrastructure provider. *Global Perspectives*, 2(1), 26941.

Liu, P. and Liu, J.M. (2020). Digital Authoritarianism in the People's Republic of China. In S. Sarsar and R. Datta (eds), Democracy in Crisis around the World, (pp 176–184). Lexington Books.

Lizárraga, F.A. (2020). The case for community wealth building. *Polis (Santiago)*, 56.

Loewenstein, A. (2015). *Disaster capitalism: Making a killing out of catastrophe.* Verso Books.

Löfflmann, G. (2024). *The politics of antagonism: Populist security narratives and the remaking of political identity.* Taylor & Francis.

López, G.A.G. (2020). Reflections on disaster colonialism: Response to Yarimar Bonilla's 'The wait of disaster'. *Political Geography*, 78, 102170.

Lovins, L.H., Wallis, S., Wijkman, A., and Fullerton, J. (2018). *A finer future: Creating an economy in service to life.* New Society Publishers.

Lowrey, A. (2018). *Give people money: How a universal basic income would end poverty, revolutionize work, and remake the world.* Crown.

Lu, K. (2013). Can individual psychology explain social phenomena? An appraisal of the theory of cultural complexes. *Psychoanalysis, Culture & Society*, 18, 386–404.

Luca, M. (2016). Reviews, reputation, and revenue: The case of Yelp. com. Harvard Business School NOM Unit Working Paper (12-016).

Lucarelli, D.B. (2012). Financialization and global imbalances: Prelude to crisis. *Review of Radical Political Economics*, 44(4), 429–447.

Lucarelli, S. (2010). Financialization as biopower. In A. Fumagalli and S. Mezzadra (eds), Crisis in the global economy: Financial markets, social struggles, and new political scenarios, (pp 119–138). Semiotext(E).

Ludwig, G. (2016). Desiring neoliberalism. *Sexuality Research and Social Policy*, 13, 417–427.

Lundskow, G. (2012). Authoritarianism and destructiveness in the tea party movement. *Critical Sociology*, 38(4), 529–547.

Luo, Z. and Li, M. (2022). Participatory censorship: How online fandom community facilitates authoritarian rule. *New Media & Society*, 14614448221113923.

Lupton, D. (2016a). The diverse domains of quantified selves: Self-tracking modes and dataveillance. *Economy and Society*, 45(1), 101–122.

Lupton, D. (2016b). *The quantified self.* John Wiley & Sons.

Lupton, D. (2017). Digital health and health care. In S. Rushton and J.R. Youde (eds), *Routledge handbook of health geography* (pp 172–183). Routledge.

Lupton, D. (2019). *Data selves: More-than-human perspectives.* John Wiley & Sons.

Lupton, D. and Maslen, S. (2018). The more-than-human sensorium: From embodied and emplaced sensing to machine-guided tracking. In C. Lury, R. Fensham, A. Heller-Nicholas, S. Lammes, A. Last, M. Michael, et al (eds), *Routledge handbook of interdisciplinary research methods* (pp 148–158). Routledge.

Lynn III, W.J. (2014). The end of the military-industrial complex: How the Pentagon is adapting to globalization. *Foreign Affairs*, 93, 104.

Lysandrou, P. (2016). The colonization of the future: An alternative view of financialization and its portents. *Journal of Post Keynesian Economics*, 39(4), 444–472.

MacDonald, R. and Giazitzoglu, A. (2019). Youth, enterprise and precarity: Or, what is, and what is wrong with, the 'gig economy'? *Journal of Sociology*, 55(4), 724–740.

Mačiulienė, M. and Skaržauskienė, A. (2020). Building the capacities of civic tech communities through digital data analytics. *Journal of Innovation & Knowledge*, 5(4), 244–250.

MacKinnon, C.A. (2011). Trafficking, prostitution, and inequality. *Harvard Civil Rights-Civil Liberties Law Review*, 46, 271–309.

MacKinnon, D. (2012). Reinventing the state: Neoliberalism, state transformation, and economic governance. In T.J. Barnes, J. Peck, and E. Sheppard (eds), *The Wiley-Blackwell companion to economic geography* (pp 344–357). Blackwell.

MacLean, N. (2017). *Democracy in chains: The deep history of the radical right's stealth plan for America*. Penguin.

Madden, M., Gilman, M., Levy, K., and Marwick, A. (2017). Privacy, poverty, and big data: A matrix of vulnerabilities for poor Americans. *Washington University Law Review*, 95, 53.

Mader, P. and Mader, P. (2015). The financialization of poverty. In *The political economy of microfinance: Financializing poverty* (pp 78–120). Palgrave Macmillan.

Mafeje, A. (1981). On the articulation of modes of production. *Journal of Southern African Studies*, 8(1), 123–138.

Magnet, S. (2019). Rituals of communication and security. In B.C. Taylor, and H. Bean (eds), *The handbook of communication and security* (pp 342–353). Routledge.

Maher, H. (2023). The free market as fantasy: A Lacanian approach to the problem of neoliberal resilience. *International Studies Quarterly*, 67(3), sqad050.

Maidment, M.R. (2006). *Doing time on the outside: Deconstructing the benevolent community*. University of Toronto Press.

Malabou, C. (2020). Cryptocurrencies: Anarchist turn or strengthening of surveillance capitalism? From Bitcoin to Libra (R. Boncardo, trans). *Australian Humanities Review*, 66.

Mang, P., & Reed, B. (2012). Designing from place: A regenerative framework and methodology. *Building Research & Information*, 40(1), 23–38.

Manley, J. and Whyman, P.B. (eds) (2021). *The Preston model and community wealth building: Creating a socio-economic democracy for the future*. Routledge.

Mann, S. and Ferenbok, J. (2013). New media and the power politics of sousveillance in a surveillance-dominated world. *Surveillance & Society*, 11(1/2), 18–34.

Mann, W. (2018). Creditor rights and innovation: Evidence from patent collateral. *Journal of Financial Economics*, 130(1), 25–47.

Mare, A. (2020). Internet shutdowns in Africa: State-ordered internet shutdowns and digital authoritarianism in Zimbabwe. *International Journal of Communication*, 14(20), 4244–4263.

Maréchal, N. (2017). Networked authoritarianism and the geopolitics of information: Understanding Russian internet policy. *Media and Communication*, 5(1), 29–41.

Marques, J.S. (2014). Social and solidarity economy: Between emancipation and reproduction (No. 2). UNRISD Occasional Paper: Potential and Limits of Social and Solidarity Economy.

Martin, A. and Petro, P. (eds) (2006). *Rethinking global security: Media, popular culture, and the 'War on terror'*. Rutgers University Press.

Martinez, D.E. (2011). Beyond disciplinary enclosures: Management control in the society of control. *Critical Perspectives on Accounting*, 22(2), 200–211.

Marvin, S. and Luque-Ayala, A. (2017). Urban operating systems: Diagramming the city. *International Journal of Urban and Regional Research*, 41(1), 84–103.

Marwick, A.E. and Lewis, R. (2017). *Media manipulation and disinformation online*. Data & Society Research Institute.

Marwick, A., Kuo, R., Zug, M., Anderson, J., Gundlach, C., and Tucker, J.A. (2022). Complex network shaping of COVID-19 disinformation: Actors, messages and structural signatures. *The International Journal of Press/Politics*.

Marx, K. (1867). *Capital: A critique of political economy*. Verlag Meissner.

Masco, J. (2015). The age of fallout. *History of the Present*, 5(2), 137–168.

Massey, A. (2019). Persistent public management reform: An egregore of liberal authoritarianism? *Public Money & Management*, 39(1), 9–17.

Masullo, J. and Morisi, D. (2024). The human costs of the war on drugs: Attitudes towards militarization of security in Mexico. *Comparative Political Studies*, 57(6), 887–920.

Massumi, B. (2015). *Ontopower: Wars, powers, and the state of perception*. Duke University Press.

Matfess, H. (2015). Rwanda and Ethiopia: Developmental authoritarianism and the new politics of African strong men. *African Studies Review*, 58(2), 181–204.

Matos, P. (2019). Locating precarization: The state, livelihoods and the politics of precarity in contemporary Portugal. *Dialectical Anthropology*, 43(1), 15–30.

Mattioli, F. (2018). Financialization without liquidity: In-kind payments, forced credit, and authoritarianism at the periphery of Europe. *Journal of the Royal Anthropological Institute*, 24(3), 568–588.

Mattioli, F. (2019). Debt, financialisation and politics. In J.G. Carrier (ed), *A research agenda for economic anthropology* (pp 56–73). Edward Elgar.

Mattioli, F. (2020). *Dark finance: Illiquidity and authoritarianism at the margins of Europe.* Stanford University Press.

Maturo, A.F. and Moretti, V. (2018). *Digital health and the gamification of life: How apps can promote a positive medicalization.* Emerald Publishing Limited.

Mayer, B. (2014). Sub specie de homine: A study in Freierian nonconformism. *Educational Theory,* 64(1), 41–56.

McCann, B.J. (2017). *The mark of criminality: Rhetoric, race, and gangsta rap in the war-on-crime era.* University of Alabama Press.

McCartin, J.A. (2011). *Collision course: Ronald Reagan, the air traffic controllers, and the strike that changed America.* Oxford University Press.

McCluskey, M.T. (2017). Are we economic engines too: Precarity, productivity and gender. *The University of Toledo Law Review,* 49, 631.

McDaniel, J.L. and Pease, K. (eds) (2021). *Predictive policing and artificial intelligence.* Routledge.

McDonald, M. (2018). US hegemony, the 'war on terror' and security in the Asia-Pacific. In A. Burke and M. McDonald (eds), *Critical security in the Asia-Pacific* (pp 198–212). Manchester University Press.

McDoom, O.S. (2022). Securocratic state-building: The rationales, rebuttals, and risks behind the extraordinary rise of Rwanda after the genocide. *African Affairs,* 121(485), 535–567.

McDowell, L., Batnitzky, A., and Dyer, S. (2009). Precarious work and economic migration: Emerging immigrant divisions of labour in Greater London's service sector. *International Journal of Urban and Regional Research,* 33(1), 3–25.

McElroy, E. and Vergerio, M. (2022). Automating gentrification: Landlord technologies and housing justice organizing in New York City homes. *Environment and Planning D: Society and Space,* 40(4), 607–626.

McIlroy, B. (1993). The repression of communities: Visual representations of Northern Ireland during the Thatcher years. In L. Friedman (ed), *Fires were started: British cinema and Thatcherism* (pp 92–108). Wallflower Press.

McKay, B.M. (2017). Agrarian extractivism in Bolivia. *World Development,* 97, 199–211.

McMichael, P. (2017). *Development and social change: A global perspective* (6th ed.). SAGE.

McNally, D. (2009). From financial crisis to world-slump: Accumulation, financialisation, and the global slowdown. *Historical Materialism,* 17(2), 35–83.

McNeill, F. (2018). *Pervasive punishment: Making sense of mass supervision.* Emerald Publishing Limited.

McNeill, F. (2020). Penal and welfare conditionality: Discipline or degradation? *Social Policy & Administration,* 54(2), 295–310.

McNeil-Willson, R. (2022). Understanding the #plandemic: Core framings on Twitter and what this tells us about countering online far right COVID-19 conspiracies. *First Monday*, 27(5).

Meissner, M. and Meissner, M. (2017a). Conclusion: Financialization, spectral absence and the politics of myth. In M. Meissner, *Narrating the global financial crisis: Urban imaginaries and the politics of myth* (pp 221–227). Springer.

Meissner, M. and Meissner, M. (2017b). Introduction: Myths of finance and the city. In M. Meissner, *Narrating the global financial crisis: Urban imaginaries and the politics of myth* (pp 1–16). Springer.

Melman, S. (1974). *The Permanent War Economy: American capitalism in decline.* Simon & Schuster.

Meltzer, B.D. and Sunstein, C.R. (1983). Public employee strikes, executive discretion, and the air traffic controllers. *University of Chicago Law Review*, 50, 731.

Michalsen, V. (2019). Abolitionist feminism as prisons close: Fighting the racist and misogynist surveillance 'child welfare' system. *The Prison Journal*, 99(4), 504–511.

Mignolo, W.D. (2011). *The darker side of western modernity: Global futures, decolonial options.* Duke University Press.

Milan, S. (2013). *Social movements and their technologies: Wiring social change.* Springer.

Miliband, R. (1965). Marx and the state. *Socialist Register*, 2, 278–296.

Millar, K.M. (2017). Toward a critical politics of precarity. *Sociology Compass*, 11(6), e12483.

Miller, K. (2014). Total surveillance, big data, and predictive crime technology: Privacy's perfect storm. *Journal of Technology Law & Policy*, 19, 105.

Miller, R.J. and Stuart, F. (2017). Carceral citizenship: Race, rights and responsibility in the age of mass supervision. *Theoretical Criminology*, 21(4), 532–548.

Milne, S. (2014). *The enemy within.* Verso Books.

Miraftab, F. (2011). Faraway intimate development: Global restructuring of social reproduction. *Journal of Planning Education and Research*, 31(4), 392–405.

Mirowski, P. (2013). *Never let a serious crisis go to waste: How neoliberalism survived the financial meltdown.* Verso Books.

Mishura, A. and Ageeva, S. (2022). Financialisation and the authoritarian state: The case of Russia. *Cambridge Journal of Economics*, 46(5), 1109–1140.

Misra, J. (2021). *The intersectionality of precarity. Contemporary Sociology: A Journal of Reviews*, 50(2), 104–108.

Mohanty, C.T. (1984). Under western eyes: Feminist scholarship and colonial discourses. *Boundary 2*, 12(3), 333–358.

Möhlmannn, M., Alves de Lima Salge, C., and Marabelli, M. (2023). Algorithm sensemaking: How platform workers make sense of algorithmic management. *Journal of the Association for Information Systems*, 24(1), 35–64.

Monahan, T. (2006). Counter-surveillance as political intervention? *Social Semiotics*, 16(4), 515–534.

Monbiot, G. (2016). Neoliberalism: The ideology at the root of all our problems. *The Guardian*, 15 April.

Montag, W. (1995). 'The soul is the prison of the body': Althusser and Foucault, 1970–1975. *Yale French Studies*, 88, 53–77.

Montford, K. and Taylor, C. (eds) (2021). *Building abolition: Decarceration and social justice*. Routledge.

Montgomery, R. and Griffiths, T. (2015). The use of private security services for policing. *Public Safety Canada*, R041.

Moore, P.V. (2019). Watching the watchers: Surveillance at work and notes for trade unionists. *International Journal of Labour Research*, 9(1/2), 103–122.

Moore, P.V. and Robinson, A. (2016). The quantified self: What counts in the neoliberal workplace. *New Media & Society*, 18(11), 2774–2792.

Morales, W.Q. (1989). The war on drugs: A new US national security doctrine? *Third World Quarterly*, 11(3), 147–169.

Morgan, D. (1984). Terminal flight: The air traffic controllers' strike of 1981. *Journal of American Studies*, 18(2), 165–183.

Morozov, E. (2019). Digital socialism? The calculation debate in the age of big data. *New Left Review*, 116, 33–67.

Morozov, V. (2022). Uneven worlds of hegemony: Towards a discursive ontology of societal multiplicity. *International Relations*, 36(1), 83–103.

Morrison, E. (2016). *Discipline and desire: Surveillance technologies in performance*. University of Michigan Press.

Moskos Jr, C.C. (1974). The concept of the military-industrial complex: Radical critique or liberal bogey? *Social Problems*, 21(4), 498–512.

Moulier-Boutang, Y. (2011). *Cognitive capitalism*. Polity.

Mozur, P., Kessel, J.M., and Chan, M. (2019). Made in China, exported to the world: The surveillance state. *The New York Times* (24 April).

Mudde, C. and Kaltwasser, C.R. (eds) (2012). *Populism in Europe and the Americas: Threat or corrective for democracy?* Cambridge University Press.

Mullenite, J. (2019). Infrastructure and authoritarianism in the land of waters: A genealogy of flood control in Guyana. *Annals of the American Association of Geographers*, 109(2), 502–510.

Müller, M.M. (2016). *The punitive city: Privatized policing and protection in neoliberal Mexico*. Bloomsbury Publishing.

Mumby, D.K. (1989). Ideology & the social construction of meaning: A communication perspective. *Communication Quarterly*, 37(4), 291–304.

Muntaner, C. (2018). Digital platforms, gig economy, precarious employment, and the invisible hand of social class. *International Journal of Health Services*, 48(4), 597–600.

Murakami Wood, D. (ed) (2006). *A report on the surveillance society*. Surveillance Studies Network.

Murray, B. (1999). No welfare for Lockheed or Maximus. *LA Weekly* (29 July).

Nafus, D. and Sherman, J. (2014). This one does not go up to 11: The quantified self movement as an alternative big data practice. *International Journal of Communication*, 8, 11.

Neal, A.W. (2009). *Exceptionalism and the politics of counter-terrorism: Liberty, security and the war on terror*. Routledge.

Neff, G. and Nafus, D. (2016). *Self-tracking*. MIT Press.

Negri, A. and Hardt, M. (2000). *Empire*. Harvard University Press.

Neilson, B. and Rossiter, N. (2008). Precarity as a political concept, or, Fordism as exception. *Theory, Culture & Society*, 25(7–8), 51–72.

Neilson, D. (2015). Class, precarity, and anxiety under neoliberal global capitalism: From denial to resistance. *Theory & Psychology*, 25(2), 184–201.

Neimark, B., Mahanty, S., Dressler, W., and Hicks, C. (2020). Not just participation: The rise of the eco-precariat in the green economy. *Antipode*, 52(2), 496–521.

Neocleous, M. (2007). Security, liberty and the myth of balance: Towards a critique of security politics. *Contemporary Political Theory*, 6, 131–149.

Nethercote, M. (2023). Platform landlords: Renters, personal data and new digital footholds of urban control. *Digital Geography and Society*, 5, 100060.

Newlands, G. (2021). Algorithmic surveillance in the gig economy: The organization of work through Lefebvrian conceived space. *Organization Studies*, 42(5), 719–737.

Newman, S. (2004). New reflections on the theory of power: A Lacanian perspective. *Contemporary Political Theory*, 3, 148–167.

Nguyen, D. (2019). Algorithmic governmentality and the dilemma of transparency in Vietnam's smart cities. *East Asian Science, Technology and Society: An International Journal*, 13(4), 519–542.

Norris, P. and Inglehart, R. (2019). *Cultural backlash: Trump, Brexit, and authoritarian populism*. Cambridge University Press.

Nunes, D.M. (2023). Imperialism in the financial capital era: Forgotten contributions from Marxist dependency theory. *Review of Radical Political Economics*, 04866134231189835.

Nunnally, S.C. (2020). (Re)defining the black body in the era of Black Lives Matter: The politics of blackness, old and new. *Politics Groups Identities*, 6(1), 138–152.

Obi, C. (2010). Oil as the 'curse' of conflict in Africa: Peering through the smoke and mirrors. *Review of African Political Economy*, 37(126), 483–495.

Odendaal, N. (2016). Towards the digital city in South Africa: Issues and constraints. *Journal of Urban Technology*, 13(3), 29–48.

O'Donnell, G. (1978). Reflections on the patterns of change in the bureaucratic-authoritarian state. *Latin American Research Review*, 13(1), 3–38.

O'Donnell, G. (2023). *Bureaucratic authoritarianism: Argentina 1966–1973 in comparative perspective*. University of California Press.

O'Hara, K. and Hall, W. (2018). Four internets: The geopolitics of digital governance. CIGI Papers. Centre for International Governance Innovation, Chatham House.

Oneal, J.R. (1994). The affinity of foreign investors for authoritarian regimes. *Political Research Quarterly*, 47(3), 565–588.

O'Neil, C. (2016). *Weapons of math destruction: How big data increases inequality and threatens democracy*. Crown.

Ong, A. (2006a). Mutations in citizenship. *Theory, Culture & Society*, 23(2–3), 499–505.

Ong, A. (2006b). *Neoliberalism as exception: Mutations in citizenship and sovereignty*. Duke University Press.

Ongweso, E. (2020). Police and big tech are partners in crime: We need to abolish them both. *Vice*, 25 June.

Öniş, Z. (1991). The logic of the developmental state. *Comparative Politics*, 24(1), 109–126.

Oppenheim, L. (2018). *Politics in Chile: Democracy, authoritarianism, and the search for development*. Routledge.

Ormrod, J.S. and Ormrod, J.S. (2014). Fantasy in Lacanian theory. In J. Ormrod, *Fantasy and social movements* (pp 98–133). Brill.

Orren, B. (2019). India's data wild west: The Aadhaar system and its questionable data protections. *North Carolina Journal of International Law*, 45, 619.

Ossewaarde, M. and Reijers, W. (2017). The illusion of the digital commons: 'False consciousness' in online alternative economies. *Organization*, 24(5), 609–628.

Osuna, S. (2020). Transnational moral panic: Neoliberalism and the spectre of MS-13. *Race & Class*, 61(4), 3–28.

Oswick, C., Harney, S., and Hanlon, G. (2008). The new securocracy and the 'police concept' of public sector worker identity. *International Journal of Public Administration*, 31(9), 1024–1036.

Ottosen, R. (2009). The military-industrial complex revisited: Computer games as war propaganda. *Television & New Media*, 10(1), 122–125.

Ozalp, H., Ozcan, P., Dinckol, D., Zachariadis, M., and Gawer, A. (2022). 'Digital colonization' of highly regulated industries: An analysis of big tech platforms' entry into health care and education. *California Management Review*, 64(4), 78–107.

Palacios, J.M.S. (2017). US–México border states and the US military–industrial complex: A global space for expanding transnational capital. *Regions and Cohesion*, 7(1), 87–121.

Pallesen, E. and Aakjær, M. (2020). More for less? Sharing economy as a driver of public welfare innovation. *Technology Innovation Management Review*, 10(5), 19–27.

Palmer, M.H. (2006). *Creating indigital peripheries: The Bureau of Indian Affairs, geographic information systems, and the digitization of Indian Country*. The University of Oklahoma.

Palomera, J. (2014). Reciprocity, commodification, and poverty in the era of financialization. *Current Anthropology*, 55(S9), S105–S115.

Pangrazio, L. and Sefton-Green, J. (2021). Digital rights, digital citizenship and digital literacy: What's the difference? *Journal of New Approaches in Educational Research*, 10(1), 15–27.

Panitch, L. and Gindin, S. (2013). The integration of China into global capitalism. *International Critical Thought*, 3(2), 146–158.

Pantzar, M. and Ruckenstein, M. (2015). The heart of everyday analytics: Emotional, material and practical extensions in self-tracking market. *Consumption Markets & Culture*, 18(1), 92–109.

Papacharissi, Z. (2021). *After democracy: Imagining our political future*. Yale University Press.

Papageorgiou, I. and Papanicolaou, G. (2013). Theorising the prison–industrial complex. In *New directions in crime and deviancy* (pp 71–84). Routledge.

Paret, M. (2016). Towards a precarity agenda. *Global Labour Journal*, 7(2), 111–122.

Parfitt, C. and Barnes, T. (2020). Rethinking economic security in a precarious world. *Critical Sociology*, 46(4–5), 487–494.

Parikka, J. (2015). *A geology of media*. University of Minnesota Press.

Park, Y.S. (2011). Revisiting the South Korean developmental state after the 1997 financial crisis. *Australian Journal of International Affairs*, 65(5), 590–606.

Parnell, S. and Robinson, J. (2012). (Re) theorizing cities from the Global South: Looking beyond neoliberalism. *Urban Geography*, 33(4), 593–617.

Parsons, A.E. (2018). *From asylum to prison: Deinstitutionalization and the rise of mass incarceration after 1945*. UNC Press Books.

Partycki, S. (2018). Network: Colonization of the Digital World. *Visnyk of VN Karazin Kharkiv National University. Series Sociological Studies of Contemporary Society: Methodology, Theory, Methods*, 40, 44–49.

Pasquale, F. (2015). *The black box society: The secret algorithms that control money and information*. Harvard University Press.

Patel, R. and Moore, J.W. (2017). *A history of the world in seven cheap things: A guide to capitalism, nature, and the future of the planet*. University of California Press.

Patomäki, H. (2017). *Disintegrative tendencies in global food production: Climate change, territorial disputes and faltering régulation.* Futuresprospektive Territorialforschung/TA.

Patomäki, H. (2021). Capitalist disintegration: The plural world of ostensible disorder and legitimation hegemony crisis. In *Cambridge capitalism: Notes for the future from the age of disruption* (pp 156–214). Cambridge University Press.

Pavelec, S.M. (ed) (2010). *The military-industrial complex and American society.* Bloomsbury Publishing USA.

Peck, J. and Theodore, N. (2007). Variegated capitalism. *Progress in Human Geography*, 31(6), 731–772.

Peck, J. and Tickell, A. (2007). Conceptualizing neoliberalism, thinking Thatcherism. *Contesting Neoliberalism: Urban Frontiers*, 26(50), 1770–1787.

Peck, J., Brenner, N., Theodore, N., Cahill, D., Cooper, M., Konings, M., et al (2018). Actually existing neoliberalism. In D. Cahill, M. Cooper, M. Konings, and D. Primrose (eds), *The SAGE handbook of neoliberalism* (pp 1–15). SAGE.

Pegg, S. (2006). Mining and poverty reduction: Transforming rhetoric into reality. *Journal of Cleaner Production*, 14(3–4), 376–387.

Pepinsky, T.B. (2008). Capital mobility and coalitional politics: Authoritarian regimes and economic adjustment in Southeast Asia. *World Politics*, 60(3), 438–474.

Pérez-Curiel, C., Segado-Boj, F., and Domínguez-Gómez, E. (2021). Social communication of disinformation in the digital age: The case of deplatforming in the networks of digital populism in Spain. *Social Sciences*, 10(10), 387.

Perret, A. (2023). Militarization and privatization of security: From the war on drugs to the fight against organized crime in Latin America. *International Review of the Red Cross*, 105(923), 828–848.

Peters, M.A. (2001). *Poststructuralism, Marxism, and neoliberalism: Between theory and politics.* Rowman & Littlefield.

Petersohn, U. (2021). Onset of new business? Private military and security companies and conflict onset in Latin America, Africa, and Southeast Asia from 1990 to 2011. *Small Wars & Insurgencies*, 32(8), 1362–1393.

Peterson, V.S. (2002). Rewriting (global) political economy as reproductive, productive, and virtual (Foucauldian) economies. *International Feminist Journal of Politics*, 4(1), 1–30.

Petit, N. (2020a). *Big tech and the digital economy: The moligopoly scenario.* Oxford University Press.

Petit, P. (2020b). 'Everywhere surveillance': Global surveillance regimes as techno-securitization. *Science as Culture*, 29(1), 30–56.

Petry, J. (2020). Financialization with Chinese characteristics? Exchanges, control and capital markets in authoritarian capitalism. *Economy and Society*, 49(2), 213–238.

Phelps, M.S. (2013). The paradox of probation: Community supervision in the age of mass incarceration. *Law & Policy*, 35(1–2), 51–80.

Phelps, M.S., Ward, A., and Frazier, D. (2021). From police reform to police abolition? How Minneapolis activists fought to make Black lives matter. *Mobilization: An International Quarterly*, 26(4), 421–441.

Pike, A. and Pollard, J. (2010). Economic geographies of financialization. *Economic Geography*, 86(1), 29–51.

Piketty, T. (2014). Capital in the twenty-first century: A multidimensional approach to the history of capital and social classes. *British Journal of Sociology*, 65(4), 736–747.

Pilisuk, M. and Hayden, T. (1965). Is there a military industrial complex which prevents peace? Consensus and countervailing power in pluralistic systems. *Journal of Social Issues*, 21(3), 67–117.

Piotrowski, M. (2018). Data desire in the anthropocene. *M/C Journal*, 21(3).

Pirie, I. (2007). *The Korean developmental state: From dirigisme to neoliberalism*. Routledge.

Pohle, J. and Thiel, T. (2020). Digital sovereignty. *Internet Policy Review*, 9(4). https://policyreview.info/concepts/digital-sovereignty

Poulantzas, N. (1978). *State, Power, Socialism*. New Left Books.

Prato, S. and Sonkin, F. (2018). Inequalities, financialization, technology: Sometimes the nearest exit is behind you. *Development*, 61(1), 1–5.

Prechel, H. and Harms, J.B. (2007). Politics and neoliberalism: Theory and ideology. *Politics and Neoliberalism: Structure, Process and Outcome*, 16, 3–17.

Price, D.H. (2014). The new surveillance normal: NSA and corporate surveillance in the age of global capitalism. *Monthly Review*, 66(3), 43–53.

Prins, N. (2018). *Collusion: How central bankers rigged the world*. Bold Type Books.

Privacy International (2021). Exclusion by design: How national ID systems make social protection inaccessible to vulnerable populations. 29 March. https://privacyinternational.org/long-read/4472/exclusion-design-hownational-id-systems-make-social-protection-inaccessible

Puar, J.K. (2007). *Terrorist assemblages: Homonationalism in queer times*. Duke University Press.

Purvis, T. and Hunt, A. (1993). Discourse, ideology, discourse, ideology, discourse, ideology. *British Journal of Sociology*, 473–499.

Quart, L. (2006). The religion of the market: Thatcherite politics and the British film of the 1980s. In L.D. Friedman (ed), *Fires were started: British cinema and Thatcherism* (pp 15–29). Wallflower Press.

Rahim, L.Z. and Barr, M.D. (2019). Introduction: Authoritarian governance in Singapore's developmental state. In L.Z. Rahim and M.D. Barr (eds), *The limits of authoritarian governance in Singapore's developmental state* (pp 1–25). Palgrave Macmillan.

Rahman, H.A. (2019). *Invisible cages: Algorithmic evaluations in online labor markets*. Stanford University.

Rains, P. and Teram, E. (1992). *Normal bad boys: Public policies, institutions, and the politics of client recruitment*. McGill-Queen's Press.

Rak, J. (2022). The global authoritarian turn, democratic vulnerability, and geo-digital competition. *Geopolitics*, 27(2), 680–686.

Rancière, J. (2014). On the theory of ideology – Althusser's politics. In T. Eagleton (ed), *Ideology* (pp 141–161). Routledge.

Rankin, S.K. (2021). Hiding homelessness: The transcarceration of homelessness. *California Law Review*, 109, 559.

Rao, U. and Nair, V. (2019). Aadhaar: Governing with biometrics. *South Asia: Journal of South Asian Studies*, 42(3), 469–481.

Rasillo, X.B. (2023). Digital commoning and post-capitalist crypto-economies: The case of FairCoop. *Geoforum*, 144, 103811.

Ravenelle, A.J. (2020). Precarious lives. *Sociological Forum*, 35(2), 543–545.

Rawal, T. (2014). Geographies of debt: The prison industrial complex and the global South. *The Global South*, 8(2), 34–48.

Rawlings, P. (1991). 'Creeping privatisation'? The police, the Conservative government and policing in the late 1980s. In R. Reiner and M. Cross (eds), *Beyond law and order: Criminal justice policy and politics into the 1990s* (pp 41–58). Palgrave Macmillan.

Raworth, K. (2017). *Doughnut economics: Seven ways to think like a 21st-century economist*. Chelsea Green Publishing.

Raychaudhuri, S. and D'Agostino, B. (2019). Modi's 'digital India' and the mother goddess: Fantasy as legitimation. *The Journal of Psychohistory*, 46(3), 207.

Raza, A.E. (2011). Legacies of the racialization of incarceration: From convict-lease to the prison industrial complex. *Journal of the Institute of Justice and International Studies*, 11, 159–170.

Reeves, J. (2012). If you see something, say something: Lateral surveillance and the uses of responsibility. *Surveillance & Society*, 10(3/4), 235–248.

Régnier, P. (2011). Developmental states and hybrid regimes in south-east Asia: the socio-economic and political challenges of global crises (1998–2008). *Asien*, 120, 10–27.

Remling, E. (2018). Logics, assumptions and genre chains: A framework for poststructuralist policy analysis. *Critical Discourse Studies*, 15(1), 1–18.

Remmer, K.L. (1986). The politics of economic stabilization: IMF standby programs in Latin America, 1954–1984. *Comparative Politics*, 19(1), 1–24.

Resnick, P. and Zeckhauser, R. (2002). Trust among strangers in Internet transactions: Empirical analysis of eBay's reputation system. In M.R. Baye (ed), *The economics of the internet and e-commerce* (pp 127–157). Emerald Group Publishing Limited.

Resnick, S.A. and Wolff, R.D. (1989). *Knowledge and class: A Marxian critique of political economy*. University of Chicago Press.

Ricaurte, P. (2019). Data epistemologies, the coloniality of power, and resistance. *Television & New Media*, 20(4), 350–365.

Richards, G. (1985). The rise and decline of military authoritarianism in Latin America: The role of stabilization policy. *SAIS Review*, 5(2), 155–171.

Richards, I. (2022). Neoliberalism, COVID-19 and conspiracy: Pandemic management strategies and the far-right social turn. *Justice, Power and Resistance*, 5(1–2), 109–126.

Rigakos, G.S. (2016). *Security/capital: A general theory of pacification*. Edinburgh University Press.

Riofrancos, T. (2023). Resource radicalisms. In B. Bustos, S. Engel-Di Mauro, G. García-López, F. Milanez, and D. Ojeda (eds), *Routledge handbook of Latin America and the environment* (pp 158–167). Routledge.

Rist, G. (2014). *The history of development: From western origins to global faith*. Bloomsbury Publishing.

Rivera, D.Z. (2022). Disaster colonialism: A commentary on disasters beyond singular events to structural violence. *International Journal of Urban and Regional Research*, 46(1), 126–135.

Robinson, P. (2017). The media and foreign policy. *Oxford Research Encyclopedia of Politics*. 26 September.

Robinson, R.N., Martins, A., Solnet, D., and Baum, T. (2019). Sustaining precarity: Critically examining tourism and employment. *Journal of Sustainable Tourism*, 27, 1008–1025.

Rodney, W. (1972). Problems of Third World development. *Ufahamu: A Journal of African Studies*, 3(2), 27–47.

Roland, A. (2021). *Delta of power: The military-industrial complex*. Johns Hopkins University Press.

Romagna, M. (2020). Hacktivism: Conceptualization, techniques, and historical view. In T.J. Holt and A.M. Bossler (eds), *The Palgrave handbook of international cybercrime and cyberdeviance* (pp 743–769). Springer International Publishing.

Rosen, E., Garboden, P.M., and Cossyleon, J.E. (2021). Racial discrimination in housing: How landlords use algorithms and home visits to screen tenants. *American Sociological Review*, 86(5), 787–822.

Rosenblat, A. (2018). *Uberland: How algorithms are rewriting the rules of work*. University of California Press.

Rosenblat, A. and Stark, L. (2016). Algorithmic labor and information asymmetries: A case study of Uber's drivers. *International Journal of Communication*, 10, 27.

Rosenman, E. and Narayan, P. (2024). Economic geography for and by whom? Rethinking expertise and accountability. *Dialogues in Human Geography*, 14(2), 307–311.

Rosky, C.J. (2003). Force, inc.: The privatization of punishment, policing, and military force in liberal states. *Connecticut Law Review*, 36, 879.

Ruckenstein, M. and Schüll, N.D. (2017). The datafication of health. *Annual Review of Anthropology*, 46(1), 261–278.

Ruhanya, P. and Gumbo, B. (2023). The securocratic state: Conceptualising the transition problem in Zimbabwe. *Third World Thematics: A TWQ Journal*, 8(4–6), 219–237.

Rundquist, B.S. (1978). On testing a military industrial complex theory. *American Politics Quarterly*, 6(1), 29–53.

Rushkoff, D. (2022). The super-rich 'preppers' planning to save themselves from the apocalypse. *The Guardian*, 4 September.

Ryder, A. (2013). Foucault and Althusser: Epistemological differences with political effects. *Foucault Studies*, 134–153.

Sadowski, J. (2019). When data is capital: Datafication, accumulation, and extraction. *Big Data & Society*, 6(1), 2053951718820549.

Sadowski, J. (2020). *Too smart: How digital capitalism is extracting data, controlling our lives, and taking over the world*. MIT Press.

Sadowski, J. and Pasquale, F.A. (2015). *The spectrum of control: A social theory of the smart city*. First Monday.

Sadowski, J. and Bendor, R. (2019). Selling smartness: Corporate narratives and the smart city as a sociotechnical imaginary. *Science, Technology, & Human Values*, 44(3), 540–563.

Sáez, L. and Gallagher, J. (2008). Authoritarianism and development in the Third World. *The Brown Journal of World Affairs*, 15, 87–101.

Saglam, S. (2022b). War machines in industry 4.0: Defence technology transfers and the financialization of military exports. *Review of International Political Economy*, 1–28.

Said, E. (1978). *Orientalism*. Pantheon Books.

Sallai, D. and Schnyder, G. (2021). What is 'authoritarian' about authoritarian capitalism? The dual erosion of the private–public divide in state-dominated business systems. *Business & Society*, 60(6), 1312–1348.

Salmela, M. and von Scheve, C. (2017). Emotional roots of right-wing political populism. *Social Science Information*, 56(4), 567–595.

Samuel, R. (1992). Mrs. Thatcher's return to Victorian values. *Proceedings of the British Academy*, 78, 9–29.

Sanchez, A. (2018). Relative precarity: Decline, hope and the politics of work. In C. Hann and J.P. Parry (eds), *Industrial Labor on the Margins of Capitalism: Precarity, Class and the Neoliberal Subject* (pp 218–240). Berghahn Books.

Sanchez, P.M. (1991). The drug war: The US military and national security. *Air Force Law Review*, 34, 109–152.

Sanderson, H. (2019). Congo, child labour and your electric car. *Financial Times* (6 July).

Sandhu, A. and Fussey, P. (2021). The 'uberization of policing'? How police negotiate and operationalise predictive policing technology. *Policing and Society*, 31(1), 66–81.

Sannon, S., Sun, B., and Cosley, D. (2022). Privacy, surveillance, and power in the gig economy. In *Proceedings of the 2022 CHI conference on human factors in computing systems* (pp 1–15), April.

Sassen, S. (2006). When national territory is home to the global: Old borders to novel borderings. *New Political Economy*, 10(4), 523–541.

Saud, M. and Margono, H. (2021). Indonesia's rise in digital democracy and youth's political participation. *Journal of Information Technology & Politics*, 18(4), 443–454.

Saull, R. (2015). Capitalist development and the rise and 'fall' of the far-right. *Critical Sociology*, 41(4–5), 619–639.

Sawyer, M. (2013). What is financialization? *International Journal of Political Economy*, 42(4), 5–18.

Schack, T. (2011). Twenty-first-century drug warriors: The press, privateers and the for-profit waging of the war on drugs. *Media, War & Conflict*, 4(2), 142–161.

Schamis, H.E. (1991). Reconceptualizing Latin American authoritarianism in the 1970s: From bureaucratic-authoritarianism to neoconservatism. *Comparative Politics*, 23(2), 201–220.

Schept, J. (2022). *Coal, Cages, Crisis: The Rise of the Prison Economy in Central Appalachia*. New York University Press.

Schierup, C.U. and Jørgensen, M.B. (2016). An introduction to the special issue. Politics of precarity: Migrant conditions, struggles and experiences. *Critical Sociology*, 42(7–8), 947–958.

Schletz, M., Cardoso, A., Prata Dias, G., and Salomo, S. (2020). How can blockchain technology accelerate energy efficiency interventions? A use case comparison. *Energies*, 13(22), 5869.

Schlosberg, J. (2017). *The media-technology-military industrial complex*. Open Democracy.

Schlosser, E. (1998). The prison-industrial complex. *The Atlantic Monthly*, 282(6), 51–77.

Schneider, B.R. (2015). The developmental state in Brazil: Comparative and historical perspectives. *Revista de Economia Política*, 35(1), 114–132.

Scholz, T. (2012). *Digital labor: The Internet as playground and factory*. Routledge.

Schor, J.B., Attwood-Charles, W., Cansoy, M., Ladegaard, I., and Wengronowitz, R. (2020). Dependence and precarity in the platform economy. *Theory and Society*, 49, 833–861.

Schram, S.F. (2015). *The return of ordinary capitalism: Neoliberalism, precarity, occupy*. Oxford University Press.

Schüll, N.D. (2012). *Addiction by Design: Machine Gambling in Las Vegas*. Princeton University Press.

Schüll, N.D. (2016). Data for life: Wearable technology and the design of self-care. *BioSocieties*, 11, 317–333.

Schulze, H., Hohner, J., Greipl, S., Girgnhuber, M., Desta, I., and Rieger, D. (2022). Far-right conspiracy groups on fringe platforms: A longitudinal analysis of radicalization dynamics on Telegram. *Convergence: The International Journal of Research into New Media Technologies*, 28(4), 1103–1126.

Scott, A.J. (2012). *A world in emergence: Cities and regions in the 21st century*. Edward Elgar Publishing.

Scott, J.C. (1998). *Seeing like a state: How certain schemes to improve the human condition have failed*. Yale University Press.

Semenzin, S. (2023). 'Blockchain for good': Exploring the notion of social good inside the blockchain scene. *Big Data & Society*, 10(2), 1–14.

Serra, J. (1979). Three mistaken theses regarding the connection between industrialization and authoritarian regimes. In D. Collier (ed), *The new authoritarianism in Latin America* (pp 99–163). Princeton University Press.

Seymour, K. (2024). Circling the divide: Gendered invisibility, precarity, and professional service work in a UK business school. *Gender, Work & Organization*, 31(5), 1873–1893.

Shaikh, A. (2016). *Capitalism: Competition, conflict, crises*. Oxford University Press.

Shapiro, A. (2018). Between autonomy and control: Strategies of arbitrage in the 'on-demand' economy. *New Media & Society*, 20(8), 2954–2971.

Sharon, T. (2017). Self-tracking for health and the quantified self: Re-articulating autonomy, solidarity, and authenticity in an age of personalized healthcare. *Philosophy & Technology*, 30(1), 93–121.

Shehabi, A., Smith, S., Masanet, E., and Koomey, J. (2016). Datacenters leverage disciplined separate potentials for operational improvements. Current sustainable/renewable energy reports, 1–10.

Selbin, E. (2019). Resistance and revolution in the age of authoritarian revanchism: The power of revolutionary imaginaries in the austerity-security state era. *Millennium*, 47(3), 483–496.

Selg, P. and Ventsel, A. (2008). Towards a semiotic theory of hegemony: Naming as hegemonic operation in Lotman and Laclau. *Sign Systems Studies*, 36(1), 167–183.

Selke, S. (ed) (2016). *Lifelogging: Digital self-tracking and lifelogging – between disruptive technology and cultural transformation*. Springer.

Sharp, J. (2011). A subaltern critical geopolitics of the war on terror: Postcolonial security in Tanzania. *Geoforum*, 42(3), 297–305.

Shih, V.C. (2020). *Economic shocks and authoritarian stability: Duration, financial control, and institutions*. University of Michigan Press.

Shin, K.Y. (2013). Economic crisis, neoliberal reforms, and the rise of precarious work in South Korea. *American Behavioral Scientist*, 57(3), 335–353.

Shires, J. (2021). The implementation of digital surveillance infrastructures in the Gulf. *Digital Activism and Authoritarian Adaptation in the Middle East*, 43, 16–21.

Shkaratan, O. and Fontanel, J. (1998). Conversion and personnel in the Russian military-industrial-complex. *Defence and Peace Economics*, 9(4), 367–379.

Shorrock, T. (2008). *Spies for hire: The secret world of intelligence outsourcing*. Simon & Schuster.

Shwayri, S.T. (2013). A model Korean ubiquitous eco-city? The politics of making Songdo. *Journal of Urban Technology*, 20(1), 39–55.

Silva, E. (1993). Capitalist coalitions, the state, and neoliberal economic restructuring: Chile, 1973–88. *World Politics*, 45(4), 526–559.

Silvey, R. and Parreñas, R. (2020). Precarity chains: Cycles of domestic worker migration from Southeast Asia to the Middle East. *Journal of Ethnic and Migration Studies*, 46(16), 3457–3471.

Sim, S. (2017). *Insatiable: The rise and rise of the greedocracy*. Reaktion Books.

Simmons, L. (2014). Profiting from punishment: Public education and the school security market. *Social Justice*, 41(138), 81–95.

Singer, D. (1990). The power of ideology. *Monthly Review*, 41(11), 43–48.

Singer, P.W. (2008). *Corporate warriors: The rise of the privatized military industry*. Cornell University Press.

Singer, P.W. (2017). *Corporate warriors: The rise of the privatized military industry*. Cornell University Press.

Singer, T. and Kimbles, S.L. (2004). The emerging theory of cultural complexes. In J. Cambray and L. Carter (eds), *Analytical psychology* (pp 188–215). Routledge.

Sitrin, M. and Azzellini, D. (2014). *They can't represent us! Reinventing democracy from Greece to Occupy*. Verso Books.

Skaržauskienė, A. and Mačiulienė, M. (2020). Mapping international civic technologies platforms. *Informatics*, 7(4), 46–59.

Smith, A. and Martín, P.P. (2022). Going beyond the smart city? Implementing technopolitical platforms for urban democracy in Madrid and Barcelona. In L. Mora, M. Deakin, X. Zhang, M. Batty, M. de Jong, P. Santi, et al (eds), *Sustainable smart city transitions* (pp 280–299). Routledge.

Smith, D.N. (2019). Authoritarianism reimagined: The riddle of Trump's base. *The Sociological Quarterly*, 60(2), 210–223.

Smith, D.T. (2015). From the military-industrial complex to the national security state. *Australian Journal of Political Science*, 50(3), 576–590.

Smith, E. and Hattery, A.J. (2010). African American men and the prison industrial complex. *Western Journal of Black Studies*, 34(4), 387–398.

Snyder, J. (2018). Alternative modernities on the road to nowhere. In T. Meyer and J.L de Sales Marques (eds), *Multiple modernities and good governance* (pp 43–59). Routledge.

Soederberg, S. (2004). *The politics of the new international financial architecture: Reimposing neoliberal domination in the global south.* Zed Books.

Solimano, A. (2012). *Chile and the neoliberal trap: The post-Pinochet era.* Cambridge University Press.

Soss, J., Fording, R.C., and Schram, S. (2011). *Disciplining the poor: Neoliberal paternalism and the persistent power of race.* University of Chicago Press.

Soto, O.F. (2021). On the outs: Global capitalism and transcarceration. *Social Justice*, 48(1), 53–124.

South, N. (1988). *Policing for profit: The private security sector.* SAGE.

South, N. (1994). Privatizing policing in the European marker: Some issues for theory, policy, and research. *European Sociological Review*, 10(3), 219–233.

Spivak, G.C. (1988). Can the subaltern speak? In C. Nelson and L. Grossberg (eds), *Marxism and the interpretation of culture* (pp 271–313). University of Illinois Press.

Springer, S. (2010). Neoliberalism and geography: Expansions, variegations, formations. *Geography Compass*, 4(8), 1025–1038.

Springer, S. (2012). Neoliberalism as discourse: Between Foucauldian political economy and Marxian poststructuralism. *Critical Discourse Studies*, 9(2), 133–147.

Sproll, M. and Wehr, I. (2014). Capitalist peripheries: Perspectives on precarisation from the global south and north. *Journal Fur Entwicklungspolitik*, 30(4), 4–13.

Srnicek, N. (2017). *Platform capitalism.* Polity.

Srnicek, N. and Williams, A. (2015). *Inventing the future: Postcapitalism and a world without work.* Verso Books.

Standing, G. (2011). *The precariat: The new dangerous class.* Bloomsbury Academic.

Stark, L. and Levy, K. (2018). The surveillant web: Data mining and algorithmic surveillance. *Annual Review of Law and Social Science*, 14, 203–222.

Stavrakakis, Y. (2007). *The Lacanian left: Essays on psychoanalysis and politics.* State University of New York Press.

Steinberg, J., Loyle, C.L., Carugati, F., Schackleford, S.J., Duzet, F., and Anderson, C. (2021). Domestic digital repression and cyber peace. *Cyber Peace*, 22.

Stern, A. (2016). *Raising the floor: How a universal basic income can renew our economy and rebuild the American dream.* Public Affairs.

Stiglitz, J.E. (2010). Risk and global economic architecture: Why full financial integration may be undesirable. *American Economic Review*, 100(2), 388–392.

Storey, A. (2008). The shock of the new? Disaster and dystopia. *Capitalism Nature Socialism*, 19(1), 121–137.

Stoycheff, E., Burgess, G.S., and Martucci, M.C. (2020). Online censorship and digital surveillance: The relationship between suppression technologies and democratization across countries. *Information, Communication & Society*, 23(4), 474–490.

Strauss, K. (2020). Labour geography III: Precarity, racial capitalisms and infrastructure. *Progress in Human Geography*, 44(6), 1212–1224.

Streeck, W. (2017). *How will capitalism end? Essays on a failing system*. Verso Books.

Streeter, K.A. (2004). *'Coin blood into gold': The development of prison-industrial complex in Georgia and Tennessee*. The University of North Carolina at Asheville.

Sturm, T. and Albrecht, T. (2021). Constituent Covid-19 apocalypses: Contagious conspiracism, 5G, and viral vaccinations. *Anthropology & Medicine*, 28(1), 122–139.

Suarez-Villa, L. (2012). *Technocapitalism: A critical perspective on technological innovation and corporatism*. Temple University Press.

Summers, L.H. (2016). The age of secular stagnation: What it is and what to do about it. *Foreign Affairs*, 95(2), 2–9.

Sunstein, C.R. (2014). *Why nudge? The politics of libertarian paternalism*. Yale University Press.

Susser, D. (2022). Data and the good? *Surveillance & Society*, 20(3), 297–301.

Svampa, M. (2019). *Neo-extractivism in Latin America: Socio-environmental conflicts, the territorial turn, and new political narratives*. Cambridge University Press.

Svendsen, A.D. (2009). *Intelligence cooperation and the war on terror: Anglo-American security relations after 9/11*. Routledge.

Svolik, M.W. (2019). When polarization trumps civic virtue: Partisan conflict and the subversion of democracy by incumbents. *Quarterly Journal of Political Science*, 14(1), 3–31.

Swagel, P. (2015). Legal, political, and institutional constraints on the financial crisis policy response. *Journal of Economic Perspectives*, 29(2), 107–122.

Swales, S. (2022). Neoliberalism and liminality: Perverse cruelties in the age of the capitalist discourse. In M. Lee (ed), *Lacan's cruelty: Perversion beyond philosophy, culture and clinic* (pp 185–211). Springer International Publishing.

Tabb, W.K. (2021). Financialization, a key contradiction of the neoliberal social structure of accumulation. In T. McDonough, C. McMahon, and D.M. Kotz (eds), *Handbook on social structure of accumulation theory* (pp 224–241). Edward Elgar Publishing.

Taibbi, M. (2010). *Griftopia: Bubble machines, vampire squids, and the long con that is breaking America*. Spiegel & Grau.

Tang, A. (2020). Inside Taiwan's new digital democracy. *The Economist*, (19 March). https://www.economist.com/open-future/2019/03/12/inside-taiwans-new-digital-democracy

Tansel, C.B. (ed) (2017). *States of discipline: Authoritarian neoliberalism and the contested reproduction of capitalist order*. Rowman & Littlefield.

Tassinari, A. and Maccarrone, V. (2020). Riders on the storm: Workplace solidarity among gig economy couriers in Italy and the UK. *Work, Employment and Society*, 34(1), 35–54.

Taylor, C. and Dobbins, T. (2021). Social media: A (new) contested terrain between sousveillance and surveillance in the digital workplace. *New Technology, Work and Employment*, 36(3), 263–284.

Tellmann, U. (2009). Foucault and the invisible economy. *Foucault Studies*, 5–24.

Teräs, M., Suoranta, J., Teräs, H., and Curcher, M. (2020). Post-Covid-19 education and education technology 'solutionism': A seller's market. *Postdigital Science and Education*, 2(3), 863–878.

Thaler, R.H. and Sunstein, C.R. (2008). *Nudge: Improving decisions about health, wealth, and happiness.* Yale University Press.

Thatcher, J., O'Sullivan, D., and Mahmoudi, D. (2016). Data colonialism through accumulation by dispossession: New metaphors for daily data. *Environment and Planning D: Society and Space*, 34(6), 990–1006.

Therborn, G. (1999). *The ideology of power and the power of ideology* (vol 24). Verso.

Thomassen, L. (2005). Antagonism, hegemony and ideology after heterogeneity. *Journal of Political Ideologies*, 10(3), 289–309.

Thrasher, J. (2019). Democracy unchained: Contractualism, individualism, and independence in Buchanan's democratic theory. *Homo Oeconomicus*, 36(1), 25–40.

Thrift, N. (2011). Lifeworld Inc – and what to do about it. *Environment and Planning D: Society and Space*, 29(1), 5–26.

Thrift, N. (2014). The 'sentient' city and what it may portend. *Big Data & Society*, 1(1), 1–21.

Ticona, J. and Mateescu, A. (2018a). Trusted strangers: Carework platforms' cultural entrepreneurship in the on-demand economy. *New Media & Society*, 20(11), 4384–4404.

Ticona, J., and Mateescu, A. (2018b). Trusted truckers: Uber work, algorithmic recruitment, and hierarchies of control. *Data & Society*, 8.

Tidwell, A.S. and Smith, J.M. (2015). Morals, materials, and technoscience: The energy security imaginary in the United States. *Science, Technology, & Human Values*, 40(5), 687–711.

Tismaneanu, V. (2009). *Fantasies of salvation: Democracy, nationalism, and myth in post-communist Europe.* Princeton University Press.

Todolí-Signes, A. (2017). The end of the subordinate worker? The on-demand economy, the gig economy, and the need for protection for crowdworkers. *International Journal of Comparative Labour Law and Industrial Relations*, 33(2).

Tokat, B.E. (2022). The global data race: Geopolitics of data, artificial intelligence, and corporate hegemony. *International Studies Review*, 24(3).

Topal, R. (2022). The rise of digital repression: How technology is reshaping power, politics, and resistance. *The Information Society*, 38(1), 77–78.

Tronto, J. (2017). There is an alternative: Homines curans and the limits of neoliberalism. *International Journal of Care and Caring*, 1(1), 27–43.

Tsing, A. (2009). Supply chains and the human condition. *Rethinking Marxism*, 21(2), 148–176.

Tufekci, Z. (2017). *Twitter and tear gas: The power and fragility of networked protest*. Yale University Press.

Turner, B.S. (2002). Max Weber on individualism, bureaucracy and despotism: Political authoritarianism and contemporary politics. In L. Ray and M. Reed (eds), *Organizing modernity* (pp 122–140). Routledge.

Turner, F. (2019). The rise of the internet and a new age of authoritarianism. *Harper's Magazine*, 29, 25–33.

Tyler, I. (2013). *Revolting subjects: Social abjection and resistance in neoliberal Britain*. Bloomsbury Publishing.

Ubel, P., Abernethy, A., and Zafar, S.Y. (2019). Public commentary on rating websites for rating US health care physicians. *JAMA Network Open*, 2(1), e186945–e186945.

Ulbricht, L. (2020). Scraping the demos. Digitalization, web scraping and the democratic project. *Democratization*, 27(3), 426–442.

Ulfstjerne, M.A. (2020). BoB and the blockchain: Anticipatory infrastructures of the cashless society. In A. Sen, J. Lindquist, and M. Kolling (eds), *Who's cashing in? Contemporary perspectives on new monies and global cashlessness* (pp 89–104). Berghahn Books.

Upham, P., Sovacool, B., and Monyei, C. (2022). Digital bricolage: Infrastructuring lower carbon digital space via Nordic datacentre development. *Political Geography*, 96, 102617.

Vaidhyanathan, S. (2018). *Antisocial media: How Facebook disconnects us and undermines democracy*. Oxford University Press.

Valdés, J.G. (1995). *Pinochet's economists: The Chicago school of economics in Chile*. Cambridge University Press.

Vallas, S. (2015). Accounting for Precarity: Recent Studies of Labor Market Uncertainty. *Contemporary Sociology*, 44(4), 463–469.

Valle, A.M. (2021). Justice in the living market: Subjectivation processes in neoliberalism. *Knowledge Cultures*, 9(1), 75–94.

Valsiner, J. (1995). Discourse complexes and relations between social sciences and societies. *Culture & Psychology*, 1(4), 411–422.

Van der Zwan, N. (2014). Making sense of financialization. *Socio-economic Review*, 12(1), 99–129.

Van Dijck, J. (2014). Datafication, dataism and dataveillance: Big data between scientific paradigm and ideology. *Surveillance & Society*, 12(2), 197–208.

Vanolo, A. (2014). Smartmentality: The smart city as disciplinary strategy. *Urban Studies*, 51(5), 883–898.

Van Parijs, P. and Vanderborght, Y. (2017). *Basic income: A radical proposal for a free society and a sane economy*. Harvard University Press.

Van Steden, R. and Sarre, R. (2007). The growth of private security: Trends in the European Union. *Security Journal*, 20, 222–235.

Van Zwieten, M. (2011). Danger close: Contesting ideologies and contemporary military conflict in first person shooters. DiGRA Conference, September.

Varoufakis, Y. (2015). *The global minotaur: America, the true origins of the financial crisis and the future of the world economy*. Zed Books.

Vaughn, L. (2008a). *Beginning racial integration: Privileging exploitation at the University of Texas*. Routledge.

Veltmeyer, H. and Petras, J. (2014). *The new extractivism: A post-neoliberal development model or imperialism of the twenty-first century?* Zed Books.

Venkatesh, N. (2021). Surveillance capitalism: A Marx-inspired account. *Philosophy*, 96(3), 359–385.

Vicdan, H. (2020). Platformization of COVID and the rise of biosocial surveillance. *Markets, Globalization and Development Review*, 5(3), 1–9.

Vieira, V.R. (2014). Invisible legacies: Brazil's and South Korea's shift from ISI towards export strategies under authoritarian rule. *Journal of International Relations and Development*, 17, 157–190.

Vij, R. (2019). The global subject of precarity. *Globalizations*, 16(4), 506–524.

Vilenica, A., Škobić, M., and Pantović, N. (2023). CHF-indexed housing debts in Serbia: Dependent financialization, housing precarity and housing struggles. *City*, 27(3–4), 636–653.

Vinen, R. (2013). *Thatcher's Britain: The politics and social upheaval of the Thatcher era*. Simon & Schuster.

Wacquant, L. (2008). The place of the prison in the new government of poverty. In M.L. Frampton, I.H. Lopez, and J. Simon (eds), *After the war on crime: Race, democracy, and a new reconstruction* (pp 23–36). New York University Press.

Wacquant, L.J. (2009). *Prisons of poverty* (vol 23). University of Minnesota Press.

Wagner, J.R. (2021). Circulating value: Convergences of datafication, financialization, and urbanization. *Urban Transformations*, 3(1), 4.

Wahl, D.C. (2016). *Designing regenerative cultures*. Triarchy Press.

Waite, L. (2009). A place and space for a critical geography of precarity? *Geography Compass*, 3(1), 412–433.

Walcott, R. (2021). *On property: Policing, prisons, and the call for abolition* (vol 2). Biblioasis.

Walker, C. and Whyte, D. (2005). Contracting out war? Private military companies, law and regulation in the United Kingdom. *International & Comparative Law Quarterly*, 54(3), 651–689.

Walker, R. (2018). Tech city: Myths of Silicon Valley and globalization 1. In *Annales de geographie* (No 5, pp 561–587). Cairn/Publilog.

Wallerstein, I. (2004). *World-systems analysis: An introduction.* Duke University Press.

Wardle, B. (2016). You complete me: The Lacanian subject and three forms of ideological fantasy. *Journal of Political Ideologies,* 21(3), 302–319.

Wasson, H. and Grieveson, L. (eds) (2018). *Cinema's military industrial complex.* University of California Press.

Watson, V. (2015). The allure of 'smart city' rhetoric: India and Africa. *Dialogues in Human Geography,* 5(1), 36–39.

Watt, P. and Zepeda, R. (2012). *Drug war Mexico: Politics, neoliberalism and violence in the new narcoeconomy.* Bloomsbury Publishing.

Watts, M.J. (2004). Antinomies of community: some thoughts on geography, resources and empire. *Transactions of the Institute of British Geographers,* 29(2), 195–216.

Webb, M. (2020). *Coding democracy: How hackers are disrupting power, surveillance, and authoritarianism.* MIT Press.

Webster, J.G. (2010). User information regimes: How social media shape patterns of consumption. *Northwestern University Law Review,* 104, 593–612.

Westcott, M., Clibborn, S., and Wright, C.F. (2019). Financialisation and the growth of low-wage, insecure work. In R. Lansbury, A. Johnson, and D. van den Broek (eds), *Contemporary issues in work and organisations* (pp 127–142). Routledge.

Westermeier, C. (2020). Money is data: The platformization of financial transactions. *Information, Communication & Society,* 23(14), 2047–2063.

Wexler, A. (2017). *The gig is up: Side hustle your way to financial freedom.* Gingertopia.

White, A. (2015). The politics of police 'privatization': A multiple streams approach. *Criminology & Criminal Justice,* 15(3), 283–299.

White, C.S. (2020). Wielding social media in the cyber-arena: Globalism, nationalism, and civic education. *Research in Social Sciences and Technology,* 5(1), 1–21.

White, E. (2023). What does finance democracy look like? Thinking beyond fintech and regtech. *Transnational Legal Theory,* 14(3), 245–269.

White, G. (1995). Towards a democratic developmental state. *IDS Bulletin,* 26(2), 27–36.

Whitener, B. (2019). *Crisis cultures: The rise of finance in Mexico and Brazil.* University of Pittsburgh Press.

Whittaker, M. (2020). *The secret rules of the internet.* The Verge.

Wicaksono, T. and Perwita, A.A.B. (2020). The military industrial complex in a developing country: Lessons from the republic of Turkey. *Jurnal Hubungan Internasional,* 9(1), 53–67.

Wijermars, M. and Lokot, T. (2022). Is Telegram a 'harbinger of freedom'? The performance, practices, and perception of platforms as political actors in authoritarian states. *Post-Soviet Affairs,* 38(1–2), 125–145.

Williams, R. (1977). *Marxism and literature* (vol 392). Oxford Paperbacks.

Willim, R. (2017). Imperfect imaginaries: Digitisation, mundanisation, and the ungraspable. In G. Koch (ed), *Digitisation* (pp 53–77). Routledge.

Wilson, A. and Tewdwr-Jones, M. (2021). *Digital participatory planning: Citizen engagement, democracy, and design.* Routledge.

Wilson, S. and Ebert, N. (2013). Precarious work: Economic, sociological and political perspectives. *The Economic and Labour Relations Review*, 24(3), 263–278.

Winlow, S., Hall, S., and Treadwell, J. (2017). *The rise of the right: English nationalism and the transformation of working-class politics.* Policy Press.

Winston, P., Burwick, A., McConnell, S., and Roper, R. (2002). *Privatization of welfare services: A review of the literature.* Mathematica Policy Research.

Witko, C. (2016). The politics of financialization in the United States, 1949–2005. *British Journal of Political Science*, 46(2), 349–370.

Wodak, R. (2015). *The politics of fear: What right-wing populist discourses mean.* SAGE.

Wolfson, M.H. and Epstein, G.A. (eds) (2013). *The handbook of the political economy of financial crises.* Oxford University Press.

Wolpe, H. (ed) (2023). *The articulation of modes of production: Essays from economy and society.* Taylor & Francis.

Wong, J. (2005). Re-making the developmental state in Taiwan: The challenges of biotechnology. *International Political Science Review*, 26(2), 169–191.

Wong, J. (2020). Authoritarian durability in East Asia's developmental states. In V.C. Shih (ed), *Economic Shocks and Authoritarian Stability: Duration, Financial Control, and Institutions* (p 189). University of Michigan Press.

Wong, S.Y. and Dobson, A.S. (2019). We're just data: Exploring China's social credit system in relation to digital platform ratings cultures in Western markets. *Global Media and China*, 4(2), 220–232.

Wood, A., Graham, M., Lehdonvirta, V. and Hjorth, I. (2019). Good gig, bad gig: autonomy and algorithmic control in the global gig economy. *Work, Employment and Society*, 33(1), 56–75.

Wood, A.J. and Lehdonvirta, V. (2021). Antagonism beyond employment: How the 'subordinated agency' of labour platforms generates conflict in the remote gig economy. *Socio-Economic Review*, 19(4), 1369–1396.

Wood, A.J., Graham, M., Lehdonvirta, V., and Hjorth, I. (2019). Networked but commodified: The (dis) embeddedness of digital labour in the gig economy. *Sociology*, 53(5), 931–950.

Woodcock, J. (2020). The algorithmic panopticon at Deliveroo: Measurement, precarity, and the illusion of control. *Ephemera: Theory & Politics in Organizations*, 20(3), 67–95.

Woodcock, J. and Johnson, M.R. (2018). Gamification: What it is, and how to fight it. *The Sociological Review*, 66(3), 542–558.

Woodhams, S. (2020). China, Africa, and the private surveillance industry. *Georgetown Journal of International Affairs*, 21, 158–165.

Worth, N. (2016). Feeling precarious: Millennial women and work. *Environment and Planning D: Society and Space*, 34(4), 601–616.

Wray, I. (2021). The essential state: Pandemic, norms and values, and the new authoritarianism. *Planning Theory*, 20(4), 372–389.

Wright, S. (1991). The new technologies of political repression: A new case for arms control. *Philosophy and Social Action: Philosophy, Science and Society*, 17(3–4), 31–62.

Yalman, G.L. (2021). Crisis in or of neoliberalism? A brief encounter with the debate on the authoritarian turn. In E. Babacan, M. Kutun, E. Pinar, and Z. Yilmaz (eds), *Regime change in Turkey* (pp 15–31). Routledge.

Yang, G. (2016). Narrative agency in hashtag activism: The case of #BlackLivesMatter. *Media and Communication*, 4(4), 13–17.

Yar, S. and Bromwich, J.E. (2019). Tales from the teenage cancel culture. *The New York Times*, 2 November.

Yen, C.P. and Hung, T.W. (2021). Achieving equity with predictive policing algorithms: A social safety net perspective. *Science and Engineering Ethics*, 27, 1–16.

Yerramsetti, S. (2022). Public sector digitalisation and stealth intrusions upon individual freedoms and democratic accountability. *Asia Pacific Journal of Public Administration*, 1–19.

Yesil, B. (2011). Recording and reporting: Camera phones, citizen journalism and the fight for democracy. In R. Firmino, F. Duarte, and C. Ultramar (eds), *ICTs for Mobile and Ubiquitous Urban Infrastructures: Surveillance, Locative Media, and Global Networks* (pp 272–293). IGI Global.

Yeung, H.W.C. (2017). Rethinking the East Asian developmental state in its historical context: Finance, geopolitics and bureaucracy. *Area Development and Policy*, 2(1), 1–23.

Yilmaz, I., Uslu, N., Çavdar, A., Erdogan, E., and Giourieva, J. (2022). Religious populism, cyberspace, and digital authoritarianism across the Muslim world. *Politics and Religion*, 1–30.

Yonita, S.R. and Darmawan, A. (2021). The role of anonymous cyberactivism in the Black Lives Matter movement in the United States (2014–2020). *Insignia: Journal of International Relations*, 1–15.

Youdell, D. (2006). Subjectivation and performative politics – Butler thinking Althusser and Foucault: Intelligibility, agency and the raced–nationed–religioned subjects of education. *British Journal of Sociology of Education*, 27(4), 511–528.

Zake, I. (2002). The construction of national (ist) subject: Applying the ideas of Louis Althusser and Michel Foucault to nationalism. *Social Thought & Research*, 217–246.

Zembylas, M. (2019). The ethics and politics of precarity: Risks and productive possibilities of a critical pedagogy for precarity. *Studies in Philosophy and Education*, 38(2), 95–111.

Zeng, J. and Schäfer, M.S. (2021). Conceptualizing 'dark platforms': Covid-19-related conspiracy theories on 8kun and Gab. *Digital Journalism*, 9(9), 1321–1343.

Zervas, G., Proserpio, D., and Byers, J.W. (2017). The rise of the sharing economy: Estimating the impact of Airbnb on the hotel industry. *Journal of Marketing Research*, 54(5), 687–705.

Zhang, C. (2020). Governing (through) trustworthiness: Technologies of power and subjectification in China's social credit system. *Critical Asian Studies*, 52(4), 565–588.

Zhang, F. (2018). The Chinese developmental state: Standard accounts and new characteristics. *Journal of International Relations and Development*, 21, 739–768.

Zhang, J. and Peck, J. (2016). Variegated capitalism, Chinese style: Regional models, multi-scalar constructions. *Regional Studies*, 50(1), 52–78.

Zhang, J. and Davis, W. (2022). Converging authoritarianisms: An analysis of illiberal populism and neoliberal authoritarianism. *Fudan Journal of the Humanities and Social Sciences*, 15(2), 289–313.

Ziai, A. (ed) (2007). *Exploring post-development: Theory and practice, problems and perspectives*. Routledge.

Zimmermann, F.B. (2020). COVID-19 in Brazil: Bolsonaro's far-right authoritarianism in a pandemic. *Australian Institute of International Affairs*, 16 April. https://www.internationalaffairs.org.au/australianoutlook/20579/

Žižek, S. (1989). *The sublime object of ideology*. Verso Books.

Žižek, S. (1997). *The abyss of freedom*. University of Michigan Press.

Zuboff, S. (2019a). *The age of surveillance capitalism: The fight for a human future at the new frontier of power*. Profile Books.

Zuboff, S. (2019b). Surveillance capitalism and the challenge of collective action. *New Labor Forum*, 28(1), 10–29.

Zuboff, S. (2023). The age of surveillance capitalism. In *Social theory re-wired* (pp 203–213). Routledge.

domination 87–89
  prohibition 94–96
profiting from terror 96–98
authoritarianism vi–vii
  bureaucratic 73–75
  'communicative' 146
  financial
    connection between securitization
      and 58–60
    empowering 54–55, 58
    key mechanisms 8–9
  rebooting global 147–149
  see also digital authoritarianism

B

'Baker Plan' 72
Bank of Bob 187
behaviour, modifying and shaping 46,
    123–124, 129–131, 140, 142
  data collection and analysis 28, 46,
    130–131, 139
  in era of self-control 131–133
  nudge theory and 130–131
  vast markets in 140
Big Brother Inc. 7–12
  complex security 10–12
Big Tech vii, 8, 9, 50–51, 54, 165, 171
  Amazon 54, 55, 136, 138, 167, 169
  Apple 134, 171
  digital nudging 130–131
  Facebook 130–131, 147, 167, 183
  financial growth 165–166
  Google 54, 130, 167, 171
  partnerships 167
biological data 11, 12
biometric technologies 10, 11, 12, 38, 142,
    146, 147, 149
  Aadhaar 151–152, 153
  in administering welfare benefits 93,
    151–152
  on gig platforms 118–119
Black Lives Matter 183
blockchain 186, 187, 189
Bloom, Peter 7, 29, 32, 33, 35
Bolivia 188
Bolsonaro, Jair 158, 171
Brazil 74–75, 148, 150, 158, 171
bureaucratic–authoritarian regimes 73–75

C

Cambodia 147, 148
Cambridge Consultants 112–113
cancel culture 164, 165, 166
capitalism vi–vii, 2, 7
  complexes bolstering social logics of 26–27
  counter-narratives to ideology of capitalist
    securitization 180–182
  intertwining of authoritarianism
    and 145–147

key term 4–5, 6
  as mobile technology 28
  modes of production 27–28
  navigating different forms 38–42
  post- 178–179, 182, 187, 188
  repressive 75–78
  resisting alternatives to 177
  socio-economic and psychological
    dimensions of modern 3–4, 5–6
  valorizing technology 179
  see also surveillance capitalism
capitalist class, transnational 41, 114–115, 121
carceral state
  abolitionist movements to
    dismantle 190–191
  expanding reach 168–169, 173–174
  global expansion 90–92, 108
  see also prison–industrial complex
care economy 180, 181–182
  technologies to restructure 177–178
Central America 77
Chile 63, 73–74
China vii, 10, 147, 148
  exporting of digital authoritarianism 83–84
  Social Credit System 146, 151, 152, 153
  state-directed capitalism 39, 41, 148
civil liberties, erosion of 69, 73, 76, 96,
    99, 167
classes, precarious 114–115
Cobham 111
Cold War 64, 70, 73, 74, 82
Colombia 94–95
colonization, internal 133–135, 140,
    155–156
'common sense', hegemonic 26–27
'communicative authoritarianism' 146
community wealth building 191, 192, 193
complex
  hegemony 24–27, 30
    and complexification 27–30, 32
  historical transitions 64–67
  perpetual 36–38
  political economies 21–24
  repression 34–36
  security 10–12
  social production 104–107
complexes 3, 5–6
  as drivers of change 85–87
  psycho–social 5–6, 30–33, 44
    cultural complexes 31–32, 33
    discourse complexes 31–32
  socio–economic 5–6, 10, 32, 33, 36
complexification 27–30
  cultural 30
  economic 30
  political 30
  of punishment 89–92
  of welfare 92–94, 101
  see also power, complexifying